Philosophy Within Its Proper Bounds

Philosophy Within Its Proper Bounds

Edouard Machery

OXFORD
UNIVERSITY PRESS

OXFORD
UNIVERSITY PRESS

Great Clarendon Street, Oxford, OX2 6DP,
United Kingdom

Oxford University Press is a department of the University of Oxford.
It furthers the University's objective of excellence in research, scholarship,
and education by publishing worldwide. Oxford is a registered trade mark of
Oxford University Press in the UK and in certain other countries

First Edition published in 2017

Impression: 2

Published in the United States of America by Oxford University Press
198 Madison Avenue, New York, NY 10016, United States of America

British Library Cataloguing in Publication Data
Data available

Library of Congress Control Number: 2017936516

ISBN 978-0-19-880752-0

Printed in Great Britain by
CPI Group (UK) Ltd, Croydon, CR0 4YY

A mes parents,
Pierre et Dominique Machery

Contents

Acknowledgments

This won't surprise you if you're already an author: It takes a village to write a book, and authors take on so many debts that it may be more convenient to pretend to be an intellectual island. But I won't travel that path, acknowledging instead my many debts.

The impetus for this book comes from an invitation by Michael Strevens and David Chalmers to present some work in the Mind and Language seminar they organized at NYU in 2013. The shortcomings of my presentation convinced me of the need to write a book on the topic. I thought the book would be sweet and short, but sometimes reality bites, and a longer, more detailed treatment ended up being necessary.

Many philosophers have generously taken the time to comment on older versions of this book, and I have extensively benefited from their generosity. Students, colleagues, and visitors at Pitt suffered through the first version of the manuscript in a reading group at the end of 2014, and their feedback was extraordinary: Thanks to Mikio Akagi, Joshua Alexander, Jim Bogen, David Colaço, Matteo Colombo, Taku Iwatsuki, Joe McCaffrey, Jasmin Özel, Alison Springle, and Zina Ward. Many thanks too to the participants to the reading group at Washington University during my semester-long visit in the winter of 2015: Mike Dacey, Eric Hochstein, Anya Plutynski, Felipe Romero, Rick Shang, Brian Talbot, and Tomek Wisocky. I am particularly grateful to Brian Talbot, who raised challenging objections for each of the chapters. Mark Sprevak organized a seminar meeting on a version of Chapter 3 during my visit at Edinburgh in 2014 and, again, a reading group on the whole book in 2016. The discussion of Chapter 3 with Mikkel Gerken, Michela Massimi, Andrea Polionoli, Stephen Ryan, and Mark Sprevak led me to rewrite this chapter entirely (thanks guys!). I have also been thinking about, and sometimes struggling with, the comments from the 2016 reading group for months: Thanks to Ian Bisset, Jesper Kallestrup, Stephen Ryan, Rick Sendelbeck, Mark Sprevak, Orestis Spyridon, and Annie Webster. Sascha Benjamin Fink organized a wonderful one-day workshop on the book manuscript at the Berlin School of Brain and Mind during the fall of 2015. Thanks to all the participants: in addition to Sascha Benjamin Fink himself, Raphael Becker, Dimitri Coelho Mollo, Matthijs Endt, Ramiro Glauer, Markus Hoffmann, Rhea Holzer, Joachim Horvath, Lena Kästner, Juan R. Loaiza, Stephan Pohl, and Lara Pourabdolrahim. Corinne Bloch Mullins organized a reading group at Marquette and sent me some comments resulting from the participants' discussion. Thanks to the participants to this reading group, including Yoon Choi, Anthony Peressini, and Margaret Walker. Wesley Buckwalter wrote some detailed feedback on Chapter 4 and Joe Milburn on Chapters 1 and 3; Jennifer Nagel made some helpful remarks about Chapter 1. Stefano Cossara read the near final version of the whole book and helped me reformulate some key claims. Thanks for the detailed, sympathetic feedback from the two anonymous reviewers for

Oxford University Press: One only wishes all reviewers were as smart and understanding. Finally, many thanks to John Doris, who met with me on a weekly basis over breakfast to discuss each chapter during my semester-long visit at Washington University: These meetings were one of the intellectual (and gastronomical) highlights of my visit!

Other philosophers have given me feedback on particular claims or arguments in the book. I consulted with Eric Hatleback, Peter Machamer, Paolo Palmieri, and Elay Shech for the history-of-science examples discussed in Chapter 3. My colleagues in the Department of History and Philosophy of Science at the University of Pittsburgh also responded to my request for examples of scientific instruments lacking calibration and hopefulness. Facebook hivemind was put to contribution for issues related to the literature on disagreement discussed in Chapter 4: Thanks to Endre Begby, Carlo Martini, Andrés Páez, Darrell Rowbottom, and Greg Wheeler for answering my questions. My email exchange with John Turri helped me better understand his criticisms of the Gettier cases written by philosophers. Michael Strevens had searching questions about Chapter 7 and its relation with *Doing without Concepts*.

I have given many talks based on the materials of this book. I'd like to single out an early lecture as well as an informal seminar meeting at Syracuse generously organized by Kevan Edwards and the keynote lecture at the UK conference in experimental philosophy in Nottingham during the summer of 2015.

Steve Stich's fingerprints are all over this book, as will be apparent to many. I am delighted to have yet another occasion to acknowledge my intellectual debts! My family was a source of joy and sorrow while writing this book: My father, Pierre, passed away, and my daughter, Uliana, was born. I dedicate this book to my parents, Pierre and Dominique Machery.

List of Figures

List of Tables

If we find those who are engaged in metaphysical pursuits, unable to come to an understanding as to the method which they ought to follow; if we find them, after the most elaborate preparations, invariably brought to a stand before the goal is reached, and compelled to retrace their steps and strike into fresh paths, we may then feel quite sure that they are far from having attained to the certainty of scientific progress and may rather be said to be merely groping about in the dark. In these circumstances we shall render an important service to reason if we succeed in simply indicating the path along which it must travel, in order to arrive at any results—even if it should be found necessary to abandon many of those aims which, without reflection, have been proposed for its attainment.

Kant, *Critique of Pure Reason*, Preface to the Second Edition

Introduction

There are people around who have Very Strong Views ("modal intuitions," these views are called) about whether there could be cats in a world in which all the domestic felines are Martian robots, and whether there could be Homer in a world where nobody wrote the *Odyssey* or the *Iliad*. Ducky for them; their epistemic condition is enviable, but I don't myself aspire to it.

(Fodor, *Psychosemantics*, p. 16)

The aim of *Philosophy Within Its Proper Bounds* is simple, albeit ambitious, arrogant some may say: curbing philosophers' flights of fancy and reorienting philosophy toward more humble, but ultimately more important intellectual endeavors. I argue that resolving many traditional and contemporary philosophical issues is beyond our epistemic reach: We cannot know whether dualism is true (supposing that actual psychological events happen to be physical events), whether pain is identical to some complicated neural state (supposing that actual pains are identical to neural states), what knowledge really is, what makes an action morally permissible, whether causation just is some relation of counterfactual dependence between events, whether I remain the same person because of the continuity of the self, and whether necessarily an action is free only if the agent could have acted otherwise. These philosophical issues and similar ones should be dismissed, I conclude.

This conclusion may seem dire, and I expect serious pushback from philosophers, but it is in fact cause for rejoicing: There are important issues in the neighborhood of most of the dismissed philosophical issues, and *these* are within our epistemic reach. Even if we cannot know whether pain is identical to some neural state, supposing facts about the actual world do not settle the issue, we can still learn whether according to our best science pain is identical to a neural state. Even if we cannot know whether causation can be identified with a relation of counterfactual dependence, we can still understand the properties that are characteristic of causal relations in a large range of actual systems, and we can understand why scientists proceed as they do to establish causal claims. Equally important, the dismissal of such philosophical issues would free time and resources for bringing back to prominence a once-central intellectual endeavor: *conceptual analysis*. In recent years, conceptual analysis has unfortunately been associated with the search for analytic truths and a priori knowledge, but this conception is too narrow, and overlooks the traditional goals of conceptual analysis: clarifying and assessing ideas.

Resolving many traditional and contemporary philosophical issues requires some modal knowledge (i.e., knowledge about what is necessary and possible). Typically, epistemologists are not after what knowledge is like in the actual world; they have little to say about its contingent properties—those properties knowledge has, but would not if the world were different. They are not even after what knowledge is like for creatures like us, for creatures obeying the laws of nature; they have little to say about what promotes or hinders knowledge for minds like us—minds obeying the same psychological laws—and more generally about the net of causal laws knowledge is embedded in (Bishop & Trout, 2005). No, what philosophers are after is what knowledge must be, what knowledge is, or at least requires, in every possible world. Similarly, most moral philosophers do not want to explain what makes something morally permissible in the actual world or for creatures with our psychology; they are after what permissibility must be. Philosophers too rarely debate what free will and responsibility would be for minds constituted like ours; rather, they are usually concerned with, e.g., whether necessarily an action is free only if the agent could have acted otherwise or whether necessarily an agent is responsible for her action only if she is the source of her action. Resolving many central issues in the history of philosophy and in contemporary philosophy also turns on knowing what would be the case in situations utterly different from those governed by the laws of nature. If physicalism is true, necessarily every psychological event is a physical event, and you could not have a physical duplicate that would not also be a psychological duplicate, but if dualism is true, there could be physical duplicates that are not psychological duplicates, something that could probably only happen if the laws of nature did not hold. If type identity theory is true, every psychological property is a physical property, and the instantiation of a psychological property must be identical to the instantiation of one and the same physical property, but if the multiple realizability hypothesis is true, two instantiations of a single psychological property could be identical to the instantiations of two distinct physical properties. Thus, the truth of the multiple realizability hypothesis does not depend only on the actual relation between psychological and physical properties, and instead of trying to disentangle what science tells us about the relations between psychological and physical properties, it may seem more expedient to attempt to determine how they could be related if the world were very different from the world described by science.

Such philosophical concerns, theories, and issues are *modally immodest*: Addressing them requires epistemic access to metaphysical possibilities and necessities. One of the main aims of this book is to defend a form of *modal skepticism*: While there may be such facts, I will argue that we cannot know many of the metaphysical possibilities and necessities of philosophical interest. And if we can't, then modally immodest issues cannot be resolved, and modally immodest philosophical views supported.

The reader will need to follow me through an extensive detour to reach this modal skepticism. Much of the book assesses the main philosophical method for identifying the modal facts bearing on modally immodest philosophical views: *the method of cases*. Philosophers rely on the method of cases when they consider actual or hypothetical situations (described by cases) and determine what facts hold in these situations. These facts then bear, more or less directly, on competing philosophical views.

The method of cases has a long, prestigious history, and it is arguably already used by Plato: The Ring of Gyges story in *The Republic* is a plausible example. It is so important in contemporary philosophy that I could probably fill a whole book by quoting philosophical cases (e.g., Tittle, 2005), and even if I limited myself to the most famous and influential cases, I could perhaps cite a few dozen cases. Admittedly, it is used more often in some areas of philosophy than others. As a first approximation, the more naturalistic the research area, the less frequently it is used. It is rarely used in the philosophy of biology or in the philosophy of cognitive science, and it is uncommon (though occasionally used) in the philosophy of science. It is commonly used in epistemology, in some areas of the philosophy of language, and in ethics.

Consider Gettier's (1963) classic article, which describes several cases in order to undermine the Justified-True-Belief analysis of knowledge he claims to find in Plato. "Case I" reads as follows (1963, 122):

Suppose that Smith and Jones have applied for a certain job. And suppose that Smith has strong evidence for the following conjunctive proposition:

(d)   Jones is the man who will get the job, and Jones has ten coins in his pocket.

Smith's evidence for (d) might be that the president of the company assured him that Jones would in the end be selected, and that he, Smith, had counted the coins in Jones's pocket ten minutes ago.

Proposition (d) entails:

(e)   The man who will get the job has ten coins in his pocket.

Let us suppose that Smith sees the entailment from (d) to (e), and accepts (e) on the grounds of (d), for which he has strong evidence. In this case, Smith is clearly justified in believing that (e) is true. But imagine, further, that unknown to Smith, he himself, not Jones, will get the job. And, also, unknown to Smith, he himself has ten coins in his pocket. Proposition (e) is then true, though proposition (d), from which Smith inferred (e), is false. In our example, then, all of the following are true: (i) (e) is true, (ii) Smith believes that (e) is true, and (iii) Smith is justified in believing that (e) is true. But it is equally clear that Smith does not know that (e) is true; for (e) is true in virtue of the number of coins in Smith's pocket, while Smith does not know how many coins are in Smith's pocket, and bases his belief in (e) on a count of the coins in Jones's pocket, whom he falsely believes to be the man who will get the job.

Gettier concludes that it is not the case that necessarily someone knows that *p* if and only if she has a justified true belief that *p*.

Dretske's cleverly disguised zebra case plays an important role in the assessment of the closure of knowledge under known entailment. He describes the case as follows (1970, 105–6):

Let me give you another example—a silly one, but no more silly than a great number of skeptical arguments with which we are all familiar. You take your son to the zoo, see several zebras, and, when questioned by your son, tell him they are zebras. Do you know they are zebras? Well, most of us would have little hesitation in saying that we did know this. We know what zebras look like, and, besides, this is the city zoo and the animals are in a pen clearly marked "Zebras." Yet, something's being a zebra implies that it is not a mule and, in particular, not a mule cleverly disguised by the zoo authorities to look like a zebra. Do you know that these animals are not mules cleverly disguised by the zoo authorities to look like zebras? If you are tempted to say "Yes" to this question, think a moment about what reasons you have, what evidence you can produce in favor of this claim. The evidence you had for thinking them zebras has been effectively neutralized, since it does not count toward their not being mules cleverly disguised to look like zebras. Have you checked with the zoo authorities? Did you examine the animals closely enough to detect such a fraud? You might do this, of course, but in most cases you do nothing of the kind. You have some general uniformities on which you rely, regularities to which you give expression by such remarks as, "That isn't very likely" or "Why should the zoo authorities do that?" Granted, the hypothesis (if we may call it that) is not very plausible, given what we know about people and zoos. But the question here is not whether this alternative is plausible, not whether it is more or less plausible than that there are real zebras in the pen, but whether you know that this alternative hypothesis is false. I don't think you do. In this, I agree with the skeptic.

But since according to Dretske we would know in this situation that zebras are in the cage, knowledge is not closed under known entailment: It is not the case that necessarily if I know that p and that p entails q, then I know that q.

To show that someone's right to life does not necessarily trump someone else's right "to decide what happens in and to her body," Thomson describes the famous society of music lovers case (1971, 49):

[N]ow let me ask you to imagine this. You wake up in the morning and find yourself back to back in bed with an unconscious violinist. A famous unconscious violinist. He has been found to have a fatal kidney ailment, and the Society of Music Lovers has canvassed all the available medical records and found that you alone have the right blood type to help. They have therefore kidnapped you, and last night the violinist's circulatory system was plugged into yours, so that your kidneys can be used to extract poisons from his blood as well as your own. The director of the hospital now tells you, "Look, we're sorry the Society of Music Lovers did this to you—we would never have permitted it if we had known. But still, they did it, and the violinist now is plugged into you. To unplug you would be to kill him. But never mind, it's only for nine months. By then he will have recovered from his ailment, and can safely be unplugged from you." Is it morally incumbent on you to accede to this situation? No doubt it would be very nice of you if you did, a great kindness. But do you have to accede to it? What if it were not nine months, but nine years? Or longer still? What if the director of the hospital says, "Tough luck, I agree, but you've now got to stay in bed, with the violinist plugged into you, for the rest of your life. Because remember this. All persons have a right to life, and violinists are persons. Granted you have a right to decide what happens in and to your body, but a person's right to life outweighs your right to decide what happens in and to your body. So you cannot ever be unplugged from him." I imagine you would regard this as outrageous, which suggests that something really is wrong with that plausible-sounding argument I mentioned a moment ago.

Some doubt that the method of cases really plays a central role in philosophy. We will see in Chapter 6 that there is really no alternative to this method for assessing philosophically immodest theories, but for the time being I'd like to show that, as a matter of fact, philosophers do rely on the method of cases.

Cases play a central role in many classic articles. To give only a few examples in epistemology, applied and normative ethics, action theory, philosophy of language, and philosophy of mind, all the following classics include cases (with their citation numbers in parentheses[1]): Gettier's "Is justified true belief knowledge?" (2453), Goldman's "Discrimination and perceptual knowledge" (899), BonJour's "Externalist theories of empirical knowledge" (318), Dretske's "Epistemic operators" (805), Thomson's "A defense of abortion" (1363), Thomson's "Double effect, triple effect and the trolley problem: Squaring the circle in looping cases" (586), Frankfurt's "Alternate possibilities and moral responsibility" (1265), Evans's "The causal theory of names" (543), Block's "Troubles with functionalism" (1361), Jackson's "What Mary didn't know" (967), and Searle's "Minds, brains, and programs" (4667). Furthermore, not only do these influential articles include cases, the facts assumed to hold in the situations described by these cases also play a central role in the arguments they develop.

Relatedly, cases guide the historical development of the relevant areas of philosophy. Gettier's (1963) cases gave rise to the introduction of new conditions on justification and to the search for a fourth necessary condition in the analysis of knowledge. Proposals were assessed, and rejected, by means of further cases (for review, see Shope, 1983). BonJour's clairvoyant case and Lehrer's Truetemp case figure prominently in the discussion of reliabilism, as Goldman's (2008) entry in the *Stanford Encyclopedia of Philosophy* shows:

The second objection is that reliability isn't sufficient for justification. The principal example of this kind is due to Laurence BonJour (1980)....If someone disagrees with BonJour about the Norman case, there are other examples with similar contours in the literature that may be more persuasive. Keith Lehrer (1990) gives the case of Mr. Truetemp...

Foot's and Thomson's trolley cases have framed the debate about the nature of moral permissibility. Searle's Chinese room case is the basis of a classic objection against Strong AI.

Cases do seem to play an important role in philosophical argumentation; why, then, are some philosophers inclined to deny it? Some philosophers may confuse the proposed importance of the method of cases in philosophy with the claims that cases

---

[1] From Google Scholar (August 12, 2015).

elicit "intuitions" and that these intuitions, however understood, are what ultimately justify philosophical views. However, the intuition-based characterization of the method of cases is one of the mischaracterizations I take on at the beginning of this book. Generally, the minimalist characterization of the method of cases I will offer has no truck with intuitions, epistemic or metaphysical analyticity, or conceptual competence.

Some philosophers may respond that, if cases play a role in philosophy, it is a small one. In a sense, their role is indeed limited. The facts assumed to hold in the situations described by cases must be brought to bear on philosophical conclusions (about free will, meaning, moral permissibility, or causation), and doing this often requires long chains of reasoning. Much of philosophers' ingenuity goes into developing these long chains of reasoning. Acknowledging this point is, however, consistent with the claim that, if we did not know which facts hold in the situations described by philosophical cases, we would not be able to draw the philosophical conclusions we hope to draw.

Perhaps by saying that cases play at best a small role in philosophy, some philosophers mean that other methods are available to reach the same conclusions. I'll challenge this idea toward the end of this book (Chapter 6).

In any case, the first five chapters of *Philosophy Within Its Proper Bounds* examine whether we know or can come to know which facts hold in the situations described by philosophical cases. Can we really assume that Smith does not know that "the man who will get the job has ten coins in his pocket" in the situation described by Gettier's Case I? That Truetemp does not know that "the temperature is 104 degrees" in the situation described by Lehrer's case? That it is really impermissible to push the large person in the situation described by Thomson's footbridge version of the trolley case? That Frankfurt cases describe free actions? The present book makes a case for a negative answer. We are not entitled to assume that it is really impermissible to push the large person in the situation described by Thomson's case and that Truetemp does not know the temperature, and we should not bring the alleged facts to bear on philosophical views: Our theory of knowledge cannot be built on the facts often assumed to hold in Gettier cases or in the Truetemp case, and a theory of moral permissibility cannot be built on the facts often assumed to hold in the situations described by trolley cases. And so on, I argue, for most philosophical cases.

Fifteen years of experimental research on the judgments elicited by philosophical cases show that these are often "cognitive artifacts": They reflect the flaws of our "cognitive instruments," exactly as experimental artifacts reflect the flaws of scientific instruments. Philosophical cases also tend to elicit different responses: If these responses are a genuine sign of disagreement, we ought to take stock of this disagreement by suspending judgment; if these responses indicate instead that people are speaking at cross purposes, then we should reorient our research priorities and at least for the time being stop theorizing about justice, permissibility, causation, or personal identity.

Philosophers have of course sometimes expressed concerns about the judgments elicited by philosophical cases. Some cases, for instance, have long been known to elicit contradictory judgments when framed differently. Williams (1970) created two cases that elicit contradictory judgments about personal identity and concluded (1970, 168–9),

[T]he whole question [personal identity] seems now to be totally mysterious. For what we have just been through is of course merely one side, differently represented, of the transaction which we considered before; and it represents it as a perfectly hateful prospect, while the previous considerations represented it as something one should rationally, perhaps even cheerfully, choose out of the options there presented. It is differently presented, of course, and in two notable respects; but when we look at these two differences of presentation, can we really convince ourselves that the second presentation is wrong or misleading, thus leaving the road open to the first version which at the time seemed so convincing? Surely not.

Lewis (1986, 203) identified a pair of cases that could not be used to constrain philosophical theorizing about causation because they were "far-fetched"; rather, the theories developed in part on the basis of other cases would determine what to think about the cases: "I do not worry about either of these far-fetched cases. They both go against what we take to be the ways of this world; they violate the presuppositions of our habits of thought; it would be no surprise if our commonsense judgments about them went astray—spoils to the victor!" More recently, Gendler and Hawthorne (2005) have also noted that different formulations of the fake-barn case lead to different judgments.[2]

Philosophers have typically limited their concerns to specific cases, but similar concerns apply in fact much more widely. And if one is convinced by Williams's discussion of personal identity or Gendler and Hawthorne's discussion of fake-barn cases, one should have concerns about most philosophical cases.

I conclude from the discussion of the method of cases that we should suspend judgment in response to most philosophical cases. This radical conclusion is at odds with a more common view among critics of the method of cases: moderate restrictionism (Alexander & Weinberg, 2007; Weinberg, 2007; Alexander, 2012). A moderate restrictionist "advocates not the root and branch removal of all intuitions, but just the pruning away of some of the more poisoned philosophical branches" (Alexander & Weinberg, 2007, 16). Moderate restrictionists hold that a substantial number of cases elicit reliable judgments and they are hopeful that, perhaps with the help of experimental philosophy, we may be able to identify the class of safe-for-thinking cases. By contrast, according to the radical restrictionism defended in *Philosophy Within Its Proper Bounds*, we ought to suspend judgment in response to not only most current philosophical cases, but also the type of actual and possible cases that would be most useful for philosophizing about modally immodest philosophical issues.

It is important to be crystal clear about the content of radical restrictionism. It is not a skepticism about judgment in general or, more narrowly, about the judgments concerning the topics of philosophical interest—e.g., knowledge, causation, permissibility, or personal identity. We are pretty good at distinguishing ignoramuses from

---

[2] See also Unger (1996, e.g., on Trolley cases pp. 88ff.); Gendler (2007); Norcross (2008).

people who know what they are talking about; we often have no trouble recognizing causes; and we typically know which actions are morally permissible and which are not. Nor is radical restrictionism a skepticism about judgments elicited by texts: We do not need to meet politicians to know that many of them do not know what they are talking about—reading about them is often enough—and moral judgments about war crimes read in the *New York Times* are not under suspicion. Radical restrictionism has a narrower scope: It focuses on judgments elicited by a particular kind of text, namely the kind of case philosophers tend to use to support modally immodest philosophical views. Judgments elicited by other texts are not under suspicion, and indeed I'll be using a few cases of this second type in the book.

Also radical restrictionism isn't a form of eliminativism about the use of cases in philosophy. Cases are used for very different purposes in philosophy (Chapter 1), many of which are perfectly acceptable and will not be the focus of this book. Some of the uses that are discussed in the coming chapters are also beyond criticism: In particular, I will defend a version of conceptual analysis (Chapter 7), recommending the use of judgments about a particular type of case to study concepts of philosophical interest. Even the use of cases to answer questions such as, What is knowledge? or What does causation reduce to?, which will be the focus of much of this book, can be appropriate in some restricted circumstances. Judgments about everyday cases will not be impugned, although it is not clear how much philosophical mileage one can gain from them (Chapter 3). Finally, philosophical cases that are known to elicit consensual, unbiased judgments, if there are any, can remain in our toolbox for philosophizing.

End of the detour: Radical restrictionism undercuts modally immodest philosophical views. These views assume that we have epistemic access to the facts that hold in the situations described by cases, but we don't. We should thus abandon the hope of resolving modally immodest philosophical issues; we are unable to determine what knowledge, moral permissibility, and causation essentially are; if facts about the world do not settle the question of dualism, then we are not in a position to know whether dualism is true.

We are now free to redirect our attention toward issues that do not require some epistemic access we can't have. Of prime importance is the descriptive and prescriptive analysis of concepts. Conceptual analysis has bad press in contemporary philosophy, including among naturalistic philosophers whose work is most congenial to mine, but it is time to reassess its prospects. The vices of some particular, though influential conceptions of conceptual analysis do not generalize to the naturalized conceptual analysis defended in *Philosophy Within Its Proper Bounds*. And this form of conceptual analysis is philosophically important. It allows us to better understand ourselves and to improve the inferences we are prone to draw, and it enables us to square the world of common sense with that of science.

Finally, some may suspect that philosophizing about philosophy is a sign of philosophy's loss of vigor: Only declining fields become introspective. This suspicion is, however, misplaced. Without going as far as Sellars (1963, 3), according to whom, "It is this reflection on the place of philosophy itself in the scheme of things which is the distinctive trait of the philosopher as contrasted with the reflective specialist; and in the absence of this critical reflection on the philosophical enterprise, one is at best but a potential philosopher," philosophizing about the nature, goals, methods, and limitations of philosophy has always been part of the philosophical activity. Plato, Hume, Kant, Nietzsche, Marx, and Carnap, to give only a few examples, extensively philosophized about philosophy, and nearly every decade of the second half of the twentieth century witnessed intense, multifarious metaphilosophical debates: To allude to only some of these debates, philosophers involved in the linguistic turn extensively debated whether, and in which sense, philosophical questions were linguistic questions; the 1950s and 1960s saw scores of articles pitting the metaphilosophy of ordinary language philosophy against that of Carnap and his followers; the 1960s addressed the concerns raised by Fodor and others against ordinary language philosophy; in the 1960s, 1970s, and the 1980s philosophers of science debated the role of the history of science in the philosophy of science; the 1970s examined the prospects of reflective equilibrium; the 1980s were in part concerned with the naturalization of philosophy; the 1990s with mysterianism and with the Canberra plan and its offshoots; the 2000s with the relation between conceivability and possibility and with the significance of experimental philosophy. Dig a bit in a period of philosophy, and you'll find some active philosophy of philosophy going on.

The chapters of *Philosophy Within Its Proper Bounds* develop the themes broached in this introduction in a systematic manner.

Chapter 1, "The Method of Cases," compares three characterizations of the method of cases: exceptionalist, particularist, and minimalist characterizations. Among the most prominent exceptionalist characterizations are those that characterize the attitudes elicited by cases as expressing a conceptual competence, as epistemically analytic, as metaphysically analytic, or as irreducible intuitions. Among the most prominent particularist characterizations are those that characterize these attitudes as obvious or spontaneous judgments. Chapter 1 shows that only a minimalist characterization, according to which cases elicit everyday judgments, is philosophically adequate—it does not rely on empty notions or on notions useless to characterize the method of cases—and descriptively adequate—it captures how philosophers really use cases.

Chapter 2, "The Empirical Findings," is the first systematic review of the empirical findings suggesting that the judgments influenced by cases vary across demographic groups and are influenced by the way cases are presented. Nearly every examined case, from nearly every area of philosophy, elicits judgments varying across demographic groups or different judgments depending on how the case is presented.

Chapter 3, "Fooled by Cognitive Artifacts," examines one of the two concerns often brought up against the method of cases: The judgments elicited by cases seem epistemically deficient. This concern is captured by the first argument against the method of cases, which I call "Unreliability": Cases currently used in philosophy as well as those cases that would be particularly useful for some central philosophical purposes are likely to elicit unreliable judgments. I conclude that we ought to suspend judgment.

Chapter 4, "Enshrining *Our* Prejudices," builds upon the second concern often brought against the method of cases: People make different judgments in response to cases. Chapter 4 develops a dilemma against the method of cases: If people are genuinely disagreeing, then according to the most important views in the epistemological literature on disagreement we ought to suspend judgment in response to cases; if people are in fact talking at cross purposes, then we should reorient our research priorities; instead of theorizing about what our judgments refer to, we should first decide what is worth theorizing about—the objects of our judgments or the objects of their judgments. Both arguments, Dogmatism and Parochialism, lead to the same conclusion: We should shelve the method of cases.

Chapter 5, "Eight Defenses of the Method of Cases," examines eight different ways of defending the method of cases against Unreliability, Dogmatism, and Parochialism, and finds them wanting. I defend the experimental bona fides of experimental philosophy, provide evidence that reflective judgments do not differ from the judgments reported by experimental philosophers, show that philosophers are not expert judgers, explain why their findings generalize beyond the cases that have been examined, argue that the lesson to be drawn from experimental philosophy can't just be that judgments are fallible, explain why the prospects for a reform of the method of cases are dim, make the point that Unreliability, Dogmatism, and Parochialism do not rest on a mischaracterization of the use of cases in philosophy, and defuse the threat that if sound these three arguments would justify an unacceptable general skepticism about judgment.

Chapter 6, "Modal Ignorance and the Limits of Philosophy," examines the implications of Unreliability, Dogmatism, and Parochialism for modally immodest philosophizing: Modally immodest issues should be dismissed. Alternatives to the method of cases are critically examined: We cannot gain the required modal knowledge by relying on intuition, by analyzing the meaning of philosophically significant words, and by appealing to alleged theoretical virtues like simplicity, generality, and elegance to choose between philosophical views.

Chapter 7, "Conceptual Analysis Rebooted," proposes a new, naturalistic characterization of conceptual analysis, defends its philosophical significance, and shows that usual concerns with conceptual analysis do not apply to this revamped version. Furthermore, naturalized conceptual analysis often requires empirical tools to be pursued successfully, and an experimental method of cases 2.0 should often replace the traditional use of cases in philosophy.

1

The Method of Cases

Let's suppose, then, that there were two such rings, one worn by the just person, the other by the unjust. Now no one, it seems, would be so incorruptible that he would stay on the path of justice ... And in so behaving, he would do no differently than the unjust person, but both would pursue the same course. This, some would say, is strong evidence that no one is just willingly, but only when compelled.

Plato, *Republic* (Book 2, 360 b–d)

The first chapter of *Philosophy Within Its Proper Bounds* defends a particular characterization of the method of cases and identifies some of the roles it plays in contemporary philosophy. In Section 1.1, I examine how cases are used in philosophy. In Section 1.2, I contrast exceptionalist, particularist, and minimalist characterizations of the method of cases, and I embrace a minimalist characterization. In Section 1.3, I show that the main exceptionalist characterizations are philosophically inadequate: They rely on notions that are either empty or useless to characterize the method of cases. In Section 1.4, I further argue that only the minimalist characterizations of the method of cases are descriptively adequate: Exceptionalist and particularist characterizations do not describe correctly how philosophers use cases.

1.1 The Method of Cases

1.1.1 Philosophical cases

Cases are descriptions of actual or hypothetical situations, and philosophical cases are cases put forward by philosophers. Philosophical cases are almost always meant to elicit a judgment[1] or some other mental state about the situations they describe. The nature of the mental state elicited by philosophical cases is a matter of controversy, which will be the focus of the next sections. In this section, I will speak generally of "the attitude elicited by philosophical cases." Philosophical cases do not specify whether the proposition expressed by the elicited attitude holds in the situation

---

[1] In this book, I will usually use "judgment" and "belief" interchangeably. I take a judgment to be an occurrent belief.

described: They are neutral in this respect. The reader is meant to form an attitude about this proposition on the basis of her reading of the case.

Consider for instance the clock case (Russell, 1948, 170):

If you look at a clock which you believe to be going, but which has in fact stopped, and you happen to look at it at a moment when it is right, you will acquire a true belief as to the time of the day, but you cannot be correctly said to have knowledge.

This case, which suitably modified has often been used in contemporary epistemology, describes a hypothetical situation where the reader would form by luck a true belief about the time of the day on the basis of her visual experiences.[2] The case is neutral with respect to the proposition of philosophical interest—namely, the proposition that the reader would not know the time of the day—and, following Russell, the reader is expected to form the attitude, on the basis of her reading of the case, that in this situation she would not know the time of the day.

What kind of mental state is the reader supposed to have about the situation described by a philosophical case? Is she supposed to imagine the situation described by, e.g., the clock case? To pretend that this situation holds? To suppose that it holds? Or something else (grasp it, understand it, etc.)? And, first, how do imagination, pretense, and supposition differ from one another? I will remain by and large non-committal about such questions since the argument developed in the next chapters does not depend on answering them. The minimalist characterization of the method of cases that I will endorse in this chapter only requires that, whatever attitude one has toward the situation described by a philosophical case, the reader can, first, reason about this situation, draw inferences about it, and categorize its elements, and, second, that she can reason, infer, and categorize using the very processes we use toward situations we believe to be actual. Imagination, pretense, and supposition plausibly meet these two requirements.[3] In addition, because we could believe that the situation described by a philosophical case is actual and make a judgment about the proposition of philosophical interest on the basis of this belief, the attitude toward the situation described by a philosophical case (when it is not one of belief) should be as similar to belief as possible. Imagination, pretense, and supposition plausibly meet this third requirement.

Another issue I will remain non-committal about is the content of the attitudes elicited by philosophical cases. Philosophers have proposed many analyses of their content: According to some leading analyses, these attitudes express counterfactual conditionals, strict conditionals, or metaphysical possibilities.[4] Nothing hangs on how this content is characterized, supposing it can be characterized uniformly across philosophical cases, and the remainder of this chapter examines the nature of the attitudes elicited by cases rather than their content.

---

[2] It is sometimes said that similar cases are found in Indian epistemology, but that claim is controversial (for critical discussion, see Stoltz, 2007).

[3] E.g., Nichols & Stich (2003); Weisberg (2014).

[4] E.g., Williamson (2007); Malmgren (2011). For review, see Horvath (2015).

To characterize philosophical cases further, it is useful to draw a pair of orthogonal distinctions: the superficial vs. the target content of a case and the explicit vs. the inferred content of a case.[5] The superficial content of a case is the narrative setting of a philosophical case; it consists of the described facts and non-factual (e.g., emotional) connotations that do not matter from a philosophical point of view; it varies across versions of a given case. By contrast, the target content of a case consists of the described facts and non-factual connotations that matter from a philosophical point of view; it is invariant across versions of a case. That the agent sees a broken clock is part of the superficial content of the clock case in epistemology; that the agent has evidence that a certain proposition holds and forms on this basis the belief that this proposition holds is part of the target content of the clock case. Two Gettier cases have different superficial contents, but the same target content. The clock case is a Gettier case, and so is the following case (Zagzebski, 1994, 65–6):

Smith comes to you bragging about his new Ford, shows you the car and the bill of sale, and generally gives you lots of evidence that he owns a Ford. Basing what you think on the evidence, you believe the proposition "Smith owns a Ford," and from that you infer its disjunction with "Brown is in Barcelona," where Brown is an acquaintance and you have no reason at all to think he is in Barcelona. It turns out that Smith is lying and owns no Ford, but Brown is by chance in Barcelona. Your belief "Smith owns a Ford or Brown is in Barcelona" is true and justified, but it is hardly the case that you know it.

Both have the same target content in that the protagonist forms a justified true belief by luck, but different superficial contents. It is naturally not always clear what the target content of a philosophical case is; indeed, this can be a matter of substantial philosophical dispute. Consider the clock case: Is the fact that the evidence is a perceptual part of the target content of a case? Similarly, it is not entirely clear what counts as a Gettier case, as Weatherson puts it (2013, 68):

Some philosophers use the phrase "Gettier case" to describe any case of a justified true belief that is not knowledge. Others use it to describe just cases that look like the cases in Gettier, i.e., cases of true belief derived from justified false belief. I do not particularly have strong views on whether either of these uses is better, but I do think it is important to keep them apart.

On the other hand, some facts described by a case uncontroversially belong to either the superficial or the target content of a case. Uncontroversially, that the agent forms a justified belief is part of the target content of a Gettier case, that the agent is a man or a woman part of its superficial content. Finally, the target content is not to be identified with the features of a case that cause its readers to form a particular attitude. Philosophers do intend readers to form their attitude on the basis of the target content of a philosophical case, ignoring its superficial content, but, as we will see in Chapters 2 to 4, the superficial content of a case often influences the attitudes readers form.

---

[5] These distinctions are loosely inspired by Talbot (2013); see also Horvath (2015).

The explicit content of a case consists of the facts explicitly stated by the case; the inferred content consists of the facts a reader infers from reading the explicit content of a case. Some inferred content is superficial; some is part of the target content of the case. Readers often must infer that some facts hold in the situation described by a case since cases rarely make explicit everything that is relevant. That the agent sees a broken clock is part of the explicit content of the clock case; that the agent is not blind and is rational is part of its implicit content.

An example may be useful to illustrate all these points. (Additional examples of philosophical cases are given in this chapter.) Jackson's Mary the neuroscientist case reads as follows (1986, 130):

Mary is a brilliant scientist who is, for whatever reason, forced to investigate the world from a black and white room via a black and white television monitor. She specializes in the neurophysiology of vision and acquires, let us suppose, all the physical information there is to obtain about what goes on when we see ripe tomatoes, or the sky, and use terms like "red," "blue," and so on. She discovers, for example, just which wavelength combinations from the sky stimulate the retina, and exactly how this produces via the central nervous system the contraction of the vocal chords and expulsion of air from the lungs that results in the uttering of the sentence "The sky is blue" ... What will happen when Mary is released from her black and white room or is given a color television monitor? Will she learn anything or not?

The case ends here; Jackson then presents his verdict:

It seems just obvious that she will learn something about the world and our visual experience of it.

From this, Jackson draws the following conclusion:

But then it is inescapable that her previous knowledge was incomplete. But she had all the physical information. Ergo there is more to have than that, and Physicalism is false.

Jackson's case describes a hypothetical situation, and the reader is invited to form some attitude toward the proposition that, when she sees red for the first time, Mary learns something new. His case does not specify explicitly that Mary learns something new: It is neutral in this respect. The reader is supposed to entertain the relevant attitude on the basis of the facts explicitly specified by the case (e.g., that Mary knows which wavelength combinations from the sky stimulate the retina) and those she inferred (e.g., that Mary has never looked at herself in a mirror). That Mary is a woman is part of the superficial content of the case and is not meant to influence the attitude it elicits, that she knows every scientific fact about colors is part of the target content of the case and is meant to be taken into consideration.

1.1.2 Provocative, illustrative, formal, material, and exploratory uses of cases

Cases are used for different purposes, some of which are utterly innocuous. Cases can be used to get philosophical inquiry started by eliciting puzzling attitudes (e.g., puzzling judgments) that motivate philosophical discussion: This is their *provocative* use. It still remains puzzling why the footbridge and the switch cases elicit two opposite attitudes.

If this were their only use in philosophy, cases would just be a ladder that philosophers would kick away once serious philosophical discussion would be ongoing. Nothing objectionable there. More generally, philosophical cases can encourage readers to think through issues that they would otherwise not consider seriously or to think about them in a new light (Gendler, 2007).

An important, but still innocuous use of cases is *illustrative*: Philosophers often use cases to illustrate a philosophical theory or a philosophical argument by showing how this theory or this argument applies to the situations described by the cases or to illustrate the analysis of a concept of philosophical interest by showing how so analyzed this concept applies to these situations. A philosophical point that is hard to grasp abstractly may be more easily understood once illustrated by means of a concrete case (Gendler, 2007). While Davidson's (1987) Swampman case came to have a life on its own in the philosophy of mind literature of the early 1990s, it merely fulfills an illustrative function in Davidson's article. Here is the case (1987, 443–4):

Suppose lightning strikes a dead tree in a swamp; I am standing nearby. My body is reduced to its elements, while entirely by coincidence (and out of different molecules) the tree is turned into my physical replica. My replica, The Swampman, moves exactly as I did; according to its nature it departs the swamp, encounters and seems to recognize my friends, and appears to return their greetings in English. It moves into my house and seems to write articles on radical interpretation. No one can tell the difference.

But there is a difference. My replica can't recognize my friends; it can't recognize anything, since it never cognized anything in the first place. It can't know my friends' names (though of course it seems to), it can't remember my house. It can't mean what I do by the word "house," for example, since the sound "house" it makes was not learned in a context that would give it the right meaning—or any meaning at all. Indeed, I don't see how my replica can be said to mean anything by the sounds it makes, nor to have any thought.

In this classic paper Davidson discusses the following conditional: If one's history of causal interactions with the world determines the content of one's mental states, as externalists hold, first-person authority about one's beliefs is undermined. Davidson does not argue for the antecedent of this conditional (although he clarifies how he interprets it and contrasts his interpretation with Burge's and Putnam's externalisms), focusing instead on whether the conditional holds. The Swampman case is briefly introduced as an alternative to Putnam's Twin-Earth case before being entirely left aside in the remainder of the paper, and it is merely meant to illustrate the view that one's history of causal interactions with the world determines the content of one's mental states rather than to support it.

Other uses are less innocuous. In this book I will concentrate on two uses of philosophical cases: their formal and material use. Cases are used *formally* when the goal is to understand the meaning of some of the words (e.g., "cause") that compose the sentences asserted in response to reading cases ("Suzy's and Billy's throws caused the shattering of the bottle") or the semantic content of the concepts expressed by these words (e.g., CAUSE). Relatedly, I will call questions about meaning or semantic content "formal-mode questions." Philosophers describe actual or hypothetical situations and (implicitly or explicitly) ask readers to form some attitudes about these situations. These attitudes apply concepts of philosophical interest such as KNOWLEDGE, PERMISSIBILITY, BEAUTY, and CAUSATION to the situations described by the philosophical cases, and the sentences expressing these attitudes provide evidence about the meaning or semantic content of the relevant words or concepts. For instance, Collins et al. present the following overdetermination case (2004, 32–3):

Suzy and Billy both throw rocks at a window; the rocks strike at the same time, with exactly the same force; the window shatters. Furthermore, each rock strikes with sufficient force to shatter the window all by itself. There is some intuition here that both Suzy's and Billy's throws are causes of the shattering.

A philosopher using this overdetermination case formally would appeal to readers' use of the term "cause" or the concept CAUSE to support or undermine philosophical proposals about the meaning of this term or the semantic content of this concept.

Cases are used *materially* when philosophers use them not to discover the meaning of words or the semantic content of concepts of philosophical interest, but to understand their referents: That is, philosophers are not interested in "cause" or CAUSE, but in causation itself. Philosophers then address what I will call "material-mode questions." If a philosopher makes use of Collins and colleagues' overdetermination case materially, her goal is to support or undermine philosophical proposals about the nature of causation itself.

It has recently been proposed that philosophical cases have yet another use in philosophical discourse. Vaidya (2010) and Love (2013) note that experiments are often not meant to confirm or undermine scientific hypotheses, but fulfill instead an *exploratory* function: They allow scientists to determine new regularities or investigate the boundary conditions of accepted theories. Cases in philosophy sometimes have a similar use, Vaidya and Love propose. I will not single out this use of cases in the remainder of this book because, contrary to what Vaidya and Love assert, the challenges raised against the material use of cases straightforwardly extend to their exploratory use: If the attitudes elicited by philosophical cases are unreliable or otherwise problematic, these cases can't play any of the roles experiments play in science; in particular, they can't guide philosophical inquiry since they would then be terrible guides for exploring philosophical issues.

To end this section, let me stipulate the following terminological convention: I will use "the use of cases" to refer to any use of cases in philosophical discourse, leaving "the method of cases" for referring to the formal or material use of cases in philosophical discourse. Jackson's Mary the neuroscientist case is used to provide an argument against physicalism and its use is a good example of the method of cases; Davidson's Swampman case is a mere illustration and, by stipulation, its use is not an instance of the method of cases.

1.2 Three Competing Characterizations of the Method of Cases

The method of cases has been characterized in very different ways.[6] In this section, painting with a broad brush, I lay out three competing characterizations of the method of cases, including my own minimalist characterization.[7]

1.2.1 Exceptionalist characterizations of the method of cases

Exceptionalist characterizations of the method of cases assert that the attitudes elicited by philosophical cases differ from everyday judgments, i.e., the kind of judgment we routinely make when we apply concepts to possible instances (e.g., the judgment that a student knows the course content, that plagiarism is not permissible, or that smoking causes cancer). That is, on these views, the attitudes elicited by philosophical cases possess properties everyday judgments do not have. Exceptionalist characterizations distinguish these attitudes from everyday judgments in various ways. Some hold that these attitudes, which they often call "intuitions," are not judgments at all and are irreducible to judgments. Irreducible intuitions are also sometimes said to possess properties that everyday judgments do not have, such as, among others, a distinct phenomenology (e.g., a sense of necessity), a distinct epistemic role (e.g., judgments based on them are a priori justified), or a distinct etiology (e.g., they express one's conceptual competence—i.e., roughly, what someone must be able to do or infer or what someone must know to possess a given concept).

Exceptionalism does not require that the attitudes elicited by philosophical cases be irreducible to judgments. On some exceptionalist characterizations, these attitudes are judgments (or inclinations to judge) that possess properties that everyday judgments do not have. Some distinguish the judgments elicited by philosophical cases by their phenomenology, their semantic status (e.g., they are analytic or conceptual truths), their epistemic status (e.g., they are a priori justified), or their etiology (e.g., they express one's conceptual competence). Everyday judgments are not justified a priori, they are not analytically true, they do not express people's conceptual competence, and they do not feel as if we have to assent to them.

Some have argued that philosophers have some kind of expertise for forming attitudes (having an intuition or making a judgment) in response to philosophical cases (for critical discussion, see Section 5.3 of Chapter 5), but even if that were the case, that would not entail that such attitudes differ from everyday judgments. Expertise may just mean that philosophers are better at deploying everyday cognitive tools, exactly as people with perfect vision and myopic people just differ in how good their vision is.

---

[6] Compare, e.g., Parfit (1984, 200), Sorensen (1992), Graham & Horgan (1994), Bealer (1996, 1998), Häggqvist (1996), Jackson (1998), Hintikka (1999), Weatherson (2003), Levin (2005), Ludwig (2007), Sosa (2007), Weinberg (2007, 2014), Williamson (2007, 2011, 2016), Alexander (2012), Cappelen (2012), and Deutsch (2015).

[7] For a different approach, see Chapter 1 of Alexander (2012) and Sytsma & Livengood (2015).

Sosa's characterization of the method of cases is paradigmatically exceptionalist. On his view, the judgments elicited by philosophical cases, which he calls "rational intuitions,"[8] have the following features (2007, 101):

On my proposal, to intuit that p is to be attracted to assent simply through entertaining that representational content. The intuition is rational if and only if it derives from a competence, and the content is explicitly or implicitly modal (i.e. attributes necessity or possibility).

For Sosa, then, cases are meant to elicit an inclination to assent (that is, judge), which is characterized by its etiology ("derive from a competence") and its modal content ("explicitly or implicitly modal"). His account is exceptionalist by virtue of its etiology, since everyday judgments or inclinations to judge do not "derive from a competence" (being derived from a competence with a concept differs from simply involving a concept, as I explain in Section 1.3 below) and are not made "simply through entertaining that representational content." Consider for instance the fake-barn case (Goldman, 1976, 772–3):

Henry is driving in the countryside with his son. For the boy's edification Henry identifies various objects on the landscape as they come into view. "That's a cow," says Henry, "That's a tractor," "That's a silo," "That's a barn," etc. Henry has no doubt about the identity of these objects; in particular, he has no doubt that the last mentioned object is a barn, which indeed it is. Each of the identified objects has features characteristic of its type. Moreover, each object is fully in view, Henry has excellent eyesight, and he has enough time to look at them reasonably carefully, since there is little traffic to distract him. Given this information, would we say that Henry knows that the object is a barn? Most of us would have little hesitation in saying this, so long as we were not in a certain philosophical frame of mind. Contrast our inclination here with the inclination we would have if we were given some additional information. Suppose we are told that, unknown to Henry, the district he has just entered is full of papier-mâché facsimiles of barns. These facsimiles look from the road exactly like barns, but are really just facades, without back walls or interiors, quite incapable of being used as barns. They are so cleverly constructed that travelers invariably mistake them for barns. Having just entered the district, Henry has not encountered any facsimiles; the object he sees is a genuine barn. But if the object on that site were a facsimile, Henry would mistake it for a barn. Given this new information, we would be strongly inclined to withdraw the claim that Henry knows the object is a barn. How is this change in our assessment to be explained?

According to Sosa's exceptionalist characterization of the method of cases, this case elicits from the reader an inclination to assent to (judge it to be true) the proposition that Henry does not know that the object is a barn, an inclination to assent that is derived from her competence with the concept of knowledge. This inclination to judge differs from the deployment of the concept of knowledge in everyday circumstances (e.g., when a teacher judges that a student does not know the content of the

---

[8] Sosa does not hold that intuitions are irreducible to judgments. On his view, they are a type of judgment.

previous week's lecture), which is not derived from one's competence with the concept of knowledge.

1.2.2 Particularist characterizations of the method of cases

Particularist characterizations of the method of cases hold that the attitudes elicited by philosophical cases are a particular type of everyday judgment. They do not ascribe to these judgments properties that everyday judgments do not have, as exceptionalist characterizations do, but they single out properties that some (but not all) everyday judgments possess, and assert that the judgments elicited by the method of cases possess these properties. Some particularist characterizations may identify the latter judgments by means of their content (e.g., modal content or abstract content), their phenomenology (e.g., obviousness), their epistemic status (e.g., knowledge, justified belief, prima facie justified belief, or reliable belief), or their psychological, including etiological, properties (e.g., elicited judgments are not consciously inferred or they are fast). Some everyday judgments have a modal or abstract content (e.g., the judgment that Hillary Clinton could have been president or the judgment that love is eternal), others are obvious (e.g., the judgment that 2 plus 2 is equal to 4), and yet others are snap judgments (e.g., recognitional judgments). Particularist characterizations characterize the judgments elicited by philosophical cases by means of some of these properties.

According to a common particularist characterization, philosophical cases elicit snap judgments—that is, judgments that are not consciously inferred and that come quickly to mind.[9] Gopnik and Schwitzgebel write (1998, 77, italics in the original):

We will call any judgment an *intuitive judgment* or more briefly an *intuition*, just in case that judgment is not made on the basis of some kind of reasoning process that a person can consciously observe....So, for example, we make intuitive judgments about such things as the grammaticality of sentences, the morality of actions, the applicability of a certain term to a certain situation...In each of these cases, judgments flow spontaneously from the situations that engender them, rather than from any process of explicit reasoning.

Gopnik and Schwitzgebel take a property that some everyday judgments have—"not [being] made on the basis of some kind of reasoning process that a person can consciously observe"—and characterize the judgments elicited by the method of cases by means of this property. Consider for instance a Frankfurt case (Fischer, 2010, 316):

Because he dares to hope that the Democrats finally have a good chance of winning the White House, the benevolent but elderly neurosurgeon, Black,...has secretly inserted a chip in Jones's brain that enables Black to monitor and control Jones's activities. Black can exercise this control through a sophisticated computer that he has programmed so that, among other things, it monitors Jones's voting behavior. If Jones were to show any inclination to vote for McCain (or, let us say, anyone other than Obama), then the computer, through the chip in Jones's brain, would intervene to assure that he actually decides to vote for Obama and does so vote. But if

---

[9] Goldman & Pust (1998, 119); Weinberg et al. (2001, 19); Weinberg (2007, 318); Nagel (2012).

Jones decides on his own to vote for Obama (as Black, the old progressive would prefer), the computer does nothing but continue to monitor—without affecting—the goings-on in Jones's head. Now suppose that Jones decides to vote for Obama on his own, just as he would have if Black had not inserted the chip in his head. It seems, upon first thinking about this case, that Jones can be held morally responsible for his choice and act of voting for Obama, although he could not have chosen otherwise and he could not have done otherwise.

According to Gopnik and Schwitzgebel's particularist characterization of the method of cases, this Frankfurt case elicits a snap judgment, a judgment that is not consciously inferred from anything else. This judgment is, in this respect, similar to recognitional judgments such as the judgment that the object below me is a chair or that the object in front of me is a computer.

1.2.3   Minimalist characterizations of the method of cases

Minimalist characterizations of the method of cases hold that philosophical cases do not elicit attitudes distinct in kind from the application of concepts in everyday life.[10] That is, first, these attitudes are judgments about either actual or hypothetical situations. Second, no particular property distinguishes the judgments elicited by philosophical cases from everyday judgments. Judgments elicited by philosophical cases do not possess a phenomenology that everyday judgments do not have: In particular, we do not feel we have to make these judgments. They do not have a distinctive epistemic status: For instance, they are not justified a priori. They do not have a distinctive semantic status: They are not analytic. They do not have a distinctive etiology: They do not express our conceptual competence with the relevant concepts. Third, minimalist characterizations of the method of cases do not require the judgments elicited by philosophical cases to share any particular content (e.g., they may sometimes have a modal content, but they need not), phenomenology (e.g., obviousness), or psychological properties. For instance, minimalist characterizations do not characterize them as fast judgments that have not been consciously inferred. Some judgments elicited by philosophical cases could be consciously inferred, and others could be slow.

Naturally, judgments elicited by philosophical cases are sometimes, perhaps even often, about situations that at best rarely occur in everyday life (remember the Frankfurt case, for instance), but this does not mean that they are not of the same kind as everyday judgments. They neither possess properties that distinguish them from everyday judgments (except of course for their unusual subject matters) nor can they be identified with a particular type of everyday judgment. Similarly, when we judged that the first iPhone was a phone, our judgment had a novel subject matter, but it was

---

[10] Williamson (2004, 2007) and Cappelen (2012) have embraced minimalism and hold that it undermines the metaphilosophical significance of experimental philosophy. This book demonstrates that this second claim is mistaken (more on this in Section 5.7 of Chapter 5).

of the same kind as other applications of the concept PHONE. Generally, everyday judgments can be made about esoteric subject matters.

If philosophical cases just elicit everyday judgments, then when people judge about the situations described by these cases, they deploy their everyday capacities for recognizing the referents of the relevant concepts. People who judge that the protagonist in a Gettier case does not know the relevant proposition deploy the capacity to recognize knowledge and distinguish it from lack of knowledge, the very capacity that allows them to judge that someone knows what she is talking about or that a karaoke singer does not know the words of a song. Accordingly, according to minimalist characterizations, the judgments elicited by philosophical cases are not warranted because they are analytically epistemic or because they have a distinct epistemic status. Rather, these judgments are warranted, if they are, for the very reason that everyday judgments are warranted, whatever that is. Suppose that my judgment that an object is a chair is warranted because I am reliable at sorting chairs from nonchairs. Similarly, people (all of them? some of them? perhaps just philosophers? see Chapter 5 on this question) may be good at sorting knowledge from non-knowledge or permissibility from impermissibility, and their judgments about knowledge and permissibility may be warranted on precisely this ground. If readers are warranted to judge that the situations described by philosophical cases involve or fail to involve instances of knowledge or permissibility, it would then be because they deploy this reliable capacity to recognize knowledge or permissibility.

One may object to minimalist characterizations of the method of cases on the following grounds: If the attitude elicited by a philosophical case is simply a judgment (and not a special kind of judgment or an irreducible intuition), then considering cases would be of little use to support one's philosophical theory or undermine others' philosophical views because one's theoretical commitments influence one's judgments. If my judgment elicited by the fake-barn case is influenced by my theoretical commitment to the view that knowledge entails safety, then considering this case cannot provide support for this theoretical commitment: Circular reasoning does not improve one's epistemic standing. This concern can be dismissed swiftly. Judgments about knowledge elicited by epistemological cases need not be influenced by our explicit theoretical commitments about knowledge; they may rather be the expression of our capacity to recognize knowledge. If our judgments express our theoretical commitments—for instance, because we let our theories determine what holds in difficult cases as if they were "spoils to the victor" (Lewis, 1986, 194)—then the facts assumed to hold in the cases do not, and are not taken to support, these theoretical commitments.

As part of the argument against descriptivism, Kripke describes a hypothetical situation in which a speaker associates a proper name, "Gödel," with a description that is not true of the original bearer of the name, but that is true of someone else, called "Schmidt" in the story. Descriptivist theories of reference typically entail that in this situation "Gödel" refers to the man originally called "Schmidt," but, Kripke maintains, this is just wrong (1980, 83–4):

Suppose that Gödel was not in fact the author of [Gödel's] theorem. A man called "Schmidt"... actually did the work in question. His friend Gödel somehow got hold of the manuscript and it was thereafter attributed to Gödel. On the [descriptivist] view... when our ordinary man uses the name "Gödel," he really means to refer to Schmidt, because Schmidt is the unique person satisfying the description "the man who discovered the incompleteness of arithmetic."... But it seems we are not. We simply are not.

According to minimalist characterizations of the method of cases, Kripke judges that, in the hypothetical situation just described, "Gödel" would refer to Gödel rather than to Schmidt. Kripke here is making a judgment, and is asking his reader to make a judgment, that does not differ in kind from an everyday judgment about the reference of proper names. For instance, it does not differ in kind from the judgment one makes when correcting a misuse of the proper name of an actual person—e.g., when one says, "'Stendhal,' not 'Flaubert' is the name of the author of *La Chartreuse de Parme*"—or the misuse of the proper name of a fictional character: "'Morel,' not 'Jupien,' is the name of the violinist who is protected by Charlus." This type of judgment does not have the properties that some exceptionalist characterizations assume the judgments elicited by cases to possess—they do not express conceptual competence, they do not have any distinctive epistemic status, and they are not intuitions (supposing intuitions differ from judgments). That the situation eliciting the judgment is esoteric does not mean that the judgment differs in kind from everyday judgments. If Kripke is warranted to make this judgment, it is because he deploys his everyday capacity to recognize the reference of names and for the very reason that his everyday judgments about names are justified (perhaps because he is reliable at identifying the referents of proper names). To avoid circularity, this judgment must not reflect Kripke's theoretical commitment to a causal-historical theory of reference.

In her classic article, Thomson starts by discussing Foot's switch version of the trolley case (1985, 1395):

Some years ago, Philippa Foot drew attention to an extraordinarily interesting problem (Foot, 1978). Suppose you are the driver of a trolley. The trolley rounds a bend, and there come into view ahead five track workmen who have been repairing the track. The track goes through a bit of valley at that point, and the sides are steep, so you must stop the trolley if you are to avoid running the five men down. You step on the brakes, but alas they don't work. Now you suddenly see a spur of track leading off to the right. You can turn the trolley onto it, and thus save the five men on the straight track ahead. Unfortunately, Mrs. Foot has arranged that there is one workman on that spur of track. He can no more get off the track in time than the five can, so you will kill him if you turn the trolley onto him. Is it morally permissible for you to turn the trolley? Everyone to whom I have put this hypothetical case says, Yes, it is.

Then, Thomson compares Foot's case with other versions of the trolley case, including the footbridge case (1985, 1409):

Consider a case... in which you are standing on a footbridge over the trolley track. You can see a trolley hurtling down the track, out of control. You turn around to see where the trolley is headed, and there are five workmen on the track where it exits from under the footbridge. What to do? Being an expert on trolleys, you know of one certain way to stop an out-of-control trolley: Drop a really heavy weight in its path. But where to find one? It just so happens that standing next to you on the footbridge is a fat man, a really fat man. He is leaning over the railing, watching the trolley; all you have to do is give him a little shove, and over the railing he will go, onto the track in the path of the trolley. Would it be permissible for you to do this? Everyone to whom I have put this case says it would not be.

According to minimalist characterizations, Thomson judges, with many philosophers, that it is permissible for the driver to turn the trolley onto the side track in the situation described by the switch case, but that it is not permissible to push the large man in the situation described by the footbridge case. Her judgments do not differ in kind from the judgment a parent would make when saying to his or her child, "It's not permissible to hurt animals" or "You should not have stolen the toys of your sister." If it is warranted, it is for the same reasons these judgments are warranted.

Searle's Chinese-room thought experiment in his well-known criticism of Strong AI provides a long, but striking example of the method of cases (1980, 417–18):

Suppose that I'm locked in a room and given a large batch of Chinese writing. Suppose further-more (as is indeed the case) that I know no Chinese, either written or spoken... Now suppose further that after this first batch of Chinese writing I am given a second batch of Chinese script together with a set of rules for correlating the second batch with the first batch. The rules are in English, and I understand these rules as well as any other native speaker of English. They enable me to correlate one set of formal symbols with another set of formal symbols... Now suppose also that I am given a third batch of Chinese symbols together with some instructions, again in English, that enable me to correlate elements of this third batch with the first two batches, and these rules instruct me how to give back certain Chinese symbols with certain sorts of shapes in response to certain sorts of shapes given me in the third batch. Unknown to me, the people who are giving me all of these symbols call the first batch "a script," they call the second batch a "story," and they call the third batch "questions." Furthermore, they call the symbols I give them back in response to the third batch "answers to the questions," and the set of rules in English that they gave me, they call "the program." ... Suppose also that after a while I get so good at following the instructions for manipulating the Chinese symbols and the programmers get so good at writing the programs that from the external point of view—that is, from the point of view of somebody outside the room in which I am locked—my answers to the ques-tions are absolutely indistinguishable from those of native Chinese speakers.... I simply behave like a computer; I perform computational operations on formally specified elements.... Now the claims made by strong AI are that the programmed computer understands the stories and that the program in some sense explains human understanding. But we are now in a position to examine these claims in light of our thought experiment. As regards the first claim, it seems to me quite obvious in the example that I do not understand a word of the Chinese stories. I have inputs and outputs that are indistinguishable from those of the native Chinese speaker, and I can have any formal program you like, but I still understand nothing.

According to minimalist characterizations, the reader is invited to judge that the protagonist in the Chinese room (and, later on in Searle's article, the Chinese room itself) does not understand Chinese, despite his or her capacity to write down contextually appropriate sentences in response to queries in Chinese. This judgment does not differ in kind from the judgment one would make about a parrot that utters some sentences of English, about a student who has rote learnt a poem in a foreign language, about an app that matches a finite number of sentences in English to sentences in German, or about a simple bot that chitchats mindlessly.

1.2.4 Psychologizing the "data" in philosophical theorizing?

The three characterizations examined differ in another respect: While these characterizations do not entail any particular answer to the question, What supports or undermines philosophical theories?, their proponents are likely to answer differently.

Proponents of the exceptionalist characterizations that posit irreducible intuitions as well as proponents of the particularist characterizations that distinguish obvious ("intuitive") or snap judgments (which they also call "intuitions") from the reflective judgments involved in philosophical theorizing are likely to "psychologize the data," to use Williamson's apt phrase (2007, 4–5): They are likely to assert that philosophical theories are supported or undermined by those intuitions. The reader of the Chinese-room case has the intuition—either an attitude irreducible to judgment or a snap judgment—that in the situation described by this case John Searle would not understand Chinese, and this intuition is what supports Searle's argument against Strong Artificial Intelligence.

By contrast, a proponent of the minimalist characterization is likely to think that the fact holding in the situation described by a philosophical case—not the act of judging itself, but, if true, its truthmaker—is what supports or undermines a philosophical claim. So, for example, the fact that in the hypothetical situation described by the Gödel case "Gödel" would refer to Gödel rather than to Schmidt—and not the judgment with this content—undermines descriptivist theories of reference. The fact that it is permissible to push the switch in the situation described by the switch case and that it is impermissible to push the large person in the situation described by the footbridge—and not the judgments with these contents—bears on the philosophical theories of moral permissibility.

Prima facie, philosophical theories are indeed supported or undermined by the facts assumed to hold in the situations described by philosophical cases. After all, philosophical theories about knowledge or moral permissibility (in contrast to theories about the concepts of knowledge or moral permissibility) have nothing to say about psychological states such as judgments or intuitions about knowledge or about moral permissibility; their subject matters are instead what is involved in knowing something or what makes an action morally permissible.

A proponent of an exceptionalist or particularist characterization of the method of cases may demur. She may concede that philosophical theories are supported or undermined by the facts holding in the situations described by philosophical cases, while insisting that the intuitions elicited by these cases are what warrant judging that these facts hold. Indeed, she may ask, what else if not these intuitions could provide a warrant for these judgments?[11] If this were correct, philosophical theories would ultimately be supported or undermined by intuitions (whatever these are).

This line of response is indeed available to the proponents of the exceptionalist characterizations that posit irreducible intuitions and to the proponents of the particularist characterizations that distinguish obvious or snap judgments from the reflective judgments involved in philosophical theorizing. These philosophers are in a position to psychologize the data of relevance in philosophy. By contrast, for two reasons, a proponent of a minimalist characterization of the method of cases cannot hold that philosophical theories are supported or undermined by judgments elicited by philosophical cases. A proponent with this view would endorse the following inductive argument schema ("Psychologism"):

Psychologism

I judge that p

p

For instance, in the Gödel case, the argument would be:

I judge that in the Gödel situation "Gödel" would refer to Gödel and not Schmidt

In the Gödel situation "Gödel" would refer to Gödel and not Schmidt

In this inference, the act of judging itself—the fact that I make a particular judgment— would be the evidence for the conclusion. This conclusion would then be the premise of an argument against descriptivism:

Descriptivism is false if "Gödel" would refer to Gödel and not Schmidt in the Gödel situation

In the Gödel situation "Gödel" would refer to Gödel and not Schmidt

Descriptivism is false.

A first problem with Psychologism is that its premise is not available before its conclusion (Williamson, 2016). If the conclusion of Psychologism has not been asserted, its premise cannot be asserted either. Thus, Psychologism cannot characterize correctly the reader's warrant for assuming that facts hold in the situations described by philosophical cases. Furthermore, Psychologism would allow a reader of a case to bootstrap herself to certainty. Suppose that I come to believe to degree c that "Gödel" would refer to Gödel and not Schmidt in the situation described by the Gödel case.

---

[11] I have embraced this line of response in the past (Machery, 2011a, 194, n. 4). I now see it as misguided (see Williamson, 2016 for some apt criticisms). See also Deutsch's discussion of "the relocation problem" (2015, Chapter 3).

That is, I form the judgment that "Gödel" would refer to Gödel and not Schmidt. If Psychologism correctly characterized the reader's warrant for assuming that "Gödel" would refer to Gödel and not Schmidt in this situation, then by making this judgment I would have acquired a new reason (a judgment with confidence c) for assuming that "Gödel" would refer to Gödel and not Schmidt. In accordance with Psychologism, it would then be appropriate to strengthen my judgment that "Gödel" would refer to Gödel and not Schmidt, coming to endorse that proposition to degree $c'>c$. But then I would have just acquired a new reason for assuming that "Gödel" would refer to Gödel and not Schmidt. And so on, up to certainty.

It is natural to respond that these two arguments show that *the reader's* judgment that p cannot warrant assuming that p holds, but not that *some* judgment does not play this role. Indeed, one could reformulate Psychologism as follows (e.g., Weatherson, 2003, 2):

Socialized Psychologism

People agree that p	or	According to common sense, p
p		p

For instance, in the Gödel case, the argument could be:

People agree that in the Gödel situation "Gödel" would refer to Gödel and not Schmidt

In the Gödel situation "Gödel" would refer to Gödel and not Schmidt

On this view, the reader's warrant for assuming that a particular fact holds in the situation described by a philosophical case derives not from her judgment, but from the fact that there is a consensus about this matter. Socialized Psychologism does not suffer from the two flaws of Psychologism; it is also in line with the fact that philosophers sometimes refer to how "we" would react to a philosophical case—Kripke concludes the Gödel case by saying that "*we* are not" (my emphasis)—or allude to the consensus elicited by a case—Thomson writes that "*Everyone* to whom [she has] put this case says it would not be [permissible]" (my emphasis).

A proponent of the minimalist characterization of the method of cases may well psychologize the data of relevance in philosophy this way: On this view, philosophical theories are ultimately supported or undermined not by intuitions, but by judgments that happen to be widely shared. A sort of philosophical commonsense would then be the basis of philosophy. While this position seems consistent with the minimalist characterization, proponents of this characterization should be inclined to resist it for two (admittedly non-conclusive) reasons. First, philosophers know that some cases (e.g., the fake-barn case) fail to elicit any consensus among philosophers; second, they regularly develop new cases without attempting to check that people tend to form the same judgment in response to them.

One may wonder what warrants assuming that a particular fact (e.g., that "Gödel" would refer to Gödel rather than to Schmidt) holds in the situation described by a philosophical case if it is not an intuition or a consensual judgment? As noted earlier, a proponent of a minimalist characterization can easily dispel the air of mystery surrounding this question: If anything, what warrants the assumption that the protagonist does not know the relevant proposition in the situation described by the clock case is whatever it is that warrants everyday judgments about knowledge, such as a professor's judgment that a student does not know the course content; similarly, if anything, what warrants assuming that it is morally impermissible to push the large man in the situation described by the footbridge case is whatever it is that warrants everyday judgments about moral permissibility, such as a parent's judgment that it is morally impermissible for her child to torture her pet. Everyday judgments about knowledge and moral wrongness may be warranted because we reliably identify instances of knowledge or moral wrongness, exactly as everyday categorization judgments about chairs or computers (e.g., the judgment that the object in front of me is a computer) may be warranted because we reliably identify chairs and computers. Alternatively, everyday judgments about knowledge and moral wrongness may be warranted because they are based on the right evidence. In which case, a judgment about the situation described by a philosophical case would be warranted if it is based on the right evidence. The explicit and inferred target content of the case—for instance, that the protagonist in the clock case would have had a false belief had she looked at the clock a minute earlier or later—would constitute the evidence for the fact taken to hold in this case. Compare: I see a small red bird in front of my windows in Pittsburgh, and I infer that a cardinal is sitting in the bush in the backyard of my house. The evidence for the inferred fact (i.e., that a cardinal is sitting in the bush in the backyard of my house) is the color of the bird, its size, and its location (a northern state of the USA).

Importantly, I can remain neutral about the exact nature of the warrant for the judgments elicited by philosophical cases. Two things matter here. First, if judgments elicited by philosophical cases are warranted, whatever it is that provides warrant for everyday judgments is what provides their warrant. This first claim, of course, is not uncontroversial, and many philosophers believe that the epistemic standing of the judgments elicited by cases is out of the ordinary. Weinberg (2014, 549, my emphasis) writes that "Any notion of intuition shared across intuition theorists is better thought of as an epistemic functional notion: whatever it is (if there is anything) that does the apparently needed work of legitimating such claims as ECG [evidential common ground], *given that standard sorts of justificatory bases are inadequate.*" Weinberg and others, however, fail to acknowledge the similarity between the judgments we make in response to philosophical cases and the judgments we make in response to other texts (novels, journal articles, etc.) or conversations. If the former are justified, it is for the very reason the latter are, whatever that is (and again I can remain non-committal about that). Second, the discussion of the formal and material use of cases in the remainder of *Philosophy Within*

Its Proper Bounds does not rest on "psychologizing the data" that are of relevance in philosophy: Their non-psychological nature is fully acknowledged.

Finally, that philosophical theories are supported or undermined by the facts that hold in the situations described by philosophical cases rather than by the judgments elicited by these cases does not entail that the characteristics of these judgments or of the underlying processes are irrelevant for supporting or undermining these philosophical theories. If the judgments elicited by philosophical cases were, for some reason, systematically false, we would not be warranted to assume that some facts hold in the situations described by philosophical cases, and we would not be in a position to support or undermine the relevant philosophical theories. Consider the following analogy: While a sample's temperature may confirm or undermine a chemical hypothesis about the substance the sample is taken from, the characteristics of the thermometer are not irrelevant for the confirmation of this chemical hypothesis. If the thermometer were imprecise and biased when it is involved in measuring the temperature of this substance, we would not be warranted to assume that the temperature of the sample is such and such and the temperature reported by the thermometer would neither support nor undermine the chemical hypothesis at stake.

1.2.5 Adjudicating between the competing characterizations

I propose two adequacy conditions to adjudicate between the competing characterizations of the method of cases.

1. *Descriptive Adequacy*: A characterization of the method of cases is adequate only if it is consistent with how cases are actually used by philosophers.
2. *Philosophical Adequacy*: A characterization of the method of cases is adequate only if the notions it relies on are not empty and are useful to characterize the method of cases.

In contrast to these two adequacy conditions, philosophers' metaphilosophical views—including how they describe their own use of cases—do not bear on the adequacy of a characterization of the method of cases: That is, an adequate characterization need not be consistent with these views. Philosophers must often characterize the method of cases incorrectly since many characterizations are inconsistent with one another. It may be tempting to suggest that philosophers' metaphilosophical disagreements about how to characterize the method of cases reflect the fact that they use cases differently, but that would be a mistake. It is a common fact that philosophers use $\ulcorner X \urcorner$ similarly, but propose competing, inconsistent characterizations of $\ulcorner X \urcorner$. Conceptual analysts plausibly use "knowledge" and "cause" similarly, although they have proposed many mutually inconsistent characterizations of the concepts these words express.

As formulated, Philosophical Adequacy seems uncontroversial, but it carries less dialectical weight than Descriptive Adequacy, since philosophers are unlikely to agree about the emptiness of some philosophical notion (e.g., the distinction between analytic and synthetic truths) or about its utility or lack thereof to characterize the method of cases. Descriptive Adequacy may be challenged in three distinct ways. A philosopher could present her characterization as describing how *she* uses cases, and could insist that it does not matter how other philosophers use cases. This first challenge is flawed. Philosophizing is a social activity, and arguments using the method of cases are put forward in informal conversation, talks, articles, and books in order, presumably, to convince others. Philosophers must use cases similarly for philosophical cases to play this dialectical role. Alternatively, a philosopher could present her characterization of the method of cases as prescriptive: It would then state how philosophers should use cases, not how they are actually used. This prescriptive approach could be more or less radical: It could hold that some philosophers are already using philosophical cases properly for material and formal purposes, or it could assert that nearly all, if not all, philosophers are misusing cases. The second challenge to Descriptive Adequacy does not suffer from the flaw undermining the first challenge, but a philosopher embracing it would be engaged in a different project from mine. My goal is to understand a particular practice in philosophy—the use of philosophical cases to answer formal or material questions—in order to assess it. In addition, the prescriptive approach under consideration would still need to satisfy Philosophical Adequacy, and, as I will argue in the next section, most characterizations of the method of cases fail to do so. Minimalist characterizations, which also satisfy Descriptive Adequacy, do satisfy Philosophical Adequacy, and a proponent of the prescriptive approach may then end up agreeing with my own characterization of the method of cases. According to the third challenge, Descriptive Adequacy assumes that philosophers' material or formal use of cases is homogeneous ("the assumption of methodological homogeneity"), while it could in fact vary from philosophers to philosophers (perhaps some philosophers use irreducible intuitions, as some exceptionalist characterizations would have it, while others don't) or from topic to topic (perhaps ethical cases elicit intuitions, while cases in the philosophy of language don't). It would, however, be very surprising if the formal and material use of philosophical cases varied from topic to topic or from philosopher to philosopher. As noted, philosophizing is a social activity, philosophers argue with one another across areas of specialization, and the dialectical role of arguments based on the method of cases is incompatible with the variation hypothesized by the third challenge. It could of course be that philosophers misunderstand one another, and that both the formal and material uses of cases differ across philosophers, research areas, or research traditions; after all, philosophers do sometimes misconstrue the terminology or mischaracterize the philosophical projects of other philosophers. However, while such misconstruals and mischaracterizations happen, they are the exceptions rather than the rules. In the absence of actual evidence that both the formal and material use of cases really differ across philosophers, research areas, or research traditions, we can ignore the remote possibility that the assumption of methodological homogeneity happens to be false.

Minimalist characterizations seem to have an advantage over exceptionalist and particularist ("non-minimalist") ones. Because exceptionalist characterizations require cases to elicit a kind of attitude that differs from everyday judgments, they are more likely to appeal to empty or useless notions to characterize the elicited attitudes and thus to be philosophically inadequate. To be philosophically adequate, the notion of conceptual competence that Sosa appeals to must be acceptable—for instance, it must be possible to draw a line between what is part of conceptual competence and what is not. Because non-minimalist characterizations require the mental states elicited by philosophical cases to share a justificatory status, phenomenology, or etiology, they are more likely to be descriptively inadequate. Gopnik and Schwitzgebel's characterization, for example, is descriptively adequate only if the attitudes elicited by the Gödel case, the Frankfurt cases, the trolley cases, Searle's Chinese-room thought experiment, fake-barn cases, trolley cases, King Arthur's case, the case of the Society of Music Lovers, and Rachel's killing and letting die pair of cases are all snap judgments.

The remainder of this chapter will confirm this impression: I argue that only minimalist characterizations satisfy the two adequacy conditions just proposed, and that exceptionalist and particularist characterizations should thus be rejected.

1.3 Philosophical Adequacy

In this section, I criticize the main exceptionalist characterizations of the method of cases, focusing on their philosophical adequacy. Exceptionalist characterizations often assume that the judgments elicited by philosophical cases have lofty properties, including expressing conceptual competence, being analytically justified, being analytically true, being justified a priori, and being the product of a faculty of intuition. Many of the notions used to characterize these properties are notoriously unclear, and they are either empty or useless to characterize the method of cases. Here I will examine the characterizations that appeal to the notions of conceptual competence, epistemic analyticity, metaphysical analyticity, conceptual truth, and intuition.

1.3.1 Conceptual competence and epistemic analyticity

A number of philosophers hold that, when the method of cases is used, the mental states they elicit are derived from, express, or manifest a conceptual competence.[12] Sosa writes (2007, 102; see also 2007, 61): "When we rely on intuitions in philosophy, then, in my view we manifest a competence that enables us to get it right on a certain subject matter, by basing our beliefs on the sheer understanding of their contents." Similarly, Ludwig describes the judgment elicited by a philosophical case as follows (2007, 135; see also 2014, 225): "I will use 'intuition' to mean an occurrent judgment formed solely on the basis of competence in the concepts involved in response to a question about a scenario."

---

[12] E.g., Bealer (1998, 221–6); Sosa (1998, 2007); Ludwig (2007, 2014). For Bealer, these mental states are not judgments, but an irreducible kind of mental state—intuitions. I will ignore this complication for the time being.

Setting aside differences between the details of their views, when Sosa, Ludwig, Bealer, and others refer to judgments that derive from, manifest, or express our competence with the relevant concepts, presumably in contrast to judgments that do not do so, they endorse an epistemic distinction between two kinds of justification: The former judgments are justified merely in virtue of the fact that they involve, in the right way, particular concepts, the latter in virtue of further beliefs about, or capacities related to, the extension of the relevant concepts. For instance, the judgment that a red surface seen in canonical conditions is red or the judgment that red is a color may be justified merely in virtue of the fact that this judgment involves, in the right way, the concept RED; no further knowledge about the color red is needed for this judgment to be justi-fied. The judgment that the wavelength of red is between 620 and 750 nanometers is not simply justified because it involves RED in the right way; some empirical know-ledge about red is also required. Sosa, Ludwig, Bealer, and others also endorse the view that the judgments elicited by philosophical cases are of the first kind. Thus, these proponents of exceptionalist characterizations of the method of cases claim that the judgments elicited by philosophical cases are epistemically analytic, where a judgment is analytically justified if and only if possessing the relevant concepts is sufficient to justify it (Boghossian, 1996, 2003). If a judgment is analytically justified, then it is a priori justified. Proponents of exceptionalist characterizations can thus hold that judg-ments elicited by philosophical cases are a priori.

To anticipate the conclusion of the discussion, I will argue that either there is no such thing as conceptual competence or that, if there is such a thing, it cannot be a source of much philosophical knowledge. Three considerations support this claim: I undermine a natural reason to defend the notion of conceptual competence; I show that it is very difficult to identify what would constitute conceptual competence either because there is no such thing as conceptual competence or because it is very thin; and I challenge the idea that judgments based on conceptual competence, if there is such a thing, must be or are likely to be true. In any case, the notion of epistemic analyticity cannot play a role in characterizing the method of cases.

Let's start with two by and large uncontroversial clarifications. First, conceptual competence with concept C, if there is such a thing, is the set of inferential or recogni-tional dispositions related to the thoughts involving C or the explicit or implicit doxastic states (beliefs or belief-like states) about the reference or extension of C that are necessary and sufficient for possessing C. For instance, it may be that one possesses the concept AND if and only if one is disposed to draw the inferences specified by the introduction and elimination rules of conjunction, or perhaps if and only if one is disposed to find them primitively compelling (Peacocke, 1992):

Elimination rule of AND	*Introduction rule of* AND
p and q	p, q
p	p and q

It may also be that one possesses the concept of a cat only if one believes, implicitly or explicitly, that cats are animals. Second, one can have propositional attitudes (e.g., beliefs) about the reference or extension of *C* if and only if one possesses *C*. Thus, to have a belief about presidents, it is necessary and sufficient to have the concept of a president.

Now, how are we going to identify what constitutes the conceptual competence with a given concept? It is common to use semantic competence as a proxy for conceptual competence, and indeed some do not distinguish conceptual and semantic competence. Semantic competence with a given word *W* (if there is such a thing) consists in the dispositions or beliefs that, according to the rules governing the language *W* belongs to (let's call it "*L*"), are necessary and sufficient for a speaker to mean what *W* means in *L* when she uses *W*.

Why believe that there is any such thing as semantic competence? People respond to assertions involving *W* in two distinct ways (e.g., Grice & Strawson, 1956, 150–1): They either agree or disagree with the speaker (saying, e.g., "I disagree with you; Messi was not offside"), or they don't understand what the speaker said (saying, e.g., "I don't understand what you mean by 'offside'" or "you and I don't use 'offside' to talk about the same thing"). Let's call the first type of response "a matter-of-fact response," the second "a matter-of-word response." Matter-of-word responses are rare, but they occur. A matter-of-fact response involves an assertion about the topic of discussion, not about language, while a matter-of-word response involves a semantic ascent: It turns away from the topic of discussion, and involves an assertion about the meaning of the words used. That lay discourse includes both matter-of-fact and matter-of-word responses may suggest that one is a competent user of a given word in a natural language if and only if one is able to do specific things (e.g., draw some specific inferences, identify some specific presuppositions, compute some specific entailments, etc.) or if and only if one has (explicitly or implicitly) some particular beliefs. When a speaker does not meet these conditions (e.g., she draws some strange inferences or fails to draw some expected inferences), listeners conclude that she means something different by this word. This interpretation would vindicate the notion of semantic competence and, indirectly, the notion of conceptual competence.

However, one need not understand matter-of-word responses this way. Uncontroversially, we often judge that people use a word differently than we do or we express puzzlement about what they mean, not because they fail to display some semantic competence, but because they would have outlandish beliefs if they used the word to refer to what we do. For example, if someone uses the word "triangle," but denies many obvious facts about triangles—including the fact that a triangle's angles add up to 180 degrees—a listener may well infer that the speaker means something different by "triangle" than what she herself means. The listener's inference would not result from the speaker failing to display the knowledge or capacities involved in having the concept of a triangle—indeed, knowing the facts denied by the speaker is not constitutive of possessing this concept—but from her desire to avoid ascribing obviously false beliefs to the speaker. The suggestion then is that matter-of-word responses ("I do not understand what you mean" or "she must be talking about something else") are *only* made to avoid ascribing outlandish beliefs (in contrast to resulting from the violation of an alleged semantic competence). When someone says to a speaker, e.g., "I don't understand what you mean by 'offside,' " she simply expresses the judgment that, despite using the same word ("offside"), the speaker is talking about something different from what she is herself talking about with this word (something other than offsides) because it would be uncharitable to interpret the speaker as really talking about offsides: If she were really talking about offsides, she would have outlandish beliefs. Thus, to make sense of the existence of matter-of-word responses in addition to matter-of-fact responses, we need not assume any semantic rule specifying what speakers must be able to do or must believe in order to count as semantically competent users of a given word. That is, we don't need a notion of semantic competence in order to make sense of matter-of-word responses.

Furthermore, it is difficult to find any disposition or belief that speakers must have to be semantically competent. To be competent with words like "elm," people need not be able to distinguish elms from beeches; they need not even know that elms are trees (in contrast to some kind of plant) since people can disagree about whether elms are really trees.[13] One can explain this difficulty in three different ways. The first explanation is that there is no such thing as semantic, and a fortiori conceptual, competence; the second is that semantic, and a fortiori conceptual competence is really thin; finally, the third is that ascribing linguistic understanding when people don't have the proper knowledge or capacities (e.g., ascribing the understanding of "elm" to people unable to recognize elms) is erroneous. The first explanation strikes me as the most plausible, but if either the first or the second explanation is correct, the method of cases cannot be adequately characterized by appealing to the notion of conceptual competence. While the third option would not invalidate exceptionalist characterizations appealing to this notion, it is implausible.

In response to the challenge of finding dispositions or beliefs that are necessary for semantic competence, one could perhaps distinguish between natural kind terms, competence with which would require very little, and other terms, competence with which would be thicker. But, first, I doubt that the notion of natural kind term really identifies a semantically distinct class of words in natural languages. Two features are often taken to distinguish these words: the type of modal intuition that is illustrated by Putnam's (1975b) Twin-Earth thought experiment (Horgan & Timmons, 1991; Ludwig, 2014) and deference to experts. It is, however, not the case that all speakers share the alleged modal intuitions even for terms like "water" (Dupré, 1981; Machery et al., ms), and speakers' alleged deference to experts with respect to the proper use of terms like "water" may be a philosophical myth. Second, it is also difficult to identify any capacity or belief that speakers must have to be semantically competent with other kinds of word, such as proper names ("Gödel"), artifact terms, words denoting abstract

---

[13] Putnam (1975a); Burge (1979); Fodor (1994).

entities (e.g., "square" and "democracy"), and even closed-class words expressing logical constants such as "not" (Williamson, 2007).

Some philosophers will pick up the gauntlet, and offer examples of beliefs or capacities they take to be necessary (if not necessary and sufficient) to be semantically competent with a given word. Shouldn't one know that "oxygen" refers to a gas to be semantically competent with "oxygen," that "gold" refers to a substance to be semantically competent with "gold," that "red" refers to a color, that the truth value of a conjunction somehow depends on that of the conjuncts to be a competent user of "and"? First, many of these counterexamples are not compelling. Someone without a concept of gas can still use "oxygen" to talk about oxygen, and instead of knowing that "oxygen" refers to a gas being necessary to be semantically competent with "oxygen," most of us may just happen to have learned this fact (exactly as we learn that we breathe oxygen). Second, how are we going to know whether these claims about semantic competence are right? Without an answer to this question, the notion of semantic competence remains obscure. Third, even if these counterexamples were genuine, they would not show that semantic competence is thick enough to be philosophically interesting.

Perhaps philosophers who appeal to the notion of conceptual competence to characterize the method of cases would deny that semantic competence is a proxy for conceptual competence (Ludwig, 2014, 223), but all the points made above about words generalize to concepts. People ascribe propositional attitudes to individuals who don't distinguish elms from beeches, who don't know that elms are trees, who use propositional negation in an intuitionist manner, and who have no idea who Cicero was.

It would not do to respond that there are two different ways of having propositional attitudes about the reference or extension of C—one that does not require conceptual competence with C (explaining how one could have beliefs about beeches without knowing that beeches are trees), and one that requires conceptual competence with C—since nothing would motivate this response but the desire to save the notion of conceptual competence. In addition, how we are supposed to determine what is constitutive of conceptual competence if propositional attitude ascription is not to be taken as a guide?

Finally, why is it assumed that conceptual competence requires being in a position to form true beliefs? One is free to stipulate that it is so, but this is quite unsatisfactory. And this assumption is quite implausible if one takes semantic competence (if there is such a thing) to be a proxy for conceptual competence since, if there is such a thing, a listener's semantic competence could involve the possession of false beliefs that happen to be shared within a linguistic community. One may respond that their truth is guaranteed by how concepts pick their reference (i.e., descriptively): What they refer to satisfies the beliefs that are constitutive of conceptual competence. But, first, even if concepts refer descriptively, not all constitutive beliefs need to be made true by the reference of concepts: The concept could refer to what satisfies most of these beliefs or to the natural property that satisfies some of them. Second, concepts need not refer descriptively.

Philosophers who appeal to the notion of conceptual competence may be tempted to give examples of propositions we know or can know by forming beliefs on the basis of our conceptual competence. Don't or can't we know that "the arithmetic mean of a range of numbers lies within it," that "no one knows that the moon is larger than the earth if it is not true," "that no person is identical to two people" (Ludwig, 2014, 218) because we are competent with the relevant concepts involved in these beliefs? However, while some of these beliefs may well be known or knowable a priori (whatever a prioricity amounts to), there is no reason to believe that they are known or knowable merely in virtue of possessing the relevant concepts. If not all mathematical or logical propositions are known or knowable merely in virtue of possessing the relevant concepts, as is likely, do we really know that way that the arithmetic mean of a range of numbers lies within it? The same remark applies to the other candidate propositions: Supposing they are true and that one knows them, this knowledge need not be due to the mere possession of the concepts involved; rather it may express our best metaphysical and epistemological theory developed by the usual means of theory construction (simplicity, coherence with other beliefs, breadth, etc.—but see Chapter 6 for concerns). It won't do to respond that we know that it is necessary that, e.g., no person is identical to two people, and that theory construction could not give such modal knowledge since that latter claim lacks justification.

To recap the discussion: One does not need to appeal to the notion of semantic competence to explain the occurrence of matter-of-word responses in everyday discourse; in addition, it is difficult to find any capacity or belief that people must have to be conceptually competent, suggesting either that the notion of conceptual competence is empty or that, if it is not, conceptual competence is thin; and the connection between conceptual competence and truth is unclear. If we should be wary of the notion of conceptual competence, we should be wary of epistemic analyticity too: If there is no conceptual competence—nothing we need to believe or be able to do to possess a concept—then no judgment is epistemically analytic; furthermore, if conceptual competence is really thin, then epistemic analyticity is unlikely to be of interest to philosophy. Upshot: It would be a mistake to characterize the method of cases by appealing to the notion of conceptual competence and, by extension, to epistemic analyticity.

1.3.2 Conceptual truths and metaphysical analyticity

The exceptionalist characterizations discussed above characterized the attitudes elicited by philosophical cases in epistemic terms: Expressing our conceptual competence, these attitudes are epistemically analytic. Other exceptionalist characterizations of the method of cases characterize them in semantic terms: Their contents are conceptual truths or metaphysically analytic truths. A belief is metaphysically analytic if and only if its truth is determined only by the semantic content of the concepts that constitute it, and a sentence is metaphysically analytic if and only if its truth is determined only by the meaning of its constituents. "Bachelors are unmarried" is metaphysically analytic if and only if that sentence is true only in virtue of the meaning of "bachelor" and "unmarried" (mutatis mutandis for the belief that bachelors are unmarried). Some distinguish conceptual from analytic truths (e.g., Hacker, 2009), but they are not fully clear about what conceptual truths are if they are not analytic truths. In any case, the two concerns raised below about analytic truths would plausibly apply to conceptual truths too.

The first concern is that nobody knows how to identify analytic or conceptual truths, and how to distinguish beliefs in such truths from obvious beliefs (beliefs that seem true whenever we consider their content) and unquestionable beliefs (beliefs we cannot imagine being falsified and thus having to relinquish). Beliefs previously taken to be obvious or unquestionable (e.g., divine command theory, stasis of species, axioms of Euclidean geometry, perspective-independence of simultaneity) have been shown to be false simpliciter or in some conditions (e.g., some of the axioms of Euclidean geometry are false in some geometries), and have been relinquished. A fortiori, they were not conceptually or analytically true. The beliefs taken to be analytically or conceptually true may well be made of the same cloth.

The concern here is not that the distinction between analytic and synthetic truths is empty if it is not somehow operationalized, and it thus cannot be dismissed for a naive commitment to operationalism. Rather, the first concern has two dimensions. First, the best explanation of our incapacity to identify marks of analytic truths is that there are no such truths. What are the competing explanations? It isn't for lack of trying. And there is no reason why identifying marks of analytic truths should be harder than characterizing other semantic properties such as indexicality. Second, to determine whether the judgments elicited by philosophical cases express analytic or conceptual truths, one needs to be able to distinguish them from obvious or unquestionable propositions. We aren't, and because we aren't, the notion of metaphysical analyticity should not be put to use to characterize the method of cases.

The second concern is that, even if there are analytic or conceptual truths (it is perhaps analytically true that bachelors are unmarried), these "cut no philosophical ice...bake no philosophical bread and wash no philosophical windows" (Putnam, 1962, reprinted in 1975a, 36). The best examples of analytic truths (e.g., the true propositions that bachelors are unmarried and that vixens are female) have no philosophical import, and it is thus plausible that philosophical propositions are not analytic, or, if some philosophical truths turn out to be analytic, that most philosophical propositions are not. This implies that, even if it is not empty, the distinction between analytic and synthetic truths is of no use to characterize the method of cases.

1.3.3 Intuitions

It is common to describe the method of cases as involving intuitions, but the notion of intuition is cashed out in very different ways. Some compare intuitions to perceptual experiences, and identify them with intellectual seemings.[14] According to Bealer (1998, 207), an intuition is "a sui generis, irreducible, natural (i.e., non-Cambridge-like)

---

[14] E.g., Bealer (1996, 1998); Huemer (2005); Chudnoff (2013); Bengson (2015).

propositional attitude that occurs episodically"; furthermore (1998, 207, italics in the original), "intuition is an *intellectual* seeming, sense perception is a *sensory* seeming (an *appearing*)." As we have seen above, others identify intuitions with judgments or inclinations to judge that have a particular modal content (about what is necessarily or possibly the case) and that express our "conceptual competence" (Sosa, 2007; Ludwig, 2014). Yet others identify intuitions with specific kinds of judgment or specific kinds of inclination to judge, such as non-inferred, unreflective, immediate judgments or inclinations to judge.[15]

I will say little about this latter characterization of intuitions here since it is not exceptionalist: Some everyday judgments are indeed immediate and not inferred consciously. I can also be curt with characterizations of intuitions that appeal to a faculty of intuition (e.g., BonJour, 1998). It is all too easy to postulate faculties when it suits one's epistemology, one's metaphysics, or one's theology. That there is a faculty of intuition is an empirical claim, which can be only taken seriously if it finds support in our best sciences of the mind—psychology and neuroscience—but these have no place for a faculty of intuition. Finally, in light of the criticism of the notion of conceptual competence above, I can dismiss the characterization of intuition that appeals to this notion (e.g., Sosa, 2007; Ludwig, 2007, 2014).

We are thus left with the idea that intuitions are a distinct type of propositional attitude, irreducible to judgments, similar to perceptual experiences, and endowed with a particular phenomenology and a distinctive epistemic import. On this view, intuitions are not the expression of our conceptual competencies, they are not the product of a faculty of intuition, and their epistemic import is not due to epistemic analyticity, but to the fact that they play a role relative to judgment that is analogous to the role played by perceptual experiences (e.g., Huemer, 2005; Chudnoff, 2013).

The problem is that there is little reason to believe that there are intuitions, so understood. To justify postulating this kind of propositional attitude, philosophers often allude to cases where, while one judges, indeed knows that not *p*, it seems that *p*. For instance, the axiom of unrestricted comprehension may seem true, but it isn't. A hard-nosed consequentialist may hold that it seems impermissible to push the large person in the footbridge case, but it really is permissible; it may seem that if a ball and a bat cost \$1.10 and if the bat costs a dollar more than the ball, then the ball costs \$.10, but it doesn't (the first question of the Cognitive Reflection Test or CRT; see Frederick, 2005). Philosophers then argue that these seemings cannot be judgments since one is not contradicting oneself in any of these cases. But if they are not judgments, we need to postulate a distinct kind of propositional attitude, namely intuitions (e.g., Bealer, 1992; Chudnoff, 2013, 41).

However, this last step of the argument fails because there is an alternative explanation of the cases alluded to by philosophers (e.g., the axiom of unrestricted comprehension): These simply involve inclinations to judge that do not result in

---

[15] E.g, Sidgwick (1876); Gopnik & Schwitzgebel (1998); Weinberg (2007); Nagel (2012).

judgments (e.g., Williamson, 2007, 217). When we consider the axiom of unrestricted comprehension, we have an inclination to judge that it is true, but this inclination is countervailed and we do not judge that the axiom of unrestricted comprehension is true; when a hard-nosed consequentialist considers the footbridge case, she has an inclination to judge it impermissible to push the large person, but her inclination is countervailed.

This alternative explanation better explains the analogy between perceptual illusions (e.g., the fact that in a Müller-Lyer illusion it seems that the two lines are unequal, while we judge that they are equal) and the cases alluded by philosophers (e.g., the fact that the axiom of unrestricted comprehension seems true, while we judge it isn't). Three components are constitutive of perceptual illusions: the perceptual experience (e.g., as of the two lines being unequal), whatever it is that makes the sentence "it seems that the lines are unequal" true (let's call the relevant state "the seeming"), and the judgment that the lines are equal. What is the nature of this seeming? It is just an inclination to judge: Based on one's experience, one is inclined to judge that the lines are unequal. This inclination results from the processes leading to perceptual judgments triggered by the perceptual experience, as happens in any ordinary perceptual experience. The inclination elicited by the perceptual experience is not acted upon, and we form instead the belief that the lines are equal based on our further knowledge. Now consider the axiom of unrestricted comprehension: One understands the sentence expressing this axiom; one is inclined to judge that it is true, an inclination that makes the sentence "it seems that for any condition φ there is a set S such that S contains all and only the objects that satisfy φ" true; one forms a judgment at odds with this inclination. To preserve the analogy with perceptual illusions, one need not introduce intuitions; in fact, there is no room for intuitions at all, just for inclinations to judge, if one takes seriously the analogy with perceptual illusions. The counterpart of the perception is the understanding, imagining, or grasping of a situation or proposition; in both cases, the seeming is an inclination to judge; in both cases, the inclination is not acted upon, but rather one forms a judgment based on further information. So understood, what is going on in the cases alluded by philosophers and similar cases is an instance of a very familiar process: One imagines or conceives a situation (perhaps as a result of a newspaper article); one is inclined to form a judgment that p based on one's imagination or conception; one does not act on this imagination or conception because one knows better.

Furthermore, those who think that epistemic virtues matter for the assessment of explanations should acknowledge that it is better to explain the cases alluded to by philosophers by means of inclinations to judge rather than by means of intuitions for two reasons: The former explanation is more parsimonious and has broader scope.[16] First, it is more parsimonious because it does not require the postulation of a new, irreducible kind of mental state; second, and more important, it is consistent with our

---

[16] I am somewhat skeptical of the epistemic significance of alleged theoretical virtues such as parsimony (Section 6.3 of Chapter 6).

understanding of what is going on in numerous similar cases. Consider the fact that it seems that if a ball and a bat cost $1.10 and if the bat costs 1 dollar more than the ball, then the ball costs $.10. Psychologists have a standard explanation of this seeming: Some features of the sentence are cues that trigger a judgment heuristic, resulting in an inclination to judge that the ball costs $.10. One explains similarly why in the Linda case it seems that Linda is more likely to be a bank teller and a feminist than just a feminist (Tversky & Kahneman, 1974): The description of Linda triggers a judgment heuristic (the representativeness heuristic). Similarly, one can explain the seeming that occurs to the bite-the-bullet kind of consequentialist in the footbridge case by appealing to an influential account of moral judgment in moral psychology (Greene, 2014): The footbridge case elicits an aversive emotional reaction, which is itself a cue for moral judgment. As a result of this aversive emotion, people, including the hard-nosed consequentialist, have an inclination to judge that it is impermissible to push the large person.

To block the extension of the psychological explanation in terms of judgmental cues from the bat-and-ball case to alleged cases of intuitions, a believer in intuitions could deny that the attitude elicited by the question, "If a ball and a bat cost $1.10 and if the bat costs 1 dollar more than the ball, how much does it cost?", is an intuition. Thus, Chudnoff (2013, 8, italics in the original) has claimed that "on the face of it, this error [i.e., people answering 10 cents instead of 5 cents] occurs precisely because he [i.e., the reader] is *not* aware of, and does *not* have an experience that even purports to make him aware of, the arithmetical relations involved," but this claim is unconvincing. First, Chudnoff may not be able to distinguish the intuition elicited by the comprehension axiom (a genuine intuition) from the attitude elicited by the bat-and-ball case (not an intuition) since the central reason for positing intuitions as an irreducible kind of attitude—i.e., something seems to be the case, while we judge it is not—applies to both cases equally. Second, I do not know what Chudnoff means by "awareness of" the content of the intuition. Is being aware of the content of an intuition simply representing that content? But if that is so, why wouldn't the bat-and-ball case elicit an intuition? And if awareness amounts to something else, what is that exactly? Next, Chudnoff's argument seems to be that, had the reader been aware of the arithmetic relations involved (whatever that amounts to— perhaps just represented), she would have gotten it right, but since she did not get it right, she must have failed to have the proper awareness, and the bat-and-ball case fails to count as an intuition. However, Chudnoff gives no reason for the assumption that, had the reader been aware of the arithmetic relations involved, she would have gotten it right, and this assumption is not particularly credible: It often happens that we represent some asserted mathematical relation while not knowing whether the assertion is true. Finally, while I do not know how to determine whether a mental state "purports to make us aware of its subject matter," I see no way of clarifying this idea in such a way that the seeming elicited by the comprehension axiom (taken by Chudnoff to be a genuine intuition) would "purport to make us aware of its subject matter," while the seeming elicited by the bat-and-ball case would not.

Chudnoff (2013, 42–3) has also developed the following dilemma against the attempt to reduce seemings to inclinations to judge. Either the inclination to judge is unconscious or it is not. Because the intuition is conscious, the attempted reduction fails if the inclination to judge is unconscious; if the inclination to judge is conscious, then it is puzzling that philosophers who posit intuitions do not recognize them for what they are. As Chudnoff says (2013, 42), "I know what it is like to have these inclinations. When I consider (All Ordinals) [viz. There is a set {x: x is an ordinal} containing all the ordinals] I do not experience anything like one of these inclinations. Only a convincing error theory would tempt me to revise this claim." This argument fails, however: Surely, philosophers who claim that intuitions are mere inclinations to judge know what an inclination to judge is, and take themselves to recognize such inclinations in the relevant seemings. It would take "a convincing error theory" to show that these philosophers are mistaken, and Chudnoff and others have not provided one.

I have discussed a few important exceptionalist characterizations of the method of cases, which appeal to conceptual competence, epistemic analyticity, metaphysic analyticity, and a non-reductive view of intuitions. All these characterizations are committed to empty notions or to notions that under examination turn out to be useless to characterize the method of cases, and they should thus be rejected.

1.4 Descriptive Adequacy

I now turn to the critical weakness of the exceptionalist and particularist characterizations of the method of cases: They are simply descriptively inadequate. In general, there is no indication that philosophers who appeal to the method of cases think that the attitudes elicited by philosophical cases possess the properties non-minimalist characterizations single out. Typically, these mental states are presented as judgments, not as an irreducible kind of mental state (e.g., intuitions à la Bealer); these judgments are not said to be a priori justified; they are rarely described as having a modal content; they are not connected in any way with conceptual competence. Remember Kripke's assertion about the Gödel case: "We simply are not," not "It is a priori that we are not" or "It is necessary that we are not," or anything of this ilk. Similarly, Searle writes, "It seems to me quite obvious in the example that I do not understand a word of the Chinese stories," not "It is a priori true that I do not understand a word of the Chinese stories."

Of course, it may be that philosophers conceive of the attitudes elicited by philosophical cases along the lines of some non-minimalist characterization or other, but simply did not feel the need to make it explicit. Or it may be that the elicited mental states have the characteristics specified by this or that non-minimalist characterization, but that philosophers are not clear about the nature of the attitudes their own cases elicit.

However, it is in fact doubtful that the mental states elicited by cases during philosophical argumentation really have the properties singled out by non-minimalist characterizations. To start with the claim that they are intuitions, there is much to agree with Cappelen's recent discussion of intuitions and the method of cases (2012). Most philosophers do not refer to a distinct propositional attitude or to a distinct kind of judgment, one with a distinct warrant-conferring power, when they refer to what is intuitive or when they say, "Intuitively, p" or "it seems that p." Rather, these expressions (particularly, "it seems that p") sometimes work as hedges, expressing a qualified judgment or the thought that the judgment is in need of further support; sometimes, they play no role at all and are a mere stylistic habit (see the end of the Gödel case quoted earlier). Similarly, how plausible is it that the judgments elicited by the Gödel case, the Frankfurt cases, the trolley cases, Searle's Chinese-room thought experiment, fake-barn cases, trolley cases, King Arthur's case, and the case of the Society of Music Lovers *all* have a modal content (even implicitly) or *all* have the same etiology (expressing a conceptual competence)?

This descriptive inadequacy of non-minimalist characterizations becomes clearer when one examines the judgments elicited by particular philosophical cases. While some non-minimalist characterizations (e.g., Sosa, 2007) hold that the judgments elicited by philosophical cases have a modal content, this isn't the case of the judgment elicited by the Gödel case: The reader is not meant to judge that "Gödel" *necessarily* refers to the man originally called "Gödel" in the situation described by the Gödel case (i.e., that "Gödel" refers to the man originally called "Gödel" in every possible world consistent with this situation) since, as Kripke himself makes it clear, it is a contingent fact that proper names refer causally-historically and since languages in which all proper names refer descriptively are possible. The same point could be made about the judgment elicited by Burge's arthritis case. It would do no good to point out that the judgment elicited by the Gödel case has a modal content because it is a counterfactual judgment: If Gödel had not proved the incompleteness of arithmetic, etc., then "Gödel" would still refer to Gödel. The Gödel case would work equally well if it described an actual situation.

It is questionable whether other philosophical cases elicit a judgment with a modal content, and in any case the dialectical function of these cases does not require such content. The Chinese-room thought experiment does not elicit the judgment that *necessarily* or *possibly* the protagonist in the room or the room itself does not speak Chinese, and, in any case, whether or not it does is irrelevant for Searle's point: His argument against good old-fashioned AI only requires that, in the actual world, being able to make appropriate assertions in response to questions is not sufficient for understanding a language.

Some non-minimalist characterizations also refer to a specific modal phenomenology that characterizes the attitudes elicited by philosophical cases: In particular, it is often alleged that these attitudes are held with a sense of necessity. Bealer (1998, 207) writes that "when we have a rational intuition—say, that if P, then not not P—it presents itself as necessary." This characterization is ambiguous—either the content of the intuition itself is modal (we intuit that necessarily p) or the phenomenology is as of necessity—but either way it too seems descriptively hopeless. Reporting on my own phenomenology, many cases (e.g., the loop case) do not elicit any such experience, and, in any case, this seems utterly irrelevant for their dialectical functions. More generally, it is outlandish to assert that the judgments elicited by philosophical cases share a common phenomenology.

Some may have a particular phenomenology, but some don't, and, to report again my own introspection, different cases elicit different phenomenologies.

Other non-minimalist characterizations hold that the attitudes elicited by philosophical cases must "manifest," be "derived" from, or be "the expression of" one's conceptual competence with the relevant concept, but it is hard to see what conceptual competence (supposing that notion is not empty) is appealed to when one makes a judgment about the Gödel case: It is not plausibly a conceptual competence with the concept of the proper name "Gödel" since it is not fully clear what a conceptual competence with a particular word would be; nor is it plausibly a conceptual competence with proper names in general since, while we have some implicit knowledge about how to use proper names, this knowledge is not well characterized as having a concept of proper names (we do have a concept of proper names, but it does not guide our use of proper names in the natural languages we happen to speak). Furthermore, other cases elicit disagreement among philosophers: For instance, many philosophers who have discussed fake-barn cases have maintained that the protagonist does not know that he or she sees a barn, but not all philosophers agree.[17] There are at least three ways to explain this disagreement among those philosophers: They have different concepts of knowledge; they have the same concept of knowledge, but one side of the controversy fails to apply it properly; they have the same concept, but their judgments are not exclusively based on their conceptual competence, but also on additional beliefs about knowledge that vary across philosophers. The first two options are implausible since, first, Lycan's and Goldman's uses of "knowledge," which presumably express their concept of knowledge, are plausibly similar in many circumstances outside the department of philosophy's seminar room and since, second, it is unclear which side would be misapplying their concept of knowledge. So, the third option is the most plausible interpretation of the disagreement among philosophers, and for at least the cases eliciting such disagreement it is not the case that judgments are solely made on the basis of conceptual competence or sheer understanding of the expressed proposition. Nor is it the case that these judgments are epistemically analytic.

While some non-minimalist characterizations hold that the judgments elicited by cases are, in the usual terminology, intuitions in the sense of, roughly, snap judgments, experimental evidence suggests that the judgments elicited by at least some philosophical cases are plausibly consciously inferred. Cushman et al. (2006) have shown that people are able to give reasons for their judgments for at least some versions of the trolley cases. People may thus have consciously inferred these judgments on the basis of these reasons, although alternatively they may simply have been good at providing post hoc reconstructions of their judgments (for additional supportive discussion of this evidence, see Paxton & Greene, 2010, 518). Lombrozo (2009) provides evidence that people's explicit endorsement of consequentialist principles predict their answers in trolley-style dilemmas. Greene's theory of moral judgments suggests that the

---

[17] Pro: Goldman (1976); Lewis (1996). Con: Millikan (1984); Lycan (2006).

judgments elicited by trolley cases (the type of stimuli used in his research) are the products of two potentially conflicting systems, one of which consists of "controlled cognitive processes that look more like moral reasoning" (Paxton & Greene, 2010, 513; see also Greene, 2014). So, on Greene's view, at least some judgments in response to philosophical cases are not snap judgments. Indeed, Paxton and Greene (2010) note that people are relatively slower at responding to difficult moral dilemmas (such as the footbridge case), consistent with the idea that they are thinking through their response. Paxton et al. (2012) also show that the judgments elicited by trolley-style cases are influenced by variables that impact reasoning. Of course, such findings do not show that the judgments elicited by *all* cases are slow and reflective, but the proponent of the minimalist characterization should not make such a strong claim; rather she should just claim that not *all* judgments are fast and the product of unconscious, automatic processes. Second, philosophical cases are exactly the type of situation that tends to elicit careful and slow judgments: They are unusual and they look tricky. How often do people consider whether someone who could not distinguish a zebra from a cleverly disguised mule knows that she is actually seeing a zebra? So, the particularist characterization that characterizes the attitudes elicited by philosophical cases as snap judgments that are not inferred consciously is descriptively inadequate. (However, to anticipate the very end of this book (Section 7.6 of Chapter 7), this type of judgment may have an important role to play when philosophical cases are used to answer formal-mode philosophical questions.)

I have not reviewed here all the existing exceptionalist and particularist character-izations, to say nothing of the merely possible ones, but the kind of consideration discussed above suggests that philosophical cases elicit judgments that do not differ in kind from the judgments we make about the same topics (knowledge, justice, beauty, explanation, permissibility, or causation) in everyday circumstances.

Finally, exceptionalist characterizations of the method of cases have possibly led some philosophers to misunderstand the material use of cases. They fail to see how philosophical cases can be justifiably used if the goal is not to analyze the meaning of the relevant terms (e.g., "knowledge") or the semantic content of concepts (KNOWLEDGE). Balaguer (2009, 4–5) writes:

> [T]his methodology would make little sense if we weren't at least partially engaged in trying to uncover ordinary-language meaning. For while it's plausible to suppose that our intuitions reliably track facts about ordinary-language meaning, it's not very plausible to suppose that they reliably track other kinds of facts.

I offer a response to, and a diagnosis of, Balaguer's mistake. The response has two steps. First, Balaguer's last claim is erroneous: If one is not a moral skeptic, there is nothing strange in assuming that in at least some circumstances people can correctly distinguish morally permissible actions from morally impermissible ones; similarly, if one is not a skeptic about responsibility, there is nothing strange in assuming that in at least some circumstances people can correctly distinguish responsible agents from non-responsible ones such as children and people in the grip of dementia. These capacities can be deployed when one is thinking about the situations described by philosophical cases, allowing readers to assume that particular facts hold in these situations. But then the method of cases "makes sense" even if one is not trying to "uncover" the meaning of predicates of philosophical interest: Deploying our recognitional capacities to judge about actual or hypothetical situations, one attempts to learn about knowledge, permissibility, responsibility, or causation. Of course—noting this is the second step of the response to Balaguer—the method of cases "would make little sense if" words in philosophical cases did not have their usual meaning. When a reader is asked about knowledge in an epistemological case, "knowledge" must mean what it usually means when one talks about knowledge in usual circumstances. Otherwise, the genuine recognitional capacity the reader deploys in ascribing knowledge in her everyday life would be of no use to identify knowledge in a situation described by an epistemological case (e.g., a fake-barn case). But using a word with its usual meaning and "trying to uncover ordinary-language meaning" are two distinct things, and only the first is required for the material use of cases to make sense. Turning to the (somewhat speculative) diagnosis: The kind of mistake illustrated by Balaguer's position may be due to thinking of the attitudes elicited by philosophical cases as intuitions instead of as everyday judgments. If one thinks of these attitudes as a distinct kind of mental state, their justification becomes mysterious (one can't simply allude to what justifies everyday judgments). To explain it, philosophers often turn to some of their favorite chimeras—the knowledge of the meaning of words (e.g., the meaning of "responsibility") that native speakers are supposed to possess (in contrast to the knowledge of synthetic propositions), the knowledge of the rules of language that govern the use of these words, or conceptual competence with the relevant concepts (e.g., KNOWLEDGE)—but if one is skeptical of the claim that intuitions are justified because they reflect such knowledge and competence, the material use of cases is bound to look puzzling. By contrast, if one thinks of the attitudes elicited by philosophical cases as simply judgments, in line with minimalist characterizations, then their role in the method of cases can prima facie be justified by appealing to the genuine capacities we deploy when we judge in everyday life. Nothing mysterious there.

1.5 Conclusion

Presenting actual or hypothetical cases plays an important role in many parts of contemporary philosophy, and this practice has a venerable history; some even view it as the distinctive methodological feature of philosophy. How to characterize this practice remains controversial, however, but only a minimalist characterization, according to which philosophical cases elicit everyday judgments, avoids any commitment to philosophically empty or useless notions (conceptual competence, epistemic or metaphysical analyticity, and intuition as an irreducible kind of mental state) and, more important dialectically, adequately describes what philosophers are actually doing.

2

The Empirical Findings

I will begin the discussion of the method of cases by considering the material use of cases—i.e., when philosophers theorize about knowledge, permissibility, or justice themselves instead of the concepts thereof. The idea, as we have seen in Chapter 1, is that, by considering cases, philosophers come to know, or come to be justified in believing that, some particular facts hold in the situations described by these cases and can thus be assumed, at least defeasibly, in a philosophical argument. The implications or philosophical significance of these facts are then a matter of philosophical argumentation. The claim that a fact holds in a particular situation can naturally be defeated by arguments or other cases.

An influential tradition within experimental philosophy—sometimes called "the negative program" or "restrictionist program" (Alexander & Weinberg, 2007)—has challenged this role of the method of cases.[1] The goal of the present chapter is to review the empirical findings that fuel this challenge. I provide the first detailed review of the experimental findings about the factors that influence the judgments elicited by philosophical cases. It is as complete as possible, although it is probably not exhaustive. The literature reviewed here is culled from experimental philosophers', but also psychologists' (particularly, moral psychologists') research. This literature has focused on two types of influence: first, the influence of demographic variables, such as culture, gender, age, personality, and socio-economic status on the judgments elicited by philosophical cases ("demographic effects"); second, the influence of the order of presentation of cases, of their wording, and of situational cues on these judgments ("presentation effects"). As we will see in this chapter, very few cases seem immune to both forms of influence: When the judgments elicited by a philosophical case appear to be immune to demographic variables, they are often influenced by presentation variables, and vice versa.

We should not pay simply attention to the influence of demographic or presentation variables on the judgments elicited by philosophical cases; we should also examine *how much* these variables influence judgment. If their influence were small, i.e., if they made people just somewhat more or less likely to make a given judgment or if

---

[1] e.g., Weinberg et al. (2001); Machery et al. (2004); Weinberg (2007); Swain et al. (2008); Machery (2011a, 2015b); Feltz & Cokely (2012); Alexander (2012); Stich & Tobia (2016).

they influenced to only a small extent how strongly somebody holds this judgment, their influence would not be remarkable.

Naturally, we need benchmarks to decide whether the influence of a variable is small or large. Psychologists use conventional benchmarks because their measures (viz., their "dependent variables") do not have an intuitive interpretation. A moderate effect size is an effect whose size is typical for psychology; a small effect size is an effect size that is smaller, a large effect size one that is larger. This distinction has been quantified for different effect size measures (Cohen, 1992). Cohen's d is a common and useful effect size measure; it is defined as the difference between the means of two conditions divided by either the standard deviation of the control condition or the pooled standard deviation. $d = 1$ means that the mean of the experimental condition is one standard deviation away from the mean of the control condition. Using this measure, the effect size is small when d is equal to 0.2, moderate when it is equal to 0.5, large when it is equal to 0.8. A moderate effect size means that the mean of the experimental condition is at the 69 percentile of the control condition, a large effect size that that the mean of the experimental condition is at the 79 percentile of the control condition. That is, a moderate effect size means that 50 percent of people in the experimental condition have a larger score than 69 percent of people in the control condition (mutatis mutandis for a large effect). Focusing on the size of gender differences in psychology, Hyde (2005) distinguishes five categories: close-to-zero ($d \leq 0.10$), small ($0.11 < d < 0.35$), moderate ($0.36 < d < 0.65$), large ($0.66 < d < 1.00$), and very large ($d > 1.00$). Given her focus on demographic difference, Hyde's benchmarks are particularly useful, and in any case, they largely agree with Cohen's.

When the dependent variable is a percentage (e.g., the percentage of people agreeing that the character does not know the relevant proposition in the situation described by a Gettier case), the difference between the percentages in the various conditions has a natural interpretation. I propose the following benchmarks: A difference equal or lower than 20 percent is a small difference that has little philosophical significance; if the difference between two groups is between 20 and 30 percent, it is moderate; if it is larger than 30 percent, it qualifies as interestingly large. For a summary, see Table 2.1.

It is also useful to anchor our intuitions about effect sizes with benchmarks drawn from other domains. In grade 4, girls read better than boys, and the effect size corresponds to roughly a fifth of a standard deviation ($d = 0.18$).[2] This corresponds to a small effect in Cohen's and in Hyde's classification, but it is already large enough to be a concern.[3] In grade 8, the effect size is a bit larger than a fourth of a standard deviation ($d = 0.28$). This corresponds to a moderate effect in Cohen's classification and to a small

---

[2] Source: U.S. Department of Education, Institute of Education Sciences, National Center for Education Statistics, National Assessment of Educational Progress (NAEP), 2002 Reading Assessment and 2000 Mathematics Assessment.

[3] Source: 2012 Report on Boys' Reading Commission by the All-Party Parliamentary Literacy Group Commission (compiled by the National Literacy Trust and available at https://www.literacytrust.org.uk/assets/0001/4056/Boys_Commission_Report.pdf).

Table 2.1. Effect sizes summary

	Small	Moderate	Large
Cohen's d	.2	.5	.8
Difference between percentages	<20%	20%≤difference<30%	≥30%

effect in Hyde's. Smoking versus not smoking explains around 2 percent of the variance in longevity, corresponding to an effect that is small in Cohen's classification ($d = 0.28$) (Vacha-Haase & Thompson, 2004).

One may of course be skeptical that the psychological classification of an effect size says much about its philosophical significance: Why would a large effect, by the conventions of psychology, be of large philosophical significance? While small effects could be of importance for some philosophical arguments, the larger the difference between the judgments made by two demographic groups or the larger the effect the presentation of a case has on a judgment, the more significant the effect will be for the arguments that will be developed in the following two chapters. But perhaps effects that are large by the conventions of psychology are still too small to matter philosophically? Any effect size short of a very large effect in Hyde's classification could be of no consequence for philosophy. While this concern is reasonable, the benchmarks proposed earlier are adequate for assessing philosophical significance. For instance, a "moderate" difference between two populations, such as a 20 percent difference, means that for many distributions the majority in one population will endorse one judgment (e.g., an instance of double prevention is a genuine case of causation), while the majority in another population will endorse the contradictory judgment (an instance of double prevention is not a genuine case of causation): 65 percent vs. 45 percent; 60 percent vs. 40 percent, etc. For other distributions, one population will be as close to consensus as possible, while there will be significant disagreement in the other population: for instance, 85 percent vs. 65 percent. This point is naturally clearer for a large difference (e.g., a 30 percent difference).

Our critic may concede the point for percentages and other intuitively meaningful measures, but object that it does not generalize to the standard effect sizes in psychology such as d because these measures depend on the variation in participants' answers. As a result, even a small difference between the means in two conditions can result in a large or even very large effect size if there is very little variation in each condition (Horne & Livengood, 2017). While this point is in principle correct, it does not apply to the type of findings reported in this chapter and in experimental philosophy in general: Variance is nearly always substantial in experimental philosophy studies.

In this chapter, I will comment on the effect size of the findings reported. When the authors did not report the effect sizes, I have computed them whenever this was possible. For the sake of simplicity, when computing Cohen's d, I have usually taken the standard deviation of one of the conditions as the denominator instead of the pooled standard deviation. This decision makes little difference for most of the effect sizes reported below. I have also converted many other effect sizes into *d*'s.

This chapter proceeds as follows. Sections 2.1 to 2.5 examine the role of demographic variables. Sections 2.6 and 2.7 examine order effects, framing effects, and the influence of situational cues. Section 2.8 synthesizes the findings.

2.1 Culture

Culture has attracted a lot of attention among experimental philosophers in large part because of its connection to Parochialism, an argument against the method of cases that will be discussed in Chapter 4.

2.1.1 Language

Judgments about the reference of *proper names* in the situation described by the Gödel case are the best-supported case for an influence of culture on judgments elicited by philosophical cases. More than a decade ago, Ron Mallon, Shaun Nichols, Steve Stich, and I (Machery et al., 2004) decided to examine whether judgments about the reference of proper names vary across cultures. Influenced by psychologist Richard Nisbett's (2003) then groundbreaking cross-cultural research in psychology, according to which East Asians (primarily, Chinese, Japanese, and Koreans) and Westerners (primarily, Americans) tend to have different cognitive styles, we hypothesized that judgments about reference vary across cultures. One especially intriguing difference is, allegedly, that, while East Asians are inclined to "make categorical judgments on the basis of similarity," Westerners are "more disposed to focus on causation in describing the world and classifying things" (Machery et al., 2004, B5). This led us to hypothesize that East Asians may be more likely to make descriptivist judgments (i.e., judgments consistent with descriptivist theories of reference) than Westerners. On a descriptivist theory, the referent has to satisfy the description, but it need not be causally related to the use of the term. In contrast, on Kripke's causal-historical theory, the referent need not satisfy the associated description; rather, it should only figure in the causal history (and in the causal explanation) of the speaker's current use of the word.

To test the hypothesis that East Asians may be more likely to make descriptivist judgments than Westerners, we presented participants in Hong Kong and in the United States with vignettes closely inspired by Kripke's (1980) Gödel case (quoted in Chapter 1), such as the following vignette (for further detail, see Machery et al., 2004):

Gödel Case
Suppose that John has learned in college that Gödel is the man who proved an important mathematical theorem, called the incompleteness of arithmetic. John is quite good at mathematics and he can give an accurate statement of the incompleteness theorem, which he attributes to Gödel as the discoverer. But this is the only thing that he has heard about Gödel. Now suppose

that Gödel was not the author of this theorem. A man called "Schmidt," whose body was found in Vienna under mysterious circumstances many years ago, actually did the work in question. His friend Gödel somehow got hold of the manuscript and claimed credit for the work, which was thereafter attributed to Gödel. Thus, he has been known as the man who proved the incompleteness of arithmetic. Most people who have heard the name "Gödel" are like John; the claim that Gödel discovered the incompleteness theorem is the only thing they have ever heard about Gödel. When John uses the name "Gödel," is he talking about:

(A) the person who really discovered the incompleteness of arithmetic? or
(B) the person who got hold of the manuscript and claimed credit for the work?

Another case, the Tsu Ch'ung Chih case, had the same structure, but used names of Chinese individuals.

As we had predicted, Chinese were more likely to make descriptivist judgments about the Gödel and the Tsu Ch'ung Chih cases than Americans. In fact, most Americans made causal-historical or "Kripkean" judgments, whereas most Chinese made descriptivist judgments (Figure 2.1).

In contrast to some other lines of cross-cultural research in experimental philosophy, Machery and colleagues' early, influential finding has been extensively replicated, and follow-up studies have provided further empirical support to the hypothesis that judgments about the reference of proper names vary across cultures (Figure 2.1). Machery et al. (2010) have shown that Chinese participants make similar judgments when Gödel-style cases are presented in English (as was originally done in Machery et al., 2004) and in Chinese (see also Machery et al., 2015). Beebe and Undercoffer (2015, 2016) have independently replicated Machery et al.'s original finding, and they have shown that it is robust: It is still found when the formulation of the vignettes

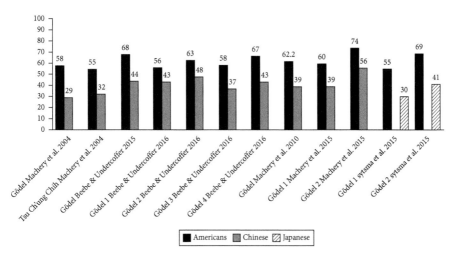

Figure 2.1 Percentages of Kripkean judgments in Gödel cases (based on Machery et al., 2004; Beebe & Undercoffer, 2015, 2016; Machery et al., 2010; Machery et al., 2015; Sytsma et al., 2015).

and of the response options is varied. In further support to Machery et al.'s cultural hypothesis, Sytsma et al. (2015) have also shown that, just like Chinese, Japanese tend to make descriptivist judgments about the reference of proper names in Gödel cases. The vignettes were presented in Japanese to Japanese participants, and the proportion of Kripkean answers varied from 30 percent to 41 percent among Japanese, depending on the details of the vignettes. Averaging across all the studies, and weighing them equally, the average difference is 22 percent, a moderate to large effect.

Beebe and Undercoffer (2016) also provide suggestive evidence that East Asians may be more likely to make descriptivist judgments about reference in Jonah cases. In a Jonah case, a proper name is associated with an entirely false description, and people are asked whether the proper name refers to anything or fails to refer. Machery et al. (2004) did not find any cross-cultural difference in judgments about Jonah cases, using two lengthy and (with hindsight) unwieldy cases. The first Jonah case reads as follows:

Jonah Case

In high-school, German students learn that Attila founded Germany in the second century A.D. They are taught that Attila was the king of a nomadic tribe that migrated from the east to settle in what would become Germany. Germans also believe that Attila was a merciless warrior and leader who expelled the Romans from Germany, and that after his victory against the Romans, Attila organized a large and prosperous kingdom.

Now suppose that none of this is true. No merciless warrior expelled the Romans from Germany, and Germany was not founded by a single individual. Actually, the facts are the following. In the fourth century A.D., a nobleman of low rank, called "Raditra," ruled a small and peaceful area in what today is Poland, several hundred miles from Germany. Raditra was a wise and gentle man who managed to preserve the peace in the small land he was ruling. For this reason, he quickly became the main character of many stories and legends. These stories were passed on from one generation of peasants to the next. But often when the story was passed on the peasants would embellish it, adding imaginary details and dropping some true facts to make the story more exciting. From a peaceful nobleman of low rank, Raditra was gradually transformed into a warrior fighting for his land. When the legend reached Germany, it told of a merciless warrior who was victorious against the Romans. By the eighth century A.D., the story told of an Eastern king who expelled the Romans and founded Germany. By that time, not a single true fact remained in the story.

Meanwhile, as the story was told and retold, the name "Raditra" was slowly altered: it was successively replaced by "Aditra," then by "Arritrak" in the sixth century, by "Arrita" and "Arrila" in the seventh, and finally by "Attila." The story about the glorious life of Attila was written down in the eighth century by a scrupulous Catholic monk, from whom all our beliefs are derived. Of course, Germans know nothing about these real events. They believe a story about a merciless Eastern king who expelled the Romans and founded Germany.

When a contemporary German high-school student says "Attila was the king who drove the Romans from Germany," is he actually talking about the wise and gentle nobleman, Raditra, who is the original source of the Attila legend, or is he talking about a fictional person, someone who does not really exist?

Beebe and Undercoffer (2016) present participants with Machery et al.'s Jonah cases, but modify the response options. Instead of giving participants the choice between "[The speaker] is talking about Raditra" and "He is talking about a fictional person who does not really exist," the choice was between "He is talking about Raditra" and "He is not talking about Raditra." As predicted by the cultural hypothesis put forward by Machery et al. (2004) and in line with the results in Gödel cases, Jonah cases happen to be more likely to elicit descriptivist judgments from Chinese (66 percent) than from Americans (53 percent), a small effect (Figure 2.2).

Finally, Machery et al. (2009) have shown that in Gödel cases judgments about the reference of proper names and judgments about the truth-value of sentences involving these names are in sync with one another: In a given culture, when people tend to report, say, descriptivist judgments about the reference of "Gödel" in the Gödel case, they tend on average to judge that a sentence such as "Gödel was a great mathematician" uttered in this case would be true (Figure 2.3).

Cultural variation is also found with cases examining *natural kind terms*. Machery et al. (ms) have recently examined cases loosely inspired by Putnam's (1975a, b) cases (although the focus of the study was on psychological essentialism rather than on Putnam's semantic theses). In the lemon case (from Study 1 of Machery et al., ms), the superficial properties of a fruit (lemons) are modified while its genetic code remains unchanged; participants are asked whether the fruits are still lemons:

Lemon Case
Suppose that following an explosion in a large chemical factory in Brazil, some gases spread all over the world. These gases are innocuous (i.e., harmless) for humans and animals. Although they do not affect the genetic structure of lemons, they react with the pigments in the peel of lemons and with the flesh of lemons. As a result of this reaction, all lemons on

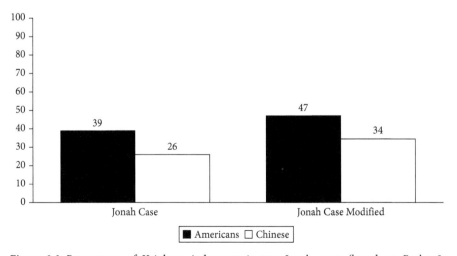

Figure 2.2 Percentages of Kripkean judgments in two Jonah cases (based on Beebe & Undercoffer, 2016).

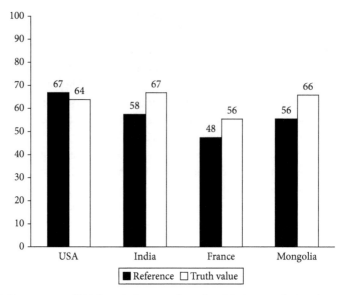

Figure 2.3 Percentages of Kripkean judgments (based on Machery et al., 2009).

Earth turn from yellow to orange and this change is permanent. Moreover, their size increases and they end up being permanently twice as big as they previously were. Their taste is also modified: they now taste exactly like oranges. Would you say that in those conditions there are still lemons?

YES, there are still lemons

NO, there are no more lemons

Participants who answer "Yes" seem to judge, in line with Putnam's externalism, that the extension of natural kind terms is determined by scientifically discoverable properties of the kind *lemon*. I will say that they are making an "externalist" judgment. Participants who answer "No" seem to judge that the extension of natural kind terms is determined by the superficial properties of the kind members, properties they seem to view as constitutive of kind membership. I will say that they are making an "internalist" judgment.

In the water case (from Study 1 of Machery et al., ms), inspired by Putnam's (1975a) Twin-Earth thought experiment, astronauts discover a substance that shares the superficial properties of another substance (water), but not its chemical structure; participants are asked whether the liquid is water:

Water Case

Suppose that in the future, astronauts find on a distant, inhabited planet a liquid, called "mantup" by the inhabitants of this planet. The chemical composition of mantup is H_3Sl_2. Although mantup's chemical composition is different from the chemical we call "water" on Earth, this liquid is in all other respects indistinguishable from water. Mantup tastes like water and it quenches thirst like water. Like water, it does not have any specific odor. It freezes at 0 degree Celsius and boils at 100 degrees Celsius. The oceans, seas, and lakes on this planet contain this liquid and it also rains this liquid. In brief, mantup interacts with everything in the same way that water does. Would you say that in those conditions, mantup is water?

Participants who answer "Yes" make an internalist judgment, while participants who follow Putnam's judgment about the Twin-Earth thought experiment in answering "No" make an externalist judgment.

The judgments elicited by these vignettes vary substantially across ten cultures (for further detail, see Machery et al., ms). The proportion of externalist judgments about the water case varies from about 30 percent in India to 75 percent in Portugal, South Korea, France, and Brazil. The proportion of externalist judgments about the lemon case varies from about 15 percent in Italy to about 65 percent in Indonesia.

2.1.2 Epistemology

Turning to epistemology, in an early, influential article, Weinberg et al. (2001) report variation in epistemological judgments among Americans of various ethnic backgrounds (Figure 2.4). In particular, they report that East Asian Americans (12 percent of knowledge ascription) were more likely than Caucasian Americans (32 percent) to deny knowledge in a Truetemp case. (This trend is reversed in other formulations of the Truetemp case, but the differences there are not significant.) More striking, East Asian Americans (57 percent of knowledge ascription) and Americans whose family come from the Indian subcontinent (61 percent) tend to ascribe knowledge in the

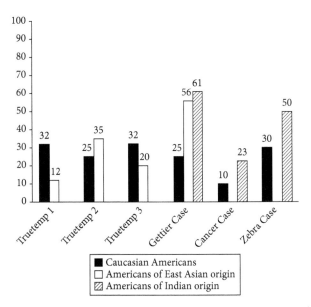

Figure 2.4 Percentages of knowledge ascriptions (based on Weinberg et al., 2001).

Buick version of the Gettier case, while only a small minority of Caucasian Americans (26 percent) does so. Finally, Americans whose family came from the Indian subcontinent (50 percent) are more likely than Caucasian Americans (26 percent) to ascribe knowledge to the character in Drestke's Zebra case.

It would thus seem that reliabilist judgments are less likely among East Asian than Caucasian Americans, that the latter are more likely to distinguish knowledge from mere true justified belief than East Asian Americans and Americans whose family came from the Indian subcontinent, and that Caucasian Americans are more likely to be sensitive to merely possible defeaters than Americans whose family comes from the Indian subcontinent.

Despite having been extensively discussed, Weinberg and colleagues' research suffers from severe limitations. First, all participants were American. Second, the sample sizes (e.g., N = 25 for Americans of East Asian ancestry in the first Truetemp case, N = 23 for Americans of East Asian ancestry in the Gettier case, and N = 23 for Americans whose family comes from the Indian subcontinent) were small. Third, only very recently have there been attempts to replicate some of the results of this influential study, and these replications have yielded results partly at odds with those of Weinberg and colleagues. Turri (2013) reports that, when Indian participants recruited on Amazon Turk were presented with the Buick case in stages (instead of all at once), 85 percent of participants shared the Gettier intuition. However, Turri's study itself is not without problems. The sample size (N = 27) is small; in contrast to American participants (Buhrmester et al., 2011), answers obtained from Indian participants on Amazon Turk may not be representative; and the vignette was presented in English. Nagel et al. (2013) also report tentatively being unable to find any difference between ethnic groups in their sample of Canadian participants, but all their participants were Canadian, the vignettes were presented in English, and the power of their test is not reported. Seyedsayamdost (2015a) and Kim and Yuan (2015) also fail to replicate various studies in Weinberg et al. (2001). Of note is the fact that Seyedsayamdost (2015a) has failed to replicate *all* the results in Weinberg's study that were reported above.

More convincing than all these studies is Machery et al., forthcoming a (see also Machery et al., forthcoming c). Participants in four different cultures were presented with two Gettier cases loosely inspired by some cases used by Nagel et al. (2013): India, Brazil, Japan, and the USA. A large majority of participants in these four cultures reject the ascription of knowledge to the characters in the Gettier cases (Figure 2.5).

Where do we stand? In light of the recent replication failures, the findings reported by Weinberg and colleagues provide no evidence that judgments elicited by *the Truetemp, Gettier, zebra,* and *cancer cases* vary across cultures. Does this mean that in contrast to cases in the philosophy of language, the judgments elicited by epistemological cases are not subject to cultural variation? No. Waterman et al. (forthcoming) have recently examined whether people across cultures are equally sensitive to skeptical pressures. In two experiments, participants in India, China, and the USA were presented with *a zebra-like vignette* and asked to agree or disagree on a 6-point Likert

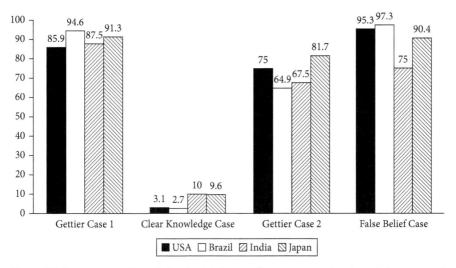

Figure 2.5 Percentages of knowledge denials for two Gettier cases, a clear knowledge case, and a false belief case (based on Machery et al., forthcoming a).

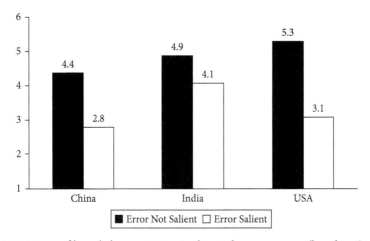

Figure 2.6 Means of knowledge ascriptions in skeptical-pressure cases (based on Study 2 of Waterman et al., forthcoming).

scale. Participants from the three countries agreed more with ascribing knowledge to the characters in the cases when the possibility of error was not raised than when it was raised, but in line with Weinberg et al.'s results, Chinese and Americans were more sensitive to the presence or absence of a possibility of error than Indians (Figure 2.6). The effect size for Americans ($d = 1.43$) is nearly 2.5 times larger than the effect size for Indians ($d = 0.6$). Furthermore, a majority of Chinese and Americans, but only a minority of Indians, withdrew knowledge ascription in zebra-like cases.

2.1.3 Mind

No reported finding.

2.1.4 Metaphysics

No reported finding.

2.1.5 Ethics

Early work suggested that judgments in response to *trolley cases* vary little across most cultures. According to Hauser et al. (2007), judgments about the switch and footbridge cases are similar in several countries, including the USA, Brazil, and India, and across ethnicities (Figure 2.7; see also O'Neill & Petrinovich, 1998 for a comparison between Taiwan and the USA and Petrinovich et al., 1993 for ethnicity).

Unfortunately, Hauser and colleagues do not report cross-cultural statistics for the other cases they examined (versions of the loop case). Similarly, Moore et al. (2011) do not find any difference between Chinese and Americans on a battery of twenty-four switch-, footbridge-, and lifeboat-like scenarios asking questions about "moral acceptability" (see also Mikhail, 2011), but their sample size is small, and the power of the test is not reported. I estimate the power of the test at 0.56, assuming a moderate effect size (power computed by means of G*Power3; Faul et al., 2007). Abarbanell and Hauser (2010) report that a Mayan population also judged action in footbridge-like dilemmas worse than the action in switch-like dilemmas, although they did not compare responses by Westerners and Mayans.

A few recent articles have, however, yielded different results. According to Ahlenius and Tännsjö (2012), Americans, Russians, and Chinese are not equally likely to judge

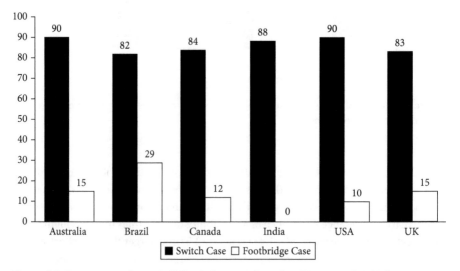

Figure 2.7 Percentages of permissibility judgments (based on Hauser et al., 2007).

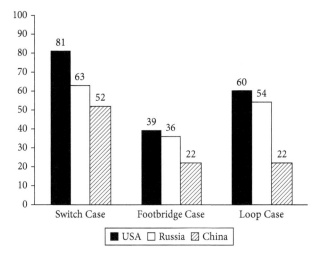

Figure 2.8 Percentages of "should" judgments (based on Ahlenius & Tännsjö, 2012).

that the agent should act in response to the switch, footbridge, and loop cases. The effect sizes are noticeable (about 25–30 percent across cases between the USA and China; Figure 2.8).

In line with these results, but using a different experimental paradigm and a different question, Gold et al. (2014) provide consistent evidence that Chinese (about 50 percent) are less likely than English (about 80 percent) to view reorienting a threat in a version of the switch case as being right. However, their vignette-based study 2 failed to find a consistent cultural difference; in particular, no difference was found for the wrongness of the action in the switch case.

Xiang (2014) has recently presented the footbridge case to Tibetan Buddhist monks and lay Tibetans, both of whom judge it permissible to push the large person to save five people (Figure 2.9). The difference with Westerners is very large. The judgments of Tibetan monks are also remarkably in line with their explicit moral teachings (in particular, with the *skill in means sutra*).

Finally, Michelin et al. (2010) report that bilingual Slovenian-Italians living in Italy (>60 percent) are significantly more likely than monolingual Italians (40 percent) to judge that one should push the large person in the footbridge case. No difference was found with the switch case.

Cultural variation is not limited to the distinction between causing harm as a means or as a side effect. According to Abarbanell and Hauser (2010), Mayans living in Tenejapa, an indigenous community in Chiapas, do not distinguish *action and omission* in cases structurally similar to trolley cases. It is not clear whether they would also overlook this distinction for cases that are more similar to the cases used by philosophers to examine the action/omission distinction (e.g., Rachels, 1975).

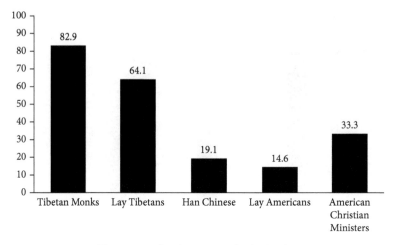

Figure 2.9 Percentages of "appropriate" judgments in the footbridge case (Xiang, 2014).

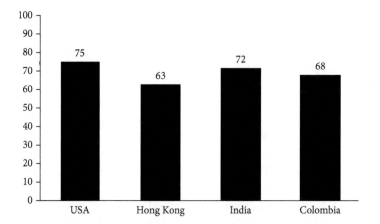

Figure 2.10 Percentages of incompatibilist judgments (based on Sarkissian et al., 2010).

Moving beyond sacrificial dilemmas such as the trolley cases, culture also influences judgments elicited by Nozick's (1974) *experience-machine case* (Olivola et al., ms). South Koreans are more than 200 percent more likely than Americans to agree to plug into the experience machine.

2.1.6 Action theory

According to Sarkissian et al. (2010), people make similar *incompatibilist judgments* about moral responsibility in the USA, India, Colombia, and Hong Kong when they are asked whether in a deterministic universe, "it is possible for a person to be fully morally responsible for their actions" (Figure 2.10). However, the question here is not about a particular case, and the significance of their finding for the present project is limited.

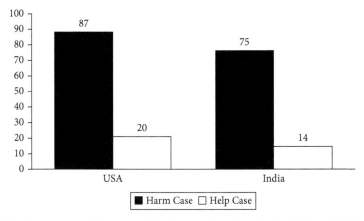

Figure 2.11 Percentages of "intentional" judgments (based on Knobe & Burra, 2006).

Table 2.2. Summary of the evidence about culture effects ("Y" for yes, "N" for no, "Mixed" indicating that the evidence goes in both directions)

Case	Field	Variation	Effect Size
Gödel case	Language	Y	Large
Jonah case	Language	Y	Small
Water case	Language	Y	Large
Lemon case	Language	Y	Large
Gettier case	Epistemology	N	-
Truetemp case	Epistemology	N	-
Zebra case	Epistemology	Y	Large[4]
Switch case	Ethics	Mixed	Possibly large
Footbridge case	Ethics	Y	Large
Loop case	Ethics	Y	Large
Action/omission cases	Ethics	Y	Large
Experience machine	Ethics	Y	Large
Harm and help cases	Action theory	Y	Large

Knobe and Burra (2006) also show that the *harm and help cases* elicit a similar pattern of judgments among Indians and Americans (Figure 2.11), but Robbins, Shepard, and Rochat (2017) have shown that it is not found in at least two small scale societies.

2.1.7 Summary

As far as we know, the judgments elicited by several cases are not influenced by culture, including the Gettier case and the Truetemp case, but cultural influence is found across nearly all the areas of philosophy that have been examined, and the effects tend to be on the larger side (Table 2.2).

---

[4] Based on the fact that the effect size for Americans is more than double the effect size for Indians.

2.2 Gender

2.2.1 Language

In a widely discussed article, Buckwalter and Stich (2015) claim that several philosophically important cases, across several areas of philosophy, elicit different judgments from men and women. In particular, they report that men are more likely than women to judge in *a Twin-Earth case* that "water" on Earth and Twin-Earth means the same (means: 5.6 vs. 4.5 on a 7-point scale, 7 indicating that "water" means the same thing; $d = 0.49$; a moderate effect size).

Surprisingly, however, Machery et al. (ms) find in two distinct studies the opposite gender effect on judgments elicited by the water case (but not with the lemon case): Men were more likely than women to make an externalist judgment. (The former's odds are about 50 percent larger than the latter's odds, corresponding to a small effect, $d = 0.2$.) While Machery and colleagues used a different question than Buckwalter and Stich (see Section 2.1.1 above), the difference is nonetheless surprising. In addition, Adleberg et al. (2015) have recently failed to replicate Buckwalter and Stich's result.

More generally, Adleberg and colleagues examine fourteen cases that, according to Buckwalter and Stich, result in gender differences (including the cases reported in this section and a variation on the trolley cases examined by Zamzow & Nichols, 2009), and they report that, when the significance level is shifted to control for multiple testing, *none* of these cases yields a significant result. The power of their tests, assuming an uncorrected $\alpha = 0.05$, is large for moderate effects (>0.8), although small for small effects (< 0.35). Furthermore, Adleberg and colleagues report being unable to find any systematic gender effect in a literature review (although gender is occasionally reported to have an influence on judgments). Similarly, Seyedsayamdost (2015b) summarizes several failed attempts to replicate Buckwalter and Stich's findings. Unfortunately, the power of his tests is low assuming a small effect size, and from low to acceptable assuming a moderate effect size.

Seyedsayamdost (2015b) also reports finding no gender effect for *a Gödel case*. Examining some of my data sets on the Gödel case, I do not find any gender effect either.

2.2.2 Epistemology

In the area of epistemology, Buckwalter and Stich (2015) report that women are less likely than men to refrain from ascribing knowledge when *a skeptical threat*—the possibility of being a brain in vat—has been raised (means: 6.7 vs. 5.6 on a 7-point scale, 7 indicating complete agreement with knowledge; $d = 0.81$, a large effect size; Figure 2.12). Adleberg and colleagues replicate this finding, although they note that the effect is not significant when one controls for the number of tests by decreasing the significance level. Given that this decrease seriously reduces the power of the test, the correction may not be a good idea, particularly since the goal is to replicate past results. On the other hand, two studies in Seyedsayamdost (2015b) fail to replicate the result reported by Buckwalter and Stich.

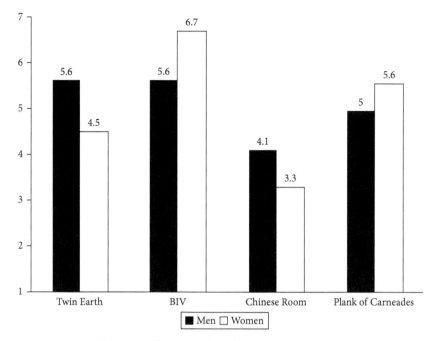

Figure 2.12 Mean judgments in four cases (based on Buckwalter & Stich, 2015).

Focusing on other cases, Wright (2010) reports that gender does not influence judgments elicited by the *Truetemp* and *fake-barn cases*. Consistent with Wright's results, gender does not influence judgments elicited by the fake-barn case in Colaço et al. (2014). Nagel et al. (2013) and Seyedsayamdost (2015b) do not find any gender effect with *Gettier cases* (see also Machery et al., forthcoming c). In addition, Seyedsayamdost (2015b) also report finding no gender effect with a Truetemp case, a zebra case, and a smoking conspiracy case.

2.2.3 Mind

According to Buckwalter and Stich (2015), men are more likely than women to say that in *the Chinese-room case* the system composed of the character and the manual understands Chinese (means: 4.1 vs. 3.3 on a 7-point scale, with 4 anchored at "In-between"; $d = 0.37$; a small to moderate effect size; Figure 2.12). Adleberg et al. (2015) and two studies in Seyedsayamdost (2015b) fail to replicate this finding.

2.2.4 Metaphysics

No reported finding.

2.2.5 Ethics

According to Buckwalter and Stich (2015), in *the plank of Carneades case* (in which one of two shipwrecked sailors pushes the other one off from a floating plank because only one of them can survive) men are less likely than women to say that the agent was blameworthy (means: 5.0 vs. 5.6 on a 7-point scale, with 7 anchored at "extremely blameworthy"; $d = 0.49$, a small to moderate effect size; Figure 2.12). However, Adleberg et al. (2015) and two studies in Seyedsayamdost (2015b) fail to replicate this finding.

Zamzow and Nichols (2009) report that gender influences judgments made in response to *the switch case*: Women find it less morally acceptable than men to kill a child or a sister to save five people, while men find it less morally acceptable than women to kill a brother to save five people. Petrinovich et al. (1993) also report finding some small gender differences with the *switch* and *lifeboat cases*. For instance, women (21 percent) are somewhat less likely than men (31 percent) to push the large man in the footbridge case. Petrinovich and O'Neill (1996) also report finding a framing effect about the switch case (described below) more often among female than male participants. Similarly, Fumagali et al. (2010) report a significant, but small gender difference in moral dilemmas such as the *transplant case* (about 10 percent): So-called "characteristically utilitarian" responses are somewhat more common among men.[5] Bartels and Pizarro (2011) also report a similar small correlation between gender and choosing the characteristically utilitarian response in moral dilemmas ($r = 0.25$).

Unfortunately, Petrinovich and O'Neill (1996), Fumagali et al. (2010), and Bartels and Pizarro (2011) elicit judgments about what actions one would take instead of what one finds permissible, appropriate, or mandatory. Gender differences may be limited to the former. In addition, Lombrozo (2009; switch and footbridge cases) and Gleichgerrcht & Young (2013; switch and footbridge cases), who ask for permissibility rather than action, as well as Adleberg et al. (2015; switch case), who ask for both acceptability and action, do not find any gender difference.

However, Friesdorf et al. (2015) meta-analyze forty studies with more than 6,000 participants, and find moderate to moderate-to-large differences between men and women in dilemmas describing the possibility of causing some harm to prevent a greater harm (e.g., the trolley cases, the crybaby case, the lifeboat case, etc.). Men are moderately more likely to choose the characteristically utilitarian answers than women ($d = 0.5$, a moderate effect size; see also Gao & Tang, 2013 and Gold et al., 2014 on the switch case). According to Friesdorf and colleagues' process dissociation analysis, this preference is driven by women's greater characteristically deontological inclination (a moderate to large effect) more than by men's greater characteristically utilitarian inclination (a small effect). According to Friesdorf et al., the studies focused on the "appropriateness" of the action.

Friesdorf and colleagues' findings are in line with the results reported by Banerjee et al. (2010). Gender predicted participants' response for nine of ten of the sets of cases they were presented with. In particular, men made more characteristically utilitarian

---

[5] A judgment made in response to a moral dilemma is "characteristically utilitarian" if and only if it finds it appropriate or permissible to cause harm to prevent a greater harm; it is "characteristically deontological" otherwise.

judgments than women. The effect sizes range from small to moderate. Banerjee et al. dismiss these effects, claiming that the "differences were consistently associated with extremely small effect sizes," and they "conclude that gender, education, politics and religion are likely to be relatively insignificant for moral judgments of unfamiliar scenarios" (2010, 253). This conclusion is, however, not supported by their results. While none of the demographic effects was large, many were from small to moderate, in line with Friesdorf and colleagues' findings. They are larger than the effect of smoking on longevity and similar to the effect of gender on reading in grades 4 and 8.

Friesdorf and colleagues' finding may seem at odds with Hauser et al.'s (2007) finding that men's and women's permissibility judgments in response to the switch and footbridge cases as well as to two variants of the loop case do not differ, but this need not be the case, since Friesdorf and colleagues examined more cases than just these four cases.

Moving beyond sacrificial dilemmas such as the trolley cases, gender also influences judgments elicited by *the experience-machine case* (Olivola et al., ms). Men are about twice as likely than women to agree to plug into the experience machine.

2.2.6 Action theory

Cokely and Feltz (2009) found that gender did not influence the asymmetry between judgments elicited by Knobe's *harm and help cases*.

2.2.7 Summary

As far as we know, gender effects are rare (Table 2.3), but they are found in ethics. In particular, Friesdorf et al.'s large meta-analysis and other articles suggest that men and women respond differently to moral dilemmas pitting a characteristically

Table 2.3. Summary of the evidence about gender effects

Case	Field	Variation	Effect Size
Gödel case	Language	N	-
Twin-Earth case	Language	Mixed	-
Gettier case	Epistemology	N	-
Truetemp case	Epistemology	N	-
Fake-barn case	Epistemology	N	-
BIV case (skeptical pressure)	Epistemology	Mixed	Possibly large
Zebra case	Epistemology	N	-
Cancer case	Epistemology	N	-
Chinese room case	Mind	N	-
Switch case	Ethics	Y	Moderate
Footbridge case	Ethics	Y	Moderate
Crybaby case	Ethics	Y	Moderate
Plank of Carneades case	Ethics	N	-
Experience machine	Ethics	Y	Large
Harm and help cases (asymmetry)	Action theory	N	-

consequentialist judgment against a characteristically deontological judgment, and that the effect size is moderate. Men and women also appear to respond differently to the experience machine case.

2.3 Age

Very little attention has been paid to how judgments elicited by philosophical cases vary across the lifespan, but some findings suggest that age too influences them.

2.3.1 Language

There is no reported finding in the published literature. Examining some of my data sets on the Gödel case, I did not find any age effect. Age did not influence answers to the lemon or water case in Machery et al. (ms).

2.3.2 Epistemology

Colaço et al. (2014) have recently examined whether age influences knowledge ascription in the fake-barn case. Participants were presented with the following case:

Fake-Barn Case
Gerald is driving through the countryside with his young son Andrew. Along the way he sees numerous objects and points them out to his son. "That's a cow, Andrew," Gerald says, "and that over there is a house where farmers live." Gerald has no doubt about what the objects are. What Gerald and Andrew do not realize is the area they are driving through was recently hit by a very serious tornado. This tornado did not harm any of the animals, but did destroy most buildings. In an effort to maintain the rural area's tourist industry, local townspeople built house facades in the place of destroyed houses. These facades look exactly like real houses from the road, but are only for looks and cannot be used as actual housing.

This case could end with one of the following two endings:

Having just entered the tornado-ravaged area, Gerald has not yet encountered any house facades. When he tells Andrew "That's a house," the object he sees and points at is a real house that has survived the tornado.

Or

Though he has only recently entered the tornado-ravaged area, Gerald has already encountered a large number of house facades. However, when he tells Andrew "That's a house," the object he sees and points at is a real house that has survived the tornado.

Participants were then asked whether Gerald knew he saw a house. Colaço et al. (2014) find that the probability to ascribe knowledge in these fake-barn cases decreases with age. Younger participants are equally likely to ascribe knowledge in response to the fake-barn case (mean: 4.9 on a 7-point [0-6] scale, anchored at 6 with "knows") and in cases where the protagonist undoubtedly has knowledge, but, just like most philosophers, people over thirty do not ascribe knowledge in the former cases (mean: 3.6, not significantly above the mid point). The effect size is moderate. Turri reports a similar age effect for men, but not women, but Knobe fails to replicate this finding.[6] It is thus at best uncertain whether there is really an age effect with the fake-barn case.

2.3.3 Mind

No reported finding.

2.3.4 Metaphysics

No reported finding.

2.3.5 Ethics

According to Hauser et al. (2007), age has a small influence on judgments elicited by *the loop case*, with younger people somewhat less likely to find it permissible to switch the trolley on a side-track when someone on this track will be used as a means to stop the runaway trolley ($d = 0.24$, a small effect). On the other hand, judgments about *the switch and footbridge cases* do not vary as a function of age. Similarly, Gleichgerrcht and Young (2013) find no age effect with the footbridge, switch, and *crybaby* cases. Gold et al. (2014a) report that in their first study, but not in their second, older people are more likely to judge the action to be wrong in their version of the switch case.

Moving beyond sacrificial dilemmas such as the trolley cases, age appears to influence judgments elicited by *the experience-machine case* (Olivola et al., ms). The odds ratio of plugging into the experience machine decreases by about 3 percent per year. The odds ratio of a sixty-year-old person would be 120 percent smaller than the odd ratio of a twenty-year-old person (corresponding to $d = 0.43$, a moderate effect size).

2.3.6 Action theory

No reported finding.

2.3.7 Summary

There is little research on the possible influence of age on judgments made in response to philosophical cases. The only two examples where such influence is attested are the loop case and the experience machine case (Table 2.4). Age does not seem to influence the judgments made in response to other cases in ethics, and there is no other well-established evidence in support of an influence of age on judgments elicited by philosophical cases.

---

[6] http://philosophycommons.typepad.com/xphi/2014/06/do-older-people-have-different-epistemic-intuitions-than-younger-people-a-study-on-fake-barn-intuiti.html.

Table 2.4. Summary of the evidence about age effects

Case	Field	Variation	Effect Size
Gödel case	Language	N	-
Fake barn case	Epistemology	Mixed	Moderate
Switch case	Ethics	N	-
Footbridge case	Ethics	N	-
Loop case	Ethics	Y	Small
Crybaby case	Ethics	N	-
Experience machine	Ethics	Y	Large

2.4 Personality

2.4.1 Language

No reported finding.

2.4.2 Epistemology

Machery et al. (forthcoming c) report an effect of personality on judgments in response to the Gettier case.

2.4.3 Mind

No reported finding.

2.4.4 Metaphysics

No reported finding.

2.4.5 Ethics

According to Bartels and Pizarro (2011), people's scores on a psychopathy scale predict their judgments about a range of moral cases, including *the switch, footbridge, crybaby,* and *lifeboat cases* (see also Glenn et al., 2010; Koenigs et al., 2012; Gao & Tang, 2013; Wiech et al., 2013). Bartels and Pizarro report correlations around 0.2–0.3 (small to moderate). Similarly, Gleichgerrcht and Young (2013; see also Choe & Min, 2011; Crockett et al., 2010) show that participants who make characteristically consequentialist judgments in response to both the switch and footbridge cases have less empathy than people who make either characteristically deontological judgments or people who give the usual pattern of answers to the two cases ($d = 0.51$, a moderate effect). Furthermore, people who have a lower empathic reaction are more likely to judge that they would smother the child in the crybaby case ($d = 0.46$, a moderate effect). A similar pattern is found for *the transplant case* ($d = 0.64$, a moderate to large effect).

On the other hand, both articles (as well as some of the other articles cited above) examine which action people think they would choose in the situations described by the cases, and they do not show that personality affects judgments about what is morally permissible or required (Tassy et al., 2013). Kahane et al. (2015) address this problem.

They report similar results with questions probing the wrongness of the action and whether one should perform the action (correlation with psychopathy, $r = -0.3$, a moderate effect). Similarly, Glenn et al. (2010) report an association between psychopathy and the characteristically deontological answer using a question about the appropriateness of the action (with scenarios involving the trolley cases, the lifeboat case, and others).

Psychopathy and lack of empathy are not the only personality traits to influence judgments elicited by moral cases. One's dispositions to disgust and anger also has a small influence on judgments elicited by switch, lifeboat, crying baby, footbridge, and other sacrificial dilemmas (see Table 8 of Choe & Min, 2011 for a list of case-by-case effects).

2.4.6 Action theory

For several years, Feltz and Cokely have been amassing data showing that personality has an influence on the judgments elicited by philosophical cases (for review, Feltz & Cokely, 2012). Feltz and Cokely (2009) present evidence that one of the five fundamental personality dimensions—extraversion—influences judgments about free will and moral responsibility: Extraverts are more likely than introverts to judge that an individual committing a crime is responsible and free in a deterministic world. While extraversion explained only a moderate amount of the variance (around 10 percent; $d = 0.65$, a moderate to large effect), the difference between people high and low on extraversion was large ($0.6 < d < 0.8$). Using other scenarios, Nadelhoffer et al. (2009) have, however, failed to find an influence of extraversion on judgment of free will, although they found an influence on judgment about desert.

Cokely & Feltz (2009) have also shown that extraversion influences the extent to which one makes different judgment in Knobe's (2003) *harm and help cases*: While extraversion explains only a small proportion of the variance in judgments about intentionality, the asymmetry is much larger among people high in extraversion than among people low in extraversion ($d = 0.5$, a moderate effect).

2.4.7 Summary

Personality happens to have a moderate influence on judgments elicited by cases drawn from moral philosophy or action theory (Table 2.5). There is no evidence that

Table 2.5. Summary of the evidence about personality effects

Case	Field	Variation	Effect Size
Gettier case	Epistemology	Y	Small
Switch case	Ethics	Y	Moderate
Footbridge case	Ethics	Y	Moderate
Crybaby case	Ethics	Y	Moderate
Lifeboat case	Ethics	Y	Moderate
Transplant case	Ethics	Y	Moderate to large
Compatibilism case	Action theory	Y	Moderate to large
Harm and help cases	Action theory	Y	Moderate

personality influences judgments elicited by cases that are drawn from other areas of philosophy.

2.5 Other Demographic Effects

Like age, there has been little research on the influence of other demographic variables, including political orientation, religious affiliation, religiosity, and socio-economic status (often operationalized by means of participants' level of education) on judgments elicited by philosophical cases. Here, I review the few pertinent findings.

2.5.1 Language

Machery et al. (ms) find that education influences externalist judgments in response to the *water case*: More educated people are substantially more likely to make an externalist judgment about a liquid that looks like water, but has a different chemical structure. The odds that participants with an undergraduate degree will make an externalist judgment are 54 percent larger, and those of participants with an MA 73 percent larger than the odds of participants with a high school education (a small effect, $d = 0.24$ and $d = 0.3$). However, education does not influence people's judgments about *the lemon case*.

2.5.2 Epistemology

According to Weinberg et al. (2001), SES influences the judgments elicited by the unrealized possibility of misleading evidence, such as the zebra case, but Seyedsayamdost (2015a) fails to replicate these results.

2.5.3 Mind

No reported finding.

2.5.4 Metaphysics

No reported finding.

2.5.5 Ethics

Banerjee et al. (2010) show that political orientation, religiosity, and religious affiliation vs. no religious affiliation has a small to moderate effect on many moral cases, including trolley-like and lifeboat-like cases (for the discussion of Banerjee and colleagues' misleading interpretation of their results, see Section 2.2.5). Young et al. (2013) report similar effects for Christian fundamentalism and political conservatism. Psychological style and characteristics also influence answers to such cases: People who rely on intuitions (Bartels, 2008) and people with less working memory (Moore et al., 2008) are more likely to give characteristically deontological answers. Lombrozo (2009) reports that people vary in their consequentialist or deontological leanings, and that these predict their permissibility judgments in response to switch and footbridge cases (small to moderate effects). Finally, Côté et al. (2013) provide evidence that people with a high SES make more characteristically utilitarian judgments in response to the footbridge, but not the switch case.

On the other hand, Banerjee et al. (2010) also report that education, current religion, the number of moral philosophy courses taken, and of moral philosophy books read had no systematic impact on judgments elicited by trolley-like and lifeboat-like cases. Similarly, according to Hauser et al. (2007), permissibility judgments elicited by the footbridge, switch, and loop cases do not vary as a function of education. Gleichgerrcht & Young (2013) and Fumagali et al. (2010) mention similar results with the footbridge and switch cases, asking how participants would act (instead of asking about permissibility).

Moving beyond sacrificial dilemmas such as the trolley cases, religion has no influence on judgments elicited by the experience-machine case (Olivola et al., ms).

2.5.6 Action theory

According to Pinillos et al. (2011), the size of the asymmetry between the harm and the help case depends on people's reflectivity, defined as the tendency to rely on one's gut intuitions (more on reflectivity in Section 5.2 of Chapter 5). The difference is small.

2.5.7 Summary

A multitude of factors may influence the judgments elicited by philosophical cases, but only very few have been examined for cases drawn from the philosophy of language, epistemology, metaphysics, and mind. On the other hand, there is clear evidence that many factors influence the judgments made in response to various types of sacrificial dilemmas in ethics (Table 2.6).

Table 2.6. Summary of the evidence about other demographic effects

Case	Field	Factor Influencing Judgment	Effect Size
Twin-Earth case	Language	Education	Small
Zebra case	Epistemology	N	-
Switch case	Ethics	Moral orientation	Small to moderate
Footbridge case	Ethics	Political orientation, religiosity, religious affiliation, Christian fundamentalism, political conservatism, moral orientation	Moderate
Loop case	Ethics	N	-
Lifeboat case	Ethics	Political orientation, religiosity, religious affiliation, Christian fundamentalism, political conservatism	Moderate
Crybaby case	Ethics	Political orientation, religiosity, religious affiliation, Christian fundamentalism, political conservatism	Moderate
Harm and help cases	Action theory	Reflectivity	Small

2.6 Order Effects

A large body of evidence shows that judgments elicited by a range of philosophical cases are subject to order effects: People make different judgments when they are presented with two or more cases in one order compared to the same cases presented in another order.

2.6.1 Language

No reported finding.

2.6.2 Epistemology

Swain et al. (2008) present participants with four scenarios: the Truetemp case, a case of lack of knowledge, a case of knowledge, and a fake-barn case. The lack-of-knowledge case involves a character guessing whether a coin will land tails or heads up, while the knowledge case involves a scientist forming a true belief on the basis of extensive evidence. The four scenarios are presented in eight different orders. Swain and colleagues report that judgments elicited by the Truetemp case (but not by the fake-barn case) are sensitive to the case preceding it: Participants are more likely to ascribe knowledge in *the Truetemp case* when preceded by a lack-of-knowledge case (3.3 on a 5-point scale, 5 being knowledge) than by the knowledge case (2.6). While these findings are suggestive, the experimental design is not fully satisfactory (the presence of fake-barn case complicates the interpretation of the results) and many of the reported results are not significant (*p*-values above 0.05). However, Wright (2010) has replicated Swain and colleagues' finding, using a dichotomous question about knowledge (Yes/No) and fully counterbalancing presentation order: In Study 1, 40 percent of participants ascribe knowledge in a Truetemp case after a knowledge case, but 55 percent after a lack-of-knowledge case, a small to moderate effect (Figure 2.13).

In contrast to Swain et al., Wright also find that people are more likely to ascribe knowledge in *a fake-barn case* after a Truetemp case than after a knowledge or lack-of-knowledge case, a moderate effect (Figure 2.14).

Importantly, presentation order does not influence knowledge ascription in either the knowledge or lack-of-knowledge case. Study 2 replicates the sensitivity of judgments elicited by the Truetemp case to presentation order (knowledge: 84 percent after a case where the character is guessing vs. 57 percent after a knowledge case, a moderate to large effect), and extended this sensitivity to a moral case. Wright also replicates the finding that presentation order does not influence judgments elicited by either the knowledge or lack-of-knowledge case.

Wright's Study 2 presents evidence that in a version of *the Gettier case* (involving "non-authentic evidence"), judgments are not sensitive to the order of the cases, but more recent work has shown that Gettier cases are in fact also subject to order effects (Machery et al., forthcoming b). In Study 2 of Machery et al. (forthcoming b), participants are presented with a Gettier case in one of two orders: Either the Gettier case precedes a case

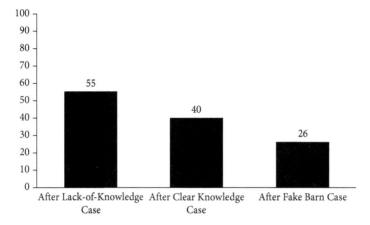

Figure 2.13 Percentages of knowledge ascriptions in a Truetemp case (based on Wright, 2010).

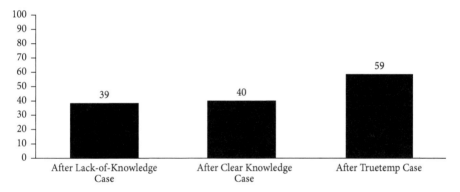

Figure 2.14 Percentages of knowledge ascriptions in a fake-barn case (based on Wright, 2010).

describing a justified false belief or it follows it. Participants are asked whether to ascribe knowledge in two different ways: The first question (called "Knowledge 1") contrasts knowledge and no knowledge (the two possible answers being "Yes, [s]he knows" and "No, [s]he doesn't know"); the second question (called "Knowledge 2") contrasts knowledge and the impression that one knows without having any knowledge (the two possible answers being "[Protagonist] knows that [relevant proposition]," and (ii) [Protagonist] feels like s[he] knows that [relevant proposition] but [s]he doesn't actually know [this]). People are more likely to ascribe knowledge when the Gettier case follows the justified false belief case than when it comes first (Figure 2.15). The effect size is small.

Study 1 in Machery et al. (forthcoming b) shows that this effect is robust across cultures, as a similar order effect was found in the USA, India, Japan, and Brazil.

2.6.3 Mind

No reported finding.

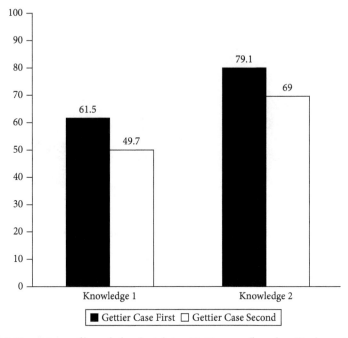

Figure 2.15 Percentages of knowledge denials in a Gettier case (based on Machery et al., forthcoming b).

2.6.4 Metaphysics

No reported finding.

2.6.5 Ethics

Petrinovich and O'Neill (1996) examine whether presentation order influences the judgments elicited by *the switch case*. In one condition, the switch case is presented before a case where by scanning a healthy patient, information could be gathered that would prevent five patients from dying, although the healthy patient would die ("the scan case"), and a transplant case. In another condition, the transplant case comes first, followed by the scan case and the switch case. Participants are more likely to agree to push the switch in the former condition (2.9 on a 10-point scale anchored at –5 with "strongly disagree" and at 5 with "strongly agree") than in the latter (1.5)—a moderate effect size ($d = 0.58$). By contrast, judgments about the two other cases are not influenced by the order of presentation. In another study, Petrinovich and O'Neill present the switch case, a version of the switch case involving pushing a button, and the footbridge case in this and in the reversed order. Order influences the judgments elicited by the two switch cases, but not those elicited by the footbridge case. An issue with Petrinovich and O'Neill's studies is that participants were asked, "What would you do?," and had to rate their agreement with an action (or an inaction) instead of judging the permissibility of the action or inaction.

Follow-up studies have remedied this problem. In Lanteri et al. (2008), people are more likely to judge that it is "morally acceptable" to pull the switch when the switch case is presented before the footbridge case (94 percent) than after (78 percent), while judgments elicited by the footbridge case were not influenced (46 vs. 48 percent). Lanteri and colleagues also find that whether the character's action is judged to be morally obligatory and intentional depends on presentation order in the switch case, but not in the footbridge case. Lombrozo (2009), using a question about permissibility ($d = 0.6$; a moderate effect), and Wiegmann et al. (2012), using a question about what should be done, report a similar effect.[7] The size of the effect reported in Wiegmann et al. (2012) is worth noting: Participants are twice as likely to push the switch when the switch case comes first compared to last (68 percent vs. 32 percent).

Wiegmann et al. (2012) also report that judgments elicited by *the footbridge case* were not influenced by the order of presentation (see also Wiegmann et al., ms). However, a version of the footbridge case, involving opening a trap instead of pushing the individual, results in an order effect (48 percent vs. 20 percent), when the case was presented before the standard footbridge case in contrast to after it. In their third study, Wiegmann et al. (ms) provide evidence that when people are allowed to modify their original judgment after having seen the footbridge and switch case (in both presentation orders), only judgments elicited by the latter case are revised.

Finally, in Liao et al. (2012), judgments elicited by *the loop case* vary with its context: People are more likely to agree that it is morally permissible to send a runaway trolley on a loop, where it would be stopped by hitting a person, after having read the switch case (3.8 on a 6 point scale anchored at 6 with "strongly agree") than the footbridge case (3.1)—a small effect ($d = 0.25$).

2.6.6 Action theory

Judgments about *the harm* and *help cases* are influenced by the order of presentation of these two cases. Feltz and Cokely (2011) report that, when the two cases are presented successively, the size of the asymmetry depends on the order of presentation: It is smaller (although still real) when the help case is presented first ($d = 0.7$) than presented second ($d = 1.03$) (Figure 2.16). The change in the intentionality judgments are moderate for the help case ($d = 0.5$) and large for the harm case ($d = 0.9$).

Similarly, Cushman and Mele (2008) provide evidence that people are less likely to judge that the agent brought about the side effect intentionally in the harm case when this case follows, rather than precedes, the help case.

---

[7] See also Schwitzgebel & Cushman (2012, 2015); Wiegmann & Waldmann (2014); Wiegmann et al. (ms).

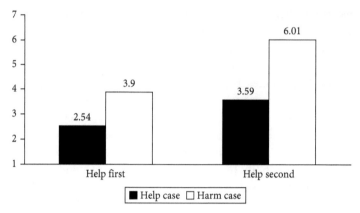

Figure 2.16 Mean intentionality judgments in the harm and help cases (based on Feltz & Cokely, 2011).

2.6.7 The objection from learning

Order effects are apparently commonly found among judgments elicited by philosophical cases, and they will play a role in the argument developed in Chapter 3: Unreliability. One may, however, wonder whether such effects in any way reveal some deficiency we make in response to cases. Horne and Livengood (2017) note that studies reporting an order effect typically compare participants' judgments in response to a target case (e.g., the Gettier case) when it is presented first or when it follows another case ("the contextual case"). Any difference between these two conditions, they maintain, may be due to participants *learning* something important when they read the contextual case. That is, participants may not have the same pertinent information when they read the target case alone and when they read it after the contextual case. If they don't, then it is not irrational to give a different answer to the target case when it comes first and when it comes second; rather, one judges differently in the latter condition because one has learned something by reading the contextual case (this is "an updating effect," as Horne and Livengood call it). To show that there is a genuine order effect, not simply an updating effect, one should present participants with both the target and the contextual case in two different orders: target case first, contextual case second vs. contextual case first, target case second. Once they have read the two cases, participants would assess the situation described by the target case. An order effect would be established if they judge differently: Because participants have the same relevant information, the difference could not be chalked up to learning. However, as Horne and colleagues note, few experiments have followed this experimental design.

Horne and Livengood are right that the effects observed in the studies reviewed in Section 2.6 could in principle be due to learning rather than to order of presentation. However, for many of these studies, this possibility seems unlikely because there is nothing to be learned in the contextual case. For instance, regarding the order effect involving the Gettier case that was reported in Section 2.6.1 (Machery et al., forthcoming b), what is it that participants could learn by considering the justified false belief case that would make it rational to judge differently when a Gettier case is presented after such a case and when it is presented independently?

Horne and colleagues will respond, I suppose, that I am dismissing too quickly the updating-effect possibility, and they may argue that their updating-effect hypothesis accounts well for some of the alleged order effects. Horne et al. (2013) show that a simple learning model—Hogarth and Einhorn's (1992) Belief-Adjustment model— explains the asymmetry between reading the footbridge case before the switch case (leading to a change in response to the switch case) and reading the switch case before the footbridge case (inducing no change in response to the footbridge case). In Hogarth and Einhorn's model, the influence a piece of evidence has on one's belief that p depends on how strongly one believes that p. If one leans toward believing p, then a confirmatory piece of evidence will reinforce the belief less than a falsifying piece of evidence would falsify it. If people incline toward believing that they should be ready to do everything to minimize the overall harm done to people ("the consequentialist principle"), and if their response to the switch and footbridge case provide the same amount of, respectively, confirmatory and falsifying evidence for this belief, then reading the footbridge case first should weaken the belief in the consequentialist principle more than reading the switch case would strengthen it. People who read the footbridge case before the switch case should then be less willing to push the switch (since they adhere less to the consequentialist principle), while people who read the switch case before the footbridge case should then be roughly equally reluctant to push the large man (since their belief in the consequentialist principle has barely been reinforced). As a result, "if people strongly endorse the beliefs that underlie their judgments about the Footbridge and Trolley dilemmas, then the asymmetry in the Footbridge-Trolley ordering effect could be a direct consequence of how people weigh evidence" (Horne et al., 2013, 708).

Unfortunately, the findings presented by Horne et al. themselves (2013) undermine this ingenious proposal. In their first study, agreement with the principle, "In life or death situations, one should always take whatever means is necessary to save the most lives," is lower after the switch case than in a control condition (where they read a morally neutral case); while the difference isn't significant, it is trending that way ($p = 0.07$) and would probably be significant with a larger data set; in any case it is not larger than in the control condition, contrary to what the Belief-Adjustment model predicts. In Study 2, people do not endorse less the principle "You should never kill another person" after having read the switch case compared to a control condition, contrary to the prediction of the Belief-Adjustment model; if anything, they endorse the principle more, although again the difference is not significant.

Another challenge to building critical arguments on order effects concedes that the effects reported in experimental philosophy are genuine order effects (and not simply updating effects), but would insist that such effects are rational (Horne & Livengood, 2017). What characterizes order effects is that change in belief is not commutative: Seeing two pieces of evidence, A and B, in the order A-B has a different effect on belief from seeing them in the order B-A. Many theories about rational belief updating require commutativity: In particular, Bayesian conditionalization is commutative. The order of the evidence does not matter: If at t_1 two Bayesian thinkers start from the same prior degree of belief, are exposed to the same body of evidence in two different orders, and update by conditionalization, they should end up with the same degree of belief at t_2. If conditionalization is the correct normative theory of belief change, then order effects are irrational. However, according to some theories, rational belief updating is not commutative: The order in which evidence is presented makes a difference in rational degrees of belief. In particular, in contrast to conditionalization, which assumes that the evidence is known, Jeffrey-conditionalization, which explains how an agent could update her belief on the basis of uncertain evidence, is not commutative.

Jeffrey-conditionalization is controversial (precisely because it is not commutative), but it would perhaps be too easy to dismiss this objection on this ground. A better response would note that Jeffrey-conditionalization and conditionalization for evidence that is certain work identically. When reading a philosophical case, the evidence is either the explicit or the implicit target content. The explicit target content is stipulated: The reader is told, e.g., that it is 4:00 p.m. in the clock case and that the character forms a belief that it is 4:00 p.m. It would be strange if the reader were uncertain about the facts that hold by stipulation. When we read in *Le Rouge et le Noir* that Julien Sorel is born in Verrières, we are not uncertain about that proposition: We accept it as a fact. But perhaps the reader could be uncertain about the target implicit content since it is not stipulated, but must be inferred on the basis of what is stipulated by the author of the philosophical case. But the reader can be certain that some of the relevant inferred propositions hold given the context: In the clock case, for example, we can infer with certainty that the character is rational. Of course, some of the propositions that constitute the target content may not be certain, in particular when the case is unusual (Section 3.5.3 of Chapter 3). However, the more common it is that readers are uncertain about philosophically pertinent aspects of the situations described by cases, the less dialectically useful cases are: Philosophers may not be responding to the same set of propositions (Alexander & Weinberg, 2007). So, appealing to Jeffrey-conditionalization may vindicate the rationality of order effects, but that would be at the expense of the dialectical utility of cases. In addition, we may not be certain about many propositions that constitute the inferred superficial content: For instance, we must be uncertain about the ethnicity of the character in the clock case. But if these propositions influence the judgments elicited by the philosophical cases, then these judgments should not be trusted, and appealing to the influence of such propositions cannot be part of an argument aiming at defending the method of cases.

Table 2.7. Summary of the evidence about order effects

Case	Field	Order Effect	Effect Size
Clear knowledge case	Epistemology	N	-
Clear lack-of-knowledge case	Epistemology	N	-
Gettier case	Epistemology	Y	Small
Truetemp case	Epistemology	Y	Moderate
Fake-barn case	Epistemology	Y	Moderate to large
Switch case	Ethics	Y	Moderate to large
Footbridge case	Ethics	N	-
Footbridge case (button)	Ethics	Y	Large
Loop case	Ethics	Y	Small
Help and harm cases	Action theory	Y	Moderate to Large

2.6.8 Summary

Across areas of philosophy, the judgments elicited by most philosophical cases are subject to order effects (Table 2.7). Their size varies: Some are small (e.g., Gettier case), others large (e.g., harm case).

2.7 Framing Effects

2.7.1 Language

Machery et al. (ms) report that the judgments elicited by the lemon case are influenced by the way the question is framed. Participants were presented with the lemon case, and then they were asked four different questions. Despite their different wordings and response options, all four questions essentially asked participants whether the transformed fruits (which had retained their genetic properties) were still lemons or not:

Would you say that in those conditions there are still lemons?
YES, there are still lemons   NO, there are no more lemons

Would you say that in those conditions lemons are now oranges?
YES, lemons are now oranges   NO, lemons are not now oranges

Would you say that in those conditions lemons have become oranges?
YES, lemons have become oranges   NO, lemons have not become oranges

What are they now, lemons or oranges?
LEMONS   ORANGES

Participants' externalist judgments were influenced by the formulation of the response option. A significant minority (24 percent) of participants assigned to the first response option gave externalist responses, while people were about evenly divided for the three other response options. The difference is moderate in size.

2.7.2 Epistemology

In Study 2 of Machery et al. (forthcoming b), participants were presented with two distinct *Gettier cases*: the clock case and the hospital case.

Hospital Case
Paul Jones was worried because it was 10 p.m. and his wife Mary was not home from work yet. Usually she is home by 6 p.m. He tried her cell phone but just kept getting her voicemail. Starting to worry that something might have happened to her, he decided to call some local hospitals to ask whether any patient by the name of "Mary Jones" had been admitted that evening. At the University Hospital, the person who answered his call confirmed that someone by that name had been admitted with major but not life-threatening injuries following a car crash. Paul grabbed his coat and rushed out to drive to University Hospital. As it turned out, the patient at University Hospital was not Paul's wife, but another woman with the same name. In fact, Paul's wife had a heart attack as she was leaving work, and was at that moment receiving treatment in Metropolitan Hospital, a few miles away.

Clock Case
Wanda is out for a weekend afternoon walk. As she passes near the train station, she wonders what time it is. She glances up at the clock on the train station wall, sees that it says 4:15 p.m., and concludes that it is 4:15 p.m. What she doesn't realize is that this clock is broken and has been showing 4:15 p.m. for the last two days. But by sheer coincidence, it is in fact 4:15 p.m. just at the moment when she glances at the clock.

These two cases differ only in their irrelevant superficial content. Participants are asked two questions, Knowledge 1 and Knowledge 2 (see Section 2.6 above). Participants were less likely to judge that the character does not know the relevant proposition when reading the clock case than the hospital case (Figure 2.17). Study 3 replicates this result. The effect size is large.

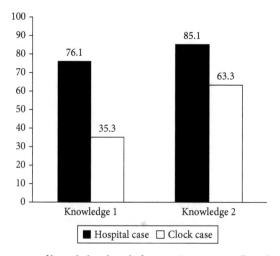

Figure 2.17 Percentages of knowledge denials for two Gettier cases (based on Machery et al., forthcoming b).

Study 1 in Machery et al. (forthcoming b) shows that this effect is robust across cultures, as a similar framing effect was found in the USA, India, Japan, and Brazil.

Beebe and Buckwalter (2010) have shown that knowledge ascription about a means depends on the moral valence of this means—an effect known as "the epistemic side-effect effect." Consider for instance the following two cases (differences in brackets):

Epistemic Help and Harm Cases
The vice-president of a company went to the chairman of the board and said, "We are thinking of starting a new program. It will help us increase profits, and it will also [help/harm] the environment." The chairman of the board answered, "I don't care at all about [helping/harming] the environment. I just want to make as much profit as I can. Let's start the new program." They started the new program. Sure enough, the environment was [helped/harmed].

Participants are much more likely to ascribe knowledge in the harm version than in the help version ($d = 0.6$, a moderate to large effect).

Buckwalter (2014) shows that the epistemic side-effect effect results in a framing effect with the Gettier case. Consider the following two Gettier cases:

Two Gettier Cases
The mayor of a small town is trying to decide whether or not to sign a new contract with a local corporation. The math is all very complex, but all his economic strategists think that there's a relatively good chance that one outcome is that it will [create/cut] jobs for workers in the community. The mayor says, "All I really care about is campaign contributions, not people's jobs, and I am sure to get millions from the corporation if I agree." So, he decides to sign their contract. The corporation, however, didn't take any chances. They secretly switched the contract with a totally different one right before the mayor signed it. By changing all the fine print, in some cases the opposite of what the mayor thought he was signing, the corporation could be sure it got what it wanted. Sure enough, shortly after the mayor signed the contract, a number of members of the community [got/lost] jobs, and the mayor received a huge donation to his re-election campaign.

People were likely to ascribe knowledge in the harm version of this Gettier case, and the effect size was very large ($d = 1.32$; Figure 2.18).

Turri and Friedman (2014) present compelling evidence that the judgments elicited by *lottery cases* depend on how the cases are framed. For instance, in Study 2 they present participants with the following two cases:

Odd News
Ellen bought a ticket in this week's Super Lotto. Her numbers are 49-20-3-15-37-29-8. Ellen just finished watching the evening news and they reported that a completely different number won. And she recalls from her statistics class that there is only a 1-in-10,000,000 (one-in-ten-million) chance that a newscaster will misreport the winning number. On that basis, Ellen concludes that her ticket lost. And she is right: her ticket lost.

Odds
Ellen bought a ticket in this week's Super Lotto. Her numbers are 49-20-3-15-37-29-8. Ellen wasn't able to watch the evening news where they reported which number won. But she recalls

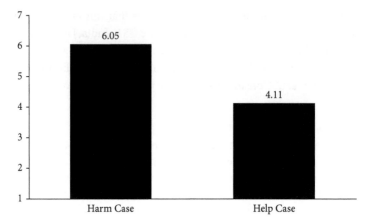

Figure 2.18 Mean knowledge ascriptions in Gettier cases (based on Buckwalter, 2014).

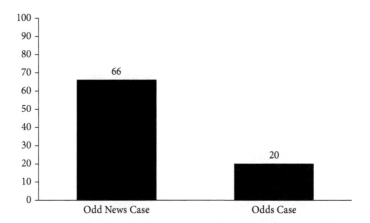

Figure 2.19 Mean knowledge ascriptions in lottery-style cases (based on Turri & Friedman, 2014).

from her statistics class that there is only a 1-in-10,000,000 (one-in-ten-million) chance that a Super Lotto ticket will win. On that basis, Ellen concludes that her ticket lost. And she is right: her ticket lost.

Few participants ascribe knowledge in response to Odds (in line with philosophers' consensus about lottery cases), while a majority ascribes knowledge in response to Odd News (Figure 2.19).

2.7.3 Mind

No finding reported.

2.7.4 Metaphysics

No finding reported.

2.7.5 Ethics

Petrinovich and O'Neill (1996) report that judgments elicited by *the switch case* vary when the choice is framed in terms of saving vs. killing people. In the action condition, participants read either "Throw the switch, which will result in the death of the one innocent person on the side track" or "Throw the switch, which will result in the five innocent people on the main track being saved." In the inaction condition they read either "Do nothing, which will result in the death of the five innocent people" or "Do nothing, which will result in the one innocent person being saved." In both the action and inaction conditions, participants were much more likely to agree with the statement when it described the action as saving people instead of killing people. The effect size of the kill/save manipulation is large, the manipulation accounting for about a quarter of the total variance. Petrinovich and O'Neill (1996) replicate this finding with a distinct sample.

In addition, according to Nadelhoffer and Feltz (2008), judgments elicited by the switch case are influenced by whether the case is formulated about a fictional character ("John") or in the second person ("you")—a phenomenon known as the actor-observer bias. 65 percent of participants judge it permissible for them to hit the switch versus 90 percent for a fictional agent (a moderate to large effect). Tobia et al. (2013) report similar results. People also respond differently to the switch case when the choice is to be made by a bystander or by a passenger. It is substantially more permissible in the latter case (84 percent) than in the former (65 percent, a small to moderate effect; see also Gold et al., 2014).

Cikara et al. (2010) provide evidence that whether the action described by *the footbridge case* is acceptable depends on our attitudes toward both the person on the footbridge and the individuals on the tracks. It is more acceptable to sacrifice people low in warmth and competence, such as homeless individuals, and less acceptable to save them (the difference between sacrificing an individual high in warmth and competence and an individual low in both is small to moderate, $d = 0.28$). The influence of these attitudes is surprisingly large. While most people think it is not permissible to push the large person when she is not described, most (84 percent) happen to judge it is permissible to push a low-warmth, low-competence individual to save five high-warmth, high-competence individuals.

How the superficial content of a case influences the judgments elicited by moral cases sometimes depends on moral and political attitudes. According to Uhlmann et al. (2009), liberals are more likely to push the large man when he has a stereotypically white name, e.g., "Chip Ellsworth III," in order to save 100 members of the Harlem Jazz Orchestra than when he has a prototypically black name, "Tyrone Payton," in order to save 100 members of the New York Philharmonic.

An actor-observer asymmetry is also found with Williams's *Jim and the Indians case* (Tobia et al., 2013). Participants (undergraduates) are more likely to say that a fictional character ("Jim") is morally obligated to shoot one person to save a greater number (53 percent) than they themselves ("you") are obligated (19 percent), a large effect.

In addition to the variation induced by manipulating the vignettes, contextual factors also influence judgments about cases eliciting moral judgments. In particular, a large body of evidence suggests that situational cues or causal factors influencing people's affective states—emotions or moods—have a substantial effect on people's moral judgments about cases. I'll limit myself to a few illustrative examples, but the pertinent literature in moral psychology is quite large.

Valdesolo and DeSteno (2006) present participants with a five-minute comedy clip (drawn from Saturday Night Live) or with a neutral control clip, and they then read the footbridge and switch cases (counterbalancing for order). Participants who see the comedy clip are almost three times as likely to judge it morally appropriate to push the character in the footbridge case (24 percent) than those who see the control clip (9 percent), while the manipulation has no effect on the switch case (for a replication and sophisticated discussion, see Strohminger et al., 2011). Pastötter et al. (2013) have replicated this effect, also showing that the effect of mood manipulation on judgments about the footbridge case depends on its wording—more precisely on whether the judgment bears on acting or on failing to act (an instance of the omission bias). People are more likely to judge it appropriate to push the man in the footbridge case when a positive mood rather than a negative mood is induced; by contrast, people are less likely to judge it appropriate to refrain from pushing the man when a negative mood rather than a positive mood is induced.

Tobia et al. (2013) present participants with short vignettes involving disgusting actions, such as the following:

A man leaves work, unwrapping a sandwich for lunch. As he is about to bite into the sandwich, he notices that part of the bread is moldy. Rather than eating it, he gives the sandwich to a homeless man who is asking for spare change.

Participants (either professional philosophers or undergraduates) are asked to assess how wrong the action was. For half of the participants, the vignettes are printed on a paper that had been sprayed with Lysol, while for the other half the paper had been sprayed with water. Half of the vignettes are formulated using the second person (e.g., "You leave work…"), while the other half are about a third party (e.g., "A man leaves work…," as above). The scent of Lysol influences all participants' judgments about the wrongness of the described actions, although in different ways for philosophers and non-philosophers (see also Helzer & Pizarro, 2011). In particular, non-philosophers' wrongness judgments about the actions described in both second-person and third-person vignettes are more severe when the paper smelled of Lysol.

Perhaps more surprisingly, language makes a difference. People tend to give a different answer in response to footbridge and switch cases in their native and in a foreign language (Costa et al., 2014). The proportion of characteristically utilitarian answers in the footbridge case increased by nearly 50 percent (from 20 percent to 33 percent) in Costa et al.'s first study and by a larger percentage in their second study (from 18 percent to 44 percent). No difference was found for the switch case. This is the kind of effect that I would be quite skeptical of, were it not for the fact that it has been replicated (Geipel et al., 2015), and is in line with a more general influence of language on judgment and decision making (Hadjichristidis et al., 2015). The size of the effect is moderate. Incidentally, the language effect is not found with the crybaby case.

Sacrificial cases are not the only cases in ethics giving rise to a framing effect. Unger's (1996) *envelope* and *Mercedes cases*, used to argue against the lack of duty to help people, are subject to a framing effect. Musen (2010) shows that various variables influence whether participants find it morally obligatory to provide help in the situation described by Unger's envelope case: the proximity of the persons in need of help ($d = 0.7$; a large effect), whether one would help by giving money or goods, whether information about the persons in need is indirectly obtained or is obtained by direct contact, and whether the need is an emergency or a chronic state. Various variables influence whether participants find it morally obligatory to provide help in the situation described by Unger's Mercedes case—particularly whether one would lose money as a means to help somebody or a side effect of helping her ($d = 0.5$; a moderate effect).

Bradner et al. (ms) show that lay people agree with the proposition that it is permissible to unplug the second person (e.g., the conductor) in versions of Thomson's (1971) *Society of Music Lovers case* only when this second person has no familial relationship with the main character of the vignette. When the second person is a half-sibling of the main character, people find the proposed action impermissible.

Turning to judgments elicited by *the experience machine case*, de Brigard (2010) has provided some evidence that judgments about whether to plug into the experience machine are influenced by the way the choice is described. People are unwilling to plug into the experience machine, but they are also unwilling to unplug from it when they are told to imagine that they are already plugged. De Brigard appeals to the status quo bias to explain judgments about the experience machine: We are biased to prefer our current situation. Furthermore, participants' willingness to unplug depends on what their life outside the machine would be: They are unlikely to unplug if they would then have a very unpleasant life (the negative condition; Figure 2.20). The effect is very large.

2.7.6 Action theory

Nichols and Knobe (2007) examine whether judgments about responsibility and free will differ when the question is asked abstractly (e.g., in a deterministic universe, "is it possible for a person to be fully morally responsible for their actions?") or about a concrete situation involving the morally reprehensible action of a particular individual (e.g., in a deterministic universe, "is Bill fully morally responsible for killing his wife and children?"). They show that people tend to make compatibilist judgments about concrete situations, while making incompatibilist abstract judgments (see also Roskies & Nichols, 2008).

In an experiment loosely inspired by Knobe's (2003, 2006) results about the harm and help cases, Feltz et al. (2012; see particularly experiment 1) show that judgments

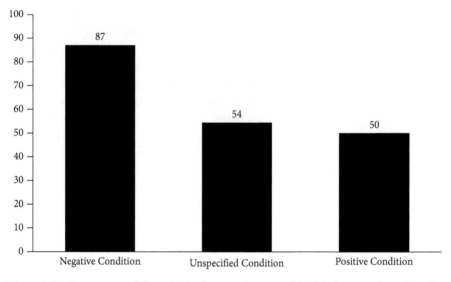

Figure 2.20 Percentages of "remain in the experience machine" judgments (based on De Brigard, 2010).

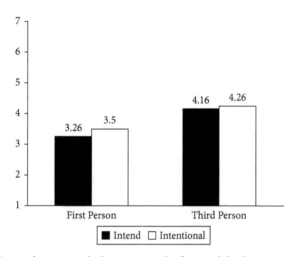

Figure 2.21 Mean judgments in the harm case in the first- and third-person conditions (based on Feltz et al., 2012).

about whether an action is intended or intentionally brought about differ when participants actually accomplish the action and when they are told about the action, agreeing more on a 7-point scale (anchored at "1" with "disagree" and at "7" with "agree") with the claim that the action was intended or intentionally brought about in the latter case (Figure 2.21). The effect size is small to moderate ($d = 0.4$ for "intend" and $d = 0.34$ for "intentional").

Table 2.8. Summary of the evidence about presentation effects

Case	Field	Framing	Effect Size
Lemon case	Language	Y	Moderate
Gettier case	Epistemology	Y	Moderate
Lottery case	Epistemology	Y	Large
Switch case	Ethics	Y	Moderate to large
Footbridge case	Ethics	Y	Large
Jim and the Indians case	Ethics	Y	Large
Envelope case	Ethics	Y	Large
Mercedes case	Ethics	Y	Large
Society of Music Lovers	Ethics	Y	Large
Experience machine case	Ethics	Y	Large
Responsibility/free will cases	Action theory	Y	Large
Help and harm cases	Action theory	Y	Small to moderate

2.7.7 Summary

Across areas of philosophy, judgments elicited by philosophical cases are influenced by framing and situational cues. The effect sizes are typically surprisingly large (Table 2.8).

2.8 Summary

Table 2.9 summarizes the results reviewed in this chapter. "No" indicates that the influence of a given variable has been tested, and was not found; if the influence of a given variable has not been tested, the table reports "Unknown"; the various effect sizes reported in this chapter are also summarized. The last column indicates whether a philosophically significant effect—i.e., one that is at least moderate—has been found.

A few points are noteworthy. First, experimental philosophers and psychologists have only examined a limited number of cases: Less than thirty out of the dozens of reasonably well-known cases. Furthermore, even fewer cases have been systematically examined, as is evident by the frequency of the "Unknown" value in Table 2.9. Cases drawn from moral philosophy are more likely to have been examined, and they have been more systematically studied, in large part because psychologists have used them to study moral psychology. Cases drawn from metaphysics have been by and large ignored, and the philosophy of mind has not been mined. In these respects, the empirical record could be more extensive. It could also be stronger, with better experimental designs (see Section 5.1 of Chapter 5), the replication of surprising effects, and the systematic variation of the vignettes used to obtain presentation and demographic effects so as to be better able to explain them. As a result, the arguments based on this empirical record, which will be developed in the next two chapters, must assume that it is representative of the phenomena that characterize the judgments elicited by philosophical cases in general.

Table 2.9. Summary of the evidence for demographic and presentation effects

Case	Field	Culture	Gender	Age	Personality	Order	Framing	Presence of a Meaningful Effect
Gödel	Language	Large	No	No	Unknown	Unknown	Unknown	✓
Jonah	Language	Small	Unknown	Unknown	Unknown	Unknown	Unknown	✓
Water	Language	Large	Mixed	No	Unknown	Unknown	Unknown	✓
Lemon	Language	Large	No	No	Unknown	Unknown	Moderate	✓
Twin-Earth	Language	Unknown	No	Unknown	Unknown	Unknown	Unknown	
Gettier	Epistemology	No	No	Unknown	Small	Small	Moderate	✓
Fake-barn	Epistemology	Unknown	No	Mixed	Unknown	Moderate to large	Unknown	✓
Truetemp	Epistemology	No	No	Unknown	Unknown	Moderate to large	Unknown	✓
Zebra	Epistemology	Large	No	Unknown	Unknown	Unknown	Unknown	✓
Cancer	Epistemology	No	Unknown	Unknown	Unknown	Unknown	Unknown	✓
BIV	Epistemology	Unknown	Mixed	Unknown	Unknown	Unknown	Unknown	
Lottery	Epistemology	Unknown	Unknown	Unknown	Unknown	Unknown	Large	✓
Chinese room	Mind	Unknown	No	Unknown	Unknown	Unknown	Unknown	
Switch	Ethics	Mixed	Moderate	Unknown	Moderate	Moderate to large	Moderate to large	✓
Footbridge	Ethics	Large	Moderate	No	Moderate	No	Large	✓

Footbridge (button)	Ethics	Unknown	Unknown	Unknown	Unknown	Large	Unknown	✓
Loop	Ethics	Large	Unknown	Unknown	Unknown	Small	Unknown	✓
Lifeboat	Ethics	Unknown	No	Small	Moderate	Unknown	Unknown	✓
Transplant	Ethics	Unknown	Unknown	Unknown	Moderate to large	Unknown	Unknown	✓
Jim and the Indians	Ethics	Unknown	Unknown	Unknown	Unknown	Unknown	Large	✓
Crybaby	Ethics	Unknown	Moderate	No	Moderate	Unknown	Unknown	✓
Society of Music Lovers	Ethics	Unknown	Unknown	Unknown	Unknown	Unknown	Large	✓
Action/omission	Ethics	Large	Unknown	Unknown	Unknown	Unknown	Unknown	✓
Envelope	Ethics	Unknown	Unknown	Unknown	Unknown	Unknown	Large	✓
Mercedes	Ethics	Unknown	Unknown	Unknown	Unknown	Unknown	Large	✓
Experience machine	Ethics	Large	Large	Large	Unknown	Unknown	Large	✓
Compatibilism	Action	No	Unknown	Unknown	Moderate to large	Unknown	Large	✓
Harm and help	Action	Large	No	Unknown	Moderate	Moderate to large	Small to moderate	✓

Nearly all the cases that have been examined are influenced either by demographic or by presentation variables, and this influence is frequently large (for further discussion of the size of this influence, see Section 3.3.4 in Chapter 3). This is true of epistemological, moral, and action-theory cases. Variation and instability (due to presentation variables such as different framings or different orders of presentation) are thus both substantial and widespread, at least among the cases that have been examined.

This variation and instability is of a different order than the variation and instability found in other domains of cognition. (Remember that I am comparing the judgments elicited by philosophical cases—and *not* the judgments about topics of philosophical interest such as knowledge, rightness, permissibility, and causation in general—to the judgments in other domains of cognition, such as perceptual judgments.) Perceptual judgments such as length estimation are sensitive to order effects (Stevens & Galanter, 1957; see Horne & Livengood, 2017, for further references), and judgments about color similarity and difference are apparently influenced by language (e.g., Winawer et al., 2007 and citations therein). But these effects are often small—this is the case of the effect of order on length estimation—and of no practical significance. When it comes to the judgments elicited by philosophical cases, many effects are of moderate or moderate to large size, which is already significant from a philosophical point of view. Sizeable effects found in the study of perceptual judgments are limited to peculiar circumstances. We should be reasonably skeptical of our inclinations to make perceptual judgments in these circumstances exactly as, I will argue, we should be skeptical of the judgments elicited by these philosophical cases.

Horne and Livengood (2017) have recently challenged the claim that the variation and instability in judgments elicited by philosophical cases are of a different order than the variation and instability found in other domains of cognition (a claim they call the "differential exhibition response"). They focus on order effects, but their challenge generalizes to all the effects reviewed in this chapter. They note that establishing the differential exhibition response would require meta-analyses that not only have not been done, but may not even be doable (given their size, complexity, etc.), and they conclude that we just do not know whether the differential exhibition response is correct. They also note that there are indications speaking against it. Psychologists routinely counterbalance their stimuli, suggesting that they expect order effects to be common, while Hogarth and Einhorn (1992) have found order effects in nearly all the studies they reviewed.

However, the experimental practice of counterbalancing does not mean that psychologists believe that order effects are widespread; rather, they believe that order effects may happen and they want to control for a potential confound. Psychologists do not seem overly concerned with framing effects: They often (though admittedly not always) treat their stimuli as representative and generalize from them. Hogarth and Einhorn (1992) have found widespread order effects in their literature review, but these effects may not be sufficiently large to matter from a practical point of view; furthermore, the experimental circumstances in which these effects were found may not be externally valid, and the frequency of order effects in the lab may not indicate that order effects are common in everyday circumstances. (Demographic and presentation effects do not suffer from this second issue since the experimental conditions—reading a case and making a judgment—are similar, though admittedly not identical to what philosophers do when they read a case in an article.) Turning now to the first point, it is true that no systematic study of presentation effects in various domains has ever been done, and it would be a daunting task to complete such study, but the differential exhibition response is much more plausible than Horne and Livengood acknowledge. While practically insignificant variation and instability may be common in many domains of cognition, sizeable effects must be limited to particular circumstances or else most of our judgments (including our perceptual judgments) would be questionable. I see no reason to take the latter skepticism seriously.

2.9 Conclusion

To conclude, let's consider two bold claims made by Bealer in a famous article (1996, 125):

[A] person's concrete cases intuitions are largely consistent with one another. (We confine our-selves to concrete-case intuitions, for it is to these that the standard justificatory procedure assigns primary evidential weight.) To be sure, a given person's concrete-case intuitions occa-sionally appear to be inconsistent with one another, but so do our observations and even our pure sense experiences. This is hardly enough to throw out observation and sense experience as sources of evidence.

[A]lthough different people do have conflicting intuitions from time to time, there is an impressive corroboration by others of one's elementary logical, mathematical, conceptual, and modal intuitions. The situation is much the same with observation: different people have con-flicting observations from time to time, but this is hardly enough to throw out observation as a source of evidence.

The widespread and large influence of presentation effects on judgments elicited by philosophical cases belies the first claim, the demographic diversity in such judgments the second claim (at least with respect to what Bealer calls "conceptual and modal intu-itions"). Judgments elicited by philosophical cases vary, and they can be pushed around.

3

Fooled by Cognitive Artifacts

[T]here is no reason to trust our intuitions about what we would say in situations in which some of our relatively secure beliefs have proved false.

(Fodor, 1964, 205–6)

In this chapter and in the next two chapters, I examine the material use of philosophical cases. Two kinds of concern have been raised about this use: the concern that in light of the demographic and presentation effects reviewed in Chapter 2 judgments elicited by philosophical cases should not be trusted, and the concern that users of the method of cases fail to react appropriately to the diversity of judgments elicited by cases. In this chapter, I consider the former concern—which is the basis of the argument from unreliability ("Unreliability")—before turning to the second concern in Chapter 4—which is the basis of the argument from disagreement ("Dogmatism") and of the argument from parochialism ("Parochialism").

Unreliability establishes that, given the kind of case philosophers tend to use, the method of cases is an unreliable way of finding about knowledge, causation, free will, and other topics of philosophical interest: When philosophers attempt to settle material-mode disputes by means of cases, the concepts of philosophical interest (CAUSATION, RESPONSIBILITY, JUSTIFICATION, or PERMISSIBILITY) are typically applied in circumstances where, for a variety of reasons, concept application is unreliable, albeit being typically reliable elsewhere. Thus, judgments elicited by typical philosophical cases are similar to experimental artifacts—outcomes of experimental manipulations that are not due to the phenomena experimentally investigated, but to the (often otherwise reliable) experimental tools used to investigate them. As I will say, judgments elicited by philosophical cases are often "cognitive artifacts." Philosophers relying on these cases are like astronomers who would take instrumental artifacts at face value when they theorize about astronomical phenomena, or biologists who would take the deformations produced by microscopes for real phenomena.

I begin by showing that the judgments elicited by the philosophical cases that have been examined by experimental philosophers are unreliable before inducing from these cases to the broader class of philosophical cases. In support of this induction,

I identify several characteristics that explain why the cases examined by experimental philosophers elicit unreliable judgments ("the disturbing characteristics"), and I argue that philosophical cases tend to share these characteristics. Furthermore, while some of these characteristics are accidental—cases without these characteristics would work equally well for philosophical purposes—others are not: Philosophical cases are likely to possess non-accidental disturbing characteristics, because these characteristics contribute to their dialectical utility. As I will say, the unreliability of the judgments elicited by philosophical cases is "fundamental." If Unreliability is correct, then we philosophers are like astronomers who, unbeknownst to them, often have no other means for theorizing about the sky than massively deforming telescopes.

The issue that Unreliability brings to the fore is not that there is something intrinsically wrong with using cases in philosophy. Indeed, how could that even be the case? If minimalist characterizations of the method of cases are correct, what philosophers do is merely judge about situations described by short stories ("cases") instead of about experienced situations. And surely there is nothing suspicious *in general* in judging about situations that are described. We do it all the time, and our judgments are warranted. No, the issue Unreliability brings to the fore is that there is something problematic with the type of case used by philosophers: These cases tend to produce cognitive artifacts, often for non-accidental reasons.

Here is how I will proceed. In Section 3.1, I describe an argument schema against the method of cases. I settle on an instantiation of this argument schema, Unreliability, and I defend its first premise in Section 3.2: Unreliable judgments are severely deficient from an epistemic point of view. In Section 3.3, I defend its second premise: Judgments elicited by most of the philosophical cases that have been examined by experimental philosophers are unreliable. In Section 3.4, I examine two approaches for generalizing from the cases examined by experimental philosophers to most philosophical cases. At the end of Section 3.4, we will be able to conclude that philosophers are not warranted to assume that facts of philosophical interest (e.g., that the protagonist in an epistemological case does not know some proposition, that an action in an ethical case is permissible, that a protagonist is not free, or that an event described by a metaphysical case is a cause) hold in the situations described by most current philosophical cases, but, for all that I will have said, this lack of warrant may merely be an accidental feature of the cases that philosophers happen to have been using. In Section 3.5, I examine another approach to generalizing beyond the cases examined by experimental philosophers: I identify some of the characteristics that explain why the cases examined by experimental philosophers elicit unreliable judgments, and I show that these characteristics are, first, widespread and, second, non-accidental. For several important dialectical purposes in material-mode philosophical debate, cases unblemished by disturbing characteristics are unavailable. Section 3.6 responds to objections.

3.1 The Typical Argument Schema

3.1.1 The Argument Schema

Critics of the method of cases have put forward several arguments, formulated with varying degrees of precision. Many of those are variations upon the following argument schema:

Argument Schema

1.   Judgments that lack epistemic property P are severely deficient from an epistemic point of view.

2.   Judgments elicited by most of the philosophical cases that have been examined by experimental philosophers lack P.

3.   If the judgments elicited by most of the philosophical cases that have been examined by experimental philosophers lack P, then the judgments elicited by most philosophical cases plausibly lack P.

4.   We ought to refrain from making a judgment of a particular kind K (i.e., we ought to suspend judgment of kind K) when most judgments of this kind are plausibly severely deficient from an epistemic point of view, except when this judgment is known to be an exception.

5.   Hence, except when a philosophical case is known to elicit a judgment possessing P, philosophers ought to suspend judgment about the situations described by philosophical cases.

Cummins (1998) embraces Argument Schema when he writes (125): "Philosophical intuition is epistemologically useless, since it can be calibrated only when it is not needed." On his view, what judgments elicited by philosophical cases lack (precisely when it is needed) is calibration (a source of evidence is calibrated if and only if it has been compared to, and made to agree with, another source of evidence known to be reliable). Focusing on another epistemic property, hopefulness (a source of evidence is hopeful if and only if one has the capacity to detect misleading outputs), Weinberg also embraces Argument Schema (2007, 340):

So ought we trust intuitions in philosophy? The first part of my answer is: no, when the intuitions are participating in practices that are hopeless, lacking any substantive means of error-detection and error-correction; and yes, when the intuition is embedded in practices that are hopeful.

In the remainder of this section, I briefly comment on Argument Schema. The remainder of the chapter turns it into a specific argument ("Unreliability") by zeroing in on a particular epistemic property as the value of P (viz., reliability) and defends its premises.

3.1.2 Premises 1, 2, and 4

I call the second premise of Argument Schema its "inductive basis." This premise leaves room for the discovery of cases that are perfectly appropriate from an epistemic point of view: It refers only to "most of the philosophical cases that have been examined."

To support the inductive basis of Argument Schema, I will interpret the findings reported in Chapter 2 as showing that the judgments elicited by most examined cases lack a particular epistemic property, namely reliability (Section 3.2). This interpretation may seem straightforward, but some care is needed to establish it.

In light of the centrality of justification in contemporary epistemology, it is tempting to formulate Premise 1 in terms of justification—"Judgments that lack P are unjustified"—instead of epistemic deficiency (vs. appropriateness), but this temptation should be resisted since this formulation may lead philosophers to debate whether epistemic property P is necessary for justification instead of addressing the more important question: whether judgments that do not have P are epistemically deficient.

On the other hand, avoiding the notion of justification creates some difficulty for Premise 4 of Argument Schema. If judgments of kind K are not justified, then one ought to refrain from making judgments of kind K. This follows from the knowledge norm of assertion and from weaker norms such as the justification norm of assertion (supposing these norms are not merely about assertions, but also extend to what assertions express, namely judgments). By contrast, if judgments of kind K are epistemically deficient in some way or other, it is not clear that one ought to refrain from making such judgments, for almost all judgments are epistemically deficient in some way or other—e.g., we could have more evidence for our beliefs or they could be more coherent—and it is not the case that we ought to suspend judgment in these circumstances. To circumvent this difficulty, a critic of the method of cases must show that failing to have epistemic property P would render judgments *severely* deficient from an epistemic point of view, not just epistemically deficient: It is plausible that if judgments of kind K are severely deficient from an epistemic point of view, then one ought to refrain from making such judgments.

I will take Premise 4 for granted in the remainder of this chapter, but perhaps some may challenge it. Some may respond that whether Premise 4 holds depends on the relative costs of taking for granted a false judgment and of suspending judgment. Since car alarms are extremely sensitive in order to minimize the rate of false negatives at a cost of having a high rate of false positives, a car alarm going off is a false positive more often than not, but it would be unreasonable to recommend ignoring their going off on this ground. Ignoring a car alarm going off is very costly when the going off is a true positive (losing of one's car), and false positives are not costly (one simply checks on one's car). The car alarm situation is, however, not analogous to that of a philosophical case since making a false judgment in response to a philosophical case is costly: One develops erroneous philosophical theories.

Alternatively, some may object to the formulation of the exception clause of Premise 3, holding that if the case at hand does not elicit a judgment lacking epistemic property P, it is not the case that we ought to suspend judgment, whether or not we know it is an exception to the generalization asserted by Premise 3. While little hangs on how we formulate this exception clause, this objection is at odds with our usual practices: If I know that most eggs in a pack are rotten, the reasonable thing in the absence of further information is to throw the *whole* pack.

3.1.3 Premise 3

I call Premise 3 of Argument Schema its "inductive step" since it asserts the legitimacy of generalizing from the cases examined by experimental philosophers to most philosophical cases. Consistent with Premise 3, some philosophical cases may be epistemically appropriate, and one could use these cases to address material-mode disputes, provided that one is able to identify them. I comment on the significance of this concession in Section 3.1.4.

Proponents of the method of cases have repeatedly challenged Premise 3 (e.g., Williamson, 2011, 2016), and defending it is the most difficult task of this chapter. Half of Chapter 3 (Sections 3.4 and 3.5) mounts this defense, and we will revisit the issue in Section 5.8 of Chapter 5. There are two possible strategies to defend the inductive step: The direct strategy and the burden-shifting strategy. The direct strategy requires explaining why it is legitimate to induce from the limited number of cases examined by experimental philosophers to most philosophical cases. The burden-shifting strategy circumvents the need of providing an explanation: It takes the existence of cases lacking P to provide us with a reason to believe that in general the judgments elicited by philosophical cases lack P. This reason is admittedly defeasible, but until advocates of the method of cases have defeated it, Premise 3 can be asserted. According to the direct strategy, then, the existence of cases eliciting judgments lacking P is not a sufficient reason to assert Premise 3; according to the burden-shifting strategy, it is.

I have embraced the burden-shifting strategy in some of my previous work (Machery, 2011a, 203–4):

[W]e have positive reasons to think that the situations described by thought experiments do not belong to the proper domains of the capacities underlying the judgments they elicit.[1] That is, we have reasons to believe that these judgments are less reliable, and if we have no further information about their reliability, we should not treat them as evidence.

In their classic article, Weinberg et al. also embrace something like the burden-shifting strategy (2001, 429–30):

[A] sizeable group of epistemological projects...would be seriously undermined if one or more of a cluster of empirical hypotheses about epistemic intuitions turns out to be true.... [W]hile the jury is still out, there is now a substantial body of evidence suggesting that some of those empirical hypotheses are true.... Our goal is not to offer a conclusive argument demonstrating that the epistemological projects we will be criticizing are untenable. Rather, our aim is to shift the burden of argument. For far too long, epistemologists who rely heavily on epistemic intuitions have proceeded as though they could simply ignore the empirical hypotheses we will set out. We will be well satisfied if we succeed in making a plausible case for the claim that this approach is no longer acceptable.

---

[1] The notion of proper domain will be clarified in Section 3.5 of this chapter.

The direct strategy demands more of critics of the method of cases than the burden-shifting strategy. The proponents of the direct and of the burden-shifting strategy need to establish that the philosophical cases examined by experimental philosophers elicit epistemically deficient judgments, but only the former need to also justify the induction from these cases. In addition, the two strategies distribute the burden of proof differently. In the direct strategy, the burden of proof entirely weighs on the shoulders of the critic; by contrast, in the burden-shifting strategy, both the critic and the proponent of the method of cases have work to do: The former needs to establish that the judgments elicited by most philosophical cases examined by experimental philosophers lack P, the latter needs to explain why this finding does not allow generalizing to most philosophical cases. Finally, which strategy a critic of the method of cases embraces depends on which epistemic property she is interested in. If it is easy to justify the inductive step for some epistemic properties (perhaps calibration), then a critic is likely to embrace the direct strategy; if not, she is likely to embrace the burden-shifting strategy.

Proponents and critics of the method of cases are unlikely to agree about which strategy should take center stage. Critics are likely to favor the burden-shifting strategy, which requires less of them and spreads the burden of proof, while proponents are likely to hold that only the direct strategy raises a genuine challenge to the method of cases. In particular, even if proponents of the method of cases concede the second premise of Argument Schema, they may not concede Premise 3, insisting that the existence of some cases eliciting judgments lacking P provides no reason to believe that most philosophical cases elicit judgments that lack P. By contrast, a critic of the method of cases who endorses the burden-shifting strategy is likely to insist that Premise 3 can't be simply dismissed. To move beyond this dialectical impasse, in what follows I will simply follow the strategy that is the most challenging for a critic of the method of cases—viz., the direct strategy.

3.1.4 Conclusion of Argument Schema

Argument Schema is devastating for the material use of cases in contemporary philosophy. If philosophers ought to suspend judgment about whether the facts of philosophical interest hold in the situations described by most philosophical cases (e.g., that it is permissible to push the large man in the situation described by the footbridge case), then these cases cannot be used to learn about knowledge, causation, permissibility, justification, or responsibility.

Argument Schema does not show that we ought to suspend judgment about all philosophical cases: Some cases currently used in philosophy are likely to elicit epistemically appropriate judgments, and provided we know how to identify those, they could figure in material-mode philosophical discussion. What's more, many cases must elicit epistemically appropriate judgments since, as noted in the Introduction, there is no reason why in general judgments about situations that are described instead of experienced should be epistemically inappropriate. Indeed, if correct, the discussion in Section 3.5 would allow philosophers to identify cases that are less likely to elicit cognitive artifacts. Perhaps some philosophers will draw some comfort from these limitations of Argument Schema, but they should reconsider. Many current cases in contemporary philosophy are bound to elicit cognitive artifacts if Argument Schema is correct, and we should revise the conclusions based on them. Furthermore, as will be argued in Section 3.5, to fulfill some important dialectical functions in material-mode philosophical debate, cases are likely to possess those properties resulting in epistemically inappropriate judgments.

3.2 Reliability, Hopefulness, or Calibration?

Critics of the method of cases have examined several epistemic properties, including being the product of a calibrated process (Cummins, 1998), of a hopeful process (Weinberg, 2007), of a reliable process (Machery, 2011a), or of an appropriately sensitive process (Horvath, 2010; Alexander & Weinberg, 2014). Which of the epistemic properties singled out by critics of the method of cases should be put to use as the value of P in Argument Schema? Any proposal must meet two requirements:

- *Requirement 1*: Judgments lacking this property are severely deficient from an epistemic point of view.
- *Requirement 2*: The evidence collected by experimental philosophers should be relevant to determine whether the judgments elicited by philosophical cases lack this property.

In Section 3.2, I agree that of the three properties most often discussed in the literature—reliability, calibration, and hopefulness—reliability is the best candidate. I will compare reliability to the sensitivity to inappropriate influences in Section 3.3.1.

3.2.1 Reliability

T, a psychological process outputting judgments, is reliable in environment E if and only if in E either T has the disposition to produce a large proportion of true judgments or, if T is an inferential process, T has the disposition to produce a large proportion of true judgments if its inputs are true.[2] Reliability here is a dispositional property, and a process used only once can still be assessed for reliability. Furthermore, just like the reliability of non-psychological processes, the reliability of a psychological process is relative to particular environments. A fake-bill detector may be reliable (it may detect a very large proportion of fake bills) when fake bills are of low quality, but unreliable when a super-duper counterfeiter made them. One may wonder how many of the beliefs produced by T must be true for T to be reliable, but someone who insists that reliability is an important epistemic property need not give any specific number; she may respond that epistemic standing worsens as reliability goes down.

---

[2] Goldman (1979, 1988); Alston (1995).

Requirement 2 is easily met: Much of the evidence in experimental philosophy (Chapter 2) speaks to the reliability of the process of forming judgments when considering philosophical cases, although whether this body of evidence really establishes that the judgments elicited by the philosophical cases examined so far are unreliable will be discussed in Section 3.3. What about Requirement 1—viz., Judgments lacking this property are severely deficient from an epistemic point of view? On the one hand, reliability seems to meet this requirement, and the first premise of Argument Schema seems credible if "*P*" is replaced with "being the product of a reliable process." If judgments produced by an unreliable process were not severely deficient from an epistemic point of view, then choosing what to believe at random (by, e.g., throwing a coin to decide what to believe) or choosing on the basis of a process that works as designed but does not do better than a random process would result in epistemically appropriate or only moderately deficient beliefs.

On the other hand, the epistemic significance of reliability has been criticized in the epistemological literature on reliabilism, and perhaps these criticisms should lead us to reconsider whether reliability really meets Requirement 1. We can set aside those criticisms of reliabilism that claim to show, typically using the method of cases (e.g., the Truetemp case or the clairvoyant case), that reliability is not sufficient for justification or knowledge since I have avoided framing Argument Schema in terms of justification or knowledge precisely to avoid being embroiled in a discussion about what is sufficient or necessary for justification and knowledge.[3] We can also disregard internalist concerns about the external nature of reliability. For internalists, a belief that a judgment-forming process is unreliable is an undercutting defeater of the warrant the judgments produced by this process may otherwise have. So, if I can convincingly establish that the judgments elicited by most philosophical cases are unreliable, internalists would grant that the warrant these judgments might otherwise have is defeated. Finally, theories that insist that epistemic achievement is compatible with unreliability (e.g., Turri, 2015) concur on the importance of reliability in the present case. Achievement requires doing substantially better than luck, and one has a chance out of two to get it right when the choice is between *p* or not *p*. (Does the character in the Gettier case know the relevant proposition or not? Is it permissible or not to push the large person from the footbridge? Did the character do something worse in the omission version of Rachels's (1975) bathtub case?) So, achievement in the present case requires reliability.

A more challenging concern is the objection that reliability is not sufficiently well defined to have any epistemic significance. A similar objection—"the generality problem"—has been raised against reliabilist analyses of justification or knowledge.[4] For instance, Pollock (1984, 105) writes that "there is no way to construct an intelligible

---

[3] e.g., Bonjour (1980); Lehrer (1990).
[4] Pollock (1984); Feldman (1985); Conee & Feldman (1998).

notion of reliability that does the job required by the reliabilist."[5] Here I extend the generality problem beyond the analysis of justification or knowledge to the epistemic significance of reliability.

Any judgment is the outcome of a particular causal sequence of events, which can be assigned to types of process of increasing generality.[6] For instance, the particular causal sequence that results in me judging that my shirt is blue is an instance of the process type consisting in forming perceptual judgments about the color of middle-sized, foveated, close objects; it is also an instance of the process type consisting in forming perceptual judgments about middle-sized, foveated, close objects, of the process consisting in forming perceptual judgments about middle-sized, close objects, of the process consisting in forming perceptual judgments about middle-sized objects, and so on. These process types do not have the same reliability; in fact, some may be very reliable, and others quite unreliable. There is no obvious principled way of determining which process type a particular causal sequence should be assigned to for the purpose of assessing the epistemic standing of its output. It would not do to begin with what one takes to be the epistemic standing of this output (e.g., unjustified), and assign the particular causal sequence to a process type with the appropriate degree of reliability (e.g., unreliable), since whoever insists that reliability is epistemically significant (to say nothing of those who analyze justification or knowledge in terms of reliability) must be able to determine which kind of process a particular causal sequence instantiates independently of the alleged epistemic standing of its products.

To address the generality problem in the present context, it is important to keep in mind what my dialectical purpose requires. I need not reduce justification or knowledge to reliability; more generally, I do not need to hold that epistemic standing only depends on reliability. Which is for the best since it doesn't: Other properties (e.g., being unlikely to result in extreme errors) contribute to epistemic standing. What I need to show is that judgments produced by an unreliable process—i.e., judgments elicited by the method of cases—are severely deficient from an epistemic point of view. This problem is much easier to address than the generality problem raised for reliabilist accounts of justification or knowledge, for it does not concern particular judgments (which somehow need to be typed in a principled manner), but process types themselves. Because we want to know whether judgments about, e.g., causation (a type of judgment), or judgments elicited by philosophical cases (a distinct type of judgment), or judgments made by philosophers about the situations described by

---

[5] Perhaps Pollock and other critics of reliabilism did not mean to claim that reliability is not sufficiently well defined to do any epistemological work, just that it cannot do the epistemological work reliabilists want to do (i.e., analyze justification or knowledge), but the generality problem seems to extend to any epistemological role reliability could play.

[6] The problem is compounded by the fact that reliability is relativized to an environment, E. It too must be typed, which can be done in many different ways. We can ignore this complication here since a principled way of typing processes will extend to environments.

philosophical cases (yet another type of judgment), etc., are reliable, there is no need to be concerned with typing judgments: Types are given to us in the formulation of our problem.

Perhaps one may wonder why we should take into account a given type rather than another type, with possibly a different reliability attached to it. For instance, why single out the reliability of judgments elicited by philosophical cases rather than that of judgments elicited by epistemological cases or by Gettier cases? What principled reason do we have to single out one type rather than another? Such questions seem to raise the generality problem again, but appearances are misleading. We single out a given type because we have no information about partitions of this type resulting in subtypes with different reliabilities. That is, as far as we have information, reliability is invariant under partitioning (for a similar idea, see Beebe, 2004). This situation could happen for one of two reasons: First, reliability is invariant under partitioning; second, while reliability varies under some partitioning, we have no information about it. Similarly, the company that produces FakeDetect, a fake-bill detector, reports the reliability of FakeDetect machines to its potential clients in contrast to the reliability of FakeDetect machines produced by factory A vs. by factory B for one of the following reasons: (1) the reliability of FakeDetect machines produced by factory A is the same as that of FakeDetect machines produced by factory B; or (2) the reliability of FakeDetect machines produced by factory A differs from that of FakeDetect machines produced by factory B, but the company does not have the pertinent information. In either situation, only information about the class of FakeDetect machines is relevant to potential buyers of FakeDetect.

The generality problem can thus be circumvented in the present context (or when the reliability of scientific instruments or artifacts is at stake): We want to assess the reliability of a particular type—namely judgments elicited by philosophical cases—instead of that of a token judgment, and, as far as we have information, reliability is invariant under partitioning of the class of judgments elicited by philosophical cases. (As we will see in Chapter 5, some defenses of the method of cases, such as the Reflection and Expertise Defenses, deny this second conjunct.)

In fact, we can go further: We can see why the generality problem is not a genuine problem for philosophers who take reliability to be epistemically important. Internalists are typically concerned with the epistemic standing of token judgments, but reliabilists are not (or at least should not). Reliabilists assess (or should assess) the epistemic standing of types of process (those processes that we are bound to use), and they single out one type rather than another because of the available information about the invariance of reliability under partitioning.

3.2.2 Hopefulness and calibration

Here is where we stand at this point: When a judgment-forming process is unreliable, the judgments it produces are severely deficient from an epistemic point of view, and the evidence accumulated by experimental philosophers bears on the reliability of the judgments elicited by philosophical cases. So, Requirements 1 and 2 introduced at the beginning of this section are met for reliability.

Next: What about the epistemic properties other than reliability that critics of the method of cases have discussed? Let's begin with Requirement 1: Judgments lacking this property are severely deficient from an epistemic point of view. It is not as plausible to hold that a judgment is severely deficient from an epistemic point of view because it is the product of a hopeless or a non-calibrated process. No doubt, hopefulness and calibration are valuable epistemic properties, but their value is instrumental. They are valuable because they endow belief-forming processes with various desirable epistemic properties, including reliability. We trust hopeful or calibrated sources of evidence (e.g., scientific instruments) in part because they are more likely to be reliable than hopeless or non-calibrated sources.

Since hopefulness and calibration are not intrinsically valuable, when we assess judgments epistemically, it is natural to concentrate on what hopefulness and calibration are for, including reliability.

Perhaps Weinberg and Cummins could concede that hopefulness and calibration are only instrumentally valuable, but rebut the claim that we should concentrate on reliability as follows. First, they could insist that hopelessness and lack of calibration are evidence for the unreliability of a process, and that we should focus on them because we are unable to establish the unreliability of the processes underlying the judgments elicited by philosophical cases directly. Second, they could argue that the judgments produced by a process that is reliable, but neither hopeful nor calibrated, may still be severely deficient from an epistemic point of view because that process may lack some further desirable properties brought about by hopefulness and calibration (such as not resulting in catastrophic mistakes).

However, neither rebuttal justifies concentrating on hopefulness or calibration instead of reliability. While processes lacking hopefulness and calibration may be epistemically deficient in some respect or other, they are not severely so. This suggests that hopelessness and lack of calibration are weak evidence of unreliability; furthermore, if they are evidence that a process lacks some other epistemically desirable property, either they are weak evidence or lacking this property does not make a process severely deficient from an epistemic point of view.

Let's examine more closely the claim that processes lacking hopefulness and calibration are not severely deficient from an epistemic point of view. Scientific instruments at the forefront of science are typically reliable, but their calibration and hopefulness are very limited. Scientists develop novel instruments to observe or measure yet unobserved or unmeasured things (e.g., unmeasured constants). In some cases, novel instruments are tested on previously observed or measured things and then extended to unobserved or unmeasured things. While the former tests calibrate novel instruments, they are naturally not calibrated with respect to unobserved or unmeasured things, and there is no guarantee that the latter interact with instruments as the former do. Galileo did much engineering work on the telescope, turning it into a scientific instrument, and the telescope was calibrated against objects on earth (e.g., towers),[7] but it was obviously not calibrated against features of the moon's landscape (craters and mountains), and observations of the moon's landscape, of Jupiter's moons, and of the Pleiades and other constellations, all of which were reported in the *Starry Messenger* (1610), could have been qualitatively different from those of the earth—a possibility Galileo's opponents such as Martin Horky exploited to undermine his observations and conclusions. Indeed, terrestrial telescopes (with a larger field of view), developed in the 1630s, were pretty much useless for astronomical observations, and astronomical and terrestrial telescopes evolved independently during the seventeenth century. Furthermore, Galileo and early astronomers had no clear understanding of the limitations of telescopes for astronomical observation; in particular, Galileo had no theory of its functioning (Van Helden, 1974). But quickly the most important of Galileo's observations (if not the details) were independently confirmed (in 1611 by the Collegio Romano), establishing the reliability of the telescope for astronomical observation.

In other cases, novel scientific instruments are not calibrated at all because they are meant to observe or measure something that has not yet been observed or measured, and their hopefulness is very limited. Coulomb's torsion balance was developed to measure the force between two electrically charged bodies, which resulted in the measurement of the exponent (i.e., 2 in the equation below) of the distance in the denominator of what is now known as Coulomb's law (for details, see Shech & Hatleback, ms):[8]

$$|F| = k \frac{q_1 q_2}{d^2}$$

In Coulomb's torsion balance, two pith balls are initially in contact; one of them is fixed, the other can rotate in the horizontal plane. The movable pith ball is secured at the end of a horizontal wax needle that is itself suspended from its center by a thin silver wire. At the beginning of the measurement, the pith balls are charged and repel each other, resulting in an angular movement of the movable pith ball. The experimenter then turns the thin silver wire by a measurable amount. Using the laws governing the force of torsion, Coulomb was able to measure the force between two electrically charged bodies and the then unknown exponent of Coulomb's law. The torsion balance was only minimally calibrated: The balance was set up so that, with no electric charge, the angular movement of a pith ball is zero. It was also substantially hopeless. Coulomb did find by trial and error that within a particular range of parameters (characteristics of the pith ball and of the needle used to produce the electric force) he obtained repeatable results. He also had some germane knowledge; in particular, he was an expert about the torsion force of different wires, which allowed him to select a thin silver wire in his experimental setup. On the other hand, we have only recently found out,

---

[7] Van Helden (1974, 1977); Brown (1985).
[8] See also the following video: https://www.youtube.com/watch?v=_5VpIje-R54.

by re-enacting Coulomb's experiments, that even small modifications to Coulomb's own torsion balance, with his original material setup, undermine its reliability (Shech & Hatleback, ms). These two examples—Galileo's telescope and Coulomb's torsion balance—are not exceptions; rather they illustrate a common situation at the forefront of science: reliability with little calibration and hopefulness.

Of course, calibration and hopefulness are important, and scientific research typically involves calibrating instruments and getting a better understanding of their limitations, by trial and error or by theory. Calibration and hopefulness are epistemically important because they are means for ensuring that sources of evidence have desirable properties that contribute to their epistemic standing, reliability first among them. Nonetheless, observations are not severely deficient from an epistemic point of view just for being produced by instruments that are uncalibrated or hopeless.

What about Requirement 2 introduced at the beginning of this section: The evidence collected by experimental philosophers should be relevant to determine whether the judgments elicited by philosophical cases lack this property? It is prima facie curious for an experimental philosopher to focus on calibration and hopefulness since we don't need evidence about what influences judgments elicited by philosophical cases (the kind of evidence experimental philosophers have been concerned with) to determine whether a source of evidence is hopeful or calibrated. It would not do to respond that the point of experimental-philosophy studies is to establish that judgments elicited by cases are fallible (more on fallibility in Section 5.5 of Chapter 5), making thereby hopefulness epistemically important (hopefulness is not an important property for infallible or near infallible judgments) since we did not really need experiments to show that these judgments are fallible.

3.2.3 Unreliability

The discussion of the use of cases to settle material-mode issues will center on the unreliability of the judgments elicited by these cases. In Argument Schema, Premise 1 should be replaced with the following premise:

1.   Unreliable judgments are severely deficient from an epistemic point of view.

The remainder of Argument Schema should be modified accordingly:

Unreliability
1.   Unreliable judgments are severely deficient from an epistemic point of view.

2.   Judgments elicited by most of the philosophical cases that have been examined by experimental philosophers are unreliable.

3.   If the judgments elicited by most of the philosophical cases that have been examined by experimental philosophers are unreliable, then the judgments elicited by most philosophical cases are plausibly unreliable.

4.   We ought to refrain from making a judgment of a particular kind K (i.e., we ought to suspend judgment of kind K) when most judgments of this kind are plausibly

severely deficient from an epistemic point of view, except when this judgment is known to be an exception.

5.   Hence, except when a philosophical case is known to elicit a reliable judgment, philosophers ought to suspend judgment about the situations described by philosophical cases.

3.2.4 Reliability, error theories, and skepticisms

Referring to the reliability of the judgments about knowledge elicited by epistemological cases (such as Gettier cases, fake-barn cases, lottery cases, and bank cases), the reliability of the judgments about moral permissibility elicited by moral cases (such as the trolley cases and the Society of Music Lovers case), and so on for the other fields of philosophy, does not require that knowledge, justification, and responsibility be natural properties, viz., roughly properties that do not depend on human practices and mental states. Even if justification depends on human practices (perhaps, "justified" is a predicate that expresses a particular kind of approval), one can still be more or less reliable at identifying it, for instance because one can be more or less attuned to the linguistic or social norms that govern the use of "justified."

On the other hand, assessing judgments about knowledge, justification, or moral permissibility for their reliability supposes that there is something—whether natural or not—the relevant judgments are about. It makes no sense to assess judgments about witches, ghosts, or phlogiston for their reliability. Similarly, if responsibility is a fiction, it makes no sense to assess the reliability of judgments about responsibility.

The reality of many of the properties philosophers theorize about is of course controversial. Error theorists in ethics deny that there is any such thing as moral wrongness or moral permissibility (e.g., Mackie, 1977), while skeptics about responsibility find it doubtful that there is such a thing as responsibility (e.g., Rosen, 2004). If there were no such thing as responsibility, it would make no sense to assess judgments about responsibility for their reliability, and Unreliability would not bear on the prospects of the method of cases for understanding responsibility. On the other hand, if there were no such thing as responsibility, using the method of cases to understand what responsibility is (e.g., by considering Frankfurt cases) would be inappropriate, although it could perhaps still be used to study the concept or concepts of responsibility (for discussion, see Chapter 7). The problem with using cases materially to understand responsibility would then be semantic (the relevant predicates or concepts would fail to refer) or metaphysical, but not epistemological. It would also be local: Not all topics examined by means of the method of cases are as much open to controversy as responsibility or moral rightness and wrongness.

What I propose to do in this book is to bracket this semantic or metaphysical problem and to discuss only the epistemological question raised by Unreliability: Assuming that it makes sense to assess the judgments elicited by philosophical cases for reliability—an assumption that users of the method of cases must be making—are these judgments reliable? If this assumption is false, then the epistemological question is moot, and, in any case, the method of cases should be not be used to answer material-mode questions.

3.3 The Inductive Basis of Unreliability

Experimental philosophers have highlighted two kinds of factor—demographic variables (gender, age, culture, etc.) and presentation variables (order and framing)—and they have gathered a large body of evidence that these two kinds of factor influence the judgments elicited by philosophical cases. I now argue that because of this influence the judgments elicited by the philosophical cases that have been examined by experimental philosophers (see Chapter 2 for a near complete list) are unreliable.

3.3.1 From causally influenced to unreliable

Consider a variable V that causally influences the judgments people make in response to a question. Let's call J the variable for people's response to a question (the responses are the values of J). V could be people's cultural background, their education, their gender, their political affiliation, their personality, whether they are paying attention, whether they are experts in the subject matter of J, whether they are tired, and so on. V can take two or more values. If V is whether people are paying attention, it takes two values: attentive and distracted. J could be dichotomous (e.g., if the question is, Is global warming real? Yes or No?) or could have many different values (e.g., if the question is, What is the price of this item between \$0 and \$100, to the nearest \$?). If for a group of people V influences J, the probability of making a given judgment varies for different values of V. If political orientation influences one's opinion about global warming, the probability of asserting that global warming is real varies between liberals and conservatives: The former could be 90 percent likely to assert it, the latter, 70 percent. The larger the influence of V, the larger the difference between the probability of making a particular judgment across groups. If political orientation at best moderately influences one's opinion about climate change, the difference between conservatives and liberals could be, say, 10 percent; if its influence is large, the difference could be as large as, say, 50 percent.

From the fact that V influences J, it does not follow that J is unreliable. Suppose that the color of the room in which one is asked a question about global warming influences one's opinion: People in a bright room are more likely to assert that global warming is real than people in a dark room. Suppose, however, that the difference is small: 80 percent of people in a bright room assert that global warming is real, for 75 percent people in a dark room. And suppose that, as is the case, global warming is real. Then, if people are equally likely to be in a bright and dark room, 77.5 percent of people make a true judgment despite the normatively inappropriate influence of the color of the room. People in this fictional example are reliable.

When does the influence of V on J mean that J is unreliable? If V has a large influence on J and if J is dichotomous (e.g., Is it permissible to push the large man in the situation described by the footbridge case? Yes or No?), then judgments are unreliable. Suppose that 80 percent of liberals correctly assert that global warming is real for only 30 percent of conservatives. If people are equally likely to be liberal and conservative, then 55 percent of people are likely to get it right, barely better than chance. So, the judgments elicited by a given case are unreliable provided that they are influenced by at least a demographic variable or a presentation variable and provided that this influence is large.

Remarkably, that V should *not* influence J—i.e., that its influence is normatively inappropriate—plays no role in this argument. The color of the room should not influence one's opinion on global warming, but this plays no role in the argument here. What only matters here is whether its influence undermines the reliability of judgment.

3.3.2 Partitioning?

Perhaps considering aggregate reliability in the circumstances identified in the previous section is the wrong thing to do. Expertise, attention, fatigue, etc., influence judgment, and their influence can be large. Suppose that experts are much more likely (say 80 percent) than novices (say 10 percent) to form a true judgment about a difficult issue, and that on average people are quite unreliable (less than 45 percent since there are much more novices). Then, the right thing to do would be to disregard the (genuine) average unreliability of judgments about this issue. Reliability is not invariant under partitioning on the basis of expertise, and experts' judgments *are* reliable. So, instead of considering average unreliability, the right thing to do is to partition the class of judgments and to concentrate on the reliable subclass. The same point applies to attention: If attention has a large effect on judgment and renders judgment unreliable, the right reaction is to partition the class of judgments and to concentrate on attentive judgment.

Why can't we treat the influence of demographic and presentation variables on judgments elicited by philosophical cases this way? Take the case of the judgments elicited by the Gödel case: the judgment that "Gödel" refers to Schmidt or that "Gödel" refers to Gödel. If, as we have assumed (Section 3.2.4), there is a matter of fact about the reference of "Gödel" in the situation described by this case (but see Machery, 2015c), and if Westerners and Easterners tend to make different judgments, then either Westerners or Easterners tend to get it right, and the class of judgments elicited by the Gödel case is not invariant under partition. We should thus partition this class of judgments and consider only one partition.

So, why can't we treat demographic and presentation variables the way we treat expertise? In a nutshell, while the reliability of the judgments elicited by philosophical cases is indeed not invariant under partition, we should not partition this class of judgments because we do not know which partition to attend to. In contrast, we should partition the class of judgments along expertise because we know which judgments to attend to: experts'. The situation of judgments elicited by philosophical cases is thus similar to the second situation described in Section 3.2.1: The reliability of FakeDetect machines produced by factory A differs from that of FakeDetect machines produced by factory B, but the company does not have the pertinent information, and so only reports the average reliability of FakeDetect machines to its customers.

Let's consider the demographic variables first. Is it true that we do not know which cultures, gender, SES level, etc., to focus on? Don't we know that some particular demographic groups are sometimes more likely to get it right than others? Those who believe in moral progress hold that people today are more likely to make true judgments about many moral matters than our predecessors. Indeed, weren't people in past centuries less likely than us to get it right about gender equality, slavery, torture, and the permissibility of harming animals? On this view, we have some information about which culture to privilege: Past cultures are simply less likely to get it right.[9] Similarly, standpoint theorists in epistemology hold that oppressed groups, including women, racial minorities, people with disabilities, and socially and economically exploited social classes, are more likely to make true judgments about a range of issues. And doesn't age correlate with increased knowledge and experience?

These remarks do show that we may justifiably believe that some particular culture, gender group, age group, and SES group are more likely to get it right than the other demographic groups for *some* issues—so for some issues we can treat demographic variables the way we treat expertise and attention—but they do little to show that we have such warrant for the judgments elicited by philosophical cases. Any proposal that among the cultures, socio-economic groups, and age groups that have been examined, a particular group is more likely than the other groups to get it right about responsibility, moral impermissibility, and the reference of proper names in general or, more narrowly, in the situations described by philosophical cases will be hard to justify, and barring such justification, any suggestion that we (whoever this "we" refers to) are more likely to get it right than them (whoever they are) smacks of various kinds of -ism, including ethnocentrism. Indeed, it is hard to find any defense of this view in print.

Turning now to the presentation variables, we must concede that some modes of presentation that have an influence on judgment are better than others. There are good and bad ways of lecturing about any topic as there are better and worse ways of presenting a mathematical proof. But, just as was the case for demographic variables such as culture and gender, it is unreasonable to hold that we should favor particular presentation orders of philosophical cases and particular ways of describing situations of philosophical interest (i.e., particular frames) since it is hard to see which of the frames or which of the orders of presentation would make it more likely that people get it right about the situations described by philosophical cases.

---

[9] Boyd (1988); Wood (2008, 339).

3.3.3 Contextualism?

There is another way of resisting the conclusion drawn in Section 3.3.1. To determine when the influence of demographic and presentation variables undermines the reliability of judgments, I assumed that the facts of the matter were invariant. Similarly, the reality of global warming is the same for liberals and conservatives. But perhaps the situation is different for the facts holding in the situations described by philosophical cases: Perhaps the facts of the matter in the situations described by philosophical cases vary as a function of the identity of the individuals who judge about them or as a function of their contexts.

This response may be defensible for some philosophical cases. Contextualists about knowledge (and other epistemic properties) hold that the truth conditions of knowledge ascriptions depend on the context of the knowledge ascriber. Knowledge contextualists would then expect variation in the ascription of knowledge to the protagonists described by philosophical cases. Contextualist theories are conceivable in other areas of philosophy too (e.g., Björnsson & Finlay, 2010, in ethics).

This second challenge suffers from several problems. As a general response, it assumes, implausibly, that adequate contextualist theories can be developed for most of the philosophical topics of interest, and it also commits itself to a controversial semantics for moral, epistemological, or causal assertions. Furthermore, it's one thing to assert that what counts as knowledge varies across contexts; it's another one to explain why this variation holds. Similarly, it's one thing to assert that the distinction between killing and letting die is morally significant in some contexts but not others (Kamm, 2006), another one to explain why it is morally significant in precisely these contexts (Norcross, 2008). A contextualist response remains ad hoc until such explanations are provided. This response also relies on the vagueness of what counts as the context of an assertion (Swain et al., 2008): This vagueness allows the user of the method of cases to include whatever demographic variable turns out to influence judgments elicited by philosophical cases in the context of assertion. Finally, and more decisively, it undermines the dialectical utility of the method of cases since, if demographic variables influence which facts hold in the situations described by philosophical cases, philosophers can only take for granted that some particular facts hold in these situations when they are engaged with philosophers of their own gender, culture, SES, age, and so on for all the potentially pertinent variables.

3.3.4 Small effects?

Finally, Demaree-Cotton (2016) has recently argued that the presentation effects (described in Sections 2.7 and 2.8 of Chapter 2) are not sufficiently large to challenge the reliability of the judgments elicited by philosophical cases (for further challenges to the claim that evidence shows the judgments elicited by philosophical cases to be unreliable, see Nagel (2012) and Sosa (2007), which are respectively discussed in Sections 5.4 and 5.5 of Chapter 5). She concentrates on the probability that a participant would make the same judgment if the case were presented differently (if its frame were different or if it followed other cases). She computes this probability by subtracting the percentages of answers in each condition. For instance, in de Brigard's (2010) study (Section 2.7.5 of Chapter 2), the probability that a participant would give a different answer to the negative and positive versions of the experience-machine case is 37 percent (87 percent minus 50 percent); conversely, 63 percent of participants would not change their judgment. Examining a large number of studies (also reviewed in Chapter 2), Demaree-Cotton reports that in half of the studies the average probability that a participant would make the same judgment even if the case were presented differently is very high (> 80 percent) and that in 26 out of 30 studies, this probability is high (> 70 percent). She concludes that presentation effects do not make judgment unreliable since a very large proportion of participants would not be influenced by them (2016, 1): "Analysis of the evidence suggests that moral intuitions subject to framing effects are in fact much more reliable than perhaps was thought."

While Demaree-Cotton's approach is ingenious, it suffers from two flaws. First, the presentation effects add to one another. Demaree-Cotton acknowledges this possibility, but responds that there is no evidence that they do. Machery et al. (forthcoming b) present the required evidence: In four different cultures, the framing effect and the order effect they report add up. Second, Demaree-Cotton does not address the issue from the right angle (see also Section 3.3.1 of Chapter 3). What matters to determine whether the judgments elicited by a given case are reliable is not the probability that a random person would make two different judgments, were she presented with two different versions of the case; it is the average probability that the readers of the case will make a judgment of a given kind. Suppose that 50 percent of participants answer that p when a case is presented one way, and 75 percent when it is presented another way (a moderate effect according to the benchmarks given in Chapter 2). Demaree-Cotton would highlight the 75 percent of participants who would not change their judgment if they were presented with another version of the case, and she would conclude that the judgments are reliable. We should rather take into consideration the average response that p: In our fictional example, only 62.5 percent of participants give that answer, a percentage sufficiently low to question the reliability of the judgment elicited by the case.

3.4 The Inductive Step: The Unreliability Caused by Current Philosophical Cases

Unreliability generalizes beyond the cases examined by experimental philosophers to conclude that the judgments elicited by most philosophical cases are unreliable. The remainder of this chapter attempts to justify this induction, in line with the direct strategy embraced in Section 3.1. Section 3.4 presents two approaches to justifying this induction. In light of their limitation, Section 3.5 describes a third approach.

3.4.1 Inducing from typical cases

The first approach is to hold that the philosophical cases examined by experimental philosophers are typical of the kind of case philosophers use, and that their typicality justifies the conclusion that many philosophical cases elicit disagreement. A philosophical case is typical if and only if it possesses many of the properties many philosophical cases possess. For this reason, everything else being equal, typicality is a good cue for induction, and atypicality a good cue that induction should be avoided. Everything else being equal, it is reasonable to induce that some bird possesses a property if sparrows possess it, unreasonable if penguins possess it. While it is admittedly not clear what properties make typical cases typical, typicality can be recognized even when such properties are not made explicit, exactly as we can recognize a typical dog or a typical bird without knowing what makes them typical. There is little doubt that experimental philosophers have studied some of the most typical cases, but if you are inclined to doubt this claim, just ask a random sample of philosophers to list philosophical cases, and you'll find, I predict, that the cases examined by experimental philosophers will be the most commonly cited.

There are, however, at least two problems with relying on typicality to defend the inductive step of Unreliability. First, the philosophical cases examined by experimental philosophers may strike us as typical because of their availability: Because they have been discussed so much over the last ten years, they easily come to mind, and the fact that we take them to be typical does not mean that they really are typical (i.e., possess many of the properties many philosophical cases possess). Do the Gödel case and the footbridge case come so easily to mind because they are typical or because they have been discussed extensively, in part because of experimental philosophers' controversial findings? Second, supposing that the philosophical cases experimental philosophers have examined are really typical, typicality is a best a fallible cue for induction. Blue jays may have many properties many birds possess, but few other birds transport the nuts and acorns they collect for thousands of meters, and inducing gathering behavior on the basis of their typicality would often lead to mistakes. It may thus be that, while typical philosophical cases—as revealed by experimental philosophers' research—result in unreliable judgments, this is not the case of philosophical cases in general.

These two problems are not insuperable. If they were asked to give examples of philosophical cases, philosophers who have not paid attention to experimental philosophy would probably list the same cases as other philosophers. Second, induction is a risky inference. So, while the typicality of philosophical cases cannot guarantee that most philosophical cases elicit unreliable judgments, it could hardly be an objection that inferring on the basis of typicality is fallible.

3.4.2 Inducing from canonical cases

Instead of developing the defense of the first approach further, I turn to another reason why it is reasonable to induce from the philosophical cases examined by experimental philosophers to most philosophical cases: The former are canonical. They are famous, and, consciously or unconsciously, they function as templates or paradigms when philosophers write novel cases. Their paradigmatic status is sometimes conscious: For instance, action theorists consciously write cases modeled on Frankfurt's original case, and epistemologists write variants of the Gettier case. Although it is hard to know for sure, well-known cases can also influence philosophers unconsciously. At any rate, their influence probably results in many philosophical cases possessing the properties they themselves possess, including properties that undermine reliability.

One concern with basing the induction supporting Premise 3 of Unreliability on the canonical nature of the philosophical cases examined by experimental philosophers is that it limits the scope of Premise 3 to the philosophical cases in contemporary analytic philosophy, since cases written a century ago or in other philosophical traditions (e.g., non-European philosophy) are not modeled on the Gettier case or the Gödel case. Since I am mostly concerned with this tradition, this is a consequence I am willing to bear.

3.4.3 Limitations of the two approaches

The two inductive approaches (from typical or canonical cases) establish that most current cases elicit unreliable judgments. Thus, except when a case is known to elicit reliable judgments, philosophers ought to suspend judgment about the situations described by current philosophical cases. This is very bad news for a large swath of contemporary philosophy: We have to renounce drawing philosophical conclusions on the basis of the cases currently on the philosophical market, and past arguments relying on these cases should be viewed with suspicion.

It won't do to object, as Williamson (2016) does, that, until the class of problematic cases is more precisely defined (which cases exactly should be discarded?), the inductive step is of little use to philosophers. Consider the following analogy: If the U.S. Food and Drug Administration discovers that many bottles of soda produced by a factory are contaminated, the prudent thing is to recommend discarding all the bottles produced by this factory even if one is confident that some bottles are not contaminated, and one need not have a more precise definition of the class of contaminated bottles.

One may, however, feel that the argument so far leaves ample room for optimism since the problem could merely lie in the cases philosophers happen to have been using rather than in the use of cases to solve material-mode philosophical debates. Hope remains, then, that we can develop cases that are both useful for philosophers and that elicit reliable judgments.

Cases can elicit reliable judgments, no doubt about that: We can obviously be good at recognizing knowledge, responsibility, or causation in situations that are described to us instead of experienced. But would these cases be useful for philosophy? The next section examines this question.

3.5 The Inductive Step of Unreliability: Fundamental Unreliability

The third approach for justifying the inductive step of Unreliability appeals to similarity: Cases that are similar to the footbridge case, the Gödel case, and so on, elicit unreliable judgments. This approach faces an obvious obstacle: Everything being similar to everything in some respect or other, the class of cases similar to the footbridge case is ill defined until the pertinent respects have been specified, and specifying these respects just is to explain why the philosophical cases examined by experimental philosophers elicit unreliable judgments. This obstacle sets the task for this section: I examine the sources of the unreliability of the judgments elicited by the philosophical cases examined by experimental philosophers, and I show, first, that the culprit characteristics are widespread among the cases currently used by philosophers, and, second, that it is not an accident that philosophical cases tend to have these characteristics, since to bear on some central material-mode issues (to be spelt out in the remainder of this section), philosophers must appeal to cases displaying them.

3.5.1 The disturbing characteristics

Clearly, the judgments elicited by the philosophical cases that have been examined by experimental philosophers are not unreliable because they are judgments! Nor is it because of their topic: Judgments about the reference of proper names, knowledge, and responsibility (if there is such a thing) are reliable. Nor is it because judgments are elicited by cases. While judgments elicited by cases sometimes differ, and can be less reliable than the judgments elicited by experienced situations (e.g., Hertwig & Erev, 2009; Danks et al., 2014), I do not doubt that we are perfectly good at identifying cause, responsibility, moral wrongness, and proper names in many situations that are verbally described.

Perhaps one could object that making a judgment in response to a verbally described situation and in response to a philosophical case are entirely dissimilar, and that the practice of asking people to make a judgment about permissibility, causation, identity, or knowledge has no counterpart in our everyday linguistic practices (Baz, 2012, 2015). If so, then maybe judgments are unreliable because they are elicited by cases. This objection dramatically exaggerates the differences between everyday practices and the method of cases. We do describe real or actual situations to each other and ask opinions about them. In a normative (e.g., legal) context, we may describe a sequence of events and ask whether an agent caused an outcome; we assess the wrongness and permissibility of actions described to us and we debate the character of agents. We say things like "so, what do you think? Was I wrong to blah blah blah," or "Well, she told you so, but does she know it for a fact?" While the method of cases systematizes these linguistic practices, it isn't an entirely new language game.

The judgments examined by experimental philosophers must then have been unreliable because the circumstances in which these judgments are made (i.e., the cases that elicit these judgments) have characteristics that undermine the reliability of judgments that are otherwise reliable. I call them the "disturbing characteristics," and I say that cases with such characteristics are "disturbing."

The disturbing characteristics can either be properties of the situations the judgments are about (e.g., the situation described by a Gödel case) or properties of our access to these situations (e.g., the way they are described). These characteristics do not necessitate that demographic and presentation variables influence judgment; rather, they merely make it likely. Some disturbing characteristics are accidental, and cases without them could be developed; others are non-accidental: To bear on some central material-mode issues, cases must have these properties.

In addition, let's call "the proper domain" of a judgment the circumstances in which it is reliable (Machery, 2011a). The proper domain of a judgment (e.g., ascription of knowledge or responsibility) varies with the expertise of the person judging, when the subject matter of the judgment allows for expertise: The proper domain of a judgment that someone has the flu on the basis of symptoms (body aches, fever, weariness, and cough) is not the same for a physician and a lay person.

The proposal, then, is that because of their array of disturbing characteristics the philosophical cases examined by experimental philosophers are beyond the proper domains of the relevant judgments. Because these disturbing characteristics are widespread among current philosophical cases, these are likely to elicit unreliable judgments, and because they are needed for some material-mode philosophical purposes, unreliability is fundamental.

Importantly, there need not be a unique disturbing characteristic. Rather, several characteristics are likely to contribute to the unreliability of judgments. Some philosophical cases may possess all these characteristics, while others only a few. Some philosophical cases may well be free of all these characteristics, and the judgments these elicit are not vulnerable to the influence of demographic and presentation variables.

How are we going to identify the disturbing characteristics? Unfortunately, no data bears directly on what they are, in large part because experimental philosophers have not addressed this question head-on, but we can identify them indirectly. In the remainder of this chapter, I identify some likely culprits: They provide good explanations of why the judgments examined by experimental philosophers are influenced by demographic and presentation variables. I also discuss whether the proposed disturbing characteristics are accidental or non-accidental.

3.5.2   Hypothetical situations

I start by examining what is unlikely to explain the influence of demographic and presentation variables on the judgments examined by experimental philosophers. As is the case of most philosophical cases (but see, e.g., the Dedekind/Peano case in *Naming and Necessity* and the Madagascar case in Evans, 1973), the philosophical cases examined by experimental philosophers are all hypothetical: They ask readers to consider situations that are not actual. Experimental participants have been asked to imagine that a character (or sometimes themselves) near trolley tracks or on a footbridge is confronted with a runaway trolley, that a famous conductor has been kidnapped, that on some planet an unknown chemical structure (XYZ) results in a liquid identical to water in almost every respect, and that a chip implanted in someone's brain can lead her to a specific action. One could speculate that the hypothetical nature of the examined philosophical cases explains, at least in part, why the elicited judgments are unreliable, but there is in fact little reason to believe that judgments about hypothetical situations are in general unreliable: Simply consider the judgment that this book would fall instead of going up if you released your grip on it.

What's more, the judgments about hypothetical situations described by at least some philosophical cases are likely to be similar to the judgments one would make if these situations were actual. My judgment that the protagonist in a Gettier case does not know the relevant proposition is likely to be similar to the judgment I would make about an actual Gettier case.

3.5.3 The unusual nature of philosophical cases

I now turn to an important explanation of the influence of demographic and presentation variables on the judgments examined by experimental philosophers: The cases examined by philosophers tend to describe very unusual situations. A situation or event (type) is unusual if and only if we encounter it infrequently or if we rarely read texts about it. Being unusual differs from being imaginary or fictional: Some imaginary situations are not unusual, others are. Being unusual is not a modal notion either: Actual situations can be unusual (in 2003 CNN reported about a situation eerily similar to the one described by the switch case (CNN, 2003; cited in Gold et al., 2014)), and counterfactual situations need not be unusual. Finally, being unusual is not being atypical, although the two are related. We rarely, if ever, encounter or think about atypical situations in everyday life: When we encounter a situation of a given kind, it tends to possess many of the typical characteristics of its kind. However, a typical situation could be unusual.

The philosophical cases examined by experimental philosophers tend to be unusual: How often have we assigned responsibility in situations that are similar to the ones found in the free-will literature (e.g., Frankfurt cases and their many epicycles)? While many of us must have had to decide whether to cause some harm to prevent a greater harm, how often have we been confronted with a decision involving lives? Is knowledge ascription in the Truetemp case similar to a common situation where we are asked to ascribe knowledge (say when we check whether someone knows what she is talking about)?

The unusual nature of a case can be due to either its superficial or its target content. Remember that the superficial content of a case consists of the facts and non-factual (e.g., emotional) connotations that do not matter from a philosophical point of view, while the target content of a case consists of the facts and non-factual connotations that matter from a philosophical point of view. To assess some claim about, say, meaning, we may need to consider extremely unusual situations: In this case, the target content of a case (e.g., of a Twin-Earth case) is the source of its unusual nature. In other cases, it is merely the narrative setting of the case that is the source of its unusual nature. The fake-barn case is unusual in part because of its superficial content.

The unusual nature of the cases examined by experimental philosophers provides an explanation of the demographic and presentation effects reported in Chapter 2. First, the more unusual a situation, the more obscure it is what facts hold in it in addition to the facts explicitly stated. I, for one, do not really know what facts hold in the situations described by brain- or body-swapping cases in addition to those explicitly stated. Readers are likely to differ in how they conceive of these unusual situations, and demographic differences as well as salient irrelevant features—their state of mind or what they have recently read—may influence how they end up conceiving them. Irrelevant narrative elements are also likely to influence how readers fill in the cases. Thus, the uncertainty of what holds in the situations described by the cases examined by experimental philosophers probably accounts in part for the demographic and presentation effects reported in Chapter 2.

Various bits of psychology provide evidence in support of the hypothesis that while people conceive of or imagine usual situations in a similar manner, they vary in how they conceive of or imagine unusual situations. Fictional thinking is constrained by people's inclination to import the facts holding in the actual word into the fictional worlds (e.g., Nichols & Stich, 2003; Weisberg & Goodstein, 2009). The less similar the actual and fictional worlds are, the less likely people are to import the facts holding in the actual world, the more they vary in their understanding of the imaginative situation. Idiosyncratic factors, including demographic characteristics, then influence their imagination. A similar lesson emerges from the research on how people create novel complex concepts, which has typically involved bizarre complex concepts such as BABY OIL, SNAKE ROBBIN, HORSE KNIFE, STONE SQUIRREL, or CACTUS FISH.[10] While some constraints govern how people describe the instances of such unusual novel complex concepts—psychologists do not agree on the nature of these constraints— there is much variation in what people imagine them to be.

Second, demographic and presentation variables may influence the judgments about the unusual philosophical cases examined by experimental philosophers because readers may in fact be unable to grasp clearly the situations they are supposed to imagine. That readers have the impression to grasp these situations clearly is little evidence that they actually do, as teachers know all too well. As Parfit (1984, 389) notes, moral judgments about utility monsters (people whose utility gains derived from others' sacrifices would be incommensurably larger than others' utility losses) may have little philosophical significance because we may not be able to represent very large numbers clearly. (The psychology of number representation, according to which large numbers are represented logarithmically, supports this concern.) Since the confused

---

[10] For review, see e.g. Machery & Lederer (2012).

thoughts people end up entertaining are not determined by the text they read, other factors such as demographic variables and irrelevant narrative features may influence these thoughts and the judgments they end up making.

Third, because of the differences between unusual and everyday situations, the readers of the philosophical cases examined by experimental philosophers cannot rely on their memories of tried and true past judgments in everyday situations to get it right or more generally on heuristics that get it right in everyday situations. When we read a Twin-Earth case, we do not use our everyday strategy to decide whether XYZ is water. Readers must then rely on ad hoc strategies, which are likely to vary across demographic groups and to be influenced by irrelevant narrative features.

Moving beyond the cases examined by experimental philosophers, philosophical cases are often unusual: How often have we decided whether a coordinated collective of individuals possess consciousness, as we are asked to do in Block's (1978) Nation-of-China case? How often do we need to judge whether someone who knows every scientific fact about color would also know what it feels like to see red, as we are asked to do in Jackson's (1986) Mary the neuroscientist case? To say nothing of Locke's prince and the cobbler case, brain-swapping cases (Shoemaker, 1963), Routley's (1973) last-man thought experiment, and Chalmers's (1996) zombies! Many philosophical cases also describe situations involving magic (e.g., Locke's prince and the cobbler case), extraordinary coincidences (e.g., the clock case), or science-fictional situations (e.g., Frankfurt cases, Parfit's teleportation cases). That is, philosophical cases are often unusual, and we should expect the judgments they elicit to be unreliable.

Furthermore, it is not an accident that philosophical cases tend to describe unusual situations. It may be that ordinary situations only elicit canned, unreflective answers that do not genuinely involve people's capacities to recognize knowledge, causation, or permissibility, and some proponents of the method of cases have speculated that unusual cases prompt readers to make considerate judgments and to bring their recognitional capacities to bear on the task at hand. Kamm (1993, 7–8), for example, invites philosophers to test their theories against "fantastic" cases. If the considerations brought forward in this section are on the right track, philosophers will need to find another way to elicit considerate judgments and override canned judgments.

More important, at least two central dialectical practices of contemporary philosophy involve examining cases describing unusual situations. Competing philosophical views (e.g., about what knowledge entails, whether personal identity depends on body or memory permanence, or whether responsibility requires that one could have acted differently) often give the same verdict about ordinary situations. To distinguish them, philosophers *must* consider unusual situations. I elaborate on this point in the next section.

Philosophers also assess philosophical views by considering their implications about unusual situations. Many philosophical views have a modal dimension, stating what *must* be the case. Reductive theories assert identities; for example, according to the reductive theories of causation that assert the identity of causation and of a particular form of counterfactual dependence, there could not be an instance of causation that is not an instance of this form of counterfactual dependence. According to Jackson's influential argument, physicalism entails that someone who would know every physical fact would not learn anything new by seeing a new color; according to Chalmers, it entails that there could not be physical duplicates without phenomenal experience (zombies). The Principle of Alternate Possibilities holds that there could not be a free action such that one could not have acted otherwise. Many of the non-actual situations that are most telling to assess such philosophical views are unusual either because they violate the laws of nature (e.g., thought experiments involving zombies, water on Twin Earth, split brains, etc.) or because they involve situations that are extremely different from what happens in the actual world.

So, not only are current philosophical cases likely to elicit unreliable judgments, useful cases to distinguish philosophical views agreeing about ordinary situations and to assess some of their modal consequences are likely to elicit such judgments too: Unreliability is fundamental.

3.5.4 Pulling apart what usually goes together

I now turn to another explanation of the influence of demographic and presentation variables on judgments elicited by philosophical cases: The philosophical cases examined by experimental philosophers typically pull apart the properties that go together in everyday life. The footbridge case pulls apart engaging in physical violence and doing more harm than good: Usually, people who engage in physical violence do more harm than good. The Gödel case describes a situation where a proper name that is associated with a single description by a whole linguistic community happens to be false of the original bearer of the name while usually many of the descriptions associated with a proper name are true of the original bearer of the name. When knowledge is ascribed or denied in everyday life, truth, justification, and the non-lucky character of the belief-forming method go hand in hand. When people fail to know something, their beliefs are typically false and unjustified. By contrast, Gettier cases sever (among other things) truth and justification from not getting it right by luck, since they describe situations where truth comes about by luck.

The demographic and presentation effects reported in Chapter 2 are explained by paying attention to this characteristic of the philosophical cases examined by experimental philosophers. The capacities to identify knowledge, permissibility, desert, reference, responsibility, understanding, and explanation—the capacities the method of cases is supposed to rely on—may work just fine when these properties co-occur, as they tend to do in the everyday circumstances in which these capacities are meant to be deployed. For instance, it may be that we judge that someone knows something if the process by which she came to form her belief possesses many of the epistemic properties epistemologists have discussed (safety, adherence, proportionality to available evidence, etc.), even if we have no idea which of the co-occurring properties—say safety, but not adherence—is necessary for knowledge. We may also judge that someone fails to know something if the process by which she comes to form her belief possesses few of these epistemic properties. One would reliably identify knowledge and ignorance if these properties tend to co-occur in everyday life. However, the reader of an epistemological case about knowledge cannot rely on these strategies to identify knowledge and ignorance since the beliefs formed in the described situations possess some, but not all, of the pertinent epistemic properties. The reader is then compelled to take a stance about what property is essential to knowledge, probably for the first time, and this is the crack through which unreliability slips in. Different presentation conditions (due, e.g., to different frames) may lead the reader to single out different properties, and different groups may single out different properties.

Alternatively, it may be that we judge that someone knows something if her situation is similar to most memories of instances of knowledge, and that she fails to know something if her situation is similar to most memories of ignorance. Memorized instances of knowledge possess many of the epistemic properties epistemologists have discussed, memorized situations of ignorance few of them. Similarity to memories of knowledge and ignorance is useless when confronted with a philosophical case, and the reader is compelled to take a stance about what property is essential to knowledge, probably for the first time, thereby opening the door to unreliability.

Or judgments about knowledge, responsibility, or causation may be underwritten by heuristics. Heuristics are judgmental procedures that use the presence of one or a few features to produce a judgment. Sometimes, these features are merely coincidental to the truth of the judgment. For instance, whether an individual is typical of a class is often used to judge whether she is likely to belong to this class (Tversky & Kahneman, 1983). In everyday life, heuristics are reliable because the features they rely on co-occur with whatever it is that makes the resulting judgments true. This co-occurrence is likely to be disrupted when the features that go together in everyday life are pulled apart by philosophical cases. Different demographic groups may use different heuristics, and different presentation conditions of the cases may prime readers to use different heuristics, resulting in the effects discussed in Chapter 2.

Psychology provides much support for these accounts of the influence of demographic and presentation variables. Situations that split apart properties that go together in everyday life are atypical members of the kind of interest (e.g., permissible actions, knowledge, or causes) or atypical non-members of this kind. Atypical objects possess only some of the properties that are deemed to be characteristic of a given kind. Just like being unusual, atypicality is not a modal notion: Actual cases can be atypical, and merely possible cases can be typical. Being atypical is not simply being unusual. A situation or event is unusual if and only if it occurs infrequently, while some situations that are typical in all respects can be unusual. Studies show that atypical objects are classified less consistently and elicit lower consensus among people (e.g., Barsalou, 1987). Lifts move and carry people like cars and planes, but, in contrast to cars and planes, their trajectory is fixed and they can only move vertically. Lifts are atypical vehicles, while cars and planes are typical vehicles. People are much more likely to classify lifts as a type of vehicle on one occasion while denying that they are a type of vehicle on another occasion, and people disagree about whether lifts are a type of vehicle. It would not do to respond that we are excellent at classifying atypical kind members such as whales (mammals, not fish) or penguins and emus (birds, appearances notwithstanding). These are known atypical members of particular kinds: We know that whales are fish, and we override our reliance on typicality to decide whether to classify whales as a fish. The situation is entirely different for the kind of atypical situations described by philosophical cases.

Moving beyond the cases examined by experimental philosophers, philosophical cases nearly always pull apart properties that go together. Zombies pull apart behavior and experience. Frankfurt cases describe situations where making another decision would not have led to another action, while in everyday life one would have acted differently if one had made another decision.

Furthermore, it is not an accident that philosophical cases tend to pull apart properties that usually co-occur. If cases did not do this, they could not be used to adjudicate between competing philosophical theories because typically these theories agree on the everyday cases where the pertinent properties co-occur. Thus, theories of reference typically agree on the reference of proper names, since many of the numerous descriptions associated with them are true of their original bearers. An analogy with scientific experiments is useful here. Naturally occurring phenomena rarely discriminate between existing scientific theories, and scientists are compelled to devise artificial experimental conditions about which existing scientific theories make different predictions. This is a non-accidental feature of developed sciences, exactly as the appeal to cases that pull apart typically co-occurring properties is a non-accidental feature of areas of philosophy that both rely on the method of cases and are well developed.

3.5.5 The entanglement of the superficial and target content of cases

Finally, we can explain the influence of demographic and presentation variables by proposing that judgments are not only influenced by their target content, as intended, but also by their superficial content, which philosophers neither intend nor expect.

Evidence supports the influence of the superficial content of the cases examined by experimental philosophers. The permissibility judgment in the footbridge case is known to depend on how the protagonist's action is described (Greene et al., 2009): The more the protagonist uses his or her own physical force to bring about this action, the more impermissible the action is judged to be, in part because we react emotionally to harmful physical actions. Judgments about footbridge and lifeboat cases are influenced by the implied race of the person to be pushed: In a footbridge case, liberals are less likely to find it permissible to push a man named "Tyrone Payton" in order to save "100 members of the New York Philharmonic" than a man named "Chip Ellsworth III" to save "100 members of the Harlem Jazz Orchestra" (Uhlmann et al., 2009).

More generally, the framing effects discussed in Chapter 2 are just a manifestation of the proposed influence of the superficial content of cases on judgment. The proposed influence of the superficial content also explains the second type of presentation effect—i.e., order effects: The judgment elicited by the second case is anchored by the judgment influenced by the superficial content of the first case. The demographic effects reviewed in Chapter 2 are also accounted for: Demographic groups are likely to react to the superficial content of philosophical cases differently.

Two features of philosophical cases strengthen the proposed influence of the superficial content of cases on the philosophical judgments examined by experimental philosophers. These cases tend to describe hypothetical situations in vivid terms—see, for example, Thomson's description of the trolley cases (quoted in Chapter 1)—and they contain many irrelevant narrative elements. Many philosophical cases are also written (perhaps involuntarily) so as to elicit a particular judgment—the judgment that supports the writer's argument. Turri (2016) has forcefully argued that many versions of the Gettier case (including those found in Gettier, 1963) are "stilted and tendentiously described." Gettier cases often involve language and themes apt to cue attributions of ignorance, such as having the protagonist select answers at random, draw silly, contextually irrelevant inferences, or be deceived. These events are similar to paradigmatic cases of ignorance, and are likely to lead to a lack-of-knowledge judgment.

Moving beyond the cases examined by experimental philosophers, all philosophical cases have a narrative setting, many of them describe hypothetical and actual situations in a vivid and lengthy manner, and many are presented in a tendentious manner. Just consider Searle's Chinese-room thought experiment (quoted in Chapter 1), the mob and the magistrate case, the last man on Earth case, and many Frankfurt-style cases. Incidentally, the influence of superficial features on judgment shows that it is a bad idea to hone one's moral sense against works of literature:[11] Their rich narrative content is likely to lead judgment astray. Descartes was right to warn us against what we may call "Donquixotism": "[T]hose who govern their own conduct by means of examples drawn from these texts ["fables" and "histories"] are liable to fall into the extravagances of the knights of our romances, and to conceive plans that are beyond their powers" (Descartes, 1999, 4).

Furthermore, while the influence of some aspects of the superficial content of philosophical cases—such as their vivid nature and extensive narrative setting—is accidental, and while pared-down, less tendentious cases could be written, it is unlikely that the target content and the superficial content can be fully disentangled, with readers responding only to the target content of the case. We do not know enough about the processes underlying judgment, and to the extent that we understand them, we do not have enough control over them, to be able to react only to the intended target content of a case and to overlook its superficial content. The intractable entanglement of superficial and target content is the last non-accidental disturbing characteristic of philosophical cases considered here.

One may respond that to deal with the possible influence of the superficial content on their judgment philosophers should simply, and in fact do, examine several versions

---

[11] Murdoch (1970, 33); Nussbaum (1990).

of the same case, ensuring that their judgments are not influenced by the superficial content of cases. But philosophers only occasionally consider different versions of the same case to sieve any influence their superficial content may have, and they never do it systematically. Furthermore, as a matter of fact, judgments happen to vary across what are intended to be versions of the same case.[12]

One may also respond that the influence of the superficial content of cases on judgment cannot justify a skeptical attitude because this skepticism would creep too far: Whenever we make a judgment after having read or heard about a situation (in a newspaper, from a friend, on TV, etc.), the description of the situation can influence our judgment. Since by hypothesis we reliably identify the reference of proper names, ascribe responsibility, assess the moral worth of actions, or identify causes, the alleged influence of the narrative setting can only show that judgments are fallible, not that they are unreliable (an issue we will revisit in Chapter 5). This concern can be allayed: In unusual cases only, the superficial content is likely to have a pervasive influence because usual strategies are less likely to be used to make a judgment.

3.5.6 Wrapping up

Several characteristics explain why the philosophical cases examined by experimental philosophers elicit judgments biased by demographic and presentation variables: their vivid and extensive narrative setting, their tendentious presentation, the entanglement of superficial and target content, their unusual content, and the pulling apart of properties that go together in everyday circumstances, which elicit reliable judgments. There is no doubt that most philosophical cases display at least some of these characteristics, and are thus likely to elicit unreliable judgments. Furthermore, the last three disturbing characteristics are not accidental. The superficial content of cases cannot be disentangled from its target content. More important, philosophical cases describe unusual situations in order to elicit reflective judgments, and they often must do so in order to test some of the modal implications of philosophical theories. They also must pull apart properties that go together in everyday situations in order to test competing theories that agree about everyday situations. If that is right, then, in some of its most central applications, the method of cases itself should be impugned, instead of just the cases philosophers happen to have been using: The type of case needed to investigate some of the modal consequences of philosophical theories and to discriminate between competing philosophical proposals is likely to elicit unreliable judgments.

The discussion in Section 3.5 also allows us to see what "good cases"—cases that would elicit reliable judgments would look like: They would describe usual and typical situations, they would be non-tendentious, and their narrative setting would be lean. It is patent that most cases in the philosophical literature are not like that, and such cases would be useless to settle many material-mode philosophical debates.

---

[12] Williams (1970); Unger (1996); Gendler & Hawthorne (2005); Gendler (2007); Norcross (2008).

3.6 Five Objections

Finally, I consider five possible objections to the discussion of the disturbing characteristics.

3.6.1 An objection against the "unusualness" explanation

One could challenge the unusualness explanation of the demographic and presentation effects reported in Chapter 2 as follows: We often make judgments about unusual situations in, for example, science-fiction or heroic-fantasy novels and movies and there is little reason to believe that these judgments are unreliable. However, the situations described in, for example, science-fiction novels are in fact quite similar to everyday situations: A lie is a lie, whether it is made in an actual situation or in the world of *The Game of Thrones*. Generally, the fact that the narrative elements of a case are fictional does not make it unusual; it is unusual if it describes a kind of situation that we rarely encounter in our experience or from description.

It would not do either to respond, as Cappelen does (2012, 226), that "lots of strange and unusual cases are very easy to judge in a reliable way" and that "many of the *normal* (not farfetched, not unusual, not esoteric) cases are very hard." To illustrate his first point, he gives the following example (2012, 226, italics in the original):

Easy Esoteric and Farfetched Case: Suppose there are two pinks elephants in my office. Then yet another pink elephant comes into my office (and the first two pink elephants stay in the room). Question: How many pink elephants are in my office?

But, just like many of our judgments about fictional situations, this situation is patently similar to an everyday situation; it just involves an addition, while the situations we are asked to judge about in philosophical cases are often quite different from everyday situations. To illustrate his second point, Cappelen refers to Burge's (1979) arthritis case, noting that Burge highlights the "ordinariness of his cases." There are many possible responses to this example. Perhaps judgments elicited by the arthritis case are not influenced by demographic and presentation variables. Alternatively, judgments about this case may be unreliable for other reasons: Unusualness is not the only disturbing characteristic.

Perhaps, however, similarity cannot help distinguish unusual from non-unusual cases. The situation described by the footbridge case is similar to those everyday situations where we have to decide whether to commit some harm to prevent a greater harm, although it differs from them in that lives are at stake. So, why is it an unusual situation? The situation described by Cappelen's easy, esoteric, and farfetched case may well involve addition, but it involves the addition of pink elephants! So, why isn't it an unusual situation? The difference between the two situations is this: The fact that harm involves causing death in the trolley cases is germane to getting it right when one is making a permissibility judgment, while whether one is adding chairs or pink elephants is not when one is adding.

3.6.2 The objection from confidence

One can doubt that the judgments elicited by philosophical cases are unreliable since they are often made with confidence. There are two steps in this objection. It relies first on the claim that judgments elicited by philosophical cases are often made with confidence, second on the claim that in general the degree of confidence in one's judgments is calibrated with respect to their reliability, that is, the reliability of judgments is not invariant under partition along the dimension of confidence. The first step seems correct for some philosophical cases—the Gettier case and the trolley cases, for instance, elicit confident judgments—but not for all, at least among lay people. Be that as it may, what about the second step? Wright (2010) may seem to provide evidence for the claim that, at least for the judgments elicited by philosophical cases, confidence is well calibrated with respect to reliability: In particular, the participants in her first study were less confident for cases liable to order effects, such as the Truetemp and fake-barn cases.

However, for two distinct reasons, Wright's results provide little support to the objection from confidence. First, her findings undermine the very first step of the objection, since lay people's judgments about two paradigmatic philosophical cases were not made with confidence. In her first study, only ordinary cases, which would be of little use in a philosophical discussion, elicited confident judgments. Second, her findings show at best that judgments made with little confidence should not be trusted, not that judgments made with confidence should be trusted. Indeed, her own follow-up study (Wright, 2013) shows that high confidence is not to be trusted: People who are given expert information that is consistent with their spontaneous answers are less confident in their response to cases eliciting confident answers!

Moving away from Wright's study, there is a lot of evidence that confidence is a poor guide to the reliability of one's judgment. People suffer from overconfidence, that is, from the tendency to overestimate the proportion of their judgments that is correct (Arkes, 2001). Confidence also varies with factors that do not necessarily increase reliability. Einhorn and Hogarth's (1978) classic model of confidence predicts that confidence increases with experience: The more frequently one exercises one's (real or illusory) skills, the more confident one is, whether or not this exercise is successful. People who often exercise a skill that is in reality illusory should be particularly confident in their craft. As Einhorn and Hogarth put it (1978, 402), "[J]udges with greater experience…may feel considerable confidence in judgment that is no more valid than those who have little experience." Confidence is also fostered by the capacity to provide reasons for one's judgments, whether or not these reasons are any good. When many justifications are available, whether or not they improve the accuracy of judgment, people are extremely confident— a phenomenon Tetlock (2005) has aptly named "the hot air hypothesis."

3.6.3 True judgments about situations splitting apart usually co-occurring properties

Other objections specifically take on the claim that judgments about cases that pull apart properties that go together in everyday life tend to be unreliable (e.g.,

Williamson, 2016). One can first describe cases that seem to pull apart properties that go together in everyday life, but that elicit true judgments. If John has a justified, but false belief that p, he does not know that p: In this situation, justification and truth value are pulled apart (justified beliefs are often true), but we should not doubt the judgment that the person has no knowledge of p.[13] What this example shows is that pulling apart usually co-occurring properties does not always lead to unreliability, but this was never in question; rather, I am proposing that pulling apart usually co-occurring features promotes unreliability. And indeed it is easy to see what distinguishes a Gettier case from a case involving a false justified belief: Falsehood is a central component of our concept of ignorance, and we just rely on the falsehood of a belief to decide, correctly, that it is an instance of ignorance. We are not compelled to decide, more or less arbitrarily, which epistemic property is essential for knowledge and we do not need to rely on any heuristic to make this judgment.

Similarly, Williamson describes the following situation (2016, 28):

[C]onsider a woman who fights off her would-be rapist, kicking him in the groin and having him arrested. We judge that her action was morally permissible, indeed right. But this too is a case of using physical violence without doing more harm than good, and therefore pulls apart the features that go together in everyday life. According to Machery's argument, therefore, we have reason to believe that the psychological capacities underlying our application of moral concepts are unreliable in this case too, and therefore to be sceptical about our initial judgment that the woman's action was morally permissible. Surely this scepticism is unwarranted, and potentially pernicious.

It is also easy to see what distinguishes the situation described by Williamson from the situation described by the footbridge case. The former situation is a typical instance of an aggression, and elicits the canned judgment that self-defense in this situation is permissible. We are not compelled to decide, more or less arbitrarily, which property is essential for moral permissibility and we do not need to rely on any heuristic to judge that self-defense in this case is morally permissible. The situation described by the footbridge case is not a typical instance of a moral concept and does not elicit a canned judgment. We have no reason to doubt our judgment in the former situation, no reason to trust it in the situation described by the footbridge case.[14]

These two apparent counterexamples are useful to make more precise the claim that pulling apart co-occurring features promotes the unreliability of judgments. Pulling apart such features will only promote unreliability when the target of the judgment of interest (e.g., pushing the large person in the footbridge case or the belief of the protagonist in a Gettier case) does not have properties that are central to a given concept (e.g., being false for IGNORANCE) or is not a typical instance of a particular concept (e.g., AGGRESSION or RAPE in Williamson's case).

---

[13] I owe this example to Cian Dorr.

[14] Williamson's second counterexample (2016, 29)—"a man who irrationally forms beliefs simply on his guru's authority. The guru makes assertions at random; a few of them are true, so the follower forms some true beliefs"—suffers from the same problem.

3.6.4 The objection from humdrum cases

One may also object that the situations described by some philosophical cases that would be suspicious if I were correct have actual counterparts, and that it would be unreasonable to doubt the judgments elicited by these actual situations. For instance, why would the Gödel case promote unreliability by pulling apart typically co-occurring properties if the Peano-Dedekind case and other "humdrum cases" don't (Devitt, 2011, 2012)? In fact, however, the actual situations that elicit reliable judgments are typically not the counterparts of the situations described by suspicious philosophical cases. For instance, the Peano-Dedekind case is not a counterpart of the Gödel case since the former but not the latter describes a situation where experts (or the broader linguistic community) associate descriptions associated with the proper names that are true of their original bearers (Machery et al., 2013).[15]

A critic could concede that the humdrum philosophical cases that elicit reliable judgments are not exact counterparts of the suspicious philosophical cases, but insist that they too pull apart properties that co-occur, despite eliciting reliable judgments: Thus, in the Peano-Dedekind case, the causal history of "Peano" is disconnected from the beliefs speakers have about the bearer of "Peano" (e.g., that he was the first to axiomatize arithmetic). However, the properties that are pulled apart by the Gödel case may not be the beliefs of the speaker and the causal history of the proper name, but rather the beliefs experts or the linguistic community at large associate with the proper name and the causal history of this name. Speakers may be used to other speakers having false beliefs or precious little information about the referents of proper names, and thus they may not expect true beliefs and causal history to go together. But they are likely to expect the causal history of a name to be in line with the beliefs experts or the linguistic community associate with this name. If this is right, the Gödel case, but not the Peano-Dedekind case, pulls apart properties that co-occur in everyday life.

3.6.5 Blaming accidental features of cases?

Finally, one may concede that the judgments elicited by some, perhaps even many, philosophical cases are unreliable, but insist that this unreliability is only due to accidental disturbing characteristics. At the very least, the critic could object that for all I have shown this unreliability may only be due to these accidental characteristics, and that it is then an overreach to impugn the method of cases itself: Unreliability would not be fundamental.

However, first, even if unreliability is not fundamental, Unreliability leads to a dramatic conclusion: We ought to suspend judgment in response to most current philosophical cases, and thus discount their contribution to philosophical theorizing. A substantial part of the last fifty years of analytic philosophy will be thrown into

---

[15] This point also undermines Williamson's (2016) discussion of my take on the Gödel case.

doubt. Furthermore, the influence of the superficial content of cases on judgment is well established, and there is little reason to believe that the target and superficial content can be disentangled. The psychology of imagination supports the idea that unusual cases are likely to leave room for the influence of demographic and presentation variables. The similarity between the influence of atypicality on categorization judgment (e.g., Barsalou, 1987) and the findings reported in Chapter 2 (influence of presentation effects and variation across people) supports the proposal that pulling apart properties that go together in everyday situations is one of the disturbing characteristics: Unreliability is fundamental.

3.7 Conclusion

We should view with great suspicion the judgments elicited by the cases that have populated analytic philosophy over the last fifty years. The reliability of most of these judgments is undermined by demographic or presentation variables, and, in the absence of any evidence to the contrary, we should simply refrain from endorsing them. Even more worrying is the fact that philosophers must appeal to cases promoting unreliable judgment in order to fulfill at least two central material-mode goals: assessing some of the modal consequences of philosophical theories and distinguishing theories that agree about everyday situations. The ramifications of this conclusion will be explored in Chapter 6.

Unreliability makes very few assumptions about the method of cases. It does not depend on which kind of attitude philosophical cases happen to elicit. Whatever is elicited by philosophical cases, if it is unreliable, one is not warranted to take for granted the alleged facts (e.g., the alleged fact that it is impermissible to push the large person in the situation described by the footbridge case). It does not depend either on the kind of warrant the attitudes elicited by philosophical cases are meant to possess: It does not attempt to deny, say, that these judgments or attitudes have a priori warrant or are epistemically basic. So, while the minimalist characterization best characterizes the method of cases (Chapter 1), Unreliability would still threaten the method of cases if another characterization turned out to be more adequate.

We can now step back and take in the lesson of Unreliability: Tossing around judgments elicited by philosophical cases is really often little more than peddling cognitive artifacts, and taking them seriously is like taking the distortions introduced by our experimental instruments for the real effects. It's using our capacities for detecting knowledge, permissibility, responsibility, or reference beyond their proper domain.

4

Enshrining *Our* Prejudices

[E]n voyageant, [j'ai] reconnu que tous ceux qui ont des sentiments forts contraires aux nôtres, ne sont pas pour cela barbares, ni sauvages, mais que plusieurs usent, autant ou plus que nous, de raison; et [j'ai] considéré combien un même homme, avec son même esprit, étant nourri dès son enfance entre des Français ou des Allemands, devient différent de ce qu'il serait, s'il avait toujours vécu entre des Chinois ou des Cannibales.

Descartes, *Discours de la méthode* (67)

As we saw in the introduction of Chapter 3, two kinds of concern have been brought forward against the use of cases to settle material-mode philosophical disputes: the concern that in light of the demographic and presentation effects reviewed in Chapter 2 judgments elicited by philosophical cases should not be trusted, and the concern that users of the method of cases fail to react appropriately to the diversity of judgments elicited by cases. In this chapter, I develop the second concern. The diversity of judgments underlies two distinct arguments—Dogmatism and Parochialism—which together form a dilemma for the proponent of the method of cases: Either she ignores the multitude of people who disagree with us philosophers (Dogmatism) or she ignores their distinct voices and interests (Parochialism).

Generally, Dogmatism and Parochialism attempt to articulate precisely the concern that philosophizing by means of the method of cases turns philosophy into a sophisticated but unjustifiable effort to build upon *our* prejudices—that is, the prejudices of the highly peculiar demographic group that makes up academic philosophy—when reflecting about the fundamental issues that motivate philosophical thinking, such as How to think?, How to act?, and How to live together? So, the method of cases does not simply lead us to take cognitive artifacts for real phenomena (Chapter 3), it also leads us to enshrine our prejudices in our philosophical theories. In what follows, I consider Dogmatism and Parochialism in turn.

4.1 Dogmatism

The gist of Dogmatism is simple: Experimental philosophers' findings suggest that people disagree about what to say in response to many philosophical cases, and there is no reason to prefer one of the answers elicited by the cases to the other; as a result, we should suspend judgment about these cases. This argument can be presented more systematically as follows:

Dogmatism

1.   Most of the philosophical cases examined by experimental philosophers elicit disagreement.

2.   This disagreement takes place among epistemic peers.

3.   If most of the philosophical cases examined by experimental philosophers elicit disagreement among peers, then most philosophical cases would plausibly elicit disagreement among peers.

4.   If epistemic peers are likely to disagree about a philosophical case, they ought to suspend judgment about it.

5.   Hence, except for those philosophical cases known not to elicit disagreement among peers, philosophers ought to suspend judgment about the situations described by philosophical cases.

One may wonder whether Dogmatism adds anything to Unreliability on the grounds that, if one ought to suspend judgment in response to disagreement with a peer, it is because disagreement indicates that one's judgment results from an unreliable process. The relation between peer disagreement and reliability is intricate, however, and Dogmatism does not depend on disagreement indicating the unreliability of the process underlying one's judgment; one could just have made a mistake. In the remainder of this section I unpack and defend Dogmatism.

4.1.1 *The inductive basis and the inductive step of Dogmatism*

Philosophers disagree about some philosophical cases. There is no consensus about the fake-barn case among epistemologists (e.g., knowledge: Millikan, 1984; lack of knowledge: Goldman, 1976). Metaphysicians often disagree about the situations described by metaphysical cases. For instance, Wasserman (2015, section 1) canvasses four possible views about whether a statue is identical to the clay it is made of. On the other hand, many philosophical cases, such as the switch and footbridge cases, the Gettier case, the Truetemp case, and the Gödel case, elicit something like a consensus in philosophy.[1] Of course, it is almost always possible to find a philosopher who rejects

---

[1] Turri (2016) argues that this consensus may be partly illusory. Philosophers who do not share the relevant judgment (e.g., about the Gettier case) just don't publish on the topic (the analysis of knowledge), and work in other areas of philosophy. This is certainly a possibility.

the consensual judgment,[2] but still there is as much consensus about these cases as there can be in philosophy.

One of the most important contributions of experimental philosophy is to have shown that, assuming that philosophers and non-philosophers are not speaking at cross purposes (by, e.g., using the same words to mean different things), many cases that elicit a consensus among philosophers happen to elicit disagreement among lay people (Chapter 2 for review). It is true that some of the cases examined do not elicit any disagreement: For instance, about 85 percent of participants in four different countries (India, Brazil, Japan, USA) find that in some versions of the Gettier case the agent does not know the relevant proposition (Machery et al., forthcoming a). However, lay people give different answers in response to most of the examined cases: Assuming again that philosophers and non-philosophers are not speaking at cross purposes (if they are, then Dogmatism does not apply, and we are concerned with another issue, spelt out by Parochialism), many lay people make the same judgment as philosophers, but many others judge differently.

I suspect that philosophers have not taken the measure of how much disagreement there is about these cases, so it may be useful to belabor the point a bit here: The switch and footbridge cases, the fake-barn, Truetemp, and zebra cases, the Gödel and Twin-Earth cases elicit no consensus (Table 4.1).[3]

Demographic variables sometimes predict disagreement about the philosophical cases that have been studied empirically—e.g., the Gödel case tends to elicit a Kripkean judgment from Westerners, but a descriptivist judgment from East Asians—but not always: For some philosophical cases, philosophers' consensual judgments diverge from the judgments made by people who are similar in terms of cultural background, language, gender, and education. To explain the disagreement between philosophers and some non-philosophers in spite of their demographic similarity, one could propose that the consensus about philosophical cases among philosophers results from their education: The consensual judgments may be inculcated, or those who do not share them may be less likely to go into philosophy, perhaps because they are not encouraged to do so or perhaps because it is aversive not to share consensual judgments; on a more sinister note, they may even be driven out of philosophy.[4]

Of course, experimental philosophers have examined only some philosophical cases, and one may wonder whether it is permissible to induce from this limited set of cases. I will have little to say about the inductive step of Dogmatism (Premise 3) beyond the considerations presented in Sections 3.4 and 3.5 of Chapter 3. The cases examined by experimental philosophers are typical and canonical, and we can thus expect most current philosophical cases to elicit disagreement too. Furthermore, disagreement is

---

[2] See, e.g., Dupré (1981) on Putnam's Twin-Earth thought experiment; Dennett (1993) on Jackson's Mary thought experiment; Sartwell (1991) and Weatherson (2003) on the Gettier case.

[3] A case fails to elicit a consensus if at least 20 percent of participants make a judgment that differs from (what I assume to be) philosophers' consensual judgment. A smaller proportion of divergent judgments can be chalked up to inattention or confusion from a small minority of participants.

[4] e.g., Cummins (1998); Machery et al. (2004).

Table 4.1. Partial list of cases that fail to elicit a consensus

Case	Field	Agreement with philosophers	Citation
Gödel case	Language	About 60% of Americans and 40% of Chinese	Machery et al. (2004)
Jonah case	Language	About 39% of Americans and 25% of Chinese	Beebe & Undercoffer (2016)
Water case	Language	About 60% of Americans and 50% of British	Machery et al. (ms)
Fake-barn case	Epistemology	Mean answer ascribes knowledge	Colaço et al. (2014); Horvath & Wiegmann (2016)
Truetemp	Epistemology	Between about 45% and 70%	Wright (2010); Seyedsayamdost (2015a)
Zebra	Epistemology	About 70%	Seyedsayamdost (2015a)
Switch	Ethics	About 60% in Russia and Italy and 50% in China	Ahlenius & Tännsjö (2012); Geipel et al. (2015)
Footbridge	Ethics	About 70% in Brazil, 40% in Tibet, and 70% among American Christian Ministers	Hauser et al. (2007); Xiang (2014)
Loop	Ethics	About 60%	Ahlenius & Tännsjö (2012)

likely to result from the disturbing characteristics discussed in Chapter 3. These characteristics are found in many philosophical cases and are likely to be found in cases that would be used to assess some of the modal consequences of philosophical theories and to distinguish theories that agree about everyday situations.

We may wonder how widely we should generalize. There are two main possibilities. First, people may disagree about the situations described by philosophical cases *and* about everyday situations that elicit the application of concepts of philosophical interest (e.g., the concepts of justification, responsibility, permissibility, justice, desert, reference, or identity). For instance, if people have different views about desert (remember that we are assuming here that people do *not* mean different things by "desert" and its standard translations[5])—say, some may have some consequentialist view, while others have some deontological view—then they will disagree about many (though not all) situations calling for a judgment about desert. It may well be that views about at least some, perhaps even many, topics of philosophical interest vary across cultures, gender, and other demographic variables; they may also vary in a more haphazard manner. The breadth of this disagreement would justify a much more radical skepticism than

[5] It is of course difficult to draw a line between having different views about, say, desert while meaning the same thing by "desert" and meaning different things by "desert." Fortunately, I can bracket this difficulty here: Philosophers who draw the line differently will simply apply Dogmatism and Parochialism to different sets of cases.

the one defended in the book. One may then be inclined to doubt that we are any good at identifying causes, responsibility, permissibility, in contrast to what I have assumed earlier. Alternatively, it may be that people do actually agree about everyday situations eliciting the application of concepts of philosophical interest, but that there is something about philosophical cases that breeds disagreement. The discussion of the disturbing characteristics of philosophical cases in Chapter 3 explains how this could happen. Being vivid, emotionally laden, unusual, and pulling apart typically co-occurring properties, philosophical cases compel the reader to appeal to ad hoc strategies for making a judgment, and those may well vary across demographic groups or perhaps across people in a more haphazard manner. I will assume that this second possibility is correct. This assumption is in line with the argument of Chapter 3— people are usually reliable at identifying knowledge, causation, or responsibility, but philosophical cases are beyond the proper domains of their capacities—and it is consistent with existing evidence: People respond to usual, typical cases (e.g., of knowledge and of ignorance) similarly.

4.1.2 Lay people and philosophers are epistemic peers

It is not entirely uncontroversial how to characterize epistemic peers.[6] Here I will follow the usual characterization, but nothing hangs on it: x is an epistemic peer of y with respect to a particular claim if and only if x has the same amount of evidence y has, has considered it as carefully as y has, is as intelligent as y, and is immune to the reasoning biases y is immune to.[7] Of course, x—the person y counts as her epistemic peer—may actually be influenced by reasoning biases that do not influence y; she may actually have less evidence than she seems to have; or she may not have considered it as carefully as y has: In this case, y is wrong to count x as an epistemic peer. Importantly, epistemic peerness is always relative to some topic—x and y can be epistemic peers relative to one topic, but not to other topics.

Philosophers will object that, with respect to the questions raised by philosophical cases (e.g., Does the man in the Chinese room understand Chinese? Does the Chinese room understand Chinese? Is the nation of China conscious?), non-philosophers cannot be considered to be their epistemic peers. First, philosophers are better than non-philosophers at understanding what is at stake in a given case and at ignoring the irrelevant details; second, philosophers' knowledge about the issues at hand makes their judgments more reliable. This objection is important, and the success of Dogmatism hangs on rebutting it, but I will postpone examining it until Section 5.3 of Chapter 5, where it will be discussed under the heading "The Expertise Defense." For the time being, I will simply assume that non-philosophers and philosophers are epistemic peers with respect to the questions raised by philosophical cases (and in this respect only).

---

[6] E.g., Elga (2007, 499, n. 21); Sosa (2010); Worsnip (2014, 2).
[7] E.g., Kelly (2005); Christensen (2009).

Other philosophers will challenge the appeal to the literature on peer disagreement on the grounds that the notion of epistemic peer describes a situation that is so idealized that it never occurs in the actual world: The epistemological literature on disagreement among peers idly theorizes about a philosophical fiction. There is no doubt that epistemic peerness is an idealization, but in itself its idealized nature does not undermine this notion any more than the idealized nature of scientific models undermines them. The notion of epistemic peerness would be undermined if no actual situation came close enough to epistemic peerness for this notion to be useful, but the antecedent of this conditional is just false. We often found ourselves in situations that closely approximate epistemic peerness. Indeed, how else can we explain our surprise at finding intelligent people of good will coming to a conclusion different from ours? Of course, for self-serving reasons we often conclude that these intelligent people of good will turn out to be biased or perhaps not so intelligent, but when we keep such self-serving bias in check, we recognize that people equally intelligent, with the same information, can come to different conclusions.

4.1.3 Suspending judgment is the proper response to disagreement about philosophical cases

The central question in the epistemological literature on disagreement is, When two epistemic peers disagree about a given proposition (e.g., the proposition that death penalty reduces recidivism), should their confidence in their judgment always decrease or instead is it, at least sometimes, rationally permissible to remain as confident? Opinions range from Elga's (2007) Equal-Weight View, according to which each epistemic peer should give equal weight to the disagreeing party's and to her own opinion and, thus, judge that she is equally likely to be right than wrong (an extreme "conciliationist" view), to "steadfast" views, which sometimes permit one of the disagreeing parties to downgrade their opponent on the sole basis of the controversial proposition and its supporting considerations.[8]

   Fortunately, I need not take a stance on the general issue in the intricate and sprawling literature on disagreement; I merely need to show that, when it comes to disagreements elicited by philosophical cases (e.g., a Frankfurt case that elicits contradictory judgments from two parties), such disagreements do not entitle peers to downgrade their opponent, and thus should lead them to suspend judgment. This claim, I argue, follows from the leading views in the epistemological literature on disagreement. While some other views about disagreement may lead to another conclusion, if one accepts any of these leading views, one should concede Premise 4 of Dogmatism.

   According to Elga's Equal-Weight view, one could only be justified in downgrading a disagreeing party if by forming a judgment about the controversial proposition

---

[8] For conciliationist views, see e.g. Feldman (2006); Christensen (2007). For steadfast views, see e.g. Kelly (2005, 2010); Sosa (2010).

(e.g., that the death penalty reduces recidivism) one also learned that one is better than this disagreeing party at judging about it, but it is, in Elga's words (2007, 487), "absurd" that by coming to judge that *p* one could also learn how good one is at judging that *p* (to say nothing about learning that one is better than someone else). So, Premise 4 holds if the Equal-Weight view is correct, and, in spite of their consensus, philosophers should then suspend their judgment about the situations described by the relevant philosophical cases.

The Equal-Weight View is the most extreme conciliationist view, and conciliationists could merely require a decrease in one's confidence in the face of peer disagreement.[9] Proponents of the method of cases could welcome this form of conciliationism since it would allow them to acknowledge disagreement without suspending judgment. However, if the number of people disagreeing influences how much one's confidence should decrease, as is plausible, the massive amount of disagreement found by experimental philosophers should result in much lower confidence in the judgments elicited by philosophical cases (see the discussion of Kelly's steadfast view below).

But what about steadfast views? Most steadfast views agree that sometimes suspending judgment is the proper response to a disagreement between epistemic peers, but in contrast to conciliationist views like the Equal-Weight View they assert that it is not always the proper response, and that sometimes one is justified to hold one's ground and to downgrade a disagreeing party, even on the sole basis of the controversial proposition and of the considerations supporting it. So, to support Premise 4 of Dogmatism, we need to find out whether the conditions for holding one's ground are met in the case of disagreement elicited by philosophical cases. We will see that the answer is no.

Sosa (2010) describes three conditions that would justify downgrading a disagreeing party—that is, coming to the conclusion that she is after all not an epistemic peer—on the sole basis of the controversial proposition and of the considerations supporting it. First, the truthmakers of some propositions may be experientially or rationally given (Sosa, 2010, 286–7). Sosa gives the example of a first-person judgment about pain—where the judger's experience is the truthmaker of the controversial proposition— and of obvious mathematical (a triangle has three angles) or logical truths—where, according to Sosa, the truthmakers are given to us when we grasp these truths. He writes (2010, 287):

Other examples of the same epistemic phenomenon will be found in any case of the given, whether it is the phenomenal given, such as our headache, or the rational given, such as the simplest truths of arithmetic, geometry, or logic. Here again if someone denies what you affirm, you can uphold your side by appealing to the very fact affirmed. Thus, if someone claims 2 and 2 not to equal 4, or a triangle not to have three sides, we could reasonably insist on what we know. We could try to disabuse him, while downgrading his conflicting judgment. Something must be misleading him, even if we can't see what that is.

---

[9] As suggested by Christensen (2009, 759); see also, e.g., Worsnip (2014).

This first condition can safely be ignored here for two reasons. When this condition is met, the disagreement does not really occur between epistemic peers and the two disagreeing parties cannot view each other as having access to the same evidence. In addition, as Sosa himself acknowledges, very few, if any, disagreements are about this kind of situation. In particular, as argued in Chapter 1, the judgments elicited by philosophical cases are not justified (or count as knowledge) by merely grasping the propositions they express, and their truthmakers are not introspectively accessible either.

Second, Sosa notes that, in contrast to the toy examples considered by conciliationists (e.g., the addition case in Christensen, 2007), in many cases of disagreement the evidence or considerations that are pertinent for the subject matter of disagreement are not neatly packaged and cannot be detailed; rather, one's judgment is based on a host of inscrutable reasons: "We have reasons…that, acting in concert, across time, have motivated our present beliefs, but we are in no position to detail these reasons fully" (Sosa, 2010, 292). In Christensen's addition case, two parties add some numbers and, unexpectedly, end up with a different sum. In this case, the relevant considerations boil down to the numbers to be added: They are circumscribed and can be detailed. It is also natural to assume that the disagreeing parties are equally good at adding. In contrast, if two childhood friends disagree about the name of their high-school math teacher (one of Sosa's examples), the pertinent considerations are diffuse and cannot be easily detailed.

Just like the first condition, this second condition—inscrutable reasons—does not seem to be a case where genuine epistemic peers justifiably downgrade their opponents. Rather, it is a case where two disagreeing parties should not count one another as epistemic peers because they should be skeptical that they have access to the same evidence. In any case, bracketing this issue, this second condition does not apply to the disagreements elicited by philosophical cases, and thus does not justify rejecting Premise 4 of Dogmatism, since disagreements about philosophical cases are in an important respect similar to Christensen's addition case. Most of the considerations germane to judgments elicited by philosophical cases are neatly packaged in the case itself and they can be detailed: By putting forward a case, philosophers stipulate that some facts hold in some situations and wonder whether, in light of these facts, some further facts hold.

Of course, philosophical cases can no more stipulate all the relevant facts than novels can make explicit all the facts holding in the worlds they describe: The content of a case is in part implied (Section 1.1 of Chapter 1). The reader of a philosophical case just like the reader of a novel must assume that many facts hold in the situation described despite not being explicitly described. And few of these facts are explicitly entertained; rather, most are part of the implicit, background assumptions that render the story meaningful. But while they are not explicitly entertained, they are not inscrutable either. We can make explicit every fact that we deem germane to the judgment about the situation described by the case: After all, they are all stipulated facts. Similarly, two people who disagree about the personality of the main protagonist of a novel have equal access to the facts explicitly stipulated by the novelist, and while they may initially interpret differently the relevant facts about the protagonist that the novelist left implicit, they may by discussion come to agree about those too; they may make the same stipulations.

Finally, when a party double-checks her judgment—for example, when one of the disagreeing parties in Christensen's addition case double-checks her addition—she puts herself in a better epistemic situation than her opponent; she can thus downgrade her opponent epistemically and hold her ground. Sosa explains (2010, 293),

The more important difference imported by repeated re-checking is not so much that one is now sure of one's procedure and of its high reliability. The more important difference is rather that one now fails to be sure independently that the opponent's relevant reliability is a match for one's own. So, the important difference is that one no longer has sufficient independent basis for judging the two opponents to be peers on the question at hand.

When it comes to disagreements elicited by philosophical cases, this third condition for holding one's ground can also be ignored. In contrast to the addition case, there is often no procedure, and a fortiori no algorithm, to check: We often do not know how we judge in response to cases. Checking in this situation really amounts to nothing more than rereading the philosophical case, and making sure that one has not ignored some elements described in the case. So, if one can antecedently assume that the disagreeing party has read the philosophical case carefully, even when one rereads a case carefully and repeatedly, double-checking gives little reason to doubt that "the opponent's relevant reliability is a match for one's own." Were it not the case, Sosa's third condition, when applied to disagreements elicited by philosophical cases, would give us an unacceptably easy strategy for dismissing inconsistent judgments: Just reread the case! Twice if rereading it once was not enough!

I now turn to Kelly's Total-Evidence View. On this view, whether one should hold one's ground depends on whether, when one adds to one's evidence the fact that an epistemic peer disagrees with one's judgment, one's total evidence still supports the original claim (Kelly, 2010).[10] If it does not, then one should suspend judgment; if it does, then one can hold one's ground, although one must decrease one's confidence somewhat, perhaps marginally, since a new piece of evidence—the existence of a disagreement—has come to light. So, the Total-Evidence View concedes that sometimes one ought to suspend judgment, although, in contrast to conciliationist views such as the Equal-Weight View, it insists that this is not always required. For our purposes, the question is, again, How to address disagreements elicited by philosophical cases? It is not easy to use the Total-Evidence View to determine what should be done categorically in any particular circumstance (in contrast to hypothetically: if your total evidence is so and so, then you ought to do this or that), since it says nothing about what evidence really is and about how to balance one's antecedent evidence with the

---

[10] In contrast to Kelly (2010), Kelly (2005) seems to hold that the body of evidence one has before the disagreement should determine one's reaction to disagreement. This view is sometimes called "the right-reasons view."

fact that an epistemic peer disagrees with one's opinion. It is tempting to dismiss The Total-Evidence View on this ground, but this kind of concern with the Total-Evidence View is better left for another venue.

Be it as it may, the Total-Evidence View also supports Premise 4 of Dogmatism (although one must remain tentative in light of the vagueness of its implications for particular instances of disagreement). First, people disagreeing about a particular case have little evidence for their judgment: It boils down to the facts specified by the case and perhaps a few conscious principles people appeal to in reasoning to decide whether, e.g., the agent knows a particular proposition, whether an action is morally permissible, or what a proper name refers to. Thus, when philosophers add the fact that others disagree with them about the situation described by a particular case, it is unlikely that they have a large body of evidence that decisively supports their antecedent opinion. If that is so, then, according to the Total-Evidence View itself, philosophers ought to suspend judgment when considering philosophical cases. It would not do to respond that a philosopher can appeal to her views about, e.g., knowledge or moral permissibility as evidence for her judgment, which her non-philosophical opponent could not do, for these views themselves are supposed to rely on the facts assumed to hold in the cases. Appealing to these theories would thus be circular.

Second, experimental-philosophy studies show that many people—hundreds of millions if their samples are representative—would often disagree with the judgments made by philosophers. Disagreements elicited by philosophical cases are simply not comparable to situations where a maverick philosopher disagrees with her colleagues or to situations where one discovers that one's views are inconsistent with the views stated by some important philosopher; rather, they should be compared to situations where millions of people, who prima facie know as much as we do, disagree with us. That many people disagree with philosophers about the situations described by philosophical cases should be added to my antecedent body of evidence on the Total-Evidence View, further undermining the suggestion that philosophers may have a large body of evidence supporting decisively their opinion. In this case, as Kelly himself acknowledges (2010, 144), the Total-Evidence View recommends suspending judgment.

It may be tempting to respond that experimental philosophers' own research undermines this last point because it shows that at least sometimes the disagreeing judgments are not independent of one another: For instance, many people in East Asia disagree with philosophers about the Gödel case because of their common cultural background. This response won't do, however, because, if I do not treat the disagreeing judgments as independent on such grounds, I should also add to my total body of evidence the fact that my own judgments are influenced by specific demographic variables (culture, etc.), and adding this proposition seems likely to prevent my total body of evidence from supporting the claim I was originally making. It is also tempting to respond that, while millions of people may disagree with philosophers' consensual judgment, the same experimental-philosophy studies also show that millions do agree with it! I doubt this response helps much the proponent of the method of cases: That there is massive disagreement about philosophical cases is the kind of fact that, added to my antecedent body of evidence, would prevent the resulting total body of evidence from clearly supporting my controversial claim; it thus is the kind of fact that, even if the Total-Evidence View is correct, should lead me to suspend judgment.

To wrap up, the leading views about the proper reaction to disagreement—from the extreme conciliationist view embodied by the Equal-Weight View to influential steadfast views—lead to the same conclusion: Premise 4 of Dogmatism is plausible. At least, when it comes to disagreements elicited by philosophical cases (different people having different opinions about the situations described by these cases), we ought to suspend judgment.

4.1.4 The objection from different understandings

One may respond to Dogmatism by arguing that I have mislocalized the source of the disagreement among lay people. True, as Dogmatism assumes, people who disagree in response to cases mean the same thing by "knowledge," "cause," "permissible," or "responsible." But the disagreement can often, if not always, be traced to a different understanding of the situations described by the cases: In effect, people who disagree are not responding to the same situation.[11] Sosa (2009, 107–8) proposes that participants in Weinberg et al.'s famous (2001) study do "not after all disagree about the very same content." If this is the right diagnosis, the epistemology of peer disagreement does not matter for understanding the implications of the diversity found by experimental philosophers.

I have already addressed related concerns in Section 2.6.7 of Chapter 2 (while discussing order effects and Jeffrey-conditionalization). As noted, many of the pertinent facts are stipulated, which leaves little room for uncertainty or variation in how the situation described by a case is understood. Context also constrains some of the propositions that are inferred—again leaving little room for uncertainty or variation—but admittedly readers may well understand differently *other* inferred propositions, particularly for unusual cases (Section 3.5.3 of Chapter 3). But this response only saves the method of cases from Charybdis to throw it in the path of Scylla: If the situations described by cases can really be understood differently, then the method of cases becomes suspicious, since philosophers themselves may not be responding to the same set of propositions (Alexander & Weinberg, 2007). Horvath (2015, 411) responds to this line of argument that it "certainly overdramatizes the problem": People who share many characteristics in common (training, background knowledge, etc.), as philosophers do, are likely to understand the situation described by a case similarly.

---

[11] Sosa (2009); Horvath (2015).

However, disagreement in response to cases is not only found between people who belong to very different cultures, as Horvath seems to assume, but between people who are similar in many respects.

4.1.5 A second objection: Condorcet's Theorem

A number of philosophers have appealed to the Condorcet Jury Theorem to address the disagreements elicited by philosophical cases (e.g., Goldman, 2010; Talbot, 2014). The Condorcet Jury Theorem describes the probability that a group will reach the correct decision. Its original formulation shows that if the jury's members are more likely to be right than wrong, then the larger the jury the more likely it is that the majority opinion is right and that, as the number of jury members increases to infinity, the probability that the majority opinion is correct increases to one. The significance of the original formulation of the Condorcet Jury Theorem is severely limited by two assumptions about the jury's members. The jury must be homogeneous—each jury member has the same probability of making a correct decision (the competence assumption)—and decisions must be probabilistically independent conditional on the state of the world (the independence assumption). The original Condorcet Jury Theorem has little to say about disagreement elicited by philosophical cases since the independence assumption is clearly violated (Talbot, 2014; Palmira, 2015).

More recent versions of the theorem have relaxed the original competence and independence assumptions, replacing the identical probability that a jury member makes the correct decision with the average probability and examining the influence of various dependencies on the probability that the majority opinion is correct (e.g., Dietrich & Spiekermann, 2013a, b). These dependencies include sharing a common body of evidence and being influenced by common causes (opinion leader, culture, ways of framing problems, etc.).

In some of the reformulations of the Condorcet Jury Theorem, probabilistic independence conditional on the state of the world is replaced with probabilistic independence conditional on the state of the world and common causes. To derive the Condorcet Jury Theorem, one must also redefine the competence assumption (for explanation, see Dietrich & Spiekermann, 2013b, 99–100). If the probability that jury members make the right decision in easy circumstances is p ($p > \frac{1}{2}$) and the probability that they make the right decision in difficult circumstances is $1-p$ ("the symmetric characterization of competence"), then the probability that the majority group makes the right decision increases to the probability of encountering an easy decision as the number of jury members increases if the probability of encountering an easy decision is larger than the probability of encountering a difficult decision; it decreases to the probability of encountering an easy decision if the probability of encountering a difficult decision is larger than the probability of encountering an easy decision; and it is $\frac{1}{2}$ if the probability of encountering a difficult decision is equal to the probability of encountering a difficult decision. If the probability that jury members make the right decision in easy circumstances is p ($p > \frac{1}{2}$) and the probability that they make the right decision in difficult circumstances is q ($q < \frac{1}{2}$ and $q \neq 1-p$) ("the asymmetric characterization of competence"), then the probability that the majority group makes the right decision may decrease as jury size increases even if the probability of encountering an easy decision is larger than the probability of encountering a difficult decision (Dietrich & Spiekermann, 2013a, b).

The relaxations of the independence assumption provide no ammunition for a proponent of the use of cases in philosophy. If the symmetric characterization of competence holds, then the probability that the majority opinion is correct decreases as jury size increases because judging about the situations described by philosophical cases is likely to be a difficult task. If the asymmetric characterization of competence holds, this probability may decrease whether or not such judgment is difficult.

4.1.6 Conclusion

Many (though not all) philosophical cases elicit as close a consensus as there can be in philosophy about which facts hold in the situations they describe, and this consensus may have prevented philosophers from grasping the extent to which these very cases elicit disagreement among non-philosophers. But, assuming that philosophers and non-philosophers don't speak at cross purposes, it is reasonable to hold on the basis of the evidence provided by psychologists and experimental philosophers that most philosophical cases elicit a massive disagreement outside philosophy: Millions of non-philosophers would disagree with the consensual judgments if they were asked. These people are philosophers' epistemic peers when it comes to judging about the situations described by philosophical cases. (This claim was simply assumed here, but it will be defended at greater length in the next chapter.) While epistemologists have not come to any consensus about the proper response to disagreement among peers, the leading views support the claim that, when philosophical cases elicit disagreement among epistemic peers, they ought to suspend judgment. Thus, philosophers ought to suspend judgment about the situations described by most philosophical cases, and they cannot assume that particular facts hold in these situations.

Some cases that have been central to philosophical debate remain unscathed by this argument since they do not elicit any disagreement. As we have seen in Chapter 2, there is widespread consensus about some versions of the Gettier case and a few others. Dogmatism does not require philosophers to suspend judgment about these cases, although Unreliability may well require it. (For instance, remember that it is easy to frame judgments elicited by the Gettier case (Machery et al., forthcoming b).) That said, the scope of Dogmatism is wide: Few philosophical cases are known to elicit consensus. It is time for philosophers to acknowledge that people all over the world are likely to react differently to the cases eliciting a near consensus in philosophy. Furthermore, if the disturbing characteristics really breed disagreement, disagreement is likely to creep in whenever philosophers investigate the modal consequences of philosophical theories and assess competing philosophical theories that agree about usual situations. Chapter 6 will investigate the consequence of this conclusion.

4.2 Parochialism

4.2.1 The argument

Just like Dogmatism, Parochialism takes as its starting point experimental philosophers' findings that people give different answers about many philosophical cases that are consensual within philosophy. In contrast to Dogmatism, however, Parochialism does not conclude from this diversity of answers that the parties disagree, i.e., have different opinions about the same subject matter. Rather, it concludes that the parties are talking about different things—or, as I will say, that "people are talking at cross purposes"—and are thus not disagreeing.[12] So, when a party says that it is permissible to push the large person in the footbridge case and another says that it is not permissible, Parochialism assumes that despite using the same word—"permissible"—or despite using a word and a standard translation—e.g., "permissible" and "permis"—people are talking about two distinct normative properties, e.g., *permissibility* and *permissibility**. Of course, not all apparent disagreements can be understood as resulting from people talking at cross purposes, but the disagreements at stake here, some philosophers may hold, bear on propositions that are constitutive of the meaning of the relevant terms ("causation," "knowledge," etc.), if any are.[13] So, if people disagree about those propositions and are not confused, they can't mean the same thing by the pertinent words, and they don't really disagree. If people do not disagree, then the epistemological concerns raised by the disagreements among readers of cases become otiose. However, there is another problem for the method of cases in the offing: In a nutshell, why should we care about what *we* are talking about in contrast to what *they* are talking about? Why should we care whether it is *permissible* to push the large man rather than *permissible** to push him? If we care about what we are talking about only because *we* are talking about it, then the use of cases to settle material-mode controversies smacks of parochialism. But what other reason could we have? This is the gist of Parochialism. The argument can be presented as follows:

Parochialism

1. When people respond differently to the philosophical cases examined by experimental philosophers, it is because they refer to different (epistemic, moral, etc.) properties.

---

[12] Goldman (2007); Sosa (2007, 2009); Jackson (2011). For a different response to Sosa's and others' claim, see Horvath (2010).

[13] The existence of verbal disagreements does not require the validity of the analytic/synthetic distinction. Even if one rejects metaphysical and epistemological analyticity, as I did in Chapter 1, two speakers may still be talking about something different, and there is thus room for verbal disagreements (see Chalmers, 2011 for the same conclusion).

2.   If people refer to different (epistemic, moral, etc.) properties when they respond differently to the philosophical cases examined by experimental philosophers, they would plausibly do so in response to most philosophical cases.

3.   Philosophers are not justified in believing that theorizing about the (epistemic, moral, etc.) properties they refer to will allow them to achieve their philosophical goals.

4.   You ought not to decide to φ in order to ψ if you believe you are not justified to believe that φ-ing is likely to bring about ψ.

5.   Hence, philosophers ought to focus on determining whether theorizing about the (epistemic, moral, etc.) properties they refer to or about the (epistemic, moral, etc.) properties others refer to will allow them to reach their philosophical goals, stopping for the time being their theorizing about the (epistemic, moral, etc.) properties they refer to.

6.   Hence, for the time being, philosophers should not appeal to the method of cases.

Parochialism is very different from both Unreliability and Disagreement. It does not attempt to show that philosophers are not justified in judging about the situations described by philosophical cases. For all it shows, philosophers may well be reliable at deciding whether permissibility, justification, responsibility, and causation are instantiated in the situations described by philosophical cases. So, Parochialism does not conclude that philosophers ought to suspend judgment in response to these cases. Rather, it attempts to show that, *if* people really refer to different properties when using "permissible," "justified," "responsible," and "cause" (or their standard translations in other languages), then philosophers should reorient their research interests: For the time being, they should stop theorizing about the actual objects of their judgments (e.g., permissibility, justification, responsibility, and causation) and focus instead on determining whether theorizing about permissibility, justification, responsibility, and causation or about permissibility*, justification*, responsibility*, and causation* will allow them to meet their philosophical goals. So, for the time being, the method of cases should be shelved.

Some philosophers have expressed ideas related to Parochialism. Of note is a remark made by Weinberg et al. about a possible interpretation of the results of their influential experimental-philosophy study (2001, 451, italics in the original): "What our studies point to…is more than just divergent epistemic intuitions across groups; the studies point to divergent epistemic *concerns.*" Nichols (2004, 514) also refers to parochialism, but does not elaborate.

The bite of Parochialism is easy to feel when one considers Jackson's discussion of the free-will debate. Jackson writes (1998, 31, italics in the original):

What…are the interesting philosophical questions that we are seeking to address when we debate the existence of free action and its compatibility with determinism…? What we are seeking to address is whether free action *according to our ordinary conception,* or something suitably close to our ordinary conception, exists…

But what if, when they talk about free will, Westerners, or English speakers, or Australians, or Australian philosophers talk about something different from what Easterners, French speakers, or New Zealanders talk about when *they* talk about free will? Why should we care about Westerners', or English speakers', or Australians', or Australian philosophers' free will rather than Easterners', French speakers', or New Zealanders' free will*?

4.2.2 *The inductive basis and the inductive step of Parochialism*

The discussion of Premises 1 and 2 can be quick since it largely overlaps with the points made in Section 4.1 of this chapter. Even when philosophers agree about particular philosophical cases (e.g., the switch case or the Gödel case), many non-philosophers often (though not always) express different answers (a diversity that is only partly predicted by demographic variables). These non-philosophers either disagree with philosophers or they talk at cross purposes with them. Section 4.1 examined the implications of the former interpretation of the diversity found by experimental philosophers. In this section, I assume instead that the philosophical cases examined by experimental philosophers elicit different answers because people talk at cross purposes. People can talk at cross purposes for a variety of reasons. First, and most obviously, despite using the same words ("justified," "permissible," or "free") or despite using standard translations of the words used by English-speaking philosophers (in French "justifié," "permis," or "libre"), when non-philosophers offer non-standard answers, they may mean something different from philosophers (and those non-philosophers who agree with them) (Sosa, 2007; Jackson, 2011). The words may be ambiguous (as "bank" is) or, perhaps more likely, simply polysemous (as "book" is). A word is ambiguous if its different senses have nothing to do with one another, polysemous if they do. Either way, because people mean something different despite using the same word, they are plausibly talking about different things, since it is unlikely that these different senses are different modes of presentation of the same property. Second, it may be that the relevant words refer to different properties despite having the same meaning because they have a (perhaps hidden) indexical nature or because they are used in a relativist manner. Either way, when people seem to disagree about the philosophical cases experimental philosophers have examined, they are really talking about different things.

Of course, as I noted in Section 4.1, experimental philosophers have examined only some philosophical cases, and some of those cases elicit the same reaction from nearly everybody. What are our grounds for going beyond the cases that have been examined? The induction here seems straightforward. If different people don't mean the same thing by "knowledge" when they express a judgment in response to a Truetemp case, they probably don't mean the same thing in everyday circumstances when they use that word either. And people will bring their interpretation of "knowledge" to the philosophical cases not examined by experimental philosophers, including those that are yet to be written.

4.2.3 Philosophers' unjustified preference for the philosophically familiar

Let's assume for the sake of argument that people refer to different properties when they judge about the situations described by philosophical cases. (But keep in mind that one is committed to that claim only if one denies that people who respond differently to philosophical cases genuinely disagree.) Philosophers presumably refer to the same properties: reference, permissibility, responsibility, desert, justice, or knowledge—what I will call "the philosophically familiar." Others refer to reference*, permissibility*, responsibility*, desert*, justice*, or knowledge*—what I will call "the philosophically unfamiliar" (Flikschuh, 2014). Philosophers use their judgments about the instantiation of reference, permissibility, responsibility, desert, justice, or knowledge in the situations described by philosophical cases to theorize about the philosophically familiar. They unwittingly disregard the properties the judgments of those non-philosophers who seem to disagree with them (e.g., people who say that "Gödel" refers to the man originally called "Schmidt") are about, failing to theorize about those. In fact, they focus *all* their energy on theorizing about the philosophically familiar, and *none* on theorizing about the philosophically unfamiliar.

But are philosophers justified to theorize about the philosophically familiar? For example, are epistemologists justified to theorize about knowledge and justification? If they are, it cannot be because our colleagues or even the great philosophers of the past have been writing about the former (supposing that the latter were in fact talking about what we (whoever that "we" refers to) are talking about, which is debatable). That would doom epistemology to triviality. (What if our colleagues were interested in table manners?) No, it must be because knowledge and justification are connected with truth (having true beliefs and drawing valid inferences) or with the practice of holding oneself and others accountable for assertions. Similarly, are moral philosophers justified to theorize about permissibility, responsibility, and justice? Again, if they are, it cannot be because our colleagues or the great philosophers of the past have been writing about them. Rather, it must be because they are connected to an incredibly thorny issue that people are bound to face: How to live together? Generally, the topics of interest in philosophy are often connected to broader, vaguer issues that lay people, scientists, or artists themselves face. Philosophers sharpen these issues (draw distinctions, etc.), develop theories to address these sharpened issues, and develop arguments to defend those theories. I will call these broader, vaguer issues "fundamental philosophical questions."

Now, are philosophers justified to believe that theorizing about the philosophical familiar is a good way to address the fundamental philosophical questions? The argument for a negative answer goes as follows. Until the philosophically unfamiliar was made salient, we had a defeasible reason to believe it was a good way to address the fundamental philosophical questions: It was after all the only serious game in town. However, now that the philosophically unfamiliar has been made salient, it has become a relevant alternative, and while they both could be good ways to address these questions (exactly as there may be several incompatible, but equally good answers to the question, How to live?), it may also be that only one of them is a good way to address these fundamental philosophical questions. So, until we have been able to either show that the philosophically unfamiliar is an inferior approach to the fundamental questions or that both the philosophically familiar and the philosophically unfamiliar are good ways to address them, we are not justified in believing that the former is a good approach to the fundamental philosophical questions.

Three reasons make the philosophically unfamiliar a relevant alternative to the philosophically familiar. First, it isn't obvious that the best way to cast light on these questions is to theorize about reference, permissibility, and knowledge; theorizing about reference*, permissibility*, responsibility*, desert*, justice*, or knowledge* could be much more enlightening. Arguments are needed. Next, most philosophers in Western academic philosophy are not in a position to argue for the greater worth of the philosophically familiar given that they have so little acquaintance with the philosophically unfamiliar. Finally, it is unlikely that among all the actual and possible intellectual traditions, Western academic philosophers' philosophical tradition happens to have stumbled upon the best way to address fundamental philosophical questions. Contemporary Western philosophers sometimes hold that their interests— e.g., in skepticism—are grounded in universal interests, but this is very often debatable. For instance, it has been argued that nothing similar to idealism and the skepticism about the external world is found in ancient philosophy (e.g., Burnyeat, 1982), that nothing similar to Western skepticism is found in some traditions of Chinese philosophy (e.g., Hansen, 1981), that there is no analysis of knowledge in terms of justification in much of Western philosophical history (Antognazza, 2015; Dutant, 2015), and that contemporary and traditional epistemologists do no theorize about the same things (Pasnau, 2013). If anything, we should hold that the contingent interests of contemporary Western philosophers are unlikely to be the best way to address such questions. Leaving room for the philosophically unfamiliar in the seminar room and making sure that Western academic philosophers' voices do not dominate other philosophical voices may be the best strategy for getting it right in philosophy.

One may respond that philosophers have spent centuries thinking about the philosophical familiar, and that the depth and sophistication of philosophical theorizing give us a defeasible reason to assume that philosophers have identified the right properties to address the fundamental philosophical questions: After all, philosophers would have found out if it was a dead-end to theorize about those. But, first, it is far from certain that in the long history of Western philosophy philosophers have always been theorizing about the same things. For example, modern moral philosophers may not theorize about what ancient philosophers were theorizing about (Anscombe, 1958; Williams, 1985). To say nothing of non-Western philosophical traditions, which also have a long history of sophisticated thinking. Second, sophistication and length do not guarantee that philosophers are on the right track at all: Ptolemaic astronomy too (to say nothing of astrology or ESP research) had a long history and became very sophisticated.

Philosophers might also think that they are entitled to theorize about reference, permissibility, or justice rather than about reference*, permissibility*, or justice* because the former are what *their* judgments happen to be about. But this won't do. First, it is hard not to suspect that this response expresses some form of parochialism. To display parochialism is to behave as if or judge that what one values is more valuable than what others value, and to do so unjustifiably. One does not display any parochialism when one behaves as if or judges that what others value is as important as what one values or when one has good grounds for behaving as if or judging that what one values is more valuable than what others value. Parochialism differs from provincialism, which is simply a form of ignorance: One displays provincialism when ones ignores that others have contradictory beliefs or care about different things. Philosophers have no doubt suffered, and arguably still suffer, from provincialism, having ignored the cognitive diversity experimental philosophers have revealed, but provincialism is not the issue with this response. Parochialism is. Second, claiming that philosophizing about justice, knowledge, responsibility, or causation is worth doing just because *we* happen to refer to justice, knowledge, responsibility, or causation would trivialize philosophizing. Philosophizing is worth doing because what philosophers theorize about is worth theorizing about.

One may worry that Premise 3 overgeneralizes. Scientists are often confronted with competing research programs that develop incompatible accounts of the explananda, to say nothing of the merely possible accounts that happen to be unconceived often for contingent reasons (Stanford, 2010). Do scientists lack justification to believe that developing their accounts will lead them to the truth of the matter? Similarly, there are often alternative means we could have chosen to reach our goals (from goals as trivial as making a goulash or going from one part of the city to another, to lofty goals such as leading a happy life), to say nothing again of merely possible means that happen to be unconceived for contingent reasons. Do we lack justification to believe that the means we have chosen will bring about our goals? And if we answer these questions negatively, why would philosophers be unjustified to believe that theorizing about the philosophically familiar rather than the philosophically unfamiliar will allow them to achieve their philosophical goals?

In some circumstances, the alternative that becomes salient does not undermine the agent's justification for believing that the means will bring about her goal, just her justification to believe that it is the best way to bring about the goal. This is the case when the agent knows full well that her means will bring about her goal. The cook knows her recipe will result in a goulash because she has used it before, although she may not know it makes a better goulash than some alternative recipe; the pedestrian knows her route will bring her to her destination because she has taken the route before, although she may not know it is better than some alternative; the engineer knows her plans will bring about a steady bridge because they are based on well-confirmed laws of physics, although she may not know it is better than some alternative. So, of course, the cook, the pedestrian, and the engineer are justified in believing that the means chosen will bring about the desired goals. However, such situations are not comparable to that of philosophers, who do not know whether theorizing about the philosophically familiar will allow them to address the fundamental philosophical questions successfully.

Now, sometimes scientists do not know which of the competing approaches, if any, will lead to the fact of the matter. But if none of these scientific approaches is much more credible than the others, then we should draw exactly the same conclusion that we drew earlier for philosophers: Scientists are then not justified to believe that developing their preferred accounts will lead them to truth. And indeed this is the conclusion philosophers of science have often drawn (e.g., Van Fraassen, 1980): When the evidence underdetermines scientific theories, scientists should refrain from believing in them. The upshot is that the argument does generalize, but does not generalize too widely.

It would also be a mistake to challenge Premise 3 on the grounds that historical and sociological considerations are always going to play a role in shaping the topics of interest for an intellectual (scientific or philosophical) community. When there is no alternative, people are justified to play the only game in town. They can still be justified to believe that their intellectual interests will allow them to reach their goals when there are alternatives: Some alternatives (e.g., homeopathy as an alternative to drugs) can be undermined, and other alternatives may not undermine the belief that a means will bring about a goal, just the belief it is the best way to bring it about (a new route to a destination).

The concerns expressed by Parochialism are not new. Comparative philosophers, feminist philosophers, philosophers working in non-Anglo-Saxon countries ("the rest of the world"), and some historians of philosophy have often argued that non-Western philosophical traditions or more broadly, non-Western cultural traditions, past Western philosophers, female philosophers or, more generally, women, and non-Anglo Saxon philosophers can bring a different voice to philosophical discussion.[14] They address issues marginalized (when not outright ignored) in mainstream philosophy, but of possibly crucial importance to deal with fundamental philosophical questions. Ignoring their voices results in a distorted picture of the philosophical landscape. Philosophers do not realize how contingent on a particular historical, cultural, and social position their formulation of the fundamental philosophical questions and the answers they happen to consider are, and they ignore many of the options available to them when addressing these philosophical questions, limiting themselves to those few options that, for accidental reasons, happen to be deemed worth considering.

---

[14] E.g., Antognazza (2015); Burnyeat (1982); Gilligan (1982); Wiredu (1996); Gyekye (1997); Kupperman (1999); Metz (2007); Pasnau (2013); Wolters (2013).

Ethics provides a good example of the epistemic perils of ignoring other voices. Kupperman (2010, 11) explains the point clearly:

A major reason that Confucius should matter to Western ethical philosophers is that some of his concerns are markedly different from those most common in the West. A Western emphasis has been on major choices that are treated in a decontextualized way. Confucius' emphasis is on paths of life, so that context matters. Further, the nuances of personal relations get more attention than is common (with the exception of feminist ethics) in Western philosophy. What Confucius provides is a valuable aid in arriving at a more balanced sense of what ethics is concerned with.

For example, there has been little discussion of civility in the Western ethical tradition, but it may be an important phenomenon for whoever aims at addressing the question of how to live together. Ignoring civility may well lead to a distorted image of the ethical landscape.[15] Metz (2007) also notes that people from sub-Saharan countries tend to have "intuitions" (his terminology) about the normative status of some (but not all) actions that differ from Westerners'. In the political domain, consensus is prized, and majoritarianism is viewed as a deficient way of making political decisions; in relation to justice, sub-Saharan people are more likely to approve of taking goods from others in case of need, even without the latter's permission. To account for these differences, he proposes that sub-Saharan people tend to conceive of the normative status of actions distinctly, and he calls the concept applied in their judgments "UBUNTU." While Metz does not put the point this way, in line with Parochialism, one can view UBUNTU as referring to a property, *ubuntu*, that differs from rightness, but that is related to it. Ignoring *ubuntu* may well lead to a distorted image of the ethical landscape.

4.2.4 Justified belief and instrumental action

Premise 4 of Parochialism does not seem controversial. It is weaker than many widely accepted principles. For instance, it weaker than the principle that you ought not to decide to φ in order to ψ if you do not have a justified belief that φ-ing is likely to bring about ψ or that it is not rational for you to φ in order to ψ if you do not have a justified belief that φ-ing is likely to bring about ψ. Audi (1997, 71, emphasis in the original) embraces something like the latter principle when he writes that "if there is no justification for instrumental beliefs, then arguably there are no rational *instrumental* actions." These two stronger principles could perhaps be challenged: For it to be permissible to φ in order to ψ it may be sufficient that one believes that φ-ing is likely to bring about ψ. On this view, epistemic and practical rationality (or permissibility) are separated. But even somebody who would endorse this kind of view would agree that if one has a second-order belief about the lack of epistemic justification of one's first-order instrumental beliefs, one ought not to act in light of these instrumental beliefs. And this weaker principle is sufficient for establishing the conclusion of Parochialism: If philosophers

---

[15] For another example, see the discussion of ritual propriety in Sarkissian (2014).

accept premises 1 to 3, they come to believe that they are not justified in believing that theorizing about the philosophically familiar will allow them to reach their theoretical goals.

There are some counterexamples to Premise 4. If you are in a maze and must choose between turning right and left (or must prove a theorem by embracing one of two different strategies), it seems rational to choose either turn despite the fact that you believe not to be justified to believe that either will allow you to exit the maze. While this is a genuine counterexample to Premise 4, it does not undermine this premise when its scope is restricted. Admittedly, Premise 4 does not apply when we cannot come to know which option, if any, will allow us to bring about our goal and when we must make a choice. But philosophers are not in this position: They could compare and assess the prospects of the philosophically familiar and the philosophically unfamiliar to reach their philosophical goals.

4.2.5 *To achieve our philosophical goals, let's shelve the method of cases*

If, as some philosophers have argued, people who respond differently to philosophical cases really speak at cross purposes, then philosophers should redirect their intellectual effort toward finding out which of the epistemic properties, which of the moral properties, and so on, are really worth theorizing about—that is, which of them will allow them to answer the fundamental philosophical questions. The intellectually responsible thing to do, for epistemologists, is to determine whether to theorize about justification or justification* if their goal is to understand how to fix beliefs responsibly or rationally. This means that for the time being, philosophers should stop theorizing about the philosophically familiar. They have a lot of work on their plate: Philosophers have to find out about these concerns before being in a position to determine whether philosophers' narrow, contingent interests are better suited to address fundamental philosophical questions. And if philosophers stop theorizing about the philosophically familiar for the time being, then they will also shelve, for the time being (probably for a long time), the method of cases to settle material-mode issues.

Let be clear about the claim made here. The proposal is naturally not that philosophers should stop philosophizing; quite the contrary: If there is such a thing as reference*, permissibility*, or justice*, philosophers should focus much of their intellectual efforts to learn about them in order to assess whether studying them could allow them to reach their philosophical goals. Similarly, when the available evidence underdetermines competing scientific programs, it is not the case that scientists ought to stop doing science; rather, they should focus their intellectual efforts on comparing the competing programs and on testing the conflicting predictions instead of attempting to collect more evidence for their preferred models in blissful ignorance of whether or not this evidence is compatible with other models. And this is in fact exactly what scientists do.

One may wonder whether the method of cases could not be useful to compare and assess the philosophically familiar and the philosophically unfamiliar, but I doubt it, at least for the foreseeable future. What needs to be done, rather, is to learn what the philosophically unfamiliar could be: Anthropology and comparative philosophy, when the philosophically unfamiliar maps onto cultural differences, and linguistics may be more useful. And if the method of cases is to play a role, it is a much-revised, experimental version, purged of the disturbing cases, to be deployed to analyze the philosophically unfamiliar concepts such as REFERENCE*, PERMISSIBILITY*, or JUSTICE* (Chapter 7).

4.2.6 Upshot

Most philosophical cases elicit a consensus among philosophers, but experimental philosophers have shown that many non-philosophers answer differently in response to these cases. If philosophers and non-philosophers don't disagree when they give different answers in response to philosophical cases, then they make judgments about different properties. Our intellectual duty, as philosophers, is then to determine which of these properties we should really theorize about. As a byproduct of a reorientation of our philosophical interests, the method of cases will be shelved, at least for the time being.

Some philosophers, I am afraid, will dismiss the concerns captured by Parochialism as purely rhetorical, perhaps musing that theorizing about justice, fairness, permissibility, responsibility, or identity just *are* the right way to address fundamental philosophical questions, or that it is all well and good to be interested in justice*, fairness*, permissibility*, responsibility*, and identity*, but that it just isn't philosophy. A dogmatic response of this kind would be simply wrong. It embodies a sadly common exclusionary attitude toward what counts as philosophy, one that may contribute to turn scores of individuals away from it. As Solomon writes (2001, 101), "What was once a liberating concept [the concept of philosophy] has today become constricted, oppressive, and ethnocentric."

4.3 Conclusion

This chapter has presented a dilemma. Either the diverging answers elicited by philosophical cases even when those elicit a consensus in philosophy constitute a genuine disagreement or they result from people talking at cross purposes. If people genuinely disagree about philosophical cases, then according to the most influential views about peer disagreement philosophers should respond to this disagreement by suspending judgment. If people instead talk at cross purposes, then philosophers should reorient their philosophical interests, and stop theorizing about the philosophically familiar. Either way, except when cases are known to elicit a broad consensus outside philosophy, philosophers should shelve the method of cases. It does little more than lead us to build our philosophy upon our prejudices.

5

Eight Defenses of the Method of Cases

Amateur Psychology, Reflection, Expertise, Limited Influence, Fallibility, Reform, Mischaracterization, and Overgeneralization

> *The loquacious (or hot air) hypothesis.* Although knowledge beyond a bare minimum should not enhance forecasting accuracy, it should bestow on experts the cognitive reseources to generate more elaborate and convincing rationales for their forecasts. Thus, as expertise raises, confidence in forecasts should raise faster than the accuracy of forecasts, producing substantial overconfidence by the time we reach the highest rings of the expertise ladder.
>
> (Tetlock, 2005, 43)

Chapters 3 and 4 have developed arguments against the use of cases to settle material-mode philosophical debates. Most cases used over the last fifty years elicit unreliable judgments, and either they breed disagreement among epistemic peers or their use embodies a form of parochialism. Furthermore, cases that would be useful to examine some of the modal implications of philosophical theories and to distinguish philosophical views that agree about typical situations are likely to elicit unreliable judgments and to elicit divergent responses. It would seem reasonable to suspend judgment about the kind of case found throughout philosophy and to begin examining how philosophy must be transformed to accommodate this conclusion. However, the proponent of the method of cases is unlikely to concede defeat easily. In this chapter, I describe and rebut eight responses to Unreliability, Dogmatism, and Parochialism that this proponent might make.

5.1 The Amateur-Psychology Defense

5.1.1 *The defense*

It is tempting to challenge Unreliability, Dogmatism, and Parochialism by rejecting the inductive basis of these arguments. In this spirit, the Amateur-Psychology Defense asserts that experimental philosophers' studies are poor (e.g., Ludwig, 2007 and Lam, 2010 on Machery et al., 2004) and that, as a result, they fail to provide evidence that demographic and presentation variables influence the judgments elicited by the philosophical cases that have been examined (thereby undermining Unreliability) or that people genuinely provide different answers to the cases that elicit consensus among philosophers (thereby undermining Dogmatism and Parochialism). For instance, Ludwig writes (2007, 150):

This general point can be illustrated by attending to a problematic feature of the probes used in the surveys about proper names…which is how the question posed to the subjects is worded: "When John uses the name 'Gödel,' is he talking about…" For anyone at all familiar with work in the philosophy of language, it is immediately evident that the question does not clearly distinguish between two things: whom John intends to be talking about (or speaker's reference) and who the name John uses refers to, taken literally in the language he intends to be speaking (semantic reference). Experts may well negotiate this infelicity in the formulation of the question without much difficulty, but that is because they have some relevant expertise about hard-won distinctions developed in the field and will likely understand what is intended.

Williamson (2010) similarly called experimental philosophers "amateur experimentalists."[1]

Some problems are alleged to plague most studies conducted by experimental philosophers, while others are taken to be specific to particular studies. Among the former are, first and foremost, the methodological issues connected to the survey methodology—that is, with the use of short stories (cases) as stimuli and of assertions as dependent variables (e.g., Cullen, 2010; Scholl, ms). When they refer to experimental philosophers' "surveys," proponents of the Amateur-Psychology Defense occasionally intend to belittle experimental philosophers' methods, by suggesting some contrast between genuine experiments and mere surveys, but this is merely a symptom of their ignorance: Surveys are often used in genuine psychological experiments. In any case, the concern with survey methods takes two forms, which vary in their pessimism about the prospects of survey methodology to address the questions experimental philosophers are addressing (and psychological issues in general). Some seem to suggest that very little can be learned from surveys. Scholl (ms) writes that "X-phi as it is typically conducted almost never succeeds in practice—and is unlikely to succeed in principle—at…determining the nature of the processes that produce the relevant intuitions. The primary reason for this failure is that the methods that are almost-but-not-quite-universally used in this area—viz. 'survey methods'—are spectacularly ill-suited to this goal." A less pessimistic take on survey methodology is that it is fraught with difficulties, and that, while these may be tractable, experimental philosophers have not acknowledged them, and have therefore failed to address them. Cullen writes (2010, 275):

---

[1] See also Jackson (2011, 475); Woolfolk (2011, 2013).

Survey research, however, is fraught with difficulties. I review some of the relevant literature— particularly focusing on the conversational pragmatic aspects of survey research—and consider its application to common experimental philosophy surveys.

His main concern is that participants' answers to vignettes are influenced by numerous experimental details such as whether participants are asked to answer on a scale or to give a yes/no answer and how the scale is anchored, and that, having overlooked this difficulty, experimental philosophers have not dealt with it adequately.

We can illustrate the objections raised to particular studies by considering two criticisms of the cross-cultural work on judgments about reference. Both lead to the same conclusion: The cross-cultural work was poorly done, and no conclusion about the influence of culture on judgments about reference can be derived from it. As reviewed in Chapter 2, together with Ron Mallon, Shaun Nichols, and Steve Stich, I have argued that the Gödel case tends to elicit different judgments from people living in the USA and in East Asia: While Americans tend to make Kripkean judgments in response to this case, Chinese and Japanese tend to make descriptivist judgments. Perhaps the most common criticism is that the vignettes used to probe participants' judgments about reference asked questions that are ambiguous with regard to the distinction between speaker's reference and semantic reference. The semantic reference of a name is, roughly, the object to which the name refers as a matter of the linguistic conventions governing the language of which it is a part and the speaker's reference of a name is, roughly, the object to which a speaker intends to refer in using the name (Kripke, 1977).[2] If this is correct, this study might not reveal participants' judgments about the semantic reference of proper names. This criticism might seem devastating to the significance of our experimental results: If data on judgments about the reference of "Gödel" are not data on judgments about the semantic reference of "Gödel," then they have no bearing on the assessment of theories such as descriptivism or the causal-historical view, both of which are theories about the semantic reference of proper names.[3]

Lam (2010) proposed a deflationary explanation of the cross-cultural variation found by Machery et al. (2004). Noting that the Chinese participants in our study were presented with vignettes in English, he hypothesized that their descriptivist answers might be due to some difference between their linguistic competence with their first language and their linguistic competence in English. He presented new evidence that Cantonese speakers tend to make Kripkean judgments when they are presented with vignettes in Cantonese just as speakers of English do when they are presented with vignettes in English, and he concluded (2010, 320) that "[t]his new data concerning the intuitions of Cantonese speakers raises questions about whether cross-cultural variation in answers to questions on certain vignettes reveal genuine differences in intuitions, or

---

[2] Ludwig (2007), Deutsch (2009), and Ichikawa et al. (2012) raise this criticism against Machery et al. (2004). The criticism also regularly comes up in informal discussions I have had with various philosophers regarding these results.

[3] See Machery (2011b) and Machery & Stich (2012) for additional discussion of this objection.

whether differences in answers stem from non-intuitional differences, such as differences in linguistic competence."

Turning to epistemic judgments, Turri (2013) illustrates how difficult it is to ensure that participants, particularly non-philosophers, have a proper understanding of the cases they are presented with. Gettier cases were presented either step by step or all at once. Presenting the cases step by step ensured that participants grasped their structure and content. When this was done, participants turned out to be much more likely to agree with philosophers that the characters described by the cases do not know the relevant proposition. The implication of this result for the Amateur-Psychology Defense is straightforward: Participants' answers in some studies (e.g., that the protagonist knows the relevant proposition in a Gettier case) may simply result from them misunderstanding the cases.

5.1.2 Rebuttal

Skepticism toward experimental findings is very valuable, as the recent replication crisis in social psychology has reminded us (Machery & Doris, forthcoming). Empirical findings may turn out to be false positives, and empirical research is a protracted and messy enterprise. But bringing a dose of healthy skepticism to bear on empirical results is one thing, dismissing a whole field, as proponents of the Amateur-Psychology Defense do, another, and such a wholesale dismissal is entirely unjustified, as I now argue. I first address the general objection to experimental philosophy (viz., the reliance on the survey methodology undermines any conclusion one would want to draw from experimental-philosophy studies) before discussing the concerns with particular studies.

The most pessimistic claims about the shortcomings of survey methods are unfounded. First, claims about the limitations of survey methods are overblown (which is not to deny that survey-based studies raise specific methodological problems). Variation in judgments across cases as a function of carefully controlled variables provides evidence about the cues that influence judgments, and thus about the cognitive mechanisms outputting these judgments. Such information may not be sufficient to identify the mechanisms underlying judgment in full detail, but they can be put to use to identify some features of these mechanisms and to assess some competing hypotheses about them. Psychologists have used this methodology fruitfully. To give a single example among many, Kahneman, Tversky, and the researchers working in the heuristics-and-biases tradition have extensively used vignettes to provide evidence about the heuristics underlying decision and judgment (see, e.g., the yellow and blue cab case or the mammography vignette). Even if one is not convinced by this point (perhaps one does not think much of Kahneman and colleagues' work), the crucial response to the general concerns expressed by Scholl is the following one: These concerns can be entirely ignored here, for, while experimental philosophers sometimes aim at developing detailed theories of the mechanisms underlying judgment (Knobe & Nichols, 2008), the three arguments developed in Chapters 3 and 4 do not depend on meeting this goal. They only depend on whether it can be established by means of surveys that demographic and presentation variables influence judgments in response to philosophical cases and that philosophical cases do not elicit a consensus response, and it is hard to see why in principle survey methods could not establish that much.

So, what about the charge that survey methods raise difficult methodological problems and that experimental philosophers have often ignored these problems? There is no doubt that survey methods raise a host of methodological problems, but which method doesn't? Not fMRI, looking-time methods in developmental psychology, or inference to psychological processes from reaction times in behavioral psychology! Furthermore, it is certain that experimental philosophers ought to be more sensitive to the problems raised by survey methods. Still, as a general line of response to Unreliability, Dogmatism, and Parochialism, this way of unpacking the Amateur-Psychology Defense is unpromising. As shown by the numbers of articles they have published in psychology journals, experimental philosophers tend to be much more methodologically savvy than what their critics suggest, particularly those critics with no training or experience in experimental design whatsoever. Furthermore, it is very unlikely that all the data collected by experimental philosophers about demographic and presentation variables and diversity can be explained away this way. Indeed, when flaws pointed out by critics have been addressed in follow-up studies, these have often, though not always, replicated the original findings.

Let's now turn to the specific objections against particular studies (e.g., Machery et al., 2004). This type of objection tends to be more interesting than the general complaints that have just been addressed, since it prevents critics of the method of cases to be overconfident about the robustness of their empirical results. The key point of my response is that experimental philosophers have typically been concerned with addressing potential flaws in their studies, and attempts to address them have often confirmed the original results (e.g., Knobe's (2004) response to Adams & Steadman (2004)). For sure, there are exceptions to this generalization. As was noted in Chapter 2, Weinberg et al. (2001) reported that judgments about Gettier cases vary across cultures, but follow-up work has not supported this claim (Machery et al., forthcoming a).[4] Similarly, Buckwalter and Stich (2015) reported that gender influences many judgments, but follow-up work has also undermined this claim (Adleberg et al., 2015; Seyedsayamdost, 2015b). However, other pieces of research have not only been widely replicated, the methodological objections against them have also been successfully met. To address Ludwig's (2007) point that the question meant to elicit a judgment about reference in the vignettes used in Machery et al. (2004) could be understood as bearing on semantic reference or on speaker's reference, Machery et al. (2015) propose several ways to disambiguate this question, and report finding stable cross-cultural differences in judgments about the Gödel case. In one of the studies, participants are

---

[4] Kim & Yuan (2015); Seyedsayamdost (2015a); Machery et al. (forthcoming c).

presented with the usual case followed by a modified question: "When John uses the name 'Gödel,' *regardless of who he might intend to be talking about,* he is *actually* talking about (A) the person who really discovered the incompleteness of arithmetic; [or] (B) the person who got hold of the manuscript and claimed credit for the work." The point of this new formulation is not that semantic reference (but not speaker's reference) is the "actual" reference, but rather that the contrast between the two italicized clauses should make it clear that the question is not about speaker's reference. If participants have a notion of semantic reference, then they are likely to give an answer about semantic reference in response to the question so formulated. In another study, we formulate a new version of the Gödel case in which the speaker has the intention to refer to the individual who is the semantic reference of "Gödel" according to causal-historical theories of reference. If some people still answer that John is talking about the man who discovered the incompleteness of arithmetic, they must be reporting genuine descriptivist judgments about semantic reference. To do this, we added the following paragraph to the end of the Gödel case used in previous studies:

One night, John is sitting in his room, reviewing for his mathematics exam by going over the proof of the incompleteness theorem. After a while, he says to his roommate, "Gödel probably got a huge number of awards from mathematical societies!"

It would seem that the speaker intends to be talking about the man who stole the theorem: Given the information provided in the vignette, only the man who stole the theorem can be viewed as having won a huge number of awards from mathematical societies. In both studies, we found a cultural difference, as had Machery et al. (2004). There is no doubt that considered on its own each study has weaknesses and fails to provide definitive evidence, but, taken together, they provide strong evidence that genuine judgments about semantic reference vary both across and within cultures.

To address Lam's (2010) point that the vignettes in Machery et al. (2004) were simply presented in English to a sample of speakers who may not have been fully fluent, Machery et al. (2010) have shown that Chinese participants make similar judgments when Gödel cases are presented in English (as was originally done in Machery et al., 2004) and in Chinese.

5.1.3 Upshot

There is no doubt that experimental philosophers' studies could often be better from a methodological point of view. Possible confounds could be controlled more systematically, statistical analyses could be more careful and sophisticated, greater care about the philosophical significance of the work could be exercised. In fact, the quality of their studies has undoubtedly increased over the last ten years. That said, the Amateur-Psychology Defense fails to undercut Unreliability, Dogmatism, and Parochialism.

5.2 The Reflection Defense

5.2.1 *The wrong kind of judgment?*

A second way to criticize the inductive basis of Unreliability, Dogmatism, and Parochialism is to contend that experimental philosophers have been collecting data about the wrong kind of judgment. There are several ways to flesh out this criticism.

1. *The Expertise Defense.* Studies conducted by experimental philosophers do not examine the judgments made by the right kind of people. In particular, they examine the judgments of people without the pertinent knowledge or skills (e.g., paying attention to the crucial features of the vignettes). Only data about the judgments of those people with the proper philosophical knowledge, the proper understanding of the issues the cases bear on, or the proper skills—i.e., only data about the judgments of philosophers—would matter to assess whether the judgments elicited by philosophical cases are reliable or variable. This kind of response is often called "the Expertise Defense."

Williamson (2007, 191) has endorsed the Expertise Defense:[5]

Much of the evidence for cross-cultural variation in judgments on thought experiments concerns verdicts by people without philosophical training. Yet philosophy students have to learn how to apply general concepts to specific examples with careful attention to the relevant subtleties, just as law students have to learn how to analyze hypothetical cases. Levels of disagreements over thought experiments seem to be significantly lower among fully trained philosophers than among novices. That is another manifestation of the influence of past experience on epistemological judgments about thought experiments.

Similarly, concentrating on modal judgments, Hales asserts (2006, 171):

Intuitions are and should be sensitive to education and training in the relevant domain. For example, the physical intuitions of professional scientists are much more trustworthy than those of undergraduates or random persons in a bus station.

2. *The Thickness Defense* (Weinberg & Alexander, 2014). These studies report data about judgments lacking properties that the judgments elicited by cases possess when the method of cases is used in philosophical argumentation. For instance, one may object that they examine spontaneous instead of reflective judgments (whatever that contrast amounts to) or that they study judgments that are not derived from conceptual competence.

I have implicitly addressed many versions of the Thickness Defense in Chapter 1 when I defended the minimalist characterization of the method of cases, and I won't rehash these points here. Rather, in this section I discuss two versions of the Thickness

---

[5] See also, e.g., Kornblith (2007); Ludwig (2007, 2014); Horvath (2010); Williamson (2011, 2016); Devitt (2011, 2012).

Defense. In the next section, I turn to the Expertise Defense, first unpacking it and then responding to it.

5.2.2 The Reflection Defense

One could develop the Thickness Defense by noting that the judgments made in response of cases take place in a particular social context (e.g., Kauppinen, 2007): Philosophers *talk* to one another, probing their responses in various ways, to make sure that the judgments elicited reflect their considered opinion. This first version of the Thickness Defense can be set aside: There is no single social context for the use of cases in philosophy. Cases are developed and assessed in the seminar room, while reading articles on one's own, while writing papers in the solitude of one's office, while probing a few select colleagues' opinions in a university hallway, while lecturing to undergraduates and informally polling them, etc. Some are very different from surveys, others less so.

A second way of unpacking the Thickness Defense goes as follows: Philosophers who use the method of cases only appeal to the judgments generated by careful reflection on the cases themselves, and whatever it is that experimental philosophers have been studying, they have not been studying those judgments.[6] Together with Colaço, Kneer, and Alexander, I have called this defense the "Reflection Defense" (Colaço et al., ms).[7] While the notion of reflection can be characterized in many different ways, we endorsed a characterization that allows for an empirical treatment of the Reflection Defense (the "minimal characterization"): A case elicits a reflective judgment to the extent that it results from a deliberation process involving attention, focus, cognitive effort, and so on—the type of domain-general psychological resources that careful and attentive thinking requires.

5.2.3 Rebuttal

We examined whether four different ways of priming reflection, all of which have been extensively used in social psychology, would make any difference in the judgments elicited by cases:

- In the *forced delay* condition, participants were encouraged to read the vignette slowly, carefully, and to think about possible variations of the scenario.
- In the *financial incentive* condition, participants were promised double compensation in case they got the answer "right."
- In the *reasons* condition, the vignette and questions were preceded by a screen which instructed participants that they would have to provide detailed explanations of their answers.

---

[6] Kauppinen (2007); Ludwig (2007).
[7] For previous discussion, see Gonnerman et al. (2011) and Weinberg et al. (2012).

- A final condition made use of *analytic priming*: Before receiving the vignettes and questions, participants had to solve a simple mathematical puzzle—a standard procedure to trigger analytic cognition.

We also examined whether participants who are more likely to be reflective (as measured by a well-known social-psychological scale: the Rational-Experiential Inventory; see Epstein et al., 1996) and participants who take longer to respond answer differently.

We selected four different cases or pairs of cases, for which there is a consensus as to what constitutes the "correct" response amongst professional philosophers: the clock case, adaptations of Radford's (1966) famous Queen Elizabeth case (Myers-Schulz & Schwitzgebel, 2013), Beebe and Jensen's (2012) cases meant to study the ESEE knowledge effect (knowledge ascriptions regarding side effects are sensitive to the latter's general desirability; see Beebe & Buckwalter, 2010), and the Gödel case.

In a series of five experimental studies with a total of over 2500 individual subjects, we found that priming reflection, being disposed to reflective judgment, and spontaneously taking a longer time to answer had no significant effect. The responses of those more inclined towards analytic cognition (i.e. participants falling on the "rational" end of the Rational-Experiential Inventory) were no different from those of more intuitive thinkers (i.e., subjects falling on the "experiential" end of the Rational-Experiential Inventory). These results are consistent with the findings reported in previous studies, which attempted to operationalize the difference in people's disposition toward reflection by means of the Need for Cognition inventory or the Cognitive Reflection Task (Gonnerman et al., 2011; Weinberg et al., 2012; Gerken & Beebe, 2016). Experimental manipulations that encourage careful reflection through increased delay, financial incentives, reason giving, and analytic priming replicated the results produced under conditions standardly employed by experimental philosophers. Finally, response time, measured individually across all five conditions, made no difference.

Our results are compelling: The empirical assumption encapsulated in the reflection defense, when "reflection" is understood minimally, is mistaken: People who, by themselves or as a result of some circumstantial primes, engage in reflection (so understood), do not respond differently from people who don't.

A proponent of the Reflection Defense may appeal to less minimal characterizations of the notion of reflection, but not any characterization will do. It should be philosophically and descriptively adequate (Chapter 1): For instance, it can't be based on notions such as conceptual competence. Furthermore, a characterization of reflective judgments should not make it the case that *by stipulation* the findings alluded to by proponents of the restrictionist challenge happen to bear only on non-reflective judgments. Stipulative victories are no victories at all, and it should be an empirical question whether reflective judgments suffer from the vagaries evidenced by fifteen years of experimental philosophy.

5.2.4 Upshot

While it is possible that proponents of the Reflection Defense might appeal to some less minimal characterizations of reflection, I see at this point no reason for thinking that there is any such characterization that is (1) acceptable and (2) would make a difference to the judgments philosophical cases elicit.

5.3 The Expertise Defense

5.3.1 The defense

There are at least two reasons why philosophers could be better at making judgments in response to cases than lay people.[8] First, philosophers could have a superior grasp of philosophical concepts, such as the concepts of truth, knowledge, necessity, possibility, and phenomenal consciousness (e.g., Singer, 1972, 117). What a better grasp of concepts amounts to depends on what concepts are, but there is no need to specify this notion in greater detail for present purposes. Note, however, that this better grasp of concepts may be simply a matter of using them more appropriately: People who have a better grasp of a concept may, but need not, be better at describing what is involved in having this concept; they may, but need not, be better at justifying their concept use. Instead, a better grasp of a concept may simply consist in being better at applying this concept to its occurrences, at drawing the proper inferences, and at avoiding confusions even if one is not better at justifying concept use than non-experts. If philosophers have such practical knowledge, the Expertise Defense would be on solid ground. I will call this view "the mastery model." Ludwig (2007, 149) seems to embrace this model when he writes that "This [viz., the training relevant to give a correct answer in thought experiments] is not a matter of acquiring new concepts! It is a matter of gaining greater sensitivity to the structure of the concepts through reflective exercises with problems involving those concepts." Alternatively, instead of having a better grasp of the concepts of truth or knowledge, they may have better theories about truth or knowledge (Devitt, 2011, 426). These superior theories would allow philosophers to draw proper inferences about truth or knowledge, to be better at recognizing truth or knowledge, and so on. Nothing hangs on describing the mastery model in terms of concepts or theories.

Second, philosophers could have a superior familiarity with thought experimenting. They could be better at ignoring the irrelevant (e.g., narrative) aspects of thought experiments and at singling out their pertinent features. They may also be better at understanding how a concept applies to the type of unusual situation described by a thought experiment. I will call this view "the thought-experimenting model." Ludwig

---

[8] For further discussion, see, e.g., Horvath (2010); Weinberg et al. (2010); Machery (2011a, 2015b); Alexander (2012); Nado (2014b, 2015); Ryberg (2013); Rini (2014, 2015); Andow (2015); Mizrahi (2015); Buckwalter (2016); Horvath & Wiegmann (2016).

defends this second model when he writes (2007, 153) that "expertise both in the relevant fields and in the methodology and conduct of thought experiments is clearly relevant to reliability." Williamson (2011, 216) concurs, asserting that "the expertise defence does not imply that a good philosophical education involves the cultivation of a mysterious sui generis faculty of rational intuition, or anything of the kind. Rather, it is supposed to improve far more mundane skills, such as careful attention to details in the description of the scenario and their potential relevance to the questions at issue."[9] Of course, both models could be correct.

The Expertise Defense is held with varying strengths. Williamson (2011) merely takes it to be a plausible hypothesis, which, as long as it has not been defeated, undermines the skeptical conclusions drawn about the method of cases by some experimental philosophers. Ludwig (2007) is less cautious, taking it as obvious that philosophizing involves an expertise at judging about the situations described by philosophical cases.

The truth of the Expertise Defense would have damaging implications for the three arguments developed in Chapters 3 and 4. It would considerably weaken Unreliability, since experimental philosophers' findings about demographic and framing effects, which underlie this argument, would likely fail to replicate when philosophers judge in response to cases. That is, the reliability of judgments elicited by philosophical cases would then not be invariant under partitioning between experts and non-experts. It would decisively undermine Dogmatism, since its Premise 2 (i.e., the claim that people who disagree about cases are epistemic peers) would then be easy to reject; and it would also considerably weaken Parochialism, since philosophers would then be in a position to argue that the issues philosophers study (e.g., knowledge vs. knowledge*) are more likely to get at the fundamental philosophical questions. It thus would not be the case that philosophers display parochialism by taking the assumed truthmakers of *their* judgments about philosophical cases to be more valuable for philosophical discussion.

5.3.2 Rebuttal

The Expertise Defense has been examined both theoretically and empirically (for review, see Nado, 2014b). Theoretical discussions have either been about who must shoulder the burden of proof (e.g., Williamson, 2011; Nado, 2014b) or about whether philosophical education satisfies the conditions that favor the development of expert judgment (Weinberg et al., 2010). Discussions of the burden of proof themselves have centered around the analogy between philosophers and scientists, an argument I call "the scientific analogy."[10] Thus, Hales writes (2006, 171):

Scientist have and rely on physical intuitions, intuitions that are trained, educated, and informed and yet are good indicators of truth for those very reasons. In the same way, the modal intuitions of professional philosophers are much more reliable than either those of inexperienced students or the "folk."

---

[9]   See also Singer (1972, 117); Kamm (1993, 8).
[10]   See also Ludwig (2007); Devitt (2011, 2012); Williamson (2011); Nado (2014b, 2015).

The scientific analogy has been cast in different ways and has been explained in more or less detail.[11] The most compelling formulation of the analogy is the following one. Scientists (e.g., paleoanthropologists) do have discipline-specific forms of expertise. For instance, paleoanthropologists excel at examining bones and at classifying them, while mathematicians follow discovery heuristics that allow them to develop new proofs. It should thus be our default expectation that philosophers too have discipline-specific forms of expertise. The upshot of this analogy is that the burden of proof is on experimental philosophers' shoulders: Until they have shown that philosophers do not have the kind of expertise that either the mastery model or the thought-experimenting model appeals to, philosophers can justifiably be assumed to possess the forms of expertise that are part and parcel of philosophizing.

Unfortunately for the proponent of the Expertise Defense, the scientific analogy is underwhelming. First, what justifies comparing philosophers to paleoanthropologists (who have a genuine expertise) rather than, say, to economists or, worse, astrologers? The scientific analogy assumes that philosophers have some expertise, and thus begs the question. Still, I do not doubt that philosophers have *some* expertise, indeed some *distinctive* expertise (Kuhn 1991; Livengood et al., 2010, discussed below), and that in some respect or other the scientific analogy is justified. However, and this is the second point, granting that philosophers have some form of expertise, why should we believe that they are expert at judging about the situations described by philosophical cases? It may well be that philosophers' expertise consists instead in clarifying concepts, drawing distinctions, providing justification for one philosophical position or another, seeing how philosophical positions relate to one another, systematizing positions, and assessing arguments. Perhaps the thought is that one can justifiably assume that philosophers excel at what philosophers do, including judging about the situations described by philosophical cases, in the same way that one can justifiably expect scientists to be good at what they do (e.g., one can expect paleoanthropologists to be good at classifying bones), but this thought is unconvincing. There are many things scientists do routinely without being particularly good at it: To give only a few examples, statistics in psychology, peer reviewing in many sciences, and probability judgments in economics. And the scientific analogy can only support the Expertise Defense if it gives us a reason to believe, not just that philosophers are somewhat better than lay people at judging in response to philosophical cases, but that they are much better. If philosophers are somewhat better, Unreliability and Parochialism would still threaten the method of cases.

Finally, one may even wonder whether the analogy makes any sense at all: Scientists' and philosophers' attitude toward their instruments are entirely disanalogous. Scientists can be confident about their observations (e.g., the temperature of a sample) because they have extensively calibrated their instruments or because they have an extensive theory of their functioning. For instance, psychologists extensively "pilot" any new

---

[11] See in particular Nado (2015) for different formulations.

experimental design (including new stimuli) before running an experiment. The contrast with philosophy is glaring: There is nothing analogous with respect to the cases used by philosophers.

The scientific analogy is underwhelming, then, but, more important, we simply should not be debating who should show what when the stakes are so high for philosophy. When some scientific method (either some tool, some principle of experimental design, or some method of data analysis) is under critical discussion, we rarely see scientists quibble about who must shoulder the burden of proof; rather, it is acknowledged to be everybody's responsibility to get things straight. For instance, during the 2014 controversy about the alleged evidence for cosmic inflation, both the naysayers and the team that reported the original findings attempted to determine whether the data could be due to cosmic dust radiation. The same is true of the retracted claim in 2014 that one could produce stem cells out of spleen cells by bathing them in acid and compressing them (*Nature*, editorial, July 2, 2014). Admittedly, it happens that one side in a scientific controversy does more work than the other. For instance, in the ongoing debate about statistical reform in the behavioral sciences, Bayesians, who militate for statistical reform, have done more work than frequentists. However, this asymmetry does not result from the former recognizing that they must shoulder the burden of proof; rather, I suspect, both sides would recognize that they have an equal responsibility to get it right. It is true that sometimes one side would deny that they have a duty to address the concerns of the other side—evolutionary theorists do not think that they have an intellectual duty to address the concerns of creationists such as Behe—but it is because the former side does not even acknowledge that there is a genuine scientific controversy. In any case, burden of proof arguments are rare in science. Why should it be any different in philosophy? Philosophers who debate who should do what or whose aim is to shift the burden of proof have an agonistic conception of philosophy, and model philosophical exchanges on legal proceedings. In contrast, I support a more collaborative approach to philosophizing, and model philosophical exchanges on (admittedly idealized) scientific exchanges. When we philosophers disagree, we share a common interest in getting to the bottom of our disagreement.

Turning to the second theoretical issue, in their influential discussion of the Expertise Defense, Weinberg and colleagues express doubts that philosophical education is conducive to the development of expert judgments about the situations described by philosophical cases because the kind of feedback that is essential for this development may well not be found in philosophical education. As they put it (2010, 341), "There is a live possibility here that philosophers' intuitions about cases do not receive anything like the kind of substantial feedback required for such virtuous tuning." Weinberg and colleagues' goal is to establish that philosophers *may* not have expert judgment, defeating the assumption shared by some defenders of the method of cases that they do. The point is not so much to shift the burden of proof back to those defenders as to defeat the presumption that a particular side of the controversy (the critics) has to take on the argumentative burden. This goal is successfully met, but the most important question for our purposes—are philosophers expert at judging about the situations described by philosophical cases?—is not settled by their article.

Weinberg and colleagues' discussion raises two issues: First, is it the case that philosophical education does not satisfy the conditions for the development of expert judgment? Budding philosophers do get a feedback of sort about their judgments (Williamson, 2011); indeed, some experimental and naturalistic philosophers have even speculated that, when their judgments diverge from the consensual judgments, budding philosophers are getting a feedback that is so negative that they are driven out of philosophy.[12] Weinberg and colleagues consider the response that budding philosophers' judgments elicited by philosophical cases could be trained against other judgments, but they reject it on the grounds that it is unclear what makes *those* judgments well tuned. However, the kind of feedback budding philosophers get may not boil down to simply comparing judgments: They are told, e.g., what to ignore and what to pay attention to in cases; for instance, in the Twin-Earth thought experiment they may be told to pay attention to the fact that the Twin Earth is not actual. Weinberg and colleagues further claim that budding philosophers are not getting the right kind of feedback in the right amount, but since they do not specify what such feedback and amount would be, their argument is hard to assess. The second issue is that the development of expert judgment among firefighters, chess players, or physicians (the kind of expert judgment about which the research appealed to by Weinberg and colleagues has been done) may not be the proper model (the right "relevant contrast domain" in Weinberg and colleagues' terminology) for understanding the development of expert judgment among philosophers. Many of these expert judgments are perceptual judgments based on pattern matching, a kind of judgment very different from the application of a concept to the situation described by a philosophical case. Mathematicians are also expert at identifying sound leads for proofs and seeing what follows from what, but it would be surprising if their expertise developed the way firefighters' or chess players' does.

Another approach to assessing the Expertise Defense would be to assess the mastery and thought-experimenting models separately. Examining the mastery model first, it is implausible that philosophers have a better grasp of many philosophical concepts than non-philosophers or at least than some non-philosophers (mutatis mutandis for better theories). (Remember that having a better grasp of a concept can be a kind of practical knowledge.) If anybody has a superior grasp of epistemological concepts, it should be scientists and statisticians rather than philosophers. The former are taught to distinguish justified experiments or inferences from unjustified ones, they apply epistemological concepts to issues of importance on a regular basis, they get feedback (from nature or from reviewers) when they are mistaken about what inferences are justified. If anybody has a superior grasp of ethical concepts, it should be judges or those individuals involved in helping people make ethically difficult choices rather

---

[12] E.g., Cummins (1998); Machery et al. (2004); Turri (2016).

than philosophers, since the former have extensive opportunity to apply these concepts. Similarly, if anybody has a superior grasp of linguistic concepts (e.g., the concept of reference), it should be linguists (perhaps historical linguists who track historical changes in the reference or extension of words).

A proponent of the mastery model may perhaps concede the superior expertise of scientists, judges, and linguists, but insist that philosophers are still more expert at deploying these concepts than lay people, which would be sufficient to unfang the alleged implications of experimental philosophers' findings about lay people's judgments. But, first, it is not enough to respond that philosophers have a somewhat better grasp of philosophical concepts than lay people. Philosophers' judgments need to be sufficiently good for them to play the role they are often supposed to fulfill. Second, if, say, scientists really have a better grasp of the concept of justification than epistemologists, then the latter should empirically study how the former use this concept. Thus, while experimental philosophers' findings about lay judgments would be unfanged, this response would undermine philosophers' way of using the method of cases (viz., by relying on their own judgments).

Finally, philosophers may have better philosophical theories of causation, identity, etc.: These may be articulated in more detail, supported by explicit and valid arguments, and possibly more accurate. But it is just implausible that they have a better grasp of many philosophical concepts than lay people; that is, that they are better at recognizing causation, identity, etc., in the situations described by philosophical cases. (Remember that on pain of circularity philosophers' theories cannot be deployed to judge in response to cases (Section 1.2.3 of Chapter 1)). For instance, why would philosophers or perhaps philosophers working on causation be better than lay people at detecting causes in actual and hypothetical situations? Similarly, "Moral philosophers, as such, have no special information not available to the general public, about what is right and what is wrong" (Broad, 1940, 115).[13] Indeed, it is remarkable that ethicists don't view their judgments about philosophical cases bearing on temporal identity as less justified than metaphysicians', that metaphysicians don't view their judgments about philosophical cases bearing on explanation as less justified than those of philosophers of science, and that philosophers of science don't view their judgments about philosophical cases bearing on permissibility as less justified than ethicists'.

In fact, claims to having a superior grasp of philosophically important concepts are not only implausible, they may sometimes be unjust. In the moral and political domains, such claims silence the voices of many—particularly of those who are more likely to be silenced (women, minorities, etc.)—while such voices are needed to engineer truly satisfying solutions to the problems raised by our living together.

I now turn to the thought-experimenting model. It is dubious that philosophers are better at thought experimenting than lay people, or, if they are, that they are sufficiently

---

[13] See also Ayer (1954).

good. Graduate students in philosophy are not taught systematically how to thought experiment, what kinds of feature to ignore in general, what kinds of feature to pay attention to in general, etc. (At best, they are told to ignore or consider particular features in specific thought experiments.) There are no textbooks for thought experimenting or graduate seminars teaching how to thought experiment. Thought experiments are often written in a way that invites errors, suggesting that philosophers have not thought hard about what a good thought experiment is or about how to write one. In particular, thought experiments often contain philosophically irrelevant narrative elements, which may have a distorting influence on judgments (Machery, 2011a; Section 3.5 of Chapter 3).

Fortunately, we need not solve the theoretical controversies just discussed to make progress about the assessment of the Expertise Defense, since a growing body of evidence suggests that philosophers' judgments too are influenced by presentation and demographic variables. I will start by describing some indirect evidence, before turning to some more direct evidence.

Proponents of the Expertise Defense who hold the mastery model or those who insist on the continuity between the judgments elicited by cases and everyday judgments may find congenial the claim that philosophers should be better at using concepts not only when they consider philosophical cases, but also in everyday situations. That is, proponents of the Expertise Defense may find congenial the claim that philosophers' everyday judgments about permissibility, causation, or responsibility should be more reliable that lay people's (assuming that the latter's judgments are not perfectly reliable), although philosophers' improved grasp of concepts could conceivably manifest itself only in difficult contexts, including when they have to assess the situations described by philosophical cases. It is also reasonable (though again debatable) to assume that, if philosophers' judgments are more reliable than ordinary people's because of the expertise philosophers have acquired, the judgments philosophers make about their particular area of expertise should tend to be more reliable than the judgments of philosophers working in other areas of philosophy—for instance, ethicists' judgments about ethical matters (what is right or wrong, what is permissible, and what is morally required) should be more reliable than metaphysicians'. Finally, if ethicists' judgments about ethical matters are more reliable than other philosophers', then ethicists' actions should arguably (although not uncontroversially) be better than other philosophers' since ethicists' judgments have practical significance.

In recent years, a large body of evidence has accumulated that ethicists do not behave better than other philosophers. Moral philosophers are 50 percent more likely to "borrow books permanently" from libraries than other philosophers (Schwitzgebel, 2009): That is, moral philosophers are 50 percent more likely to steal books from libraries! Moral philosophers are also not more likely to abide by elementary norms of politeness (such as replying to email or behaving politely in conferences) than other philosophers (Schwitzgebel et al., 2012; Rust & Schwitzgebel, 2013; Schwitzgebel & Rust, 2014). Finally, moral philosophers, including political philosophers, are not more likely to vote than other philosophers (Schwitzgebel & Rust, 2010). Unsurprisingly, philosophers tend to think that ethicists do not behave better than other philosophers (Schwitzgebel & Rust, 2009)! This growing body of findings is indirect evidence that ethicists' judgments about ethical matters are not more reliable than other philosophers', which casts doubt on the idea that philosophical expertise improves the reliability of the judgments elicited by thought experiments. Of course, one could question the significance of Schwitzgebel's findings for the Expertise Defense on various grounds. The connection between ethicists' actions and the reliability of the judgments elicited by thought experiments is admittedly indirect, and the quality of philosophers' judgments need not be reflected in their actions. After all, moral philosophers might fail to act on their enlightened judgments for a variety of reasons, including weakness of the will and failure to pay attention to their own judgments when they act. And their superior judgment may be limited to the kind of situations described by philosophical cases: Philosophers' superiority may consist in their immunity to the disturbing characteristics.

There is, however, some more direct evidence challenging the Expertise Defense. As we saw in Chapter 2, lay people's judgments about free will and moral responsibility vary as a function of extraversion, one of the five fundamental personality dimensions recognized by contemporary personality psychologists (Feltz & Cokely, 2009). In a follow-up study, participants were asked to complete a personality test, report their judgment about whether an individual would be responsible for her action and act out of her free will in a deterministic world, and complete a test measuring their expertise about the free-will debate called "the Free Will Skill Test" (Schulz et al., 2011). Extraversion turned out to predict compatibilist judgment among both experts and lay people: Extraverts are more likely to make compatibilist judgments, whether or not they have some expertise about free will. It would thus seem that philosophers' familiarity with the free-will and moral-responsibility debates and their experience with thought experimenting do not shield them from the influence of demographic variables.

Reasoning biases also seem to influence philosophers' judgments. The actor-observer bias has been extensively examined in the judgment-and-decision-making literature in psychology: People tend to judge differently when they pass judgment about themselves or others (Jones & Nisbett, 1972).[14] This bias influences philosophers too (Tobia et al., 2013). Philosophers at the meeting of the American Philosophical Association Pacific Division in April, 2011, who all had a PhD in philosophy, were presented with Williams's Jim and the Indians case and with a switch version of the trolley case, and their answers were compared with the answers of undergraduates at Rutgers. The judgments of non-experts (i.e., undergraduates) were influenced by the actor-observer bias (as discussed in Chapter 2): They were much more likely to say that Jim is obligated to shoot the character in the story (third-person judgment) than to say that they would be

---

[14] See, however, Malle (2006) for critical discussion of this literature and for the boundary conditions of the actor-observer bias.

obligated to shoot him (first-person judgment), and they were more likely to say that it is permissible for someone else to push the switch to save the lives of five people and cause the death of one individual (third-person judgment) than for themselves (first-person judgment). What about philosophers, you may ask? Just like non-experts, philosophers gave different answers in the first- and third-person versions of the scenarios, but the pattern found with philosophers differed from the pattern found with non-experts. Philosophers turned out to be much more likely to say that *they* would be obligated to shoot the character in the story (first-person judgment) than to say that Jim would (third-person judgment), and they were more likely to say that it is permissible *for themselves* to push the switch to save the lives of five people and cause the death of one individual (first-person judgment) than for someone else (third-person judgment)! Go figure!

The actor-observer bias is not the only bias known to influence philosophers' judgments. While lay people's judgments are influenced by the order in which philosophical cases are presented, one may have been tempted to speculate that philosophers would be immune to this bias, but evidence suggests that this is not the case. Philosophers (with an MA or a PhD), non-philosopher academics (with an MA or a PhD), and non-academics were presented with seventeen philosophical cases bearing on the doctrine of double effect, moral luck, and the distinction between action and omission (Schwitzgebel & Cushman, 2012). The cases were given in two distinct orders (e.g., the switch version of the trolley case before the footbridge version or vice versa). Presentation order influenced philosophers' judgments, and the size of this influence was not smaller for philosophers than for other academics and non-academics. For instance, participants were more likely to give the same numerical answer (on a seven-point scale) to the switch and footbridge versions of the trolley case when they were shown the footbridge version before the switch version. Importantly, this was equally true of philosophers, other academics, and non-academics. Schwitzgebel & Cushman (2012, 147) concluded that their "analysis found no support for the view that philosophical expertise enhances the stability of moral judgment against order effects."[15]

Unger (1996) predicts that adding choice options to cases similar to the footbridge case (such as the heavy-skater case) would lead people to find it acceptable to push the large man.

The heavy-skater case (Unger, 1996, 87)
By sheer accident, an empty trolley, nobody aboard, is starting to roll down a certain track. Now, if you do nothing about the situation, your first option, then, in a couple of minutes, it will run over and kill six innocents who, through no fault of their own, are trapped down the line (just beyond an "elbow" in the track). (So, on your first option, you'll let the six die.) Regarding their plight, you have one other option: Further up the track, near where the trolley's starting to move, there's a path crossing the main track and, on it, there's a very heavy man on roller skates.

---

[15] Schwitzgebel & Cushman (2015) have replicated this finding; for discussion, see Rini (2014).

If you turn a remote control dial, you'll start up the skates, you'll send him in front of the trolley, and he'll be a trolley-stopper. But, the man will be crushed to death by the trolley he then stops. (So, on your second option, you'll save six lives and you'll take one.)

The resulting case is "the switches and skates case" (Unger, 1996, 90):

The switches and skates case
By sheer accident, an empty trolley, nobody aboard, is starting to roll down a certain track. Now, if you *do nothing about* the situation, your *first option*, then, in a couple of minutes, it will run over and kill six innocents who, through no fault of their own, are trapped down the line. (So, on your first option, you'll let the six die.) Regarding their plight, you have *three other* options: On your *second option*, if you push a remote control button, you'll change the position of a switch-track, switch A, and, before it gets to the six, the trolley will go onto another line, on the left-hand side of switch A's fork. On that line, three other innocents are trapped, and, if you change switch A, the trolley will roll over them. (So, on your second option, you'll save six lives and you'll take three.) On your *third option*, you'll flop a remote control toggle and change the position of another switch, switch B. Then, a very light trolley that's rolling along another track, the Feed Track, will shift onto B's lower fork. As two pretty heavy people are trapped in this light trolley, after going down this lower fork the vehicle won't only collide with the onrushing empty trolley, but, owing to the combined weight of its unwilling passengers, the collision will derail the first trolley and both trolleys will go into an uninhabited area. Still, the two trapped passengers will die in the collision. On the other hand, if you don't change switch B, the lightweight trolley will go along B's upper fork and, then, it will bypass the empty trolley, and its two passengers won't die soon. (So, on your third option, you'll save six lives and you'll take two.) Finally, you have a *fourth option*: Further up the track, near where the trolley's starting to move, there's a path crossing the main track and, on it, there's a very heavy man on roller skates. If you turn a remote control dial, you'll start up the skates, you'll send him in front of the trolley, and he'll be a trolley-stopper. But the man will be crushed to death by the trolley he then stops. (So, on your fourth option, you'll save six lives and you'll take one.)

Wiegmann et al. (ms) show that lay people are indeed more likely to choose to cause the death of someone as a means to save a larger group of people when they are presented with irrelevant options. In line with the research reviewed so far, philosophers with a PhD or an MA in philosophy were no less susceptible to this effect.

At times expertise may even make experts worse than lay people because their theoretical commitments bias their judgments. To test this hypothesis, the Gödel case was given to semanticists and philosophers of language (who are likely to have read Kripke's *Naming and Necessity*), lay people, and linguists studying the descriptions associated with words, such as anthropological linguists, historical linguists, and sociolinguists (Machery, 2012a). The judgments of linguists and philosophers of language about the reference of "Gödel" in this case turned out to be influenced by their disciplinary training (although effect sizes were small): Linguists who work in fields that highlight the descriptions associated with words (sociolinguistics, historical linguistics, and anthropological linguistics) were less likely to make Kripkean judgments than lay people, and those experts who are likely to have read *Naming and Necessity* (semanticists and philosophers of language) were more likely to make Kripkean judgments. So, the expertise of some experts about linguistic matters must bias their judgments.

In sum, philosophers' expertise does not appear to shield them from the factors that influence lay people's judgments about philosophical cases. A limitation of this body of research is that the evidence is mostly drawn from the moral domain: Philosophers too appear to be influenced by presentation variables (order and framing) and demographic variables (personality), at least when they judge about moral issues. While philosophers' judgments in other domains may not be influenced by these variables, the findings reported by Machery (2012a) tentatively speak against this possibility. Similarly, Hitchcock and Knobe (2009) found that lay people's and philosophers' judgments about causation are similarly influenced by the moral content of the cases they are presented with.

On the other hand, some evidence could perhaps be marshaled in support of the Expertise Defense. Horvath & Wiegmann (2016) rightly note that the Expertise Defense can only get off the ground if philosophers and lay people respond differently to cases, and they report that philosophers and lay people responded differently for a few epistemological cases inspired by the Gettier, fake-barn, unopened-letter (Harman, 1968), and lottery cases. However, these differences were either small (Gettier-style case) or fell on the same side of the scale (above or below the mid-point: fake-barn and lottery cases): Philosophers tend to make the same kind of judgment as lay people in response to these cases, but express greater agreement or disagreement with the sentence ascribing knowledge to the character in the vignette. If anything, these results are bad news for proponents of the Expertise Defense.

Livengood et al. (2010) examined empirically what they call "the philosophical temperament"—roughly, the epistemic virtues that philosophers distinctively possess. Focusing on reflectivity, defined as the disposition to be skeptical of one's immediate inclinations to judge, they found that at every level of education philosophers are more reflective than equally educated people. One may think that, if philosophers are really more reflective, their judgments in response to cases would be more reliable—for instance, they would be less likely to be influenced by salient but irrelevant features of cases—although this appears not to be the case. It is not obvious how to reconcile Livengood and colleagues' findings with the body of evidence summarized above. Many factors that undermine the reliability of judgment—personality and culture, for instance—may influence both immediate and reflective judgments (Colaço et al., ms; see Section 5.5.2). Instead of improving the reliability of judgments elicited by philosophical cases, reflectivity's contribution to philosophical thinking may be to allow philosophers to take unintuitive views seriously (e.g., the possibility of radical skepticism, solipsism, various forms of eliminativism, or moral skepticism) and to motivate them to provide compelling argumentative justifications for or against such unintuitive views. Similarly, philosophers' distinctive argumentative skills (Kuhn, 1991) may not improve the judgments they make in response to cases; rather, this expert skill manifests itself in the sophistication of their arguments.

5.3.3 Upshot

There is no doubt that philosophers have some expertise—they may be more willing than others to consider views that violate common sense such as skepticism or various types of eliminativism, they are particularly good at developing and assessing arguments, and they may particularly good at clarifying concepts—but there is little reason, either theoretical or empirical, to believe that they are so good at judging about the kind of situation typically described by philosophical cases that they are more resilient to the demographic and presentation effects experimental philosophers have found. It is time to call the Expertise Defense what it is: a myth.

5.4 The Limited-Influence Defense

5.4.1 The defense

The fourth strategy for challenging Unreliability, Dogmatism, and Parochialism concedes their inductive basis, but challenges their inductive step. That is, while conceding that the judgments elicited by *some* philosophical cases are unreliable or differ across groups, it rejects the inductive conclusion that judgments elicited by *most* philosophical cases are unreliable or differ across groups. Nagel has been pressing this point in two different ways. First, focusing on judgments elicited by epistemological cases, she has argued that they result from an early developing cognitive capacity: mindreading, i.e., the capacity to ascribe mental states such as beliefs and desires to oneself and others (Nagel, 2012).[16] Since mental state ascription is reliable—as shown by the fact that we are pretty good at predicting behavior by ascribing beliefs and desires—it is sensible to expect judgments about knowledge to be reliable too. This expectation weakens the inductive conclusion that judgments elicited by most philosophical cases are unreliable on the basis of the few philosophical cases where knowledge ascription goes astray. Nagel writes (2012, 511):

> If Gettier's intuitions about what Smith does or doesn't know come from our everyday mindreading capacity for ascribing states of knowledge and belief, and if this capacity is generally reliable, then our epistemic case intuitions have some positive claims to epistemic legitimacy.

Since mindreading is a universal aspect of human cognition, one could also expect the reliability of knowledge ascription to be invariant across demographic groups. Again, this expectation weakens the inductive conclusion that the judgments elicited by most philosophical cases differ across groups on the basis of the few philosophical cases where knowledge ascription varies.

In addition, Nagel and colleagues have presented empirical evidence that cases that are of key importance in epistemology (in particular, the Gettier case) elicit similar judgments from lay people and philosophers as well as little demographic variation

---

[16] For discussion, see Stich (2013) and Nagel (2013).

(Nagel et al., 2013; Machery et al., forthcoming a). These cases weaken the inductive conclusion that judgments elicited by most philosophical cases differ across demographic groups.

The Limited-Influence Defense threatens Unreliability, Dogmatism, and Parochialism. If successful, a critic of the method of cases would not be allowed to generalize beyond the cases that have been examined, and philosophers would be warranted to use other cases for their dialectical purposes.

5.4.2 Rebuttal

I will first respond to the Limited-Influence Defense that appeals to empirical findings before discussing Nagel's theoretical argument. Undoubtedly, *some* thought experiments elicit the very judgment philosophers make across various kinds of population. As we have seen (Chapter 2 and Section 5.1 of the present chapter), some findings alleged to establish that judgments elicited by philosophical cases vary have been successfully challenged: Philosophical cases tend to elicit similar judgments from men and women (but see Friesdorf et al., 2015), and some (but not all—see Starmans & Friedman, 2012) versions of the Gettier case elicit across cultures the typical philosophical judgment that the protagonist does not know the relevant proposition (Machery et al., forthcoming a).

However, among the philosophical cases that have been examined by experimental philosophers and psychologists, *all* are influenced either by demographic variables or by the way the cases are presented. For instance, some versions of the Gettier case (usually classified as being "based on authentic evidence") elicit the judgment that the protagonist actually knows the relevant proposition; those that don't (usually classified as being "based on inauthentic or apparent evidence") can be framed so as to elicit the judgment that the protagonist knows the relevant proposition. Or consider the switch version of the trolley case. While the judgment that it is not permissible to push the switch to save five people and to cause the death of a single individual as a by-product is found in many cultures that have been so far examined (but not all: see, e.g., Xiang, 2014 and the other citations in Chapter 2), this judgment too can be framed: People are less likely to judge that it is permissible to push the switch when the switch case is presented after the footbridge case. While the inductive basis of Unreliability, Dogmatism, and Parochiality is not as large as one might want, there is little reason to believe that philosophical cases will typically be immune to demographic and presentation variables.

I now turn to Nagel's theoretical argument, which suffers from two flaws. First, even if knowledge ascription is a component of a reliable and universal capacity for mind-reading, this entails neither that people conceive similarly of knowledge across cultures and languages—and thus are likely to make similar judgments in response to epistemological cases—nor that knowledge ascription is reliable. Judgments elicited by Gettier cases may be a reflection of a universal folk epistemology; people in all cultures may then possess the concept of an epistemic state that entails, but requires more than justification, truth, and belief, and in most cultures that concept may be expressed by the epistemic term commonly translated into English as "know." At the same time, while a universal folk epistemology may require a concept that is more demanding than the concept of true justified belief, it may also permit considerable variation in the details, with different cultures elaborating on the true justified belief theme in different ways. In addition, while belief and desire ascription may be reliable, knowledge ascription could be much less reliable.

Second, and most important, appealing to the general reliability and universality of judgments about knowledge or permissibility does little to undermine the inductive step of Unreliability, Dogmatism, and Parochialism. Let's grant for the sake of the argument that knowledge ascription is a universal, early developing component of a generally reliable faculty of mindreading, and that the capacities used in everyday life are used in philosophers' seminar room. The problem is that the general reliability of knowledge ascription is consistent with its unreliability when it is elicited by epistemologists' cases: A given type of judgment can be in general reliable, while being unreliable in a particular kind of circumstance. What's more, the general reliability of knowledge ascription provides no reason to expect by induction reliable knowledge ascription about the situations described by epistemological cases, since those differ from everyday situations in a myriad of ways (Section 3.5 of Chapter 3): They contain misleading irrelevant elements, they are fanciful, they look tricky, and they separate cues that go together in everyday life.

5.4.3 Upshot

Unreliability, Dogmatism, and Parochialism rely on an inductive step: They generalize from the cases that experimental philosophers have examined. Like any other generalization, this inductive step is risky, but the Limited-Influence Defense does little to undermine it.

5.5 The Fallibility Defense

5.5.1 The defense

The Fallibility Defense responds to Unreliability by conceding that demographic and presentations variables can influence the judgments elicited by philosophical cases, while denying that this entails that these judgments are unreliable.[17] Experimental philosophers' research merely shows that, just like any other kind of judgment, including perceptual judgments, the judgments elicited by cases *can, in some circumstances*, be erroneous, not that they are in general unreliable. That is, their research merely shows that these judgments are fallible, exactly as common sense and psychological research show that perceptual judgments are fallible (perhaps in more ways than one would

---

[17] E.g., Bealer (1996); Sosa (2007); Nagel (2012).

have naively expected). One should thus be cautious in judging in response to philosophical cases, exactly as one should exercise caution in making perceptual judgments.
Thus, Sosa writes (2007, 105; emphasis in the original):

[S]urely the effects of priming, framing, and other such contextual factors will affect the epistemic
status of intuition in general, only in the sort of way that they affect the epistemic status of perceptual observation in general. One would think that the ways of preserving the epistemic
importance of perception in the face of such effects on perceptual judgments would be analo-
gously available for the preservation of the epistemic importance of intuition in the face of such
effects on intuitive judgments. The upshot is that we have to be *careful* in how we use intuitions,
not that intuitions are useless.

5.5.2 Rebuttal

There are two kinds of response to the Fallibility Defense. One could concede that
experimental philosophers have merely shown that judgments elicited by philosophical
cases are fallible, not that they are unreliable, but insist that, in contrast to perceptual
judgments, one is still not entitled to rely on them.[18] The task is then to explain the
difference between perceptual judgments and judgments elicited by philosophical
cases. Alternatively, instead of challenging the perceptual analogy proposed by Sosa,
one could embrace it to conclude that one is not entitled to rely on judgments elicited
by philosophical cases. In what follows, I spell out both responses, and argue for the
superiority of the latter response.

The first response agrees with Sosa that, as far as we know, judgments about philosophical cases are only fallible, but argues that in contrast to perceptual judgments one
cannot justifiably rely on them. The reason is that we have a good understanding of the
kind of situation that elicits unreliable perceptual judgments and of what to do in
response, and that a similar understanding is lacking for the judgments elicited by
philosophical cases. In Weinberg's terminology, perceptual judgments, but not judgments elicited by philosophical cases, are hopeful (Sections 3.1 and 3.2 of Chapter 3).
Using the terminology of intuitions, Weinberg writes (2007, 334–5), "Both opponents
and defenders of intuition can agree that they are arguing about intuition's hopefulness
and focus their arguments accordingly, attempting to show that our intuition-deploying
practices do or do not possess the requisite sources of hope to anything like the degree
that scientific instruments or our other basic evidential sources (like sense perception,
testimony, or memory) do." Alexander (2012, 82) concurs: "[I]t pays to be careful, but
only when we know what it means to be careful."

The first response to the Fallibility Defense relies on what can be called "the hope
principle": Generally, one can justifiably rely on fallible judgments only when one has a
good understanding of when these judgments fail (Weinberg, 2007, 327 for a similar
principle, called "H"). And, it rejects the analogy between perceptual judgments and

---

[18] Weinberg (2007); Alexander (2012); Alexander & Weinberg (2014).

judgments elicited by philosophical cases because of the different implications of the hope principle for the former and the latter.

There are several problems with this first response. First, it concedes too much to Sosa, and undersells the significance of experimental philosophers' findings. These do not simply suggest that judgments about cases are fallible (big deal!), but that they are unreliable. Experimental philosophers have shown again and again that the judgments elicited by typical and canonical philosophical cases are influenced by either demographic or by presentation variables, and we can conclude by induction that the judgments elicited by most current philosophical cases are unreliable. In addition, disturbing cases are needed to investigate some of the modal consequences of philosophical theories and to distinguish competing views agreeing about typical situations. Second, the response to the Fallibility Defense that appeals to the hope principle can be challenged by a variant of this defense: While we may not currently know when the judgments elicited by philosophical cases fail, we may soon be in such a position, in part thanks to experimental philosophers' research. So, the real lesson to be drawn from almost two decades of research in experimental philosophy is not that we should abandon the method of cases, but that we should reform it by learning what it means to use cases judiciously. I call this response "the Reform Defense," and I examine it in the next section. Incidentally, the Reform Defense is not unwelcome to Weinberg and Alexander, whose goal is not to challenge the use of cases in philosophy in general, but to criticize the way these are currently used and to justify the contribution of experimental methods to philosophy (e.g., Weinberg, 2007, 340). (As we saw in the introduction, my views are more radical than their moderate restrictionism.) Third, and most important, the hope principle should not be accepted. As argued in Section 3.2 of Chapter 3, in the history of science novel experimental techniques (e.g., Galileo's telescope) have often been used without a good understanding of the situations in which they fail.

I now turn to the second response to the Fallibility Defense. Instead of undermining the analogy between perceptual judgments and judgments elicited by philosophical cases, as Weinberg and Alexander do, this response embraces it. Perceptual judgments have a proper domain: Within their proper domain they are reliable, and one is entitled to rely on these judgments; when they are made beyond their proper domain, they are unreliable, and one is not (or less) entitled to rely on them. For instance, we are not (or less) entitled to rely on judgments about perceptual color when we are judging about the color of distant landscapes (which appear, mistakenly, blue). Judgments about cause, responsibility, the right and the wrong, or reference too have proper domains (assuming that error theories about these topics are incorrect), and one is not (or less) entitled to rely on these judgments when they are made beyond their proper domain. The lesson to be drawn from experimental-philosophy studies is that philosophical cases have properties (the disturbing characteristics discussed in Section 3.5 of Chapter 3) that place the situations they describe beyond the proper domains of the pertinent judgments. So, as Sosa rightly remarks, it would be unreasonable to stop making judgment about causes, reference, and responsibility on the grounds that the judgments about causes, reference, and responsibility that are elicited by philosophical cases are unreliable, exactly as it would be unreasonable to stop making perceptual judgments on the grounds that perceptual illusions are misleading. However, this remark provides no more justification for making judgments in response to philosophical cases than our warrant for making perceptual judgment about typical perceptual situations provides justification for making perceptual judgments about the situations that elicit perceptual illusions.

Sosa, and perhaps Weinberg and Alexander too, are likely to insist that experimental philosophers have not shown that the situations described by philosophical cases are beyond the proper domains of the relevant judgments. Let's begin with two remarks. First, *pace* Alexander and Weinberg (2014) the claim is not that epistemic, moral, or semantic judgments are unreliable; rather, the claim is that judgments elicited by epistemic, moral, or semantic cases are unreliable. As a result, arguments to the effect that the former claim is unlikely or would be hard to establish convincingly miss the point. Second, I take it that Sosa would not require experimental philosophers to show *beyond doubt* that the judgments elicited by epistemic, moral, or semantic cases are unreliable. Unreliability relies on an induction, and all inductive conclusions leave room for doubt: Will the next crow be black? Will the next ball be red? Will the sun rise tomorrow? To show that the situations described by philosophical cases are beyond the proper domains of the pertinent judgments, Sosa and others cannot require standards that cannot be met for any inductive conclusion.

In fact, when proper standards for induction are firmly kept in mind, it's hard to see what justifies resisting the inductive conclusion that the judgments elicited by most philosophical cases are unreliable. Sosa and others could either question the inductive basis of Unreliability or, granting the inductive basis, question the inductive step. The Amateur-Psychology Defense could give a reason to question the inductive basis of Unreliability, but we have seen that this response should be resisted. To question the inductive step, Sosa and others could appeal to the Expertise Defense or to the idea that judgments about topics such as knowledge, permissibility, and responsibility are generally reliable and that we can thus assume that the judgments about philosophical cases are reliable too (the Limited-Influence Defense), but both responses are underwhelming, as we have seen in previous sections.

To make the point of the last paragraph more vivid, consider the following analogy. Kahneman and Tversky have reported several experiments where subjects (including experts) make erroneous statistical judgments (e.g., Tversky & Kahneman, 1971; Kahneman & Tversky, 1982), and have concluded that statistical judgment that is not aided by computational methods is unreliable (e.g., Kahneman, 2011, 112–13). To conclude instead that statistical judgment is merely fallible, one could either question the empirical research done by Kahneman or question the induction, perhaps on the grounds that statistical judgments are in general systematically different from those studied by heuristics-and-biases researchers (a line most strongly associated with Gigerenzer), but if none of these approaches is available, then one ought to embrace Kahneman and Tversky's conclusion.

Perhaps Sosa and others would seize upon this analogy to explain why on their view experimental philosophers have failed to establish the unreliability of judgments elicited by philosophical cases, arguing that the inductive basis of Kahneman and Tversky's conclusion is simply much stronger than the inductive basis of Unreliability: Kahneman and Tversky's experiments are better, potential confounds are taken care of, and so on. Furthermore, Sosa and others could insist that they are not endorsing the Amateur-Psychology Defense: It's not that experimental philosophers' studies are bad, but it's just that, at this point, there are too few experiments, each of which with too many uncontrolled confounds. Experimental philosophy is good as it goes, it just does not go far enough. They could even add that the standards for inducing from the inductive basis should be raised since the stakes are so high—challenging one of the most important methods of philosophy and seriously curtailing philosophical knowledge (Chapter 6): A large, if not overwhelming, amount of evidence is required to conclude that the situations described by most philosophical cases elicit unreliable, and not just fallible, judgments (e.g., Sosa, 1998, 261).

I'll first rebut the point about stakes since it cuts both ways: What is at stake is also keeping a method that has misled generations of philosophers and embracing an illusion of philosophical knowledge if the arguments developed in this book are on the right track; so perhaps instead of raising the standards for induction, we should lower them. At the very least, requiring a large or overwhelming amount of evidence is unjustified. Second, there is no doubt that Kahneman and Tversky's empirical work is of higher quality than experimental philosophers', but so what? The real issue is whether experimental philosophers' work is so limited or of so poor quality that it cannot serve as the inductive basis of Unreliability. And it just ain't so.

It wouldn't do to respond that we are in the early days of the controversy about the standing of the method of cases and that it would thus be unwise to draw any drastic conclusion at this point. The points made against the method of cases in Chapters 3 and 4 generalize concerns that have been expressed about particular cases for decades (see the Introduction). And the attacks against the method of cases led by experimental philosophers is now more than fifteen years old: It is time to take stock.

5.5.3 Upshot

The Fallibility Defense would only be convincing if either we had reasons to expect judgments elicited by philosophical cases to be reliable or if we had reasons to question experimental philosophers' studies. So, the Fallibility Defense is not an independent line of argument against Unreliability; rather, at best it depends on other responses to this argument. Since these responses are unconvincing, the Fallibility Defense is of little use for defending the method of cases.

5.6 The Reform Defense

5.6.1 The defense

Proponents of the Fallibility Defense are likely to fall back on the Reform Defense of the method of cases: Rather than suggesting that the method of cases should be abandoned, experimental philosophers' findings suggest that it should be reformed; furthermore, "meliorists" hold, they show how it can be reformed: by taking into account the phenomena experimental philosophers have been highlighting.[19] Framing effects could be counteracted by considering different formulations of a particular philosophical case; order effects by examining a case in different contexts. Furthermore, philosophers should only rely on those philosophical cases that elicit a shared judgment across many kinds of population (e.g., some versions of the Gettier case).

5.6.2 Rebuttal

As a point of fact, there has been little discussion (and even less empirically based discussion) about whether, and how, one can improve the reliability of the judgments made in response to philosophical cases (when that is a meaningful idea). Dennett is one of the few contemporary philosophers to theorize explicitly about how to develop good philosophical cases, but even he has little to say beyond some fairly vague platitudes (Dennett, 2005, 104):

But is it a good intuition pump? How could we tell? Douglas Hofstadter's classic advice to philosophers confronted by a thought experiment is to treat it the way scientists treat a phenomenon of interest: vary it, turn it over, examine it from all angles, and in different settings and conditions, just to make sure you aren't taken in by illusions of causation. Turn all the knobs, he said, and see if the thing still pumps the same intuitions.[20]

Meliorists may respond that they will provide more concrete recommendations in the future, but they suffer from an exuberant optimism. We do not know how to counteract the influence cultural background and other demographic variables have on judgment. It is true that we try to ignore our own identity when we are jurors, assess job applications, and review journal submissions, but we are typically unsuccessful. Perhaps one may think that other factors (e.g., the influence of the superficial content of cases on judgment) may be easier to counteract, but this too is debatable. I have already mentioned statistical judgments unaided by formal methods. Kahneman writes about them (2011, 5):

In spite of years of teaching and using statistics, we [Kahneman and Tversky] had not developed an intuitive sense of the reliability of statistical results observed in small samples. Our subjective judgments were biased: we were far too willing to believe research findings based on inadequate evidence and prone to collect too few observations in our own research.

---

[19] E.g., Huemer (2008); Alexander (2012); Talbot (2013); Levy (2014).
[20] For other platitudes, see, e.g., Kamm (1993, Introduction); Dennett (2013); Ludwig (2014).

That is, the biases distorting statistical judgments about data from small samples are unlikely to be counteractable, and scientists rely on computational procedures to assess the reliability of their findings instead of relying on their unaided judgments. Similarly, we should be skeptical that many of the factors undermining the reliability of the judgments elicited by philosophical cases are counteractable. Indeed, some natural solutions to improve the reliability of judgments in response to cases have be shown to be inefficient.[21] When presented with the switch, footbridge, and loop versions of the trolley case, instructing philosophers and non-philosophers alike to "take some time to consider the different moral dimensions at issue, including potential arguments for and against the position to which [they] are initially attracted . . . to consider how [they] might respond to different variants of the scenario or to different ways of describing the case," and imposing a delay between the reading of the case and the response had no influence at all on their vulnerability to order effects (Schwitzgebel & Cushman, 2015). Furthermore, as we saw in Section 5.2, various strategies to promote careful judgment making, all of which have been extensively used in psychology and behavioral economics, had no impact on lay people's judgment about various cases: Compelling participants to take their time before answering, asking them to justify their answers, priming analytic thinking by giving them a mathematical problem, and paying them for accuracy did not change people's answers to the fake-barn case, to the Gödel case, and a few other cases (Colaço et al., ms).

5.6.3 Upshot

It is tempting to conclude from experimental philosophers' research that the method of cases needs to be reformed, not abandoned, but the prospects of this suggestion do not appear to be good, and the Reform Defense can be sidestepped until concrete proposals about how to improve the method of cases are developed and backed by evidence.

5.7 The Mischaracterization Defense

5.7.1 The defense

A critic could argue that the method of cases has been mischaracterized, and conclude that, because it has been mischaracterized, the challenges articulated by Unreliability, Dogmatism, and Parochialism fail. Thus, according to Cappelen (2012), experimental philosophers assume erroneously that the method of cases consists in treating intuitions elicited by philosophical cases as evidence for or against philosophical views (see also Deutsch, 2009, 2015). Instead of intuitions (e.g., the intuition that "Gödel" refers to Gödel in the situation described by the Gödel case) being evidence for various

---

[21] Wright's (2010, 2013) work on confidence is also relevant here, but it has already been critically discussed in Section 3.5.6 of Chapter 3.

philosophical views (e.g., the causal-historical theory of reference), facts about the situations described by philosophical cases (the fact that "Gödel" refers to Gödel) are simply part of the common ground in philosophy and bear on philosophical theses. Cappelen summarizes this argument as follows (2012, 219): "A central goal of experimental philosophy is to criticize the philosophical practice of appealing to intuitions about cases" and "[t]he entire project of experimental philosophy only gets off the ground by assuming Centrality" (viz., the assumption that intuitions play a central role in philosophy). He concludes that experimental philosophy is a "big mistake."

5.7.2 Rebuttal

There are two alternative responses to the Mischaracterization Defense: One could argue against Cappelen and Deutsch that intuitions play some role in the method of cases (e.g., Chalmers, 2014; Weinberg, 2014); alternatively, one could deny that the attacks against the method of cases assume that intuitions play a role in the method of cases. In light of the minimalist characterization of the method of cases presented in Chapter 1, the second response is the best way to deal with the Mischaracterization Defense.

It is true that philosophers have been prone to characterize philosophical cases as eliciting intuitions, and experimental philosophers have often followed suit.[22] However, as we have seen in Chapter 1, this characterization is erroneous. Some ways of unpacking the notion of intuition are philosophically problematic, and the characterization of the method of cases that appeals to the notion of intuition is descriptively inadequate for almost all ways of unpacking it: It fails to capture how philosophers use philosophical cases. When considering philosophical cases, philosophers simply make judgments about the situations they describe, and take it for granted that some facts hold or would hold in these situations. As Cappelen puts it, these facts are taken to belong to "the common ground" among philosophers. It is thus unfortunate that experimental philosophers, including myself, have followed the philosophical tradition in describing the method of cases as eliciting intuitions, and have given the impression that their argument was directed at the alleged use of intuitions in philosophy. It is not; the target is the method of cases.

Despite getting much right, Cappelen errs in some important respects. Surprisingly, he has nothing to say about what warrants viewing some facts as belonging to the common ground. (In contrast, Deutsch is aware of the importance of addressing this issue.) Why are we warranted in assuming, e.g., that it is permissible to cause someone's death in the situation described by the switch version of the trolley case? It can't simply be because philosophers view them as belonging to the common ground. Assuming that p does not make one warranted to assume that p. I wish it was that easy!

Paying more attention to this question—what warrants taking some facts as belonging to the common ground?—would have helped Cappelen see that the attack against

---

[22] Machery et al. (2004); Weinberg et al. (2001); Weinberg (2007); Alexander (2012); Nado (2014a).

the method of cases does not depend on assuming that philosophical cases elicit a distinct attitude or a distinct kind of judgment (i.e., intuitions). By revealing the influence of demographic and presentation variables on judgments made in response to philosophical cases or the demographic diversity of these judgments, experimental philosophers challenge, in three different ways (spelt out by Unreliability, Dogmatism, and Parochialism), the warrant for assuming that, e.g., "Gödel" would refer to Gödel in the situation described by the Gödel case. And if they are right, such alleged facts should not be part of the common ground in philosophy.

Deutsch (2015) is more sensitive than Cappelen to the question, What warrants taking some facts as belonging to the common ground?, but his answer isn't satisfactory (Colaço & Machery, 2017). On his view, philosophers are warranted because they propose arguments in support of their judgments made in response to cases: Philosophers "*argue* for their claims about their thought experiments and hypothetical cases" (2015, xv; my emphasis).

Cappelen makes a similar observation: Philosophers often explain why the facts they take to hold in the situations described by philosophical cases really hold. For instance, Goldman (1976, 773) ends the fake-barn case with the question, "How is this change in our assessment to be explained?" Similarly, Cappelen comments on Lehrer's Truetemp case as follows (168):

Is the answer presented as a rock-bottom starting point for which arguments are not needed? Is it presented as a response that justifies, but stands in no need of justification? ... The answer to each of these questions is an unequivocal "no." The first thing Lehrer does after asking the question, "does he know that it is?," is to present several arguments for responding with "No."

However, first, while arguments may sometimes be found in published articles that support philosophers' assessment of thought experiments, it isn't the case in general, although more or less compelling arguments can always be made up post hoc. In many cases, perhaps in most, the alleged arguments are not explicitly stated. Second, many of the arguments Deutsch claims to find in support of the judgments made in response to cases merely recapitulate the features of the cases, and they are not illuminating. They often add nothing to the cases themselves. Third, Deutsch fails to notice that the arguments he finds in the articles he discusses or, when those are missing, those he reconstructs cluster into two types, which I will call "justifying arguments" and "implication arguments." Justifying arguments seek to support a particular proposition about the situation described by a thought experiment, e.g. that Smith does not know that the man who will get the job has ten coins in his pocket in Gettier's 10-coins case. By contrast, in an implication argument, a fact about a situation described by a case is assumed, and philosophers infer a philosophical proposition (about knowledge, reference, causation, etc.) because this proposition provides the best explanation of the assumed fact. Thus, implication arguments are inferences to the best explanation.

Justifying arguments and implication arguments are very different. They support different kinds of conclusion: a conclusion about which facts hold in the situation described by a case (e.g., that Smith does not know that the man who will get the job has ten coins in his pocket) versus a conclusion about a philosophical topic (e.g., that knowledge requires a proper causal relation). They also have an inverse directionality. In contrast to justifying arguments, implication arguments are not meant to provide reasons for a particular assessment of the situation described by a case; rather, they *assume* such assessment. As such, implication arguments do not provide support for the thesis that philosophers' claims in response to cases are supported by arguments.

Deutsch is sensitive to this point, but believes that it does not undermine his account (2015, 96, emphases in the original): "The order of explanation goes *both* ways, from the truth of the Gettier judgment to the truth of some more general epistemic principle, but also vice versa." This response won't do, however. In addition to mischaracterizing inferences to the best explanation, it turns the method of cases into a hopelessly circular enterprise. Starting with the first point, it just is not the case that inferences to the best explanation *both* provide support for the conclusion and provide new reasons to believe the premises. Rather, inferences to the best explanation start by taking some claim or phenomenon to be well established, and infer that some theory is right because it provides the best explanation of it. Turning to the second point, the circularity of Deutsch's method is patent. Argumentative circles need not be vicious if they are sufficiently broad, but the circles here are fairly tight.

5.7.3 Upshot

The Mischaracterization Defense is misguided; it fails to take seriously and address the genuine challenges that Unreliability, Dogmatism, and Parochialism articulate, responding instead to a strawperson.

5.8 The Overgeneralization Defense

5.8.1 The defense

Finally, one may object that Unreliability, Dogmatism, and Parochialism show too much: Supposing that the judgments elicited by philosophical cases are not a distinct type of judgment, questioning their warrant should lead us to question the reliability of *all* judgments. In Williamson's words (2007, 220): "Although, in practice, judgments skeptics are skeptical only of a few judgments or concepts at a time, the underlying forms of arguments are far more general." If judgments about what causes what or about whether someone knows something are unreliable when elicited by philosophical cases, why would they be reliable when they occur in everyday life—for example, when we judge that smoking causes cancer and when a professor judges that a student does not know the course content? And since the latter skepticism is implausible, then the former skepticism should be implausible too (Williamson, 2004, 2007, 220–4; Cappelen 2012, 225–7).

5.8.2 Rebuttal

Does the argument against the method of cases lead to an unacceptable skepticism toward all judgments? The attack against the method of cases developed in this book seems particularly vulnerable since the minimalist characterization of the method of cases, which was endorsed early on and used, among other things, to rebut the Mischaracterization Defense, holds that philosophical cases do not elicit a distinct attitude or kind of judgment, but everyday judgments.

The Overgeneralization Defense highlights an important issue. The arguments against the method of cases rest on an induction from the empirical findings about some philosophical cases (the Gettier case, the Gödel case, the switch case, etc.) to a broader class of judgments ("the target class of judgments"). The concern is that there is no principled way to circumscribe this induction to a sufficiently broad class of judgments (so that the arguments have some philosophical bite), but not to a class so broad that the arguments imply that no judgment should be trusted. The three responses considered below circumscribe the target class of judgments differently. I'll start with the most concessive response.

By and large, the first response concedes defeat: There is no way to circumscribe in a principled manner the target class of judgments without including all judgments, and as a result Unreliability, Dogmatism, and Parochialism, all of which assume the possibility of a principled circumscription, should be rejected. However, snatching a sliver of victory from the jaws of defeat, this first response adds that experimental philosophers' findings still have much polemical bite, provided that the three arguments developed in this book are replaced with piecemeal arguments. Rather than questioning the warrant for the judgments elicited by philosophical cases in general, experimental philosophers should merely claim, e.g., that the judgment about whom "Gödel" refers to in the situation described by the Gödel case is unreliable or that judgments elicited by fake-barn cases are unreliable. Because piecemeal arguments do not seek to generalize beyond the judgments elicited by the particular cases examined by experimental philosophers (the Gödel case, etc.), they do not give rise to an unacceptable generalized skepticism about judgment. Still, because these cases are philosophically important—they play noteworthy dialectical roles in major philosophical arguments (although what their roles consist in and how important they are can be a matter of controversy)—piecemeal arguments would be philosophically significant. In fact, some of the philosophical cases examined by experimental philosophers are central to important philosophical controversies, and suspending judgment about these cases would have significant consequences for these controversies. The following cases are, at the very least, suspect: the Gödel case, the Twin-Earth case, the fake-barn case, the Gettier case, the Society of Music Lovers case, the trolley cases, and the bank cases (this list is not exhaustive). If we need to suspend judgment about them, a large swath of epistemology, ethics, and the philosophy of language would grind to a halt.

The first response to the generalization argument concedes a lot to the Overgeneralization Defense, and we can do better. The second and third responses seek to generalize beyond the specific cases examined by experimental philosophers. The second response appeals to content (what the judgments are about) to generalize, the third response (which I have endorsed in this book) to context (the circumstances in which judgments are made). Let's examine the second response first. It bites the bullet: If experimental philosophers' findings show that the judgments about some property (e.g., causation) happen to be unreliable or to elicit disagreement, then no judgment about *this* property (e.g., about causation) should be trusted.[23]

Everyday judgments about causation in the social domain illustrate this second response to the Overgeneralization Defense. Social psychologists have shown that judgments about causation are systematically biased when they are applied to morally salient actions. For instance, Alicke (1992, 2000) has shown that people's desire to blame an agent can influence their judgment about her causal contribution to the production of an outcome. Consider the following vignette:

John was driving over the speed limit (about 40 m.p.h. in a 30-m.p.h. zone) in order to get home in time to hide an anniversary present for his parents that he had left out in the open before they could see it. As John came to an intersection, he failed to see a stop sign that was covered by a large branch. As a result, John hit a car that was coming from the other direction. He hit it on the driver's side, causing the driver multiple lacerations, a broken collar bone, and a fractured arm. John was uninjured in the accident.

Consider another vignette that is identical to the previous one except that the first sentence now reads as follows:

John was driving over the speed limit (about 40 m.p.h. in a 30-m.p.h. zone) in order to get home in time to hide a vial of cocaine he had left out in the open before his parents could see it.

People tend to judge that the agent has made a greater causal contribution to the outcome when presented with the second vignette than with the first. More generally, people's negative evaluation of agents, due among other things to the biases they might harbor against minorities, influences their causal judgments about the causal contribution of these agents to outcomes. We could perhaps conclude from this experimental finding that judgments about causation in a morally laden social context are unreliable, whether these are elicited by vignettes or are about real-life situations. Judges, parents, teachers, and others should perhaps distrust their own causal judgments about social situations that involve blame or social biases.

One might wonder why this content-based response does not entail an unacceptable skepticism about most judgments: If the judgments about reference, justification, knowledge, moral permissibility, or responsibility elicited by the philosophical cases

---

[23] Sinnott-Armstrong (2008) and Nadelhoffer and Feltz (2008) follow this strategy.

that experimental philosophers have examined are unreliable, then everyday judgments about reference, justification, knowledge, moral permissibility, or responsibility should also be unreliable. But I know that "Edouard Machery" refers to myself. Fortunately, the threat of global skepticism can be easily defused. Some judgments have broad proper domains, but the situations described by philosophical cases just don't belong to them. For instance, while we are good at identifying the reference of proper names in most situations, the judgment about the reference of "Gödel" in the situation described by the Gödel case is unreliable because this situation is beyond the proper domain of judgments about the reference of proper names. By contrast, other judgments such as judgments about causation in a morally laden social context have narrow proper domains, and these judgments are then unreliable. It is warranted to generalize on the basis of content only when the latter condition holds.

Third, and most importantly, context distinguishes the judgments elicited by philosophical cases from everyday judgments (Machery, 2011a). As argued in Chapter 3 and earlier in this chapter, the philosophical cases examined by experimental philosophers elicit cognitive artifacts; they result in a misfiring of otherwise reliable judgments. These philosophical cases have properties that make the judgments they elicit unreliable—the disturbing characteristics. There need not be a unique disturbing characteristic; that is, different cases may instantiate different disturbing characteristics. *Pace* Williamson, there is thus a principled reason to induce from the philosophical cases examined by experimental philosophers to the broader class of current philosophical cases or, more generally, to the class of unusual or atypical or narratively intricate cases.

It is no objection that situations similar to the situations described by philosophical cases (e.g., Gettier case—Williamson, 2007) can occur in everyday life, since that just means that some everyday situations are also liable to elicit unreliable judgments, which should not surprise us. Nor is it an objection that some philosophical cases may not possess any disturbing property. The claim is not that every philosophical case elicits a cognitive artifact or diverse responses, but that the kind of case philosophers use for dialectical purpose tends, non-accidentally, to elicit cognitive artifacts or a diversity of responses.

Nor is it compelling to respond that the advice to suspend judgment remains inapplicable until there is clear-cut evidence about what cases exactly are impugned by experimental-philosophy studies. First, we have provided reasons to believe that disturbing cases prime unreliability and disagreement. Second, even if we were unsure about how broadly to suspend judgment, we should still suspend judgment in response to all the cases in contemporary philosophy (except those known to be immune to demographic and presentation effects) because the cases examined by philosophers are typical and canonical. Similarly, if we find that some eggs are contaminated with Salmonella, we would stop eating eggs sold by the brand selling them, even if it is unclear whether all eggs are contaminated.

5.8.3 *Upshot*

Unreliability, Dogmatism, and Parochialism would be unacceptable if they entailed a general skepticism about judgment. We are good at recognizing reference, judgments about causation are often trustworthy, and (if one is not a moral skeptic) there is no reason to doubt responsibility ascription. However, Unreliability, Dogmatism, and Parochialism do not entail any general skepticism, mostly because these arguments only challenge judgments beyond their proper domains.

5.9 Conclusion

Users of the method of cases will find no reason for optimism in the defenses considered in this chapter. While some experiments run by experimental philosophers and allied psychologists have methodological problems, many of the critical results are sound and well established. It is also not the case that experimental philosophers have been collecting data about the wrong kind of judgment. Priming reflective deliberation does not lead people to judge differently in response to cases. A growing body of evidence suggests that, despite their genuine distinct epistemic skills, philosophers' judgments too are unreliable. There is little reason to doubt that the findings of experimental philosophers generalize to many philosophical cases. It is tempting to reply that, for all experimental philosophers have shown, judgments about philosophical cases are only fallible, not unreliable, but this response really relies on the other responses rebuked in this chapter. There is currently no concrete proposal to use the findings of experimental philosophy to reform the method of cases, and pessimism is in order. Since they rest on the minimalist characterization of the method of cases, Unreliability, Dogmatism, and Parochialism do not assume that a distinct kind of attitude—intuitions—play an evidential role in philosophy, and thus they do not rest on a mischaracterization of what philosophers do. Finally, experimental philosophers endorsing Unreliability, Dogmatism, and Parochialism can explain why their concerns do not extend to all judgments.

6

Modal Ignorance and the Limits of Philosophy

Intellectual progress usually occurs through sheer abandonment of questions together with the alternatives they assume…We do not solve: we get over them.

(Dewey, 1910, 19)

Suppose one suspends judgment about most current philosophical cases or, more generally, about unusual, atypical, narratively rich actual and possible cases, perhaps because one has been convinced by Unreliability, Dogmatism, and Parochialism, what implications would it have for philosophy? What bit of philosophy would be affected? Would it then be impossible to address some philosophical questions? Which kind of question? Or rather can philosophers simply fall back on another method to address the same old questions? In this chapter, I argue that the consequence of suspending judgment about cases is an extensive modal ignorance that prevents us from answering important traditional and contemporary philosophical questions.

Epistemological, ethical, and metaphysical theories are often modally immodest: Their claims are often not primarily about how things actually are or about how things must be in worlds that obey the laws of nature; rather, they are often about how things must be, period. Epistemological, ethical, and metaphysical theories are not just concerned with what knowledge, moral permissibility, personal identity, causation, and explanation actually are; nor are they concerned with what knowledge, moral permissibility, personal identity, causation, and explanation are in worlds nomologically similar to ours; rather, they are typically about what these necessarily are or at least about what they entail. Some of the most influential claims in the history of philosophy, such as physicalism and dualism, are also similarly modally immodest. Physicalists assert, roughly, that necessarily every event is a physical event, while non-physicalists, including property dualists, deny it. Act utilitarianism, traditionally understood, holds that necessarily an action is morally right if and only if, among all possible actions, it maximizes total happiness—no other possible action would produce as much net happiness (that is, happiness minus unhappiness) for all individuals affected by this action. Act utilitarianism, as well as its competitors and many variants, is modally immodest: It is a claim about what *must* be the case for an action to be morally right. And according to the Principle of Alternate Possibilities in the free-will literature, necessarily one is free or responsible only if one could have acted otherwise. Action theorists debate about *must* be the case for one to be free.

In light of the limitations of the judgments elicited by philosophical cases that were revealed by the previous chapters, I argue in this penultimate chapter that, even if there are modal facts (e.g., facts about what must be the case or about what can be the case), many of the modal facts that matter for philosophy are beyond our epistemic reach: We philosophers are not in a position to acquire the desired modal knowledge. I conclude that the large swath of traditional and contemporary philosophical projects that hang on acquiring such knowledge must be abandoned. We will never know what knowledge reduces to (if it reduces to anything) or what it entails, and we will never know whether dualism or materialism are true. Philosophers can't keep doing epistemology, ethics, or metaphysics the way they've done it for far too long.

In Section 6.1, I will clarify the argument for modal ignorance and I will discuss the search for metaphysical necessities in philosophy. In Section 6.2, I will turn to the role of cases in learning about these modal facts, and I will examine what the suspension of judgment in response to cases implies for our modal knowledge. In Section 6.3, I will argue that there are no alternatives to the method of cases for learning about the metaphysical necessities that are of interest in philosophy. In Section 6.4, I examine whether the argument developed in this chapter really justifies setting aside modally immodest philosophical issues.

Please note the following caveats. For the sake of the argument, I assume that there are modal facts, in contrast to modal fictionalism (e.g., Rosen, 1990), although I won't commit myself to any specific views about their nature. I also assume that modal sentences call for a truth-conditional semantics, and thus that there can be modal knowledge. These assumptions may not be correct, but engaging with them at any depth would call for another book.

6.1 The Argument for Modal Ignorance

6.1.1 Modal Ignorance

The argument for modal ignorance ("Modal Ignorance") is straightforward.

Modal Ignorance

1. Many central philosophical issues are about metaphysical necessities, and resolving these issues requires establishing these necessities.

2. Philosophers must appeal to unusual and atypical philosophical cases to establish these metaphysical necessities.

3. We should suspend judgment about the situations described by current philosophical cases and, more generally, by unusual and atypical philosophical cases.

4. There is no other way of learning about the pertinent metaphysical necessities and possibilities.

5. Hence, there are many philosophical issues that we cannot resolve.

Let's specify first the nature and scope of the modal skepticism involved in Modal Ignorance. As I use it, "modal skepticism" does not refer to a concern about the meaningfulness of modal notions or about the reality of modal facts. Earlier, I have granted for the sake of the argument that there are modal facts. Rather, one is a modal skeptic if and only if one doubts that we know and can come to know these modal facts. That is, according to the modal skeptic, the way we form modal beliefs does not yield knowledge, and it is mysterious how else we could acquire such knowledge.[1] Modal skepticism has many flavors, and at least three grades of modal skepticism can be distinguished:

- *Hardcore modal skepticism*: We lack knowledge of *all* necessities and possibilities.
- *Skepticism about metaphysical modalities*: We lack knowledge of *metaphysical* necessities and strict metaphysical possibilities altogether.
- *Skepticism about metaphysical modalities of philosophical interest*: We lack knowledge of many metaphysical necessities that are of philosophical interest.

A hardcore modal skeptic would deny that we know anything about what is possible and necessary; for her, knowledge is limited to what is actual. That skepticism extends to trivial counterfactual propositions such as the proposition that, if I had not let the glass fall, it would not have broken. If one is a realist about modal facts, it is hard to see what would make hardcore modal skepticism attractive. A skeptic about metaphysical modalities restricts her skepticism to one form of possibility and necessity—metaphysical necesssity and strict metaphysical possibility—acknowledging that we can know what is nomologically or logically possible and necessary. The attraction of this form of modal skepticism is easily understood: It's not immediately obvious how to know what's possible once the laws of nature are allowed to vary. A skeptic about metaphysical modalities of philosophical interest is not worried about metaphysical necesssity and strict metaphysical possibility in general. She concedes that we may know some metaphysical necessities, even some of some philosophical interest (perhaps the proposition that everything is necessarily identical to itself), but she insists that many metaphysical necessities that are of interest in philosophy are beyond our epistemic grasp. Modal Ignorance is meant to support the third grade of modal skepticism; it leaves open the possibility that some metaphysical necessities are knowable.

Second, I draw the following lesson from Modal Ignorance: If we cannot resolve some central philosophical issues, then we should "abandon" them, as Dewey puts it. We should set aside reductive analyses or proposals about entailments (e.g., the Principle

---

[1] For simplicity, I will concentrate on knowledge below, but this skepticism extends to the justification of modal beliefs.

of Alternate Possibilities), the debate between type identity theory and multiple realizability, or the concerns with physicalism. Whether this is the proper lesson to draw from Modal Ignorance will be discussed in Section 6.4 of this chapter. For the time being, keep in mind that to abandon modally immodest philosophical issue about x is *not* to abandon philosophical theorizing about x. For instance, setting aside reductive proposals about causation is not tantamount to renouncing philosophizing about causation. There is more to philosophy than resolving modally immodest philosophical issues. I illustrate this point at the end of this section.

6.1.2 Philosophy and metaphysical modalities

In the remainder of Section 6.1, I elaborate on the claim that many debates in contemporary philosophy are about what is metaphysically necessary, but I first need to clarify briefly what I mean by "metaphysical necessity," "metaphysical possibility," and "strict metaphysical possibility."[2]

First, metaphysical necessity and possibility contrast with logical necessity and possibility. Logical necessity and possibility consist in what is necessary and possible in virtue of logic. For instance, if classical logic is correct, it is impossible that a proposition and its negation both hold. Everything that is not contradictory is possible. Classical logic might not be correct, but if it is correct, classical logical necessities could not be otherwise (in contrast to nomological necessities). Metaphysical necessity and possibility differ from logical necessity and possibility in that they do not hold in virtue of logic. (It is a controversial matter in virtue of what they hold, but we need not concern us with this difficult matter for present purposes.[3])

Second, within the necessities and possibilities that do not hold in virtue of logic, metaphysical necessity and possibility contrast with nomological necessity and possibility. Nomological necessity and possibility are restricted forms of necessity and possibility: They consist in what is necessary and possible when the laws of nature are held fixed. At least when scientific theories are taken at face value, their empirical commitments are broader than just what is happening in the actual world: They do not seem to describe only what is actually occurring, but what must and can be occurring if they are true. That is, scientific theories attempt to capture a form of necessity and possiblity: nomological necessity and possibility. On the other hand, if it is right that the laws of nature themselves could be different (a controversial position that is denied by necessitarians about laws), nomological necessity and possibility do not exhaust necessity and possibility. Some things that are nomologically impossible are possible in some sense (because the laws of nature could have been different), and some necessary propositions remain necessary even when the laws of nature are not held fixed. In contrast to nomological necessity, metaphysical necessity is unrestricted or absolute. When something is possible period, it is metaphysically possible; when something is necessary period, it is metaphysically necessary.

---

[2] E.g., Rosen (2006).   [3] E.g., Fine (1994).

So, roughly, metaphysical necessities are those unrestricted necessities that do not hold in virtue of logic; metaphysical possibilities those unrestricted possibilities that do not hold in virtue of logic. (Nomological possibilities then are metaphysically possible.) Strict metaphysical possibilities are those metaphysical possibilities that are not nomologically possible.

Philosophical theories often assert or deny metaphysical necessities and their truth is contingent on what is metaphysically possible. Some philosophers would like to know what personal identity depends on: Psychological continuity? Physical continuity? Something else? When asking such questions, we are not merely asking what personal identity actually depends on, as if personal identity could depend on something else if things were different; nor are we asking what personal identity depends on in light of the laws of nature, as if personal identity could depend on something else if the laws of nature were different. Indeed, we are neither inquiring about the actual world, collecting observational data or running experiments, nor examining our best scientific theories to determine what determines personal identity. Rather, we are asking what personal identity necessarily depends on, in an unrestricted sense of "necessarily."[4] Relatedly, the truth of the competing philosophical theories of personal identity depends on what is metaphysically possible. Physicalism asserts, roughly, that necessarily every event is a physical event.

Theories that propose reductive analyses of properties, states, or conditions of philosophical interest (personal identity, knowledge, permissibility, causation, or desert) assert the identity of these properties, states, or conditions with some further properties, states, or conditions, or combinations thereof. Whether or not identities can be contingent (e.g., Goliath and Lumpl), the identities asserted by reductive analyses are meant to be metaphysically necessary. Theories that refrain from analyzing properties, states, or conditions of philosophical interest reductively still ascribe metaphysically necessary features to those. Even if one doubts the possibility to analyze knowledge reductively, one can still hold that knowledge entails safety (i.e., a state must be safe to count as an instance of knowledge). And there too the truth of the proposed reductions or claims about necessary properties depends on what is metaphysically possible.

It is true that some philosophers do not purport to identify metaphysical necessities. In particular, some ethicists and political philosophers have explicitly rejected the need to identify principles that would determine, e.g., the permissible or the mandatory in every possible situation; instead, they settle for principles applying to choices and situations occurring in the actual world.[5] Thus, Pogge writes (1990, 660, italics in the original): "What does it matter that our morality is inapplicable to the life context of fictitious Martians or of the ancient Egyptians, so long as it provides reasonable solutions to *our* problems?" Such philosophical projects, which do not require knowing metaphysical necessities, are not the target of the present argument.

---

[4] For critical discussion of this approach to personal identity, see Wilkes (1988).

[5] E.g., Rawls (1980); Hare (1981); Pogge (1990); Miller (2008). For discussion, see Elster (2011).

So, the claim defended in this chapter is that we cannot know the metaphysical necessities pivotal to many philosophical debates. In particular, we often cannot know the facts at stake in the debates about what a state, property, or condition of philosophical interest is (What is knowledge? What is causation?) or entails. The issues and problems that breed these debates should be set aside; this is what progress in philosophy would look like.

6.1.3 Contrasting different types of philosophical project

The discussion so far has been fairly abstract, and some examples may help clarify what kind of philosophical project is undermined by Modal Ignorance. These examples will also be helpful to determine what kind of philosophical project this argument leaves unscathed, and why.

Let's start with causation. It is possible to distinguish two traditions in the philosophy of causation: the metaphysical and the methodological tradition. Philosophers working in the metaphysical tradition often attempt to reduce causation to another relation. Famously, treating causation as a relation between events, Lewis (1986) proposed to reduce it to a relation of counterfactual dependence: Very roughly, event e causes e' if and only if had e not occurred, e' would not have occurred. Other philosophers have proposed other reductions. Fulfilling metaphysicians' goals requires identifying a metaphysical necessity—the identity of two relations. Metaphysical proposals are supported, at least in part, by describing actual or possible situations in which both hold; they are challenged, at least in part, by describing actual or possible situations in which one relation, but not the other, holds. For instance, Hall proposes the following late preemption case to highlight an issue with Lewis's proposal (2004, 235):

Suzy and Billy, expert rock-throwers, are engaged in a competition to see who can shatter a target bottle first. They both pick up rocks and throw them at the bottle, but Suzy throws hers a split second before Billy. Consequently Suzy's rock gets there first, shattering the bottle. Since both throws are perfectly accurate, Billy's would have shattered the bottle if Suzy's had not occurred, so the shattering is overdetermined.

(Nothing hangs on the metaphysical tradition having focused on reduction; similar points could be made if it were only concerned with identifying what causation entails.)

By contrast, an important research strand in the methodological tradition aims at identifying procedures allowing scientists to infer causal relations between variables such as smoking and developing cancer or poverty and obesity (e.g., Spirtes et al., 2000). This project begins with graphical representations of probabilistic dependencies among variables. By means of these graphs, one can predict the value of a variable conditional on another variable taking on a particular value. To give a probabilistic graph a causal interpretation, one needs to determine the probabilistic consequences of the causal relations between its variables. To do so, specific connections between causal claims and probabilistic dependencies are assumed to hold. The Causal Markov Condition states, roughly, that conditional on variable Y's direct causes, Y is probabilistically independent of every other variable (except for Y's effects). Further, Faithfulness is the converse of the Causal Markov Condition. Given a causal interpretation of probabilistic graphs, algorithms can be developed to identify the causal structure of sets of variables based on observed probabilistic dependencies. The crucial point for present purposes is that these two principles are not meant to be metaphysically necessary; rather, they are empirical generalizations, taken to be true of some, perhaps many, causal systems in the domain of science (Hausman & Woodward, 1999).

Another research strand in the methodological tradition purports to clarify what scientists have in mind when they assert causal claims, without attempting to identify the metaphysically necessary properties of causation, in particular without reducing causation or without specifying in virtue of what causation holds. This clarification is meant to help to explain why scientists look for particular types of evidence or use particular types of data analysis (e.g., in econometrics) to establish causal claims; it also has a normative component. Importantly, clarifying what scientists mean when they make causal claims need not amount to specifying the truth conditions for these claims; that is, it need not amount to determining what must be true in every possible circumstance (in philosophers' terminology, in every possible world) for these claims to be true. More modestly, it may amount to determining what they take themselves to be committed to in the actual world, whether or not these commitments would also hold in other possible worlds. (This project is very much in the spirit of the conception of conceptual analysis presented in Chapter 7.) Thus, Woodward has come to describe his research on causation as follows (2017, 197–8):

I thought [my] way of thinking about causal claims...helped to clarify what researchers in the above disciplines mean or are committed to (or are trying to establish) when they make causal claims...[I]nterpreting causal claims in this way had a normative or regulative significance: Vague or unclear causal claims may be made disambiguated by spelling out the hypothetical experiments with which they are associated. A related point is that we can often clarify the sort of evidence and other assumptions needed to establish a causal claim on the basis of non-experimental data by reflecting that this must be evidence that is sufficient to establish what the outcome of the associated experiment would be, were we able to perform it. This helps us to see why and when certain techniques such as the use of instrumental variables in econometrics can be used to reliably establish causal conclusions. I've always thought of these goals as interpretive/descriptive/semantic/methodological (methodological for short) rather than metaphysical.

Modal Ignorance challenges the metaphysical tradition in the philosophy of causation: It concludes that the knowledge that metaphysicians of causation are after is beyond our epistemic reach. By contrast, the methodological tradition in the philosophy of causation is left unscathed since methodologists make no claim about metaphysical necessities, and since bringing about their projects does not require knowing any metaphysically necessary properties of causation. (Incidentally, acquiring this knowledge would be of no use for bringing about their projects, as argued by Woodward (2017.)

Let's now turn briefly to multiple realizability. In the metaphysically inclined literature in the philosophy of mind, whether or not a property is multiply realizable depends on its modal profile: The multiple realizability thesis denies that it is meta-physically necessary that this property has a single realizer property. No effort is made to restrict the scope of metaphysical possibilities bearing on the issue of metaphysical realizability. Lewis for instance writes (1983, 123):

[T]here might be a Martian who sometimes feels pain, just as we do, but whose pain differs greatly from ours in its physical realization. His hydraulic mind contains nothing like our neurons. Rather, there are varying amounts of fluid in many inflatable cavities…When you pinch his skin you cause no firing of C-fibers—he has none—but, rather, you cause the inflation of many smallish cavities in his feet. When these cavities are inflated, he is in pain. And the effects of his pain are fitting: his thought and activity are disrupted, he groans and writhes, he is strongly motivated to stop you from pinching him and to see to it that you never do it again. In short, he feels pain but lacks the bodily states that either are pain or else accompany it in us.

By contrast, the more recent, naturalistically oriented discussions have examined whether psychological properties can have multiple realizers according to the laws of nature.[6] Shapiro explains (2004, 78):

I have recommended that we understand MRT [multiple realizability thesis] to be an empirical thesis about the nomological possibility of realizing the human mind in a non-humanlike brain and nervous system….[A]s a claim about logical possibility, MRT is not very interesting….The point is that the logical possibility of MRT…holds little significance for what is true of the actual world.

Modal Ignorance challenges the metaphysical discussion about multiple realizability in the philosophy of mind, since it raises doubts about our capacity to know the meta-physical necessities philosophers of mind have been interested in, but it leaves unscathed the empirical discussion of the nomological possibility of multiple realizability.

A range of traditional and contemporary issues are threatened if Modal Ignorance is sound, and much of what exercizes contemporary philosophers needs to be jettisoned if the lesson I draw from Modal Ignorance is correct. Fortunately, pruning philosophy this way leaves plenty of room for philosophizing about the topics of traditional philosophical interest: causation, multiple realizability, personal identity, and so on.

6.2 Philosophical Cases and Modal Knowledge (Premises 2 and 3)

How can we come to know what justification, personal identity, and causation are or what knowledge, desert, and responsibility require? The sought-after knowledge differs from garden-variety kinds of knowledge. It is neither observational nor obtained by deductive or ampliative inference from what can be observed (the way knowledge about nomological modalities may be acquired). Nor does it look like mathematical

---

[6] E.g., Bechtel and Mundale (1999); Shapiro (2004); Polger and Shapiro (2016).

knowledge (however mathematical knowledge is acquired): There is no proof about what personal identity and desert are or require.

So, how do we know what, e.g., responsibility is or entails—for instance, whether it entails that an agent must have been able to act otherwise? To establish the philosophical metaphysical necessities, philosophers tend to rely on the method of cases: The facts assumed to hold in the hypothetical situations described by philosophical cases are the basis for philosophers' claims about metaphysical necessities. A proposal about responsibility can be compared with the facts taken to hold in some possible situations, and if the proposal entails that different facts (about responsibility) hold in these situations, the proposal is undermined. For instance, philosophers can consider a possible situation where an agent could not act otherwise (the type of situation descibed by a Frankurt case); if the agent is responsible for the action, then the Principle of Alternate Possibilities is undermined. In Jackson's words (1998, 36): "The business of extracting the cases that count as Ks from a person's responses to possible cases is an exercise in hypothetico-deduction. We are seeking the hypothesis that best makes sense of their responses taking into account all the evidence." Of course, philosophers sometimes come to the alternative conclusion: They were mistaken in taking these facts to hold in the germane possible situations. There is no mechanical recipe for deciding whether to suspect a proposal about, e.g., responsibility or the facts allegedly holding in the possible situations considered; what to do depends on one's degree of confidence about this proposal and about the facts allegedly holding in these situations.

Furthermore, philosophers must appeal to a particular type of case to identify the germane modal facts. Because facts in usual situations are likely to be consistent with nearly all philosophical proposals, philosophers must consider unusual situations to assess modally immodest philosophical proposals. Possible counterexamples to reductive analyses and to claims about entailment must describe circumstances where properties that typically co-occur are split apart, such as cases where a belief is not safe, but has some of the characteristic properties of knowledge or cases where an agent could not have done otherwise while her action has some characteristic properties of free actions. The same is true of possible counterexamples to modally immodest theories like physicalism. Because such theories must be consistent not only with usual circumstances, but also with the laws of nature on pain of being incredible—if psychological events that do not co-occur with physical events were a common, actual circumstance, physicalism would not be a credible metaphysical contender—the modal situations that matter for assessing them are likely to be unusual and atypical.

The trouble is that Unreliability, Dogmatism, and Parochialism conclude, in different ways, that we ought to suspend judgment about the possible situations described by most current philosophical cases and, more generally, by unusual cases and by cases that split apart typically co-occuring properties. Unreliability suggests that such philosophical cases elicit cognitive artifacts: However good we are at identifying knowledge, responsibility, causation, and personal identity in everyday life, we are unreliable at doing it in the situations described by these philosophical cases. Dogmatism suggests that we ought to suspend judgment about the situations described by most current philosophical cases or, more generally, by unusual and atypical cases because people who are equally qualified to judge about them disagree (supposing they are not talking past one another). And (supposing people are in fact talking past one another when they seem to disagree) Parochialism suggests that we ought to suspend judgment about such situations because by judging about them we are unjustifiably behaving as if we believed that the philosophically familiar has greater relevance for fundamental philosophical questions.

If we suspend judgment about the situations described by most current and, more generally, unusual and atypical philosophical cases, then philosophical views about, e.g., moral responsibility or causation cannot be assessed by comparing them to the facts we take to hold in these situations. So, we can't assess reductive (or non-reductive) views about what personal identity is (or entails) by judging about situations involving brain transplant or about what causation is or entails by judging about situations in which rocks hit a bottle at the same time. We can't assess physicalism by trying to conceive of a zombie situation.

Some current cases—in particular, cases describing everyday situations—may elicit reliable judgment and they may not give rise to any substantial disagreement. These cases could be brought to bear on reductive analyses, proposals about entailment, and, generally, modally immodest theories. I conjecture that philosophers will not go very far with these tools.

Upshot: We philosophers are not going to learn about those metaphysical necessities and possibilities that are pertinent for philosophy by means of the method of cases. Time to move on.

6.3 Any Alternative?

While I suppose many will resist the claim that we cannot come to know metaphysical necessities by means of the method of cases, some will rather insist that the method of cases is not the primary way of learning about metaphysical necessities, including those that are of particular relevance to philosophy. Here I canvass some alternatives and I argue that they too fail to deliver the sought-after modal knowledge.

6.3.1 Intuiting metaphysical necessities and possibilities

It is sometimes said that we come to know metaphysical necessities and possibilities by means of intuition (Bealer, 1996, 1998; Chudnoff, 2013). We can directly intuit the truth-value of the modal propositions of philosophical interest—e.g., that knowledge entails safety—and as a result come to know them. To learn about the propositions about metaphysical necessities and possibilities, we need not consider cases, and the rejection of the method of cases is of little significance.

In this context, there are three main ways of characterizing intuitions (Chapter 1). They can be mental states (e.g., intellectual seemings or judgments) expressing competence with the pertinent concepts; they can be the product of a distinct faculty—the faculy of intuition; or they can be intellectual seemings (understood as a distinct kind of mental state whose characterization does not appeal to conceptual competence).

As we saw in Chapter 1, each characterization has its share of problems. The notion of conceptual competence is unacceptable or of little significance for philosophy; it is unacceptable to postulate faculties when that is convenient for one's epistemological purposes; the arguments meant to establish the existence of irreducible intellectual seemings (in contrast to that of mere inclinations to judge) fail. In addition to these points, if intellectual seemings offer only prima facie justification to beliefs (if it seems to one that p and if there is no countervailing reason, then one is prima facie justified to believe that p), as proposed, e.g., by Hales (2012, 180), then they are an unsatisfying basis for philosophical knowledge, since we want more robust justification. If the only thing metaphysicians can say on behalf of their beliefs about metaphysical necessities and possibilities is that they are justified in holding them because they seem right, then so much for metaphysical beliefs. Intuition is not even a starting point for the epistemology of philosophy.

6.3.2 Metaphysics through meaning

It is common to suggest that we can know what is metaphysically necessary and possible because of a connection between meaning and modality. Duets cannot be sung by a single singer; rather, they must involve two singers; and the singers can, but need not be, of the same gender: These modal propositions are true in virtue of the meaning of "duet" (equivalently, for present purposes, in virtue of the semantic content of DUET). In addition, whoever knows the meaning of a word is at least in a position to know the modal propositions that hold in virtue of its meaning. Whoever knows what "duet" means is in a position to know that duets cannot be sung by a single singer. Finally, we can learn the meanings of words; perhaps competent speakers know them. So, it is possible to come to know metaphysical necessities and possibilities, and plausibly those include metaphysical necessities and possibilities of philosophical interest. For instance, we might be able to come to know that knowledge entails safety by making explicit what "knowledge" means, and metaphysical knowledge does not need the method of cases.

Sophisticated theories connecting modality and meaning have been developed over the last thirty years,[7] but these efforts, as impressive as they are, are undermined by the fact that there is no distinction between analytic and synthetic truths. Perhaps the propositions true in virtue of meaning alone are those such that we cannot imagine

---

[7] For discussion, see, e.g., Block & Stalnaker (1999); Chalmers & Jackson (2001); Laurence & Margolis (2003); Schroeter (2004); Chalmers (2012).

circumstances in which we would revise our judgment about their truth-value, but this mark of analyticity has repeatedly misled us, and the best explanation of this fact is that there are no analytic truths (Chapter 1). Duets, for instance, *can* be sung by a single singer; just google "duets sung by a single singer" if you are skeptical.[8]

In what follows, I will, however, bracket the question of whether there is an analytic/synthetic distinction, and for the sake of argument I will assume that analytic and synthetic propositions can be distinguished. Keep in mind also that in this section I am not concerned with the propositions expressed by judgments about particular situations—judgments elicited by cases—but by abstract propositions, such as the proposition that knowledge entails reliability: The issue of interest is whether we can bypass the method of cases. I will argue that the meaning of terms of philosophical interest ("knowledge," "person," and "causation") rarely, if ever, determines the truth-value of abstract propositions about metaphysical necessities and possibilities that are of philosophical relevance. The meaning of "person" does not determine whether necessarily people remain the same person if and only if they are psychologically or physically continuous with their past selves. Knowing what "person" means cannot allow the metaphysician to determine what personal identity is or entails. Similarly, one cannot learn what knowledge consists in or requires by making explicit the meaning of "knowledge."

If the meaning of words of philosophical interest determined the truth-value of the relevant modal propositions, then philosophical disagreements—for instance, the disagreement about whether knowledge entails safety—would be semantic at heart. It could be that one side of the disagreement fails to grasp what the word at stake (e.g., "knowledge") really means. Or it could be that this word has several meanings, and that the two sides of the disagreement happen to associate different meanings with that word (Chalmers, 2011, Section 6). Or it could be that the two sides of the disagreement disagree about what this word should mean (Plunkett, 2015).

Solving philosophical controversy would be much easier if philosophical disagreements were at bottom semantic, but philosophical disagreements are rarely semantic. Philosophers rarely treat them this way—they rarely diffuse controversy by saying: "I see, x is using 'knowledge' in this sense, while y is using it in that sense!"—and it would be surprising if they were wrong. When philosophers happen to treat them this way,[9] they rarely command assent contrary to what happens for everyday ambiguities or polysemies: Other philosophers don't simply come to realize the verbal nature of the dispute.

The proposal that philosophical disagreements are often semantic also turns trivial differences in how words are used into differences in meaning. Epistemologists who disagree about the nature of knowledge use "knowledge" similarly in most of their everyday interactions; it's only when philosophizing about knowledge that they use

---

[8] Thanks to Colin Allen for this example.
[9] E.g., Alston (1993, 2005) for "justification" and Hall (2004) for "cause."

this word differently: For example, some would say that knowledge entails reliability, while others would deny it. Such marginal differences are not the sign of differences in meaning, since the differences in use that underlie everyday ambiguity (e.g., the ambiguity of "bank") and polysemy (e.g., the polysemy of "book") are not marginal in this way. What are they, then, if they are not the sign of differences in meaning? They result from differences in what people believe about what "knowledge" denotes (i.e., knowledge). Similarly, Maria and John can mean the same by "morally permissible" but have different beliefs about the permissiblity of the death penalty. Someone who would insist that the marginal differences at play in philosophy really are the sign of differences in meaning would commit herself to a quasi meaning holism, where all or nearly all uses of a word are constitutive of its meaning.

Finally, what Waismann (1945) was the first to call "the open texture" of words supports the contention that the meaning of words of philosophical interest does not determine the truth-value of the relevant modal propositions.[10] Waismann primarily discusses what he called "empirical concepts"—i.e., concepts expressed by mass and count terms such as "dog," "gold," and "table"—and their application to particulars or samples. In everyday circumstances, we correctly subsume a particular under a concept instead of others—e.g., we truly judge that a particular is a dog and not a cat or a table— because this particular possesses some properties (call them "P+") and lacks others (call them "P–"). However, there are possible properties (which Margalit (1979, 142) calls "prima facie stigmas"), perhaps an infinite number of them, such that if the particular possessed any of them in addition to having P+ (or most of it) and lacking P– (or most of it), then the rules governing the use of this concept (which Waismann understands as constituting its semantic content) would leave it indeterminate whether the concept applies. GOLD is one of Waismann's famous examples (1945, 122–3):

> The notion of gold seems to be defined with absolute precision, say by the spectrum of gold with its characteristic lines. Now what would you say if a substance was discovered that looked like gold, satisfied all the chemical tests for gold, whilst it emitted a new sort of radiation? "But such things do not happen." Quite so; but they might happen, and that is enough to show that we can never exclude altogether the possibility of some unforeseen situation arising in which we shall have to modify our definition. Try as we may, no concept is limited in such a way that there is no room for any doubt. We introduce a concept and limit it in some directions; for instance, we define gold in contrast to some other metals such as alloys. This suffices for our present needs, and we do not probe any farther. We tend to overlook the fact that there are always other directions in which the concept has not been defined. And if we did, we could easily imagine conditions, which would necessitate new limitations. In short, it is not possible to define a concept like gold with absolute precision, i.e. in such a way that every nook and cranny is blocked against entry of doubt. That is what is meant by the open texture of a concept.

So the open texture of words is the following phenomenon: A word has open texture if and only if there are possible worlds in which it is indeterminate whether the word applies.

---

[10] On open texture, see also Hart (1961); Margalit (1979).

It may be tempting to respond that our incapacity to decide whether to subsume the particular with the novel property (the gigantic or microscopic dogish animal or the goldish substance emitting an unusual radiation) under a concept (DOG or GOLD) results from the limitations of our empirical knowledge about this particular or the actual extension of the concept (dogs or gold), but this response would miss the point of Waismann's examples. These suggest that, even if we knew everything there is to know about the particular and the concept's extension in the actual world, we still would not know whether the particular falls under the concept. To deal with the open texture of words, something like a decision seems called for, instead of more empirical knowledge or a greater clarity about what we mean. Open texture, then, is not the superficially similar but innocuous phenomenon that our knowledge is too incomplete to judge whether to subsume the particular under the concept; rather, it is indeterminate whether the particular is to be correctly subsumed.

Similarly, open texture should not be confused with vagueness, as Waismann rightly argues. Words with sharp boundaries in ordinary conditions have an open texture; vagueness concerns the actual world, open texture possible worlds; vagueness can be eliminated by arbitrary decisions, open texture can never be fully eliminated if there are an infinite number of prima facie stigmas.

One could perhaps object that Waismann does little more than assert that words have an open texture. At best he makes it plausible by describing a few extraordinary situations and priming the reader to agree with the claim that in such situations we would not know what to say. We are, however, in a better position than Waismann to address this objection, since close empirical attention to historical linguistics (instead of toy, simplistic thought experiments about what one would say in some possible situations) reveals that words indeed have an open texture. Their open texture is particularly evident in the diversity of linguistic reactions to novel, unexpected situations: That different linguistic communities using the same word sometimes react differently when a novel situation occurs suggests that it was actually indeterminate how the word would apply in this novel situation before speakers in these communities were confronted with it. The history of "jade" nicely illustrates this phenomenon (LaPorte, 2004; Hacking, 2007), as does the history of scientific theoretical terms (Wilson, 2006) and of artifacts (Margalit, 1979). For instance, the French and the British reacted differently to the discovery of the chemical heterogeneity of what they called "jade": The former took jadeite and nephrite to be two kinds of jade, while the latter debated about whether to restrict "jade" to nephrite. This suggests that the meaning of "jade" before this discovery did not settle whether jade was defined by its chemical structure. Happenstance, political and social factors, and vague analogies with other expressions in part determine what it becomes correct to say when people are confronted with the relevant novel situations. Meaning gets invented, and the open texture of words gets chipped away bit by bit.

One could also object that words do not have an open texture because a term like "gold" or "water" necessarily refers to whatever substance possesses the molecular structure of the substance "gold" or "water" actually refers to. In every possible situation, the substance is water if and only if it is made of H_2O: No open texture there. However, the case of "jade" suggests that it is a simplistic philosophical fiction that are disposed to use "gold" and "water" this way (Hacking, 2007; see also Machery et al., ms).

While Waismann and Hart mostly examine the subsumption of particulars under concrete concepts ("vehicle" is one of Hart's examples), the notion of open texture can be extended to abstract concepts, such as those expressed by "knowledge," "causation," and "intelligence," and their application to particular conditions, states, or properties. Waismann himself writes (1945, 142):

> Knowledge as supplied by quantum mechanics was unknown two or three decades ago. Who can tell what forms of knowledge may emerge in the future? Can you anticipate all possible cases in which we may wish to use that term?

That is, there is an infinite number of possible properties such that if a mental state possessed any of them in addition to having the usual properties of, say, knowledge (e.g., safety) and lacking the properties that defeat the correct ascription of knowledge (e.g., some forms of luck), then the rules governing the use of KNOWLEDGE would leave it indeterminate whether KNOWLEDGE applies.

Let's now return to our knowledge of modal propositions of philosophical interest and to its limits. If, as a result of the open texture of "person," it is indeterminate whether a perhaps infinite number of possible situations that involve, e.g., psychological continuity between punctate selves involve the same person, then the meaning of "person" does not determine the truth-value of propositions stating what personal identity really is. Thus, if all words have an open texture, reductive identity claims cannot be supported by analyzing the meaning of the pertinent words. Even if only many words had an open texture, open texture would be an undercutting defeater of the justification analysts may otherwise have for their proposed reductive analysis, since analysts could then not exclude the possibility that the words they analyze have open texture.

One could respond, however, that mere necessity claims—e.g., that knowledge entails safety—are not undermined by the open texture of words, since this phenomenon merely shows that no combination of properties (what I called P+) can be sufficient for the correct application of a word in every possible situation. So the open texture of words challenges the attempt to base reductive theories on meaning, but not more modest theories concerned with establishing metaphysical necessities on the basis of meaning postulates (where a meaning postulate is a conditional identifying a necessary property of the individuals satisfying a word, which holds in virtue of the meaning of that word). But open texture is not limited to sufficiency; the phenomenon is more general. As Waismann puts it, the crux of the matter is that there could be possible "conditions, which would necessitate new limitations" (1945, 123), new ways of distinguishing between instances of concepts. Some properties may work as if they are necessary when we are drawing the distinctions we typically draw (a dog vs. a cat; a table vs. a chair, etc.): When we deal with these typical distinctions, it may be that a particular falls under a concept only if it possesses a given property. I call them "in-practice necessities" and contrast them with genuine meaning postulates. But when we imagine some weird situations, we stop treating in-practice necessities as if they were necessary, and it is then indeterminate whether the imagined instances that do not possess these allegedly necessary properties fall under the concept. Well-known phenomena support the proposal that open texture extends to in-practice necessities. If there are any genuine meaning postulates, the following one must be one of them:

(1)   Someone is a bachelor only if he is unmarried.

However, (1) is really an in-practice necessity: In everyday circumstances, most of us use (1) to decide how to answer administrative forms and to pay taxes. But isn't a seventy-year-old man who got married in his twenties for social reasons, never divorced, quickly lost contact with the person he married, and lived alone for nearly fifty years a bachelor? Our hesitation, similar to the hesitation we may feel when reading Waismann's cases, suggests that it is indeterminate whether he is. And if (1) just is an in-practice necessity, how many genuine meaning postulates, and, more important, how many genuine meaning postulates of philosophical interest, can there be?

To conclude, making explicit the meaning of philosophically significant words will not allow metaphysicians to come to know the metaphysical necessities and possibilities of philosophical interest. Meaning analysis is a blind alley for the epistemology of philosophy.

6.3.3 Metaphysics as modeling

An idea that has grown popular over the last decade is to compare theorizing about the metaphysical necessities of philosophical interest to scientific modeling (Paul, 2012), scientific theorizing (Sider, 2011), or mathematical theorizing (Williamson, 2007, 2013, 423 ff.). In addition to "fit" (by which I mean the relation between theory and observations, however it is conceived: consistency, entailment, etc.), scientific models and theories are commonly assessed in terms of, among others, their scope, simplicity, parsimony, ad hocness, internal coherence, coherence with other theories, practical utility, and sometimes elegance. Mathematical theories are assessed in terms of their simplicity and elegance. The suggestion, then, is to assess philosophical theories, including views about metaphysical necessities, in terms of these theoretical virtues (or a subset of those—typically metaphysicians say very little about how to use these theoretical virtues in practice). If such properties genuinely contribute to the assessment of scientific theories and models or of mathematical theories, they must also contribute to the assessment of philosophical theories: So, for instance, simpler or broader philosophical theories must be better than more complex or narrower ones. Indeed, why would the scope of theoretical virtues be limited to scientific theories and models? According to Paul (2012, 12),

In metaphysics as with science, we can also understand theories of the world as built by developing models. Such theories may include the construction of models involving idealization, abstraction and hypothetical systems, as well as more precise and complete models of complex features of the world. There are obvious parallels, for example, between the use of thought experiments as hypothetical, ideal and abstract models of features of the world, and the development of logics as precise models of features of the world. Once the models are developed, just as in science, theories are compared with respect to the elegance, simplicity and explanatory virtues of their models, and theories are chosen over their competitors using inference to the best explanation. On this way of understanding theorizing about the world, much of metaphysics, like much of science, proceeds by model-building.

In the same spirit, Sider describes his methodological commitment as follows (2011, 12):

The epistemology of metaphysics is far from clear; this any metaphysician should concede. For what it's worth, as a general epistemology of metaphysics I prefer the vague, vaguely Quinean, thought that metaphysics is continuous with science. We employ many of the same criteria—whatever those are—for theory choice within metaphysics that we employ outside of metaphysics. Admittedly, those criteria give less clear guidance in metaphysics than elsewhere; but there's no harm in following this argument where it leads: Metaphysical inquiry is by its nature comparatively speculative and uncertain.

If theoretical virtues can really be imported from science or mathematics to philosophy and metaphysics, we may after all be able to gain knowledge of the desired metaphysical possibilities and necessities. On this view, cases at most play one of the innocuous functions identified in Chapter 1 (Section 1.1): Perhaps they are merely used to get the discussion going. Perhaps, then, we can do without the method of cases.

Let's bracket the fact that metaphysicians have been vague about which theoretical virtue is supposed to play a role in theory assessment in philosophy and about how this assessment is meant to proceed. Rather, let's examine first whether the use of simplicity, elegance, or scope in science suggests that these are genuine virtues that can be imported to theory choice in philosophy. For two reasons I argue they don't: Simplicity, elegance, scope, and so on are rarely used in science; second, if they are virtues, they are only *local* virtues.

As a matter of sociological fact, the alleged theoretical virtues are much less frequently appealed to in the forefront of contemporary science than what philosophers believe (with perhaps the exception of philosophers of science). In scientific articles, scientific theories or models are infrequently assessed in terms of their simplicity or ad hocness, to say nothing of elegance. Admittedly, such assessments do occasionally happen, particularly in review articles, but it is tempting to view them as often polemical and rhetorical. What carries the weight at the forefront of contemporary science is fit. The rarity of scientific appeals to simplicity, lack of adhocness, etc., raises question about whether they are genuine theoretical virtues.

In response to the charge that appeal to these properties is often polemical and rhetorical, philosophers may note that simplicity, elegance, and ad hocness have played an important role in the history of science. The fit of Copernicus's astronomical system was only slightly better than that of Ptolemaic systems, and the latter could have been improved to fit the data as well as Copernicus's. Copernicus's system was embraced because of its lack of adhocness and elegance. Copernicus's appeal to elegance is manifest in his Preface to *On the Revolutions of the Heavenly Spheres* (cited and discussed in Norton, ms, Chapter 5; my emphasis):

> [the geocentric astronomers'] experience was just like someone taking from various places hands, feet, a head, and other pieces, very well depicted, it may be, but not for the representation of a single person; since these fragments would not belong to one another at all, *a monster* rather than a man would be put together from them.

Similarly, parsimony plays a central role in Newton's theorizing about scientific methodology (cited in Norton, ms, Chapter 6), for instance:

> Rule I
>
> We are to admit no more causes of natural things than such as are both true and sufficient to explain their appearances.

Finally, in a review article Einstein objected to Newtonian theories that their distinction between inertial and non-inertial motions was ad hoc (for insightful discussion of these three historical examples, see Norton, ms, Chapters 5 and 6).

I could perhaps dig my heels in, holding that the use of the alleged theoretical virtues in apparently successful episodes in the history of science does not decisively show that they are genuine virtues. It could have been a matter of luck that the simplest or most elegant theories turned out to be successful, and in many other circumstances in the history of science our very vague assessment of simplicity, our subjective sense of elegance, and our hard-to-define feeling that a view is ad hoc may well have led to errors, which by and large have not been enshrined in the history of science.

However, I am willing to acknowledge that the examples just reviewed suggest that the alleged theoretical virtues can really be virtuous, but I hasten to add that if they justifiably contribute to theory choice, it is only in particular circumstances. This is the second reason why it would not do to hold that the use of simplicity, elegance, or scope in science suggests that these are genuine virtues that can be imported to theory choice in philosophy. First, fit and the alleged theoretical virtues are lexicographically ordered and fit comes first. Even when scientists' methodological rules involve simplicity, its role is secondary to fit (Woodward, 2014): The point of Newton's rule is to exclude theoretical complications that do not increase fit; it does not allow to prefer simpler, but less fitting theories to more complex, but better fitting. This raises the question of how the theoretical virtues can be used in philosophy, where there is no counterpart to fit.

Second, the kind of context in which simplicity, elegance, and other alleged virtues play a role in theory choice suggests that their role is at best limited to peculiar epistemic situations. The controversy between the Copernican and Ptolemaic astronomies is telling here (as is Newton's rule): The alleged theoretical virtues were involved in theory assessment because the then available data was unable to distinguish the competing theories. I conjecture that in real scientific contexts the alleged theoretical virtues are almost only appealed to when underdetermination prevails (a situation typically temporary). This is an abnormal scientific situation—not the kind of situation where science is making progress—and it is at least questionable whether criteria of theory choice that are primarily used in abnormal situations in science should govern philosophical methodology. To be sure, some believe that underdetermination is a necessary feature of science, but what they have in mind is the claim that for any scientific theory, there is another possible theory that is, first, genuinely different (and not just a terminological variant) and, second, equally supported by all possible empirical evidence (taking for granted a non-impoverished inductive theory). We need not concern ourselves with this claim here (see Norton, 2008 for critical discussion); rather, our concern bears on the following question: When science progresses, do we often find pairs of actual theories that are equally supported by the available evidence? I think not.

Finally, Norton (ms, Chapters 5 and 6) makes a convincing case that theoretical virtues are often surrogates for complex, context-specific background conditions: We justifiably appeal to, e.g., simplicity in a given scientific context as a mere shorthand for a set of facts that we know to hold. Parsimony in cladistict inference (Sober, 2015) works this way: Given what we know about evolutionary processes, more parsimonious hypotheses are more likely to be true. If Norton is right, the alleged theoretical virtues are only virtuous in a given context—they are *local* virtues—and their successful use in some scientific contexts provides no reason for exporting them to theory choice in philosophy.

One may wonder whether Norton's claim about the surrogate nature of theoretical virtues is consistent with their lexicographical position and with their use in peculiar epistemic situations such as underdetermination. If they really are surrogates for fit, why are they secondary to fit, and why would they only be used when underdetermination prevails? To answer this question, we must distinguish two uses of simplicity: a local use of simplicity, which is legitimate when for context-specific reasons simplicity stands for fit, and a universal use of simplicity. In the former case, fit and simplicity can be traded off against each other, and simplicity is not secondary to fit. This happens, for instance, when a statistical measure of the quality of a statistical model in light of data (e.g., Akaike information criterion) trades off its closeness with the data against its number of parameters. In the second case, fit may not be a surrogate for simplicity, but its role is secondary to fit and its use is limited to peculiar epistemic circumstances.

At this point, a metaphysician may bracket her appeal to science to justify the use of of simplicity, elegance, or scope in philosophical theorizing. She may instead defend directly the use of simplicity, elegance, or scope in philosophy or argue for their virtuous nature in general. However, the nature of many alleged theoretical virtues and the justification for their role in theorizing are obscure. Supposing one can clarify their nature, there are two different strategies to justify their role: One can view them as heuristics for fit—they then derive their justification from their connection to fit and the normative status of fit—or one can hold that they stand on their own. In the latter case, the justification of theoretical virtues is typically methodological. The idea here is not that ceteris paribus one should choose a simpler theory over a more complex one, but rather that it is methodologically advantageous (for whatever reason) to scrutinize (e.g., to test) the former theory first. The alleged theoretical virtues could also be justified on other grounds, including aesthetic and practical ones. Obviously different candidate virtues can be justified differently.

The first strategy to justify the alleged theoretical virtues turns out to be thorny. They are rarely heuristics for fit, and when they turn out to be, it is in restricted contexts (they are then local virtues, as we have seen in the discussion of science earlier), a fact that forestalls their extension to theory choice in philosophy.

The second strategy to justify the alleged theoretical virtues also fails to justify their application to theory choice in philosophy. Philosophical theories, particularly those that traffic in metaphysical necessities, are rarely applied, and the justification of alleged theoretical virtues on practical grounds does not justify their extension to philosophy. Furthermore, when philosophers appeal to theoretical virtues, these are meant to contribute to theory choice, not to discovery. Thus, justifying the role of a theoretical virtue on methodological grounds does not justify their extension to philosophy, where they are supposed to play another role.

Simplicity provides a good example of the difficulties with justifying an alleged theoretical virtue in a way that allows for its use in philosophy. One could attempt to justify simplicity as a theoretical virtue on the grounds that simpler theories are more likely to fit. There is a justifiable way of measuring simplicity in some scientific contexts (i.e., the number of parameters) and a well-understood rationale for preferring, everything else being equal, simpler statistical models to more complex ones (the latter are more likely to overfit), but this way of measuring simplicity and its rationale do not extend to non-statistical scientific theories. It is obscure what simplicity amounts to for more complex scientific theories, and there is in any case no reason why simpler non-statistical scientific theories would in general be more likely to fit than more complex ones. If that is the case for scientific theories, it must a fortiori be the case for philosophical theories. Philosophers should thus not expect simplicity to play a role in philosophy on the grounds that it is a heuristic for fit. Philosophers could respond that simplicity is a theoretical virtue independently of its connection to fit: Everything else, including fit, being equal, simpler theories are just preferable to more complex ones. Supposing that one can measure or at least assess simplicity for such theories (which is debatable), this preference can be justified on practical grounds: Simpler theories are just easier to use for prediction and practical applications. However, this reason for preferring simpler to more complex theories, which is defensible in a scientific or engineering context, makes no sense for theory choice in philosophy: Philosophical theories are not used to predict and are very rarely applied (with perhaps a few exceptions such as some theories in applied ethics and the foundations of statistics). The preference for simpler theories can also be justified on methodological grounds, as is the case in science. Oriander writes in the preface to Copernicus's *On the Revolutions of the Heavenly Spheres* (cited and discussed in Norton, ms, Chapter 5), "The astronomer will take as his first choice that hypothesis which is the easiest to grasp." Similarly, Kelly's (2007) learning-theoretic research shows that, for formal theories where it is defined, simplicity plays an important role in empirical discovery. This methodological rationale for simplicity too cannot be extended to philosophy. For one thing, philosophers want theoretical virtues to play a role in theory choice, not simply as methodological tools. For another, the type of situations that, in Kelly's framework, justifies the role of simplicity has no counterpart in philosophy. At this point, philosophers may insist that the preference for simpler theories (independently of fit) can be justified on other grounds, but until they have explained what these are and shown that they extend to philosophical theories, they should refrain from claiming that it should play a role in philosophy.

I have focused on simplicity here because it is often mentioned by philosophers to explain their grounds for preferring one philosophical theory to another and because that property seems a reasonable candidate for the assessment of philosophical theories (better than, e.g., practical utility). It may be possible to assess and compare the simplicity of competing philosophical theories, although I have some doubts. In any case, supposing that such comparison is possible, the appeal to simplicity in philosophy turns out to be hard to justify. There is no reason to believe it is a proxy; philosophical theories are rarely applied; and simplicity is meant to be used for theory choice in philosophy, not discovery. If simplicity cannot be justifiably used in philosophy, the appeal to many other alleged theoretical virtues is on even shakier grounds. Those that can be easily justified in science and extended to philosophy, such as consistency, are unlikely to be of much use to choose between competing philosophical theories. Philosophers rarely hold inconsistent views, and in any case soving these inconsistencies would not be sufficient to resolve issues such as dualism. But then it is erroneous to depict the assessment of philosophical proposals as a choice based on theoretical virtues. Philosophy as modeling is a dead end for the epistemology of philosophy.

6.4 Setting Aside Modally Immodest Philosophical Issues?

As I noted earlier, I draw the following lesson from Modal Ignorance: We ought to set aside modally immodest philosophical issues since we cannot resolve them. In effect, by drawing this lesson I assume, first, that philosophers aim at *resolving* modally immodest philosophical issues, and, second, that in general people should give up on their goals when they are unable to fulfill them. The first assumption may, however, be a mistaken, even naive conception of what philosophers are trying to achieve, and the second a mistaken conception of what makes an action worthwhile.

Philosophers' goal may *not* be to resolve the modally immodest philosophical issues (e.g., physicalism vs. dualism), and if it is not, why should we recommend setting aside these issues because they can't be resolved? To support this response, a critic ought to specify philosophers' goal, at least to some extent. A critic could elaborate on this response in one of two ways. First, philosophers may in fact purport to identify the implications of modal facts for philosophical issues instead of trying to resolve these issues; that is, they really purport to establish *conditional theses*. For instance, they may aim at understanding what would follow for the relation between psychological and mental events *if* physical duplicates that are not psychological duplicates are possible. Second, the aim of philosophers may be to draw novel distinctions, identify entailment or support relations between propositions, find out that some views are incompatible with other views rather than resolving modally immodest philosophical issues. I will say that philosophers aim at *understanding* such issues rather than resolving them. Supposing that we can imagine physical duplicates that are not psychological duplicates, does that show that these duplicates are possible, and does their possibility really show that physicalism is false? Which type of physicalism is falsified by physical duplicates that are not psychological duplicates and why? Which metaphysical views about the mental and the physical are compatible with their possibility? Working through these questions leads philosophers to a deeper understanding of the issue between physicalism and dualism, and this is what philosophers care about.

It is not a stretch of imagination that a philosopher would respond to Modal Ignorance by saying, "*Of course*, we can't know whether physicalism is true, but what we've *learned* is that *if* zombies are conceivable, *then* physicalism is false." Chalmers, for instance, notes (2015, 13) that "There is also often convergence on conditional theses, asserting conditional connections between views." Similarly, it is not a stretch of the imagination to think that some philosophers would insist that the point of philosophy is to understand philosophical issues, not to resolve them. Chalmers writes (2015, 13):

It is plausible that we have a greatly increased understanding of the issues underlying the big questions [of philosophy]. We better understand the reasons for accepting and rejecting key philosophical theses. We have come to explore new views and new areas of philosophical space that we had not even conceived of earlier. We have developed new methods and better arguments.

In addition, even if philosophers' goal *is* to resolve the modally immodest philosophical issues, it may not be the case that in general people should give up on their goals when they are unable to fulfill them. This general principle assumes that the only criterion to assess the worth of one's attempt to φ is whether or not one φ-es, but there may be other criteria. In particular, attempting to φ may be worthwhile even if one is in fact unable to φ provided this attempt produces valuable side effects. In the case of philosophy, there could be various such side effects. In line with the previous paragraph, by engaging, e.g., in the controversy between dualism and physicalism, we may learn which kind of possibility of zombies, if they were indeed possible, would be compatible with which version of physicalism. Or perhaps it is simply fun to try to resolve modally immodest philosophical issues even if one cannot possibly resolve them, exactly as it is fun to try to play chess like a chessmaster even if one cannot possibly reach this level. Or perhaps one gets wiser, smarter, or more reflective while trying to resolve some modally immodest philosophical issues.

Some of the deflationary conceptions of philosophizing alluded to—in particular, the claim that philosophy is in the business of establishing conditional propositions or of fostering understanding or the claim that it provides understanding as a side effect—have currency among some philosophers, but they are unsatisfying. They are not descriptively adequate: Most philosophers commit themselves to solutions to philosophical issues rather than to mere conditionals. Chalmers makes the point as follows (2015, 14):

> I suspect that for the majority of philosophers, the primary motivation in doing philosophy is to figure out the truth about the relevant subject areas: What is the relation between mind and body? What is the nature of reality and how can we know about it? Certainly this is the primary motivation in my own case.

They also trivialize philosophy: Should we care about which version of physicalism is consistent with the possibility of physical duplicates that are not psychological duplicates if we can't ever know whether these are genuinely possible? Hardly obvious. Is understanding sufficient to justify dedicating one's life to philosophy? Perhaps yes if we philosophers had nothing better to do, but as we have seen earlier there is a lot of room for philosophizing about x even when modally immodest theories about x are beyond our epistemic reach.

6.5 Conclusion

It is natural to think that we learn what personal identity is or entails by examining whether possible situations, varying in relevant respects (e.g., physical continuity), involve personal identity. The indictment of current and, more generally, unusual and atypical cases—they foster cognitive artifacts, breed disagreement that should shake our confidence, and smack of intellectual parochialism—undermines this approach to modal epistemology, compelling us to search for alternatives. But none of the most plausible alternatives provides us with a satisfying modal epistemology for philosophy. Intuition is a mirage, meaning underdetermines metaphysical necessities (supposing analytic and synthetic propositions can be distinguished), and the alleged theoretical virtues cannot guide the development of philosophical theories. We are thus left with an extensive modal ignorance: We do not know, and cannot come to know, what, e.g., personal identity is or entails, what knowledge is or entails, whether necessarily every psychological event is a physical event, whether freedom and responsibility require the capacity to have acted otherwise, and so on. This modal ignorance strikes at the heart of influential, modally immodest philosophical projects, and a significant change of course in philosophy is called for.

7

Conceptual Analysis Rebooted

I see the point of explicating concepts...to be opening them up to rational criticism....Defective concepts distort our thought and constrain it by limiting the propositions and plans we can enterain....Philosophy, in developing and applying tools for the rational criticism of concepts, seeks to free us from these fetters, by bringing the distorting influences out into the light of conscious day, exposing the commitments implicit in our concepts as vulnerable to rational challenge and debate.

(Brandom, 2001, 77)

In Chapter 6, I argued that if we ought to suspend judgment when confronted with current or, more generally, unusual or atypical philosophical cases, then modally immodest philosophizing should be rejected: Philosophical issues that turn on metaphysical necessities—including dualism, reductionism, and reductive projects in philosophy—should often be given up, and our philosophical interests should be reoriented toward issues that do not turn on such facts. Non-ideal theories in politics, methodological work on causal inference, and the debate about the multiple realization of mental states (in contrast to their multiple realizability) illustrate such issues. Perhaps, however, readers are worried that too little is left for philosophers if their interests are so narrowly bounded. The goal of this last chapter is to reassure these readers by giving a partial answer to the question, What are philosophers to do?

To be sure, this question does not have a single answer. Naturalistic philosophers have extensively discussed the contributions philosophers can make to scientific theorizing by providing novel hypotheses and original speculations, by synthesizing swaths of empirical and theoretical works, and by suggesting or conducting empirical research. Philosophers also contribute to the methodological progress of various sciences.[1] Instead of rehashing such discussions, I will highlight one of the things philosophers may do particularly well: analyze concepts.

These days, conceptual analysis is often treated with circumspection in philosophy, and some philosophers lambast the very idea that philosophers should concern

---

[1] Friedman (2001). For an impressive example, see the research on causal inference by Spirtes et al. (2000).

themselves with analyzing concepts. While leaving room for conceptual analysis, Sosa clearly distances himself from this practice when he writes (2007, 100):

It is often claimed that analytic philosophy appeals to armchair intuitions in the service of "conceptual analysis." But this is deplorably misleading. The use of intuitions in philosophy should not be tied exclusively to conceptual analysis.

Williamson concurs (2007, 3): "[F]ew philosophical questions are conceptual questions in any distinctive sense." Naturalistic philosophers such as Kornblith, Devitt, and Papineau have often expressed more radical views. Kornblith asserts that "the proper target of philosophical analysis is simply not our concepts" (2014, 207; see also 1998, 133). Papineau pulls no punches (2011, 85): "It is a bad idea to think that any serious philosophy analyses concepts in the first place."[2] Others deny that concepts can be analyzed on the grounds that, according to classic findings in the cognitive psychology of concepts, people do not have beliefs (or subdoxastic states) about the separately necessary and jointly sufficient conditions of membership in categories (e.g., Ramsey, 1992).

By contrast, I will present a novel, thoroughly naturalized, conception of conceptual analysis, demonstrate the philosophical significance of this form of conceptual analysis, show that it does not fall prey to the objections raised by critics of conceptual analysis, and argue that the method of cases needs to be thoroughly revamped if one is to analyze concepts successfully. According to what I will call "naturalized conceptual analysis," concepts are psychological entities and the distinction between what is constitutive of a concept and what is not is drawn in psychological terms; conceptual analysis does not deliver a priori, analytic truths about the world, but empirical propositions about the mind; and it calls for an empirical, including experimental, methodology, which I will call "the method of cases 2.0."

In Section 7.1, I describe what concepts are. In Sections 7.2 and 7.3, I present two distinct types of naturalized conceptual analysis: descriptive and prescriptive analysis. In Section 7.4, I explain why naturalized conceptual analysis matters philosophically ("what it is for"). In Section 7.5, I show why naturalized conceptual analysis does not fall prey to the common objections raised against conceptual analysis. In Section 7.6, I argue that naturalized conceptual analysis cannot be satisfyingly pursued by means of the armchair method of cases, but requires empirical, including experimental, tools. Finally, in Section 7.7, I illustrate naturalized conceptual analysis with the analysis of the lay concept of innateness.

---

[2] How the tide has turned! A few decades ago, Strawson could write (1963, 514–15): "It is, no doubt, rash to attempt to describe in general the nature of philosophical problems, difficulties and questions. But at any rate this much will be broadly agreed: that they are problems, difficulties and questions about the concepts we use in various fields."

7.1 Concepts

I take concepts to be psychological entities, not abstract entities (Machery, 2005, 2009, 2010a).[3] A concept of dog is a way of thinking about dogs, a concept of triangle a way of thinking about triangles. Furthermore, I take them to be bodies of information about individuals, classes, substances, or events. That is, a concept consists in a subset of people's belief-like[4] states (which I will call "bliefs" since some of these states are only belief-like) about an individual, a class, a substance, or an event-type. A concept of dog is a body of information about dogs, a concept of triangle a body of information about triangles. Thus, concepts have some content: their referent (what they are about: dogs, triangles, etc.), and their cognitive content (the body of information about dogs, triangles, etc.).[5] Concepts are about entities, and can characterize these more or less accurately. As psychological entities, they also have non-semantic properties, for instance, a format (how the information they consist in is encoded). To illustrate, empiricists believe that the format of concepts does not differ from that of perceptual representations; amodal theorists assert it does.[6]

Concepts are typically opaque: People do not have a privileged access to the content of their concepts, and a thinker is not able to articulate the content of a concept just because she possesses it. As a result, people can have mistaken views about their own concepts, and, if asked to spell out their content (that is, to explain how they think about something), they may formulate a mistaken theory. The right way to articulate the content of a concept is to ask people to use it (e.g., to apply it) and to infer its content from its use. This articulation may require some special expertise, for instance, some expertise about what concepts are. It is also an empirical task that is often best carried through empirically (Section 7.6 below).

As noted above, concepts are a subset of people's bliefs. This subset differs from the remainder of people's bliefs about the reference of the concept in that it plays a particular role in thought and in people's understanding of the predicate lexicalizing this concept (when concepts are lexicalized). On my view, a concept is retrieved *by default* from long-term memory to play a role in cognition and language understanding (Machery, 2009, 2015a). Bliefs about *x* that are not part of a concept of *x* (background

---

[3] In *Doing without Concepts*, I argue that the notion of concept should be dropped from the theoretical apparatus of psychology. For the sake of simplicity, I will bracket this claim in the remainder of this chapter.

[4] Concepts may be constituted by propositional attitudes that do not possess some of beliefs' properties (e.g., they may not obey the rationality constraint), such as subdoxastic states.

[5] In what follows, I will be referring to the cognitive content of concepts—the body of information a concept consists in—when I use the expression "the content of concepts" simpliciter. I will not assume that this cognitive content is the meaning of the concept. When I refer, with the philosophical tradition, to the meaning of concepts, I will use the expression "the semantic content of concepts."

[6] E.g., Prinz (2002); Machery (2006, 2007, 2016b).

bliefs or information) are not retrieved by default. A body of information is retrieved by default if and only if retrieval possesses the three following properties:

- *Speed*: Default information is *quickly* retrieved from long-term memory.
- *Automaticity*: Default information is *automatically* retrieved from long-term memory.
- *Context-independence*: Default information is retrieved from long-term memory *in every context*.

The first characteristic that distinguishes default from background information is how long it takes to retrieve it from memory. The second characteristic is the nature of control: Roughly, the retrieval of a particular body of information is under intentional control when retrieval requires the intention to, and the use of some attentional resources for, accessing it. While the literature on automaticity (e.g., Bargh, 1994) often treats this dimension as categorical (a process is either controlled or automatic), control may well be a continuum. If that is the case, default bodies of information are those that are on its automatic end. The third characteristic is context-dependence: Some bodies of information are retrieved only in a particular context that primes their retrieval, while other bodies of information are retrieved in all contexts. It is not entirely clear whether context-dependence is a categorical or continuous property. If it is a continuum, default bodies of information are on its context-independent end.

The three properties of default information are logically distinct and could be combined in various ways: That is, retrieval from long-term memory could have one of them without the other. For example, context-dependent retrieval could be quick and automatic, although it could also be slow and under intentional control. On the other hand, being fast, automatic, and context-independent plausibly form a homeostatic cluster: If some body of information is retrieved in all contexts, then its retrieval can be automatic, since no attentional resources are required to decide whether to retrieve it, and its retrieval is probably fast, since the retrieval process can be simple. In fact, context-independence is the most important of the three properties that are independently necessary and jointly sufficient for a body of information to be retrieved by default, and the two other properties are consequences of context-independence. Finally, background-information retrieval does not need to be uniformly slow, under intentional control, and context-dependent. What really characterizes this type of retrieval is its context-dependence. So, while retrieval of background information is always context-dependent, it could occasionally be automatic or fast.

I have reviewed elsewhere an extensive body of evidence showing that the notion of being retrieved by default from memory is useful to characterize an important distinction within memory retrieval (Machery, 2015a; for the opposite view, see Casasanto & Lupyan, 2015; Löhr, forthcoming), and thus can be used to specify the notion of concept. I won't review this body of evidence here, and I will take for granted in what follows that one can justifiably use the notion of being retrieved by default.

Default information also differs from bliefs about the central properties of the extension of a concept. On a common account of centrality, a property is central if possessing it strongly influences our judgment about whether it is an instance of the concept. Properties believed to be necessary are central properties. It may well be that, so understood, central properties tend to be retrieved by default, but this need not be the case (for discussion Rey, 2010; Machery, 2010b). The blief that a property is central for a category may play only a marginal role in our cognitive life, and we may draw on it only in the most unusual circumstances.

So drawn (and plausibly under other ways of drawing it), the distinction between what belongs to a concept and what does not is neither semantic nor epistemological; it is through and through psychological. It is not semantic because the distinction between being part of a concept and being among the background bliefs does not map onto the analytic/synthetic distinction: It is not the case that the bliefs that are constitutive of a given concept and those that are not are true on different grounds—respectively, in virtue of meaning only and in virtue of meaning and how the world is. Rather, the truth of both kinds of blief often (or always, if the metaphysical analytic/synthetic distinction cannot be drawn, as argued in Section 1.3 of Chapter 1) depends on how the world is. It is not epistemological because the distinction between being part of a concept and being among the background bliefs does not map onto the a priori/a posteriori distinction: It is not the case that the bliefs that are part of a given concept and those that are not are justified on different grounds.

7.2 Conceptual Analysis, Descriptive

Now that I have explained what concepts are and how to identify what is constitutive of concepts, I can characterize conceptual analysis. Analyzing concepts can take many forms. First and foremost, it consists in describing the content of the bliefs that constitute a concept. It can also be prescriptive, or revisionary, rather than descriptive: It then consists in identifying some bliefs that we should adopt when we think about something. I will focus on the first form of conceptual analysis in this section before turning to prescriptive conceptual analysis in the next section.

The goal of descriptive conceptual analysis is not to find out about the world, but rather to find out about people's concepts of the world. Analyzing a concept consists in identifying a subset of people's bliefs about the members of the extension of this concept—those bliefs that are retrieved by default from long-term memory. These bliefs specify properties of the members of the extension of this concept. For instance, the bliefs constitutive of the concept of dog specify properties of dogs—perhaps what they look like or how they behave.

Traditionally, philosophers have worked with the simplest model about these constitutive bliefs, assuming that they specify properties taken to be separately necessary and jointly sufficient for falling under the concept: Philosophers have traditionally taken concepts to be definitions. But, once conceptual analysis is naturalized—i.e., once the analyst's goal is to describe the content of people's ways of thinking about classes, substances, or events—there is no reason to expect concepts to represent separately necessary and jointly sufficient properties. In fact, cognitive psychology has clearly shown that at best a few concepts are of this kind (Chapter 3 of Machery, 2009), and naturalistic conceptual analysts should expect concepts to be in line with other, more complex models of concepts. The concept-constitutive bliefs can represent typical or diagnostic properties of the members of its extension; they can describe properties of members of a class if concepts are sets of exemplars (i.e., representations of particular members of a concept's extension); etc.[7]

In line with their assumption that concepts are definitions, philosophers also assume that the represented properties influence categorization judgments additively—the influence of any represented property on whether the analyzed concept applies to a particular instance does not depend on whether other properties apply—and are equally important—all represented properties have the same influence on whether the analyzed concept applies to a particular instance. But, here too, naturalistic conceptual analysts should expect concepts to be in line with more complex models of concepts. Some represented properties can play a more important role in the application of the analyzed concept than others. Let's call the importance of each represented property "its weight" (think of the regression coefficients in a linear model of some dependent variable); the properties represented by a concept can have different weights. Furthermore, these represented properties can influence the application of the analyzed concept additively or they can interact with one another (think of interactions in the analysis of variance); for instance, a represented property could be influential only when an object possesses another represented property, and not otherwise.

The take-home message is this: There are many possible models of concepts, and there is no reason to expect concepts to satisfy philosophers' preferred, but simplistic, definition model of concepts. To be able to meet the challenge of describing their content, naturalistic conceptual analysts should familiarize themselves with the existing models of concepts (hint: read *Doing without Concepts*).

7.3 Conceptual Analysis, Prescriptive

7.3.1 Carnapian and Gramscian analyses

An important form of conceptual analysis aims at reforming concepts instead of describing them. Here too concepts are taken to be psychological entities—ways of thinking about some class or some event—and it is proposed that new concept-constitutive bliefs should replace current concept-constitutive bliefs. Influenced by the definition model of concepts, philosophers have often thought of prescriptive conceptual analyses

---

[7] Murphy (2002); Machery (2009, 2011c); Danks (2014), Chapter 4.

as providing necessary and sufficient conditions of application for the analyzed concepts, but this isn't a necessary feature of prescriptive conceptual analysis: It could instead consist in specifying a prototype with a typicality measure defined over its extension or it could consist in specifying an ideal.

Prescriptive conceptual analysis plays a role in influential philosophical projects. Carnap (1950, Chapter 1; 1963) proposes that one of philosophy's important functions is to *explicate* concepts, a task characterized as follows: "By an explication we understand the transformation of an inexact, prescientific concept, the explicandum, into an exact concept, the explicatum. The explicatum must fulfill the requirements of similarity to the explicandum, exactness, fruitfulness, and simplicity" (1950, 1).[8] In contrast to descriptive analysis, explication consists in reforming lay concepts that are of philosophical, logical, mathematical, or scientific importance, such as the concepts of number, truth (Carnap's two most common examples of explication), probability, or confirmation (Carnap's explicanda in *The Foundations of Probability*). Concepts are in need of explication when they are unclear, vague, or confused, which prevent their deployment in philosophical or scientific projects. Carnap proposes four criteria for assessing the validity of an explication: the explicatum's similarity to the explicandum (we can call this criterion "Similarity"), its exactness or precision ("Exactness"), its fruitfulness ("Fruitfulness"), and its simplicity ("Simplicity"). In *The Foundations of Probability* (1950), similarity boils down to similarity of use, particularly understood extensionally (what the explicandum and explicatum are applied to). Carnap conceives of similarity in semantic terms, that is, as similarity of meaning, but similarity has a natural counterpart in my psychological, non-semantic framework (in line with the characterization of concepts endorsed in Section 7.1): Explication should be assessed with respect to the similarity between (psychologically characterized) concepts, as evidenced by the use of concepts in various tasks. To meet the precision criterion, Carnap holds that deficient lay concepts should be formalized, but, as we will see below, the notion of explication in philosophy has sometimes been separated from this formal project (a possibility recognized by Carnap himself: see Carnap, 1963). Fruitfulness justifies deviating from the concept to be explicated (that is, meeting the first criterion to a smaller extent); what counts as fruitfulness depends on the (discipline-specific) goals of the philosopher: proving theorems in logic, increasing inductive power in some empirical sciences, or allowing for greater precision in some philosophical or scientific debate. Finally, simplicity is the least important criterion for assessing potential explications.

There may not be a set of criteria that is applicable to all explications; rather, the criteria required for assessing a proposal may depend on the circumstances surrounding the explication, including the domain the explicandum belongs to (mathematics, mathematized science, non-mathematized science, etc.) and the goals of the conceptual

---

[8] See also Quine (1960, especially paragraph 53); for a comparison of Carnap and Quine on explanation, see Lavers (2012); for recent discussion, see Justus (2012); Schupbach (2017).

reformist. Furthermore, the importance of the criteria may vary from context to context. That said, Carnap has plausibly identified four criteria that often play a role in conceptual explication. One could even defend a stronger claim: Carnap's four criteria as well as their relative importance govern by default (and thus defeasibly) conceptual explication. Similarity embodies a form of conservatism: Concepts should not be modified without reason, and when they are modified they should be modified as little as possible. This conservatism can be defended on prudential grounds: Reforming a concept may lead to a worse situation. Fruitfulness and Exactness justify explicating a concept. Finally, Simplicity may be justified on practical grounds: Simpler concepts are easier to use.

Schupbach and Sprenger's (2011) formalization of the notion of explanatory power is an excellent recent example of Carnap's formal explication. Schupbach and Sprenger start by proposing four "intuitive adequacy conditions" (107) that any formalization of the notion of explanatory power should meet, including the following one: A hypothesis provides a more powerful explanation of a piece of evidence to the extent that it makes this piece less surprising. Schupbach and Sprenger thereby assume that Similarity, Carnap's first criterion, would be met since they take these adequacy conditions to be part of the folk concept of explanatory power. In line with the discussion above, Similarity need not be understood in semantic terms (viz., the *meaning* of the formal and lay concepts of explanatory power must be similar), but can be fully captured psychologically (viz., the bliefs that constitute the formal and lay concepts of explanatory power must be similar). Schupbach and Sprenger then show that a single formalization, ε, satisfies their adequacy conditions:

$$\varepsilon(e,h) = \frac{Pr(e \mid h) - Pr(e \mid \sim h)}{Pr(e \mid h) + Pr(e \mid \sim h)}$$

Because it is formal, Carnap's second criterion for the assessment of explications is automatically met. They conclude their article by highlighting the potential applications of their measure, thereby gesturing toward meeting Fruitfulness, Carnap's third criterion.

An influential example of a non-formal explication is found in Block's (1995) article "A confusion about the function of consciousness," which distinguishes two concepts of consciousness, the concepts of access consciousness and of phenomenal consciousness, that, he argues, are mingled in folk thinking.[9] He explains (1995, 227):

Consciousness is a mongrel concept: there are a number of very different "consciousnesses." Phenomenal consciousness is experience; the phenomenally conscious aspect of a state is what it is like to be in that state. The mark of access-consciousness, by contrast, is availability for use in reasoning and rationally guiding speech and action. These concepts are often partly or totally conflated, with bad results.

---

[9] Vargas's (2015) reformism about the concept of responsibility is another compelling example.

Block's discussion is an instance of explication because it eliminates a confusion by drawing a distinction between two types of consciousness; the distinction is also meant to be useful for the neuroscience of consciousness, since it allows the formulation of scientific questions about phenomenal consciousness.

Prescriptive conceptual analysis need not be associated with Carnap's notion of explication. Sometimes, the goal is neither to clarify an unclear concept, nor to sharpen a vague concept, nor to get rid of a confusion within a concept for philosophical or scientific purposes. Sometimes, the goal is to modify a concept, even if it is clear, sharp, and free of confusions. A reason is that existing concepts may be poorly suited to some philosophical or non-philosophical needs (e.g., Craig, 1990, on the concept of knowledge). Another reason is that a concept may have undesirable moral or political consequences. For instance, our default way of thinking about race may be oppressive, or may lead to oppressive expectations and behaviors, and may thus be incompatible with our commitment to racial equality. To remedy this situation, one could propose a new concept of race, which could be justified by its desirable consequences. An example of this approach to prescriptive conceptual analysis can be found in Haslanger's well-known article, "Gender and race: (What) are they? (What) do we want them to be?" (2000). Haslanger proposes to define "woman" as follows (2000, 42–3, emphasis in the original):

S *functions as a woman* in context C iff$_{df}$

i)   S is observed or imagined in C to have certain bodily features presumed to be evidence of a female's biological role in reproduction;

ii)   that S has these features marks S within the background ideology of C as someone who ought to occupy certain kinds of social position that are in fact subordinate (and so motivates and justifies S's occupying such a position); and

iii)   the fact that S satisfies (i) and (ii) plays a role in S's systematic subordination in C, i.e., *along some dimension*, S's social position in C is oppressive, and S's satisfying (i) and (ii) plays a role in that dimension of subordination.

Perhaps the most striking, and counterintuitive, feature of this analysis is the claim that women are subordinated: Without some subordination along the dimension of sex, there would be no women. Haslanger (2006) clearly explains that she does not regard the counterintuitive nature of her analysis as a drawback, since this analysis is not meant to describe how we currently think of women, but how we should think of them. Indeed, she herself describes her project as follows (2000, 33–4):

[T]he task is not to explicate our ordinary concepts; nor is it to investigate the kind that we may or may not be tracking with our everyday conceptual apparatus; instead we begin by considering more fully the pragmatics of our talk employing the terms in question. What is the point of having these concepts? What cognitive task do they (or should they) enable us to accomplish? Are they effective tools to accomplish our (legitimate) purposes; if not, what concepts would serve these purposes better? ...

So,…the questions "What is gender?" or "What is race?" require us to consider what work we want these concepts to do for us; why do we need them at all? The responsibility is ours to define them for our purposes. In doing so we will want to be responsive to some aspects of ordinary usage (and to aspects of both the connotation and extension of the terms). However, neither ordinary usage nor empirical investigation is overriding, for there is a stipulative element to the project: *this* is the phenomenon we need to be thinking about.

I will call this second form of prescriptive analysis "Gramscian": In his letters from prison, Gramsci (2000, 216) explicitly viewed the development of a new concept of hegemony as a crucial component of the justification for political activism. Political activists must be conceptual activists, too![10]

As it was the case for Carnapian explication, constraints are needed to adjudicate between various ways of reforming a concept for some purpose, including political or social ones. It is natural to extend Carnap's criteria: The more similar a Gramscian analysis is to the concept to be reformed, the clearer it is, the more it allows us to meet our political or social goals, and the simpler it is, the better it is. These constraints may pull in opposite directions: For instance, meeting some political goal may require modifying a concept to a substantial extent and to forgo simplicity. There may not be a unique optimal trade-off, and it may be unclear which of various trade-offs is the best, if any. The importance of each constraint is likely to be context-sensitive and to depend on the goals of the reformist. In some contexts, some constraints may not even be operant: For instance, in a political context we may want a reformed concept that bears little similarity to the original concept, at least in those respects that motivate the reformist project. In line with the discussion of Carnap's first criterion above, the first constraint on Gramscian analysis, Similarity, can be understood psychologically instead of semantically (similarity of meaning); furthermore, the second constraint— Exactness—need not be understood as requiring a formal characterization of the explicanda.

7.3.2 Descriptive and prescriptive conceptual analysis

What is the relation between descriptive and prescriptive conceptual analysis? First, in practice conceptual analysis is often partly descriptive and partly prescriptive, and it is also often difficult to identify which component of an analysis is descriptive, and which is prescriptive: Analysis often describes the content of a concept and regiments it in one stroke. Still, it remains useful to distinguish prescriptive and descriptive analyses, viewed as ideal types. Second, descriptive conceptual analysis provides the background for prescriptive conceptual analysis. We want to reform a concept, and we want to reform it in a particular way, because we have some grasp of its current content. For example, descriptive claims about the concept of race are, explicitly or implicitly, the background of prescriptive claims about how this concept should be reformed (e.g., Glasgow, 2009, Chapter 4). Of course, a full-blown, detailed descriptive analysis may

---

[10] For related discussion, see, e.g., Chalmers (2011); Burgess & Plunkett (2013a, b); Plunkett (2015).

not be needed for justifying and guiding a prescriptive analysis. Third, Similarity often, perhaps by default, constrains the adequacy of prescriptive analyses. This is the case even when similarity to the concept to be reformed (understood, to repeat, psychologically, not semantically) is not the most important virtue of the competing prescriptive analyses. A full-blown, detailed descriptive conceptual analysis of a given lay concept can help adjudicate between competing analyses (for development of this idea in the context of formal Carnapian explication, see Shepherd & Justus, 2015; Schupbach, 2017).

Schupbach (2011) provides an excellent example of how descriptive analysis can be used to adjudicate between competing prescriptive analyses.[11] Schupbach asked participants to apply the concept of explanatory power to hypotheses and data, and then assessed how various formal measures of explanatory power fitted their judgments. Participants were presented with two opaque urns containing white and black balls, and they were told about the two urns' content. They then saw the experimenter flip a coin in order to determine from which urn to sample, but they were not told which urn was chosen. The experimenter then drew a ball from the chosen urn ten times (without replacement). Participants were asked various questions after each drawing; in particular, they were asked to "make a mark on an 'impact scale' representing the degree to which the hypothesis that urn A was chosen…explains the results from all of the drawings so far" (816). Schupbach then compared five formal measures of explanatory power, including Popper's (1959) and his own measure, ε, and found that ε best fitted participants' judgments about the explanatory power of the hypotheses presented (i.e., urn A was chosen vs. urn B was chosen). Schupbach concludes (2011, 828):

Schupbach and Sprenger (2011) argue that measure ε corresponds most closely to our notion of explanatory power because this measure alone satisfies several intuitive conditions of adequacy for such an account. This article augments that case for ε with empirical evidence suggesting that this measure also does the best at describing actual explanatory judgments. The case for ε as our most accurate formal analysis of explanatory power thus looks to be strong indeed.

Carnap (1950) and Strawson (1963) both hold that only one of the two forms of analysis described in this chapter was important to philosophy, but they disagree about which one. Strawson offers two main arguments in defense of his own version of descriptive conceptual analysis. The first argument goes as follows: While explicata may be useful for some scientific, logical, or mathematical purposes, in general they don't contribute to resolve or even to clarify the philosophical issues that motivate interest in their respective explicanda since they differ, sometimes substantially, from those. Strawson explains (1963, 505):

[I]t seems prima facie evident that to offer formal explanations of key terms of scientific theories to one who seeks philosophical illumination of essential concepts of non-scientific discourse,

---

[11] For critical discussion, see Glymour (2015).

is to do something utterly irrelevant, it is a sheer misunderstanding, like offering a text-book on physiology to someone who says (with a sigh) that he wished he understood the workings of the human heart.

Strawson's first argument is unconvincing. It relies on a stipulative distinction between philosophical and scientific issues—a distinction many philosophers are bound to reject: Why is it not philosophical to develop a concept of life that would be useful in biology, to explicate the concepts of population or natural selection at work in evolutionary biology, or to develop a formal confirmation theory?[12] Thus, even if the explicata were unlikely to resolve or clarify some philosophical issues (those that motivated interest in the explicanda), they may well contribute to answer others. But even the antecedent of this conditional is unclear: Strawson simply assumes that the philosophical issues of interest (say, free will or personal identity) can be resolved or clarified by the explicanda (the lay concepts), and that developing concepts that differ from those would typically prevent us from reaching this goal. No argument is given, and none is to be expected since the situation is probably as often as not the opposite. Lay concepts of interest (the explicanda) are probably as often as not confused, unclear, or vague, and the confused nature, lack of clarity, or vagueness of concepts stand in the way of philosophical progress. Explicata that are sufficiently close to the explicanda may be more useful to, indeed may be necessary for, resolving or clarifying the philosophical issues that elicit interest in the explicanda. The problems of induction and confirmation are plausible examples. It is also possible to diagnose tentatively why Strawson went awry in assuming that the explicata cannot bear on philosophical problems: His mistake may be due to a Wittgensteinian or Rylean conception of the goals of conceptual analysis, including its therapeutic goal (1963, 515). If a central goal of conceptual analysis is to show how at least some philosophical problems (e.g., the problem of free will) and some philosophical theories (e.g., incompatibilism) are rooted in philosophers' misuse of a concept, then philosophers should primarily describe the subtleties involved in the lay use of this concept. Explication is indeed of little help for meeting this goal.

By contrast, Strawson's second argument is compelling. Setting aside Carnap's own pragmatic assessment of explications, he examines whether a proponent of explication could insist that formalized concepts provide the best clarification of the explicanda. The goal here is not to meet formal or scientific goals, but rather to understand the original concepts. Following Reichenbach (1938), I will call the practice alluded to by Strawson "rational reconstruction." Strawson then argues that rational reconstruction requires, instead of eliminating the need for, a descriptive understanding of the concept to be understood (1963, 513):

If the clear mode of functioning of the constructed concepts is to cast light on problems and difficulties rooted in the unclear mode of functioning of the unconstructed concepts, then

---

[12] See, respectively, Machery (2012b); Godfrey-Smith (2009); Carnap (1950).

precisely the ways in which the constructed concepts are connected with and depart from the unconstructed concepts must be plainly shown. And how can this result be achieved without accurately describing the modes of functioning of the unconstructed concepts?

Schupbach (2017) develops this idea. One of the functions of explication (casting light on the explicandum and on philosophical problems related to the explicandum) requires descriptive conceptual analysis. Naturally, this argument does not show that prescriptive conceptual analysis is not needed, only that one of its functions requires descriptive conceptual analysis.

Ultimately, the disagreement between Carnap and Strawson stems from different views about lay concepts. In line with many ordinary language philosophers (e.g., Austin, 1956), Strawson holds that typically lay concepts fit their functions adequately, and he suggests that philosophical puzzlements result from caricaturing their flexible use. We must describe them as precisely as possible. For Carnap, lay concepts are on the contrary confused, unclear, and vague, and thus of little use for theorizing. We must reform them. My sympathies here mostly lie with Carnap: The conceptual system is full of quirks and kludges, and, while lay concepts may often be as clear as needed for their usual uses, sometimes they let us down when it comes to theorizing or to political action. Reform is then needed, but, as Strawson successfully argues, reform often requires description.

7.4   Conceptual Analysis: What Is It For?

According to foes and friends of conceptual analysis alike, the point of conceptual analysis is to deliver either analytic or conceptual truths or propositions a priori known or justifiably believed about the extensions of concepts. Thus, Devitt characterizes conceptual analysis as follows (2014, 28): "According to this popular metaphilosophy, philosophers find out about the world … by examining concepts."[13] In this respect, naturalized conceptual analysis fails: It does not even attempt to deliver analytic or conceptual truths or a priori known or justifiably believed propositions. So, what is naturalized conceptual analysis for?

The answer is clear for prescriptive conceptual analysis: Our new concepts may be more fruitful in some respect or other or they may fit our political goals better. But what about descriptive conceptual analysis? What is it for? This section highlights some of the reasons why philosophers should care about describing concepts even if conceptual analysis does not deliver analytic truths or a priori knowledge.

7.4.1 Making it explicit

Concepts are typically opaque: It is not the case that possessing a concept C is sufficient for knowing, or being able to know, its content or the inferences it underwrites, and

---

[13] E.g., Block & Stalnaker (1999); Chalmers & Jackson (2001); Laurence & Margolis (2003); Schroeter (2004).

one of the things philosophers can do, one of the functions of conceptual analysis, is to reveal the content of concepts or the inferences it underwrites. As Strawson elaborates (1963, 517),

One can ... simply be aware that one does not clearly understand how some type of expression functions, in comparison with others. Or, having noticed, or had one's attention drawn to, a certain logico-linguistic feature appearing in one particular area of discourse, one may simply wish to discover how extensive is the range of this feature, and what other comparable features are to be found.

Philosophers can characterize the role concepts play in people's cognitive life.[14]

But surely, one may object, the suggestion cannot be that philosophers ought to make the content of concepts explicit for the sake of making it explicit? To do conceptual analysis for the sake of doing conceptual analysis? There is nothing particularly interesting and particularly philosophical in making explicit the content TABLE! No, the suggestion is to focus on concepts that philosophers have long been interested in, perhaps because they play a central role in human social life (RESPONSIBILITY) or in the regulation of our own and others' beliefs (JUSTIFICATION and KNOWLEDGE), perhaps because they are connected to human nature (GOOD and BAD), or perhaps because they are connected to the fundamental philosophical questions discussed in Chapter 4.

Our critic would perhaps concede that making explicit such concepts would be interesting, while insisting that there is nothing particularly philosophical in such an endeavor. Perhaps, however, we should not be too concerned with whether an issue is philosophical or not, just with whether it is interesting! And in any case, why isn't this endeavor philosophical? It can have therapeutic utility, since at least some philosophical problems and puzzles are rooted in lay concepts and are dispelled when those lay concepts are made explicit. Ordinary language philosophers often held that philosophical puzzles emerge because philosophers misuse otherwise fine concepts, but I think such misuse is the exception rather than the rule.[15] Rather, philosophical puzzles more often emerge because of quirky features of the relevant lay concepts, of which philosophers are unaware. In such circumstances, it's not that concepts are misused, as ordinary language philosophers maintained, it's that, even when properly used, lay concepts sometimes give rise to philosophical puzzles because of their quirks. Let's illustrate this idea with an important source of philosophical puzzlement, which calls for therapeutic care. Lay people may have several co-referential concepts of philosophical interest or, to avoid the controversial claim that these concepts really co-refer, several concepts expressed by the same predicate.[16] Failing to distinguish these concepts can lead to puzzlement about the judgments using them—for instance, because these judgments

---

[14] See also Hare (1981).   [15] E.g., Ryle (1953); Strawson (1963); Baz (2012).
[16] A common predicament if the theses defended in *Doing without Concepts* are correct (Machery, 2009).

seem incompatible—and to persistent, but stalled controversies—because philosophers disagreeing with one another take for granted different assumptions that are constitutive of distinct concepts. Thus, the hypothesis that there is more than one concept of causation explains why we seem committed to incompatible claims about the properties of causation as well as why straightforward philosophical accounts of causation appear prone to counterexamples, resulting in added epicycles and convolutions (Hall, 2004; Hitchcock, 2007). Hall explains this proposal as follows (2004, 253, italics in the original):

Counterfactual dependence is causation in one sense: But in that sense of "cause," *Transitivity*, *Locality*, and *Intrinsicness* are all false. Still, they are not false simpliciter; for there is a different concept of causation—the one I call "production"—that renders them true. Thus, what we have in the standard cases of overdetermination…are not merely counterexamples to some hopeless attempt at an analysis of causation, but cases that reveal one way the concepts of dependence and production can come apart: These cases uniformly exhibit production without dependence. What we have in the cases of double prevention and causation by omission…are not merely more nails in the coffin of the counterfactual analysis, but cases that reveal the other way the two causal concepts can come apart: These cases uniformly exhibit dependence without production.

Similarly, Alston (1993) has argued that debates about the necessary conditions for epistemic justification have stalled because epistemologists engaged in this debate call on assumptions constitutive of distinct concepts of justification.

7.4.2 Assessing the validity of concepts and clarifying them

Concepts are the tracks our minds prefer to travel on. They underwrite a particular kind of inference: inferences the mind is disposed to draw, that, so to speak, spring to mind, that it only resists when attention is drawn to particular facts that defeat this disposition. More precisely, concepts underwrite inferences the mind draws by default, where the notion of default is identical to the one spelled out earlier. If the blief that dogs are animals is part of the concept of dog, then one is disposed to infer by default that Fido is an animal from the fact that it is a dog. The class of concept-underwritten inferences is distinguished in psychological terms, exactly as is the class of concept-constitutive bliefs. It is neither semantic nor epistemological. The class of concept-underwritten inferences neither articulates the semantic content of the concept (its meaning), nor does it have any distinctive justificatory status.

Unfortunately, sometimes concepts lead us astray: Not all concept-underwritten inferences are good inferences. They lead us astray in various ways, many of which are familiar to philosophers. Some concept-underwritten inferences are vicious independently of how the world is, others are vicious given the actual world. Philosophers have had much to say about the former kind of inference. Some concepts give rise to paradoxes; for instance, vague concepts give rise to sorites. Prior's (1960) TONK, which is constituted by the following two inferential rules, allows thinkers to infer anything from anything:

TONK-*introduction*	TONK-*elimination*
p	p TONK Q
P TONK q	q

Peano's concept **?**, defined on rational numbers, results in contradictions, given the usual definitions of other operations on rational numbers (Belnap, 1962):

$$\frac{a}{b}?\frac{d}{d} = df \frac{a+c}{b+d}$$

I leave it to the reader to find out what is wrong with **?**.

Philosophers have paid somewhat less attention to concept-underwritten inferences that suffer from epistemic vices other than bringing about paradoxes, trivializing inference, or producing contradictions. Of particular importance for the conduct of our cognitive life is the second way concepts lead thought astray: Concepts may lead to inferences that, given the way the world is, are unreliable. That is, the conclusions of these inferences are unlikely to be true even when their premises are true. These concepts are only contingently vicious—there may be possible worlds in which the inferences are reliable—but they are vicious all the same since we are thinking in this world. Brandom characterizes well the idea that the assessment of a concept sometimes relies on empirical knowledge. Focusing on the derogatory concept BOCHE, he writes that "concepts can be criticized on the basis of substantive beliefs. If one does not believe that the inference from German nationality to cruelty is a good one, then one must eschew the concept BOCHE" (1994, 126; on BOCHE, see also Dummett, 1973, 454).

So, philosophers should engage in naturalized conceptual analysis in order to assess the inferences concepts dispose us to draw and to modify those inferences that are in some way deficient. As Brandom says (1994, 127), "The proper question to ask in evaluating the introduction and evolution of a concept is…whether the inference embodied…is one that ought to be endorsed." I'll say that one of the points of naturalized conceptual analysis is to assess the validity of concepts. A concept is invalid if and only if the inferences it disposes us to draw are deficient in some way or other. Concepts can be invalid for many different reasons. When the validity of concepts depends on how the world is (e.g., when we are concerned with the reliability of the inferences underwritten by concepts), I'll say that the point of naturalized conceptual analysis is to assess the empirical validity of concepts. Determining whether the inferences underwritten by a concept are empirically valid, for instance, whether they are reliable, requires two things: understanding the content of a concept (i.e., what bliefs constitute it) and relevant empirical knowledge about the world.

I'll provide a detailed example of naturalized conceptual analysis in Section 7.7, but I will gesture at two examples here. Philosophers working on race have proposed various conceptual analyses of RACE.[17] An important controversy about the concept of race is whether people conclude by default that two people are biologically different from the fact that they are judged to belong to two distinct races. If people's mind does not preferentially travel on these tracks, the concept of race can straightforwardly be deployed in critical projects. If it does, then the concept of race must be modified since, as a matter of fact, races do not differ biologically: The concept of race leads us to draw erroneous conclusions from true premises, and at the very least this concept must be reformed.[18]

Turning to the lay concept of consciousness, Block (1995) describes what he takes to be misguided arguments resulting from the confused nature of this concept. He singles out Searle (Block, 1995, 240):

> Searle argues: P-consciousness is missing; so is creativity; therefore the former lack explains the latter lack. But no support at all is given for the first premise, and as we shall see, it is no stretch to suppose that what's gone wrong is that the ordinary mongrel notion of consciousness is being used; it wraps P-consciousness and A-consciousness together, and so an obvious function of A-consciousness is illicitly transferred to P-consciousness.

The analysis of the concept of consciousness is meant to prevent the inference that P-consciousness is missing from evidence showing that access is missing.

When a concept is found to be (empirically or otherwise) invalid, it needs to be reformed, if it is not to be simply eliminated. This is where descriptive conceptual analysis meets prescriptive conceptual analysis (Section 7.3).

Papineau (2014) has argued that, if concepts are not constituted by analytically true and a priori justified beliefs and if assessing the validity of concepts requires some empirical knowledge, then the distinction between concepts and theories falters, and conceptual analysis does not consist in an activity distinct from studying empirically what concepts are about. For instance, if the concept of dog is not constituted by analytically true and a priori justified beliefs about dogs and if assessing the validity of concepts requires knowing about dogs, then the distinction between the concept of dog and our theory about dogs falters, and the analysis of the concept of dog is not distinct from the empirical study of dogs. Papineau explains (2014, 172):

> If the possession of concepts requires commitments to synthetic claims, and explication of these concepts involves the assessment of these claims, then there is no difference between conceptual explication and ordinary synthetic theorizing.

In one respect, Papineau's claims are both correct. The concept-constitutive bliefs do not differ from the background knowledge-constitutive bliefs semantically and epistemologically, and the content of concepts does not differ in kind from the content of scientific theories about their extension (e.g., both make synthetic claims about, say, dogs). Furthermore, assessing the empirical validity of concepts does require synthetic

---

[17] E.g., Hardimon (2003); Machery & Faucher (2005, forthcoming); Glasgow (2009).
[18] Kelly et al. (2010).

theorizing about the world. In another respect, however, both claims are mistaken. One can appeal to the notion of being retrieved by default from memory (or to other psychological notions that single out a distinct role in thought for a subset of our bliefs) in order to distinguish concepts and theories. Furthermore, whether or not concepts and theories can be distinguished, conceptual analysis does differ from the empirical study of what concepts are about. The former involves psychology, the second not! The former involves studying how we think about dogs, the latter only studies what dogs are, not how we think about dogs.

7.4.3 Articulating the manifest and scientific images

Naturalized conceptual analysis is also central to an important aspect of philosophy in the scientific age: squaring the manifest and scientific images of the world. Sellars (1963) introduces the distinction between these two images. On his view, the manifest image represents the world as it is presented to people; its main characteristic is that it does not posit unobservables. Sellars insists that the manifest image should not be identified with a confused, irrational, prejudiced understanding of the world. Instead, the manifest image has been refined and systematized during the history of humanity; it is also what some important trends in philosophy, which Sellars called "perennial philosophy," attempt to articulate. People as "persons"—roughly rational agents acting deliberately—are central to the manifest image. The scientific image differs from the manifest image in two main respects: It posits unobservables, and it has no room for persons.

Sellars acknowledges that, so characterized, the manifest and scientific images are idealizations, but I doubt that his idealizations are useful and, thus, legitimate, and I propose to reform the characterization of the manifest and scientific images of the world. The main suggestion is to identify the manifest image with what psychologists call "folk theories": sets of often implicit principles that allow people to make sense of particular aspects of the world (e.g., Carey, 2009). Folk psychology, folk biology, and folk physics are examples of such folk theories. These can be pan-cultural—folk psychology is—or the products of particular cultures and times. This novel characterization of the manifest image improves on Sellars's since, from a very early age on, lay people are in fact naïve scientists: They spontaneously posit unobservables such as causes, souls, or germs. If the manifest image is identified with folk theories, we do not have a transparent access to its content, and making it explicit can only be done empirically. Acknowledging the need for empirical research on the content of the manifest image also improves on Sellars's approach, who speculates about the content of the manifest image without specifying any clear criteria to assess whether his speculations are on target. Finally, I find it dubious that much philosophizing is meant to recapitulate the manifest image. Turning more briefly to the shortcomings of Sellars's characterization of the scientific image, it is important to acknowledge the irreducible plurality of scientific representations.

Despite these differences between my approach and Sellars's, I embrace an important feature of his discussion: An important philosophical task is to find out where the scientific image is an extension or a refinement of the manifest image, and where these two images are incompatible. Completing this task is a necessary preliminary step for deciding what to do with the manifest image: For instance, for deciding whether to eliminate one of its elements (perhaps the idea that there are agents that act deliberately), when one fails to find any plausible counterpart in the scientific image or when the manifest image sometimes stands in the way of scientific understanding.[19] Naturalized conceptual analysis can contribute to articulate the manifest image; importantly, it can also play a role in articulating the scientific image: Scientific concepts then become the target of analysis.[20]

Some will deny that the manifest image can be assessed by reference to the scientific image, and they may even question whether they can be compared (e.g., Van Fraassen, 1999). On this view, there is no point attempting to vindicate elements of the manifest image by finding counterparts in the scientific image, and the former cannot be challenged by reference to the latter. Many different arguments have been proposed to back up such denial, and addressing them in detail is beyond the scope of this chapter. I'll be satisfied if I have convinced those who do not find these arguments convincing that naturalized conceptual analysis matters for squaring the manifest and scientific images of the world.

7.4.4 Naturalized conceptual analysis and the philosophical tradition

Contemporary conceptual analysts and their critics suffer from historical myopia, and they essentialize the goals of prominent contemporary conceptual analysts such as Lewis or Jackson, ignoring what has been an important motivation for conceptual analysis: clarifying ideas by first learning what one is actually thinking and by then assessing it. In this respect, naturalized conceptual analysis is the heir of the philosophical tradition, concerned as it was with clarifying ideas and submitting ways of thinking to severe scrutiny—not learning a priori, analytic, or necessary truths by analyzing meaning.

While I am not a historian of philosophy, many traditional philosophical projects are, in important respects, similar to the program described in the present chapter. In the *Enquiry*, Hume describes his analytic empiricist method as follows (1999, 135–6):

Complex ideas may, perhaps, be well known by definition, which is nothing but an enumeration of those parts or simple ideas, that compose them. But when we have pushed up definitions to the most simple ideas, and find still some ambiguity and obscurity; what resource are we then possessed of? By what invention can we throw light upon these ideas, and render them altogether precise and determinate to our intellectual view? Produce the impressions or original sentiments, from which the ideas are copied. These impressions are all strong and sensible. They admit not

---

[19] E.g., Shtulman (2015).   [20] E.g., Machery (2016a).

of ambiguity. They are not only placed in a full light themselves, but may throw light on their correspondent ideas, which lie in obscurity. And by this means, we may perhaps, attain a new microscope or species of optics, by which, in the moral sciences, the most minute, and most simple ideas may be so enlarged as to fall readily under our apprehension, and be equally known with the grossest and most sensible ideas, that can be the object of our enquiry.

Hume's goal is to distinguish two kinds of idea: those that are irremediably obscure such as POWER and NECESSITATION and those that can be clarified by showing how they are combinations of primitive ideas, copied from "impressions."

A pragmatist such as James shares Hume's goal of providing a method for clarifying ideas such as FREE WILL. He was less concerned than Hume with showing that apparently clear ideas are in fact empty; his main goal was to resolve never-ending philosophical issues by showing that there was in fact no difference between the competing sides. With this goal in mind, he proposes his famous "principle of pragmatism" (1904, 673–4):

[T]he tangible fact at the root of all our thought-distinctions, however subtle, is that there is no one of them so fine as to consist in anything but a possible difference of practice. To attain perfect clearness in our thoughts of an object, then, we need only consider what conceivable effects of a practical kind the object may involve—what sensations we are to expect from it, and what reactions we must prepare. Our conception of these effects, whether immediate or remote, is then for us the whole of our conception of the object, so far as that conception has positive significance at all.

For James, the clarification of ideas by means of the principle of pragmatism does not yield analytic truths or a priori knowledge. Nor is it a semantic task. A similar approach is found in Peirce's important article (2001) "How to make our ideas clear," which, as James acknowledges, was the source of the principle of pragmatism.

Other philosophers have combined descriptive and prescriptive conceptual analyses. The nineteenth-century philosopher of science Whewell's method blends these two types of conceptual analysis. He writes in the second volume of *The Philosophy of the Inductive Sciences, Founded upon their History* (1847, 6–7, emphasis in the original),

Such discussion as those in which we have been engaged concerning our fundamental Ideas, have been the course by which, historically speaking, those Conceptions which the existing sciences involve have been rendered so clear as to be fit elements of exact knowledge. The disputes concerning the various kinds and measures of *Force* were an important part of the progress of the science of Mechanics. The struggles by which philosophers attained a right general conception of *plane*, of *circular*, of *elliptical Polarization*, were some of the most difficult steps in the modern discoveries of Optics. A Conception of the *Atomic Constitution* of bodies, such as shall include what we know, and assume nothing more, is even now a matter of conflict among Chemists. The debates by which, in recent times, the Conceptions of *Species* and *Genera* have been rendered more exact, have improved the science of Botany: the imperfection of the science of Mineralogy arises in a great measure from the circumstance, that in that subject, the Conception of a *Species* is not yet fixed. In physiology, what a vast advance would that philosopher make, who should establish a precise, tenable, and consistent Conception of *Life*!

Moving on to more recent analysts, neither Carnap nor Strawson are interested in learning a priori or analytic truths about the world by analyzing the semantic content of concepts. In his work following *The Logical Construction of the World*, Carnap is concerned with developing frameworks that have desirable practical properties, and explication, particularly formal explication, was his central tool for this project. It is also remarkable that in his discussion of Carnap and of conceptual analysis (1963), Strawson does not mention a priori or analytic truths. Rather, on his view (1963, 514–18) the point of conceptual analysis is to understand the concepts we have and why we have them as well as to cure ourselves from some mistaken theories anchored in a misuse of folk concepts. More generally, Hacker (2009, 343) makes the point that ordinary language philosophers did not traffic in analytic truths at all:

Among Oxford philosophers who took "the linguistic turn," the only significant one who thought that all philosophical propositions are analytic was Ayer (at the age of 26). The manifesto of the Vienna Circle followed Wittgenstein in denying that there are any philosophical propositions. Ryle, Austin, Strawson and others did think there are, but nowhere suggested that they are analytic. All insisted that philosophy is a conceptual investigation, but none held that its task is to disclose analytic truths.

As a matter of historical fact, Hacker seems to be correct.

7.5 Objections to Conceptual Analysis

Opposition to conceptual analysis comes in different strengths. Some like Sosa merely claim that there is more to philosophy than conceptual analysis; others like Papineau (2014) claim not only that philosophers should not analyze concepts, but that, appearances notwithstanding, they don't! In this section, I briefly review the objections raised against conceptual analysis, and I show that they don't apply to naturalized conceptual analysis.

7.5.1 Ramsey: analyzing and defining

Ramsey (1992) has argued that progress in the psychology of concepts reveals the futility of traditional conceptual analysis.[21] Assuming that psychologists have shown that categorization judgments are underpinned by complex, context-sensitive cognitive structures (e.g., prototypes), he concludes that the task of providing simple definitions—which he identifies with conceptual analysis—is hopeless (1992, 65):

If being an intuitive instance of X is simply a matter of having a cluster of properties that is sufficiently similar to some prototype representation, and if there are a number of different

---

[21] See also Bishop (1992); Stich (1993).

ways this can be done, some of which may vary over different contexts, then any crisp definition comprised of some subset of these properties and treating them as necessary and sufficient is never going to pass the test of intuition.... [T]he search for a simple, nondisjunctive definition of a given philosophical concept that accords with all of our intuitions and admits of no counterexamples is a hopeless enterprise—there simply is no such thing.

A brief response will do: Naturalized conceptual analysis is clearly immune to this concern, since on this approach analyzing concepts need not consist in providing necessary and sufficient conditions for their application. Quite the contrary, more complex models of concepts are explicitly called for, ones that eschew the naïve simplicity of necessary and sufficient conditions of membership.

7.5.2 Haslanger: prescriptive vs. descriptive conceptual analysis

Haslanger has recently drawn a sharp contrast between the two kinds of conceptual analysis that were embraced in Sections 7.2 and 7.3 (2010, 169, emphasis in the original):

Contemporary discussions of race and racism devote considerable effort to giving conceptual analyses of these notions. Much of the work is concerned to investigate a priori what we mean by the terms "race" and "racism."...More recent work has started to employ empirical methods to determine the content of our "folk concepts," or "folk theory" of race and racism....In contrast to both of the these projects,...I have...argued that it is not only important to determine what we *actually* mean by these terms, but what we *should* mean, i.e., what type, if any, we should be tracking.

She then writes, in a less conciliatory manner (2010, 170), that "both the a priori and 'experimental' investigation into the concepts of race and racism are misguided."

Haslanger ties conceptual analysis to meaning and reference descriptivism— roughly the view that the meaning of a predicate like "race," or the semantic content of the concept expressed by a predicate, is a description and that the extension of this predicate is the set of entities satisfying this description—and descriptivism itself to metaphysical analyticity—the propositions that are constitutive of the description constituting the meaning of a predicate or the semantic content of the concept it expresses are analytically true of its extension. She then argues that this commitment to analyticity is incompatible with scientific change—scientific change does not involve changing the meaning of scientific terms (e.g., "mass" and "earth")—and political change—modifying beliefs about a social kind (races) or a social practice (marriage) does not consist in changing the meaning of the relevant predicates and thus in talking about something else (races* or marriage*). She writes (2010, 174),

Just as Quine and Putnam emphasized that a commitment to analyticity stands in the way of scientific progress, the same might be said of its bearing on social progress.... [E]ven if "the folk" believe that race is a biological category, on the non-descriptivist account we're exploring, those who know that it is not can still use the term "race" competently without the problematic belief or entailment.

Haslanger's characterization of conceptual analysis is unjustifiably narrow. Those who employ empirical methods to study the folk concept of race (e.g., Machery & Faucher, forthcoming) are not necessarily committed either to meaning and reference descriptivism or to analyticity. Concepts need not refer descriptively even if they have a cognitive content that can be characterized as a description (Prinz, 2002; Machery, 2010b), and the propositions that constitute their content need not be analytically true. This is particularly the case if concepts are delineated psychologically— e.g., if they are constituted by those bliefs that play a distinct, significant role in cognition. So, since naturalized conceptual analysis need not be descriptivist, it just isn't the case, *pace* Haslanger (2010, 175), that "if we reject any form of descriptivism... some of the recent philosophical work on race and racism—work that purports to be exploring the 'folk theory' or ordinary view of race—will look to be barking up the wrong tree."

Perhaps Haslanger would insist that problems similar to the ones she points out arise even when concepts are delineated psychologically. Political progress involves changing the way we think about social kinds (mutatis mutandis for scientific progress), and, if concepts are psychologically individuated bodies of bliefs, political progress amounts to changing concepts like MARRIAGE and RACE; but this implies, unacceptably, that political progress amounts to "talking about something else" (2010, 174).

There are several problems with this line of thought. First, the fact that the content of people's concepts changes does not imply that they acquire different concepts (Machery, 2010c): Each person's concept may remain the same despite its content changing, exactly as an organism remains the same when its cells are replaced, and political reform need not entail that people shed their old concepts and acquire new concepts— it only requires that their (persisting) concepts change. But let's suppose that people do acquire new concepts with political reform (e.g., MARRIAGE* and RACE*). Even then, people are not talking about different things just because they have distinct concepts, since distinct concepts can co-refer (and note that, if concepts do not refer descriptively, the fact that the content of distinct concepts differs is no obstacle to them co-referring), and, thus, political reform does not imply that people are "talking about something else." But let's even suppose that people do acquire new concepts with political reform (e.g., MARRIAGE* and RACE*) and that as a result people do talk about different things (marriage* and race*). So what? So what if two men can't really marry because marriage is a social institution that involves a man and a woman? They can marry*, and marriage* is identical to marriage except for the fact that it can involve two persons of the same gender. I just don't see why this situation would "stand in the way" of social reform, as Haslanger puts it. More generally, the social theorist should not refrain from describing her work as changing social institutions, perhaps by engineering new concepts.

Alternatively, Haslanger could turn the remark that naturalistic conceptual analysts fail to identify the meaning of a predicate like "race" or "marriage" when they determine the content of the relevant concepts into an objection against naturalized conceptual analysis. She could insist that the task of social theorists is precisely to identify the meaning of the socially relevant predicates. Indeed, she asserts (2010, 175),

Regardless of whether one employs a priori reflection or empirical psychology to explore allegedly tacit assumptions we hold about what race is, the results will not give us an account of what "race" means, for these tacit assumptions do not determine meaning.

But this argument would assume that the only important task for race or gender theorists is to determine what "race" or "gender" mean, and this would be a serious mistake. Concepts determine the inferences we are prone to draw, and our thoughts follow their tracks. Understanding these inferences in order to assess them is one of the reasons why conceptual analysis matters, whether or not it also allows us to determine the meaning of predicates like "race" (as Haslanger occasionally acknowledges (2010, 180)). Furthermore, in a Gramscian spirit, we should not be reluctant to view political action as including a form of conceptual engineering or activism (as Haslanger at times also acknowledges (2006, n. 15)). What great scientists and great social theorists or activists do is in part to give us new ways of thinking about the natural and social world, new concepts that bring with them new patterns of inference that better fit the actual world or that are politically expedient.

7.5.3 Papineau: conceptual analysis and analyticity

Papineau (2014) has argued not only that philosophers should not engage in conceptual analysis, but also that, as a matter of fact, they do not; what they do, on his view, is misdescribe their own theorizing as analyzing concepts. Papineau's claim is delightfully outrageous. On their face, many bona fide philosophical projects genuinely involve some form of conceptual analysis. These projects attempt to understand how concepts are used, what their function is (i.e., roughly, why we are using the concepts we are using), what norms govern their use, and whether their use, function, and norms are any good. They include research projects in social and political philosophy and in the philosophy of science or of the special sciences, which often involve analyzing scientific concepts (e.g., the concept of innateness, the concept of drift, etc.). Often, the goal is, explicitly, not to understand what x (e.g., fitness, drift, and innateness) is, as a material-mode theoretical project would, but to characterize the concept of x (e.g., FITNESS, DRIFT, and INNATENESS).

Papineau's argument is straightforward. Conceptual analysis of a concept of x is supposed to result in a priori justified, analytically true propositions about x, but philosophical theories about x are typically synthetic propositions, and are thus not properly described as the result of the analysis of the concept of x. I agree that the content of philosophical theories is not composed of analytic propositions. The distinction between analytic/synthetic propositions is dubious, and even if there are analytically true propositions (e.g., the proposition that to kill involves causing the death of a living creature[22]), they are trivial (Section 1.2.2 of Chapter 1 and Section 6.3.2 of Chapter 6).

This argument may have some bite against Papineau's target, but it does not undermine naturalized conceptual analysis, since this type of conceptual analysis does not attempt to identify a priori justified, analytic truths. As we've seen, on my view, the distinction between what is constitutive of a concept and what is not does not map either onto the distinction between analytic and synthetic propositions or onto the distinction between a priori and a posteriori justified propositions. Furthermore, there is no reason to limit philosophical theorizing to material-mode questions about, say, matter, time, space, consciousness, or propositional attitudes. For the reasons given in Section 7.4, we philosophers may rather be interested in formal-mode questions about, say, the concepts of matter, time, space, or consciousness. When we do so, our theories are empirical theories about the mind, although we often need to know about matter, time, space, or consciousness in order to assess the empirical validity of the relevant concepts.

7.6 The Method of Cases 2.0

7.6.1 Conceptual analysis and the method of cases

Many philosophers hold the view that the method of cases can contribute to the analysis of concepts. Graham and Horgan write (1994, 223):

The point of... [their discussion] has been to emphasize the evidential relevance, for questions of ideology, of data that is relatively close at hand, so close that competent speakers can obtain it from our armchairs....Its being armchair-obtainable does not prevent it from being empirical and hence epistemically defeasible; and also makes it eminently accessible to us philosophers, even though our methods do not involve wearing white coats or conducting field linguistics.

In his influential book *From Metaphysics to Ethics* (1998), Jackson similarly asserts that "the role of intuitions about possible cases so distinctive of conceptual analysis is precisely to make explicit our implicit folk theory and, in particular, to make explicit which properties are really central" (1998, 38). In an influential series of articles, Goldman has defended this view in detail (2007, 15, emphasis in the original; see also Goldman & Pust, 1998):

It's part of the nature of concepts (in the personal psychological sense) that possessing a concept tends to give rise to beliefs and intuitions that accord with the contents of the concept. If the content of someone's concept F implies that F does (doesn't) apply to example x, then that person is disposed to intuit that F applies (doesn't apply) to x when the issue is raised in his mind. Notice, I don't say that possessing a particular concept of knowledge makes one disposed

---

[22] Even this one is dubious since we can kill zombies.

to believe a correct *general* account of that knowledge concept. Correct general accounts are devilishly difficult to achieve, and few people try. All I am saying is that possessing a concept makes one disposed to have pro-intuitions toward correct applications and con-intuitions toward incorrect applications—correct, that is, relative to the contents of the concept as it exists in the subject's head.[23]

I'll focus on Goldman's articulation of the idea that the method of cases plays a central role in the analysis of concepts here, but the arguments below extend to other articulations. Concepts give rise to judgments that some things, including the situations described by philosophers' cases, fall or do not fall under them. These judgments are, at least in part, determined by the content of the concepts. By considering a range of cases and the judgments they elicit, philosophers can infer the content of the concepts of interest. Of course, these judgments are "not infallible evidence" (2007, 15) about the content of concepts, since various other factors, including people's beliefs about the content of their concepts (what Goldman calls "a theory of one's concept"), can also influence concept application (on this point, see Chapter 2 of Machery, 2009).

Goldman calls the judgments elicited by cases "intuitions," but the notion of intuition plays little role in his defense of conceptual analysis. For Goldman, intuitions just are judgments elicited by cases. Furthermore, his view about the relation between concepts and categorization judgments is consistent with most views about concepts, including those, like mine, strongly influenced by the psychology of concepts.

Let me specify the following terminology. In the remainder of this book, I will use "the method of cases 1.0" to refer to the method of cases as it has been used by philosophers, and "the method of cases 2.0" to refer to a revamped, empirical method of cases.

7.6.2 The poverty of the method of cases 1.0 for conceptual analysis

The method of cases 1.0 is often a poor way of analyzing concepts.[24] This claim is certainly supported inductively. While it is not entirely clear how often philosophers throughout the history of philosophy have relied on the method of cases to analyze concepts, this method has played an important role in the analytic tradition. But, as critics of conceptual analysis often note, philosophers have little to show for the time invested in analyzing concepts by means of the method of cases: How many concepts, critics ask, have been successfully analyzed? While there is some truth in this observation, a proponent of the method of cases in the formal mode could justifiably point to the consensus over some negative results—for instance, the claim that the concept of knowledge cannot be identified with the complex concept of a justified true belief or that the concept of knowledge represents knowledge as being factive. However, a more damning failure of the method of cases 1.0 is that, despite their commitment to describing the content of concepts, conceptual analysts have failed to identify even

---

[23] See also, e.g., Chalmers & Jackson (2001, 322); Schroeter (2004); Ludwig (2014).
[24] See also Nadelhoffer & Nahmias (2007).

basic features of a concept. For instance, most philosophers analyzing concepts by means of the method of cases have missed the fact that typically people do not form bliefs about necessary and sufficient membership conditions and the fact that typicality gradients are an important manifestation of concepts. How much trust can we have in a method that fails to hone in on such basic features?

While this inductive argument suggests that there is something wrong with the method of cases 1.0 as a way to analyze concepts, it does not tell us what's wrong with it. I turn to this question now, focusing on four problems. The method of cases 1.0 is not suited for examining conceptual diversity; it is poorly suited to identify the weights of the properties represented by concepts and the interactions between these properties; its capacity to identify the properties represented by concepts is limited; and it often relies on disturbing cases.

Let's begin with the first problem: The method of cases 1.0 is either individualistic or elitist. Philosophers consult their own judgments (it is then individualistic) or the judgments of their colleagues and graduate students (it is then elitist), and use these judgments to analyze concepts. Thus, even if it could successfully be put in the service of conceptual analysis, the method of cases 1.0 could only contribute to the analysis of the analyst and her colleagues' concepts, and it would be of no use to examine how some group of non-philosophers conceives of something (e.g., to understand how cognitive psychologists conceive of innateness). Furthermore, it could either be that philosophers' concepts diverge from non-philosophers' or that, while philosophers share the concepts possessed by some non-philosophers, concepts vary, perhaps systematically (e.g., as a function of demographic variables such as culture, socio-economic status, or personality), different groups having different concepts. Experimental philosophers have had a field day collecting evidence in support of either possibility (see Chapter 2; see also Livengood & Machery, 2007; Sytsma & Machery, 2010 for the first option). If that is so, conceptual analysis by means of the method of cases 1.0 will only cast light on the concepts possessed by a small sliver of humanity or it will fail to cast light on the concepts possessed by other groups, and it is unclear why we should care about the analysis of those concepts (see the discussion of Parochialism in Chapter 4). It is noteworthy that experimental syntacticians have often expressed similar concerns about the individualistic or elitist nature of the prevailing methodology in syntax (Machery & Stich, 2012): Syntacticians' acceptability judgments elicited by candidate grammatical constructions may reflect their peculiar idiolect—which few people may share— and consulting them may prevent syntacticians from paying attention to systematic dialectical variation.

There are at least two responses to this concern: One can acknowledge that individualism and elitism are problems, and one can then try to address them; alternatively, one can deny that individualism and elitism are problems, and one can embrace them as desirable features of conceptual analysis. I will examine these responses in turn. Goldman is perfectly aware of the individualistic nature of the method of cases, but he argues that, once the analyst's concepts are analyzed, she simply needs to make sure that her concepts happen to be shared by others (see also Jackson, 1998, 36–7). As he puts it (2007, 17), "we can move from concepts$_2$ [i.e., psychological concepts] to concepts$_3$, i.e., shared (psychological) concepts. This can be done if a substantial agreement is found across many individuals' concepts$_2$. Such sharing cannot be assumed at the outset, however; it must be established." This is a curious way of dealing with the first problem. If it is important that the analyzed concepts be shared by non-philosophers, then why not embrace a method, such as the experimental method of the method of cases 2.0 (Section 7.6.3), that is directly focused on non-philosophers' concepts and is able to identify systematic variation?

Perhaps the idea is that philosophers and non-philosophers are likely to share the same (or a similar) concept, and that one is justified to assume that much as long as reasons to doubt this assumption have not been explicitly proposed. Jackson goes even further, asserting (1998, 37, my emphasis) that "often we *know* that our case is typical and can generalize from it to others." Similarly, syntacticians' use of their own accept-ability judgments has recently been defended on the grounds that syntacticians' and lay people's acceptability judgments are identical for an overwhelming majority of grammatical constructions (Sprouse & Almeida, 2012; Sprouse et al., 2013). Sprouse and colleagues (2013) have shown that for about 150 minimal pairs randomly selected from ten volumes of *Linguistic Inquiry* (2001–10), informal acceptability judgments made by syntacticians and acceptability judgments experimentally collected from lay informants agree nineteen times out of twenty! In the same spirit, challenging, among other claims, Livengood and Machery's (2007) contention that philosophers' and lay people's judgments about causation by absence and causal explanation differ, Dunaway et al. (2013) have provided evidence that philosophers are able to predict lay people's judgments. For each of the four studies Dunaway and colleagues considered, they found that a substantial majority of philosophers were able to predict the pattern of answers obtained with lay people.

While we do not know exactly how often philosophers and lay people, or at least some lay people, have different concepts, there are reasons to believe that this is not an extremely rare occurrence. Divergences have been found in the few explicit compari-sons between lay people's and philosophers' use of philosophically relevant concepts.[25] In addition, several studies report that lay people use philosophically relevant concepts in a way by and large unexpected in light of the philosophical literature. One type of Gettier case elicits knowledge ascription (Starmans & Friedman, 2012; Turri et al., 2015); skeptical threats (illustrated by fake-barn cases) do not always influence knowledge ascription (Colaço et al., 2014; Turri et al., 2015); people react differently to different types of Gettier cases (Turri et al., 2015); knowledge ascription about a means depends on the moral valence of this means (Beebe & Buckwalter, 2010); knowledge ascription does not require belief ascription (Myers-Schulz & Schwitzgebel, 2013; Murray et al., 2013).

---

[25] E.g., Hitchcock & Knobe (2009); Buckwalter (2010, 2012); Feltz & Zarpentine (2010); May et al. (2010); Sytsma & Machery (2010); Reuter (2011); Cova & Pain (2012); Horvath & Wiegmann (2016).

There are sufficiently many instances of divergence that philosophers cannot simply assume that they share lay people's concepts.

But don't the results by Sprouse and colleagues provide some inductive support to this assumption? First, people's syntax (as revealed by their acceptability judgments) may be less likely to vary than philosophically relevant concepts. Second, Sprouse and colleagues' results do not show that there are no dialects such that the grammar of the speakers of these dialects (and their acceptability judgments) diverges from the grammar of syntacticians: They only show that syntacticians' acceptability judgments converge with the modal acceptability judgments among speakers of US English. In their published papers, Sprouse and colleagues do not comment on the distribution of answers among their subjects: For instance, bimodal distributions would indicate that a minority of speakers make different acceptability judgments. Third, Sprouse and colleagues' results are irrelevant when one is concerned with the concepts of a particular group of individuals (e.g., cognitive scientists' concepts of innateness).

Dunaway and colleagues (2013) do show that as a group philosophers are well attuned to how lay people as a group respond to some of the cases used by experimental philosophers. However, as Liao (2016) has compellingly shown, this does not mean that individual philosophers are well attuned to lay people's responses: In fact, a majority of philosophers made at least one mistake for the four responses they were asked to predict, and this proportion was larger among philosophers without exposure to experimental philosophy. So, Dunaway and colleagues have at best shown that if philosophers examined the reactions of many other philosophers, they would perhaps be in a position to predict lay people's judgments, not that individual philosophers can be confident that they are attuned to how lay people would respond to cases. They provide little support for the suggestion that as a rule philosophers can assume that their own judgments match lay people's.

I now turn to the second response. One can embrace the individualistic or elitist nature of conceptual analysis based on the method of cases on one of the following two grounds. First, philosophers' concepts could have properties that make them particularly worth analyzing, or non-philosophers' concepts could have properties that make them particularly bad to analyze. For instance, if one is interested in the concept of something (e.g., the concept of justice) because one is interested in that thing itself (justice itself), one may elect to focus on philosophers' concept on the grounds that it is a more accurate representation of that thing. Of course, that justification is not available if one is merely interested in concepts (in contrast to what they are about), and in any case it requires a reason to believe that philosophers' and non-philosophers' concepts have the respectively desirable and undesirable properties (see the discussion of the Expertise Defense in Section 5.3 of Chapter 5). A second reason for focusing on philosophers' concepts is simply that they are *our* concepts. Baz (2012, 323) mentions this type of view (which he does not endorse himself): "The answer to Stich's question of why we should care about what is merely our concept is accordingly simple: because it is ours, and to become clearer about it is to become clearer about those features and dimensions of ourselves and of our world to which this concept is responsive and of which it is therefore revelatory."[26]

While there may be something to be said for focusing on philosophers' concepts for the analysis of at least some concepts, it is a non-starter for most of the concepts philosophers are interested in. For many projects involving conceptual analysis, one is interested in how non-philosophers think about various topics. For instance, compatibilists and incompatibilists do not disagree about whether a technical concept of responsibility—one that philosophers would have developed—is compatible with determinism, but about whether the lay concept of responsibility—the one possessed by non-philosophers—is so compatible. After all, they ultimately want to know the significance determinism would have for our everyday practice of holding people responsible. Similarly, if one is interested in the norms governing knowledge ascription, then one is unlikely to be interested in how a small corner of humanity decides that something is knowledge.

In fact, when lay concepts happen to be widely shared across demographic groups while differing from philosophers', focusing on the properties the former refer to may, at least sometimes, be an excellent way to address fundamental philosophical questions (see Chapter 4 on the nature of fundamental philosophical questions), and moving away from them may undermine our capacity to address these questions, as ordinary language philosophers have argued. Some lay concepts allow lay people to navigate situations of philosophical significance successfully. Perhaps the lay concept of responsibility is successful in enabling people to hold each other responsible for actions; perhaps the lay concept of justification is successful in enabling people to hold themselves and others accountable for assertions. If they really are so successful, understanding what these concepts refer to may be the best strategy to address the relevant fundamental philosophical questions.

It would not do to respond that one need not think that philosophers have different concepts to embrace the individualist or elitist nature of the method of cases 1.0; rather, philosophers may have the same concepts as lay people, but just be better at deploying them (e.g., Ludwig, 2007). The discussion of the Expertise Defense in Section 5.3 of Chapter 5 suggests that this claim is probably mere wishful thinking.

The previous discussion conceded that the method of cases 1.0 could successfully be used to analyze the concepts of the analyst and her colleagues, but this concession was only made for the sake of the argument. The method of cases 1.0 is limited in three distinct ways when it comes to describing the content of concepts. First, even if the method of cases happens to be useful for identifying the properties that the referents of an analyzed concept are represented as possessing, it is of little use to identify their weights. Similarly, while the method of cases 1.0 could in principle be used to examine whether the represented properties influence concept application additively or interactively, in practice this seems impossible, since many cases would have to

---

[26] See also Grice (1989, 175).

be considered and complex relations between represented properties would have to be assessed.

Second, while the method of cases 1.0 can surely be used to identify some represented properties, it is limited in this respect as well. Typically, there are a host of possible explanations about why we are judging as we do in response to a particular case (e.g., Frankfurt cases) or why we are making two different judgments in response to a pair of cases (e.g., the bystander and footbridge cases). Philosophers have not always taken the measure of this problem, sometimes naively taking for granted a preferred explanation. For instance, Quinn (1993) assumes that the pairs of cases he considers differ in that the first case of each pair involves allowing harm to happen to bring about a greater good while the second involves causing harm, but, as Horowitz (1998) has cogently argued, the judgments elicited by Quinn's cases could differ for an entirely different reason. She indeed proposes that they are better explained by prospect theory (1998, 380):

> Quinn's intuitions can be explained fairly well by Prospect theory....to the best of my knowledge, no similarly broad and plausible psychological theory, based on the idea that people intuit a distinction between doing and allowing, is available to explain Quinn's intuitions. What we have from Quinn is introspective testimony that this is the right explanation, combined with a few anecdotal claims that other people have come to the same opinion.

To identify which of the many possible explanations is the correct one—to use the jargon of experimental design, to de-confound the search for the correct explanation—a large number of comparisons are needed, and for each possible explanatory factor examined, the other explanatory factors must be held constant—in the jargon of experimental design, these explanatory factors must be crossed in an orthogonal design. Adjudicating between confounded explanations requires looking at a large, systematically varied number of cases, which is better done in an experimental setting.

Furthermore, it is likely that not all of the factors that influence concept application have a large effect; rather, some may have only a small influence—that is, they may make it only somewhat more likely that we apply a given concept. Furthermore, interactions between factors may be also small: Whether a given factor is present or absent may only slightly modify how another factor influences the probability of applying a given concept. If one were to rely only on the method of cases 1.0, one would need to consider a large number of cases barely differing from one another with respect to the extent to which they elicit or fail to elicit concept application. Experimental syntacticians have expressed an analogous concern (Machery & Stich, 2012): Except for the most important syntactic properties, which have already been identified by existing theories, a linguist's acceptability judgments about the sentences in a minimal pair cannot be reliably used to identify syntactic features. Judgments are noisy, and it is unclear whether a small difference in acceptability (sentence A sounds slightly better than sentence B) is due to noise or to the genuine better acceptability of one of the sentences. Aggregating many judgments and analyzing them statistically solve this problem.

Finally, the method of cases 1.0 tends to rely on disturbing cases, as was argued in Section 3.5 of Chapter 3. Some disturbing characteristics may lead readers to rely on ad hoc strategies to make a judgment. When this happens, judgments do not provide evidence about the content of the concepts they deploy, since they do not rest on the bliefs that are constitutive of concepts.

7.6.3 Conceptual analysis: the experimental turn

The method of cases 2.0—presenting cases to samples of participants and analyzing their response statistically—can overcome the limitations of the method of cases 1.0. First, it does not focus on the semantic content of concepts, which has been the focus of the method of cases 1.0 (Section 1.1 of Chapter 1), since the content of concepts understood psychologically is not identified with their meaning. So, the method of cases 2.0 addresses formal-mode questions in an extended sense: It does not just focus on meaning or content, but on the psychological entities that govern spontaneous inferences, judgments, and explanations. In addition, the method of cases 2.0 is neither individualistic nor elitist, in contrast to the method of cases 1.0. When folk concepts matter, they can be examined directly. When the concepts of some group of non-philosophers (e.g., cognitive psychologists' concept of innateness) matter, they can be examined directly. Experiments can be designed to assess whether concepts vary, since different populations (different cultures, different scientific traditions, scientists vs. lay people, etc.) can be sampled from.

An experimental approach also allows philosophers to estimate the weights associated with the properties represented by a given concept, using simple statistical tools like linear regression, and whether these represented properties contribute additively or interactively to the application of the analyzed concept. In addition, it enables them to identify the causes of judgments about philosophical cases. Many cases, which differ subtly, can be compared and tracked, which is hard to do with the method of cases 1.0, and noise can be distinguished from genuine differences by aggregating many judgments. Finally, since we are not trying to distinguish between competing philosophical theories, we are not constrained to rely on disturbing cases. In particular, the entanglement of superficial and target content is likely to be less of an issue for typical cases that fall squarely within the proper domain of our concepts than for the cases that philosophers incline to use. The experimental study of the concept of innateness reviewed in Section 7.7 shows how this can be done.

Remember also that to the extent that the analyst is after people's concept of x in contrast to their background bliefs about x, she will attempt to identify the information about x that is retrieved by default from long-term memory or the inferences people are disposed to draw by default. To do so may require eliciting a particular type of judgment from participants in an experimental setting, viz. the judgments that are likely to reflect their concepts. It may be that snap judgments, which some philosophers call "intuitions" (Section 1.2 of Chapter 1), have this feature. If that were the case, the particularist characterization would be an erroneous characterization of the method of cases for material-mode purposes, but an accurate characterization of the method of cases 2.0 for the study of formal-mode questions.

It is sometimes said that experimental philosophy just is the method of cases applied to more than a single person. On the one hand, this is certainly a myopic conception of what experimental philosophy has to offer (O'Neill & Machery, 2014), but on the other hand this idea gets something right: It is the method of cases minus its crippling limitations! Experimental philosophers propose to do exactly what experimental syntacticians and pragmaticists have done, namely turning individualistic or elitist methods—syntacticians assessing, e.g., the acceptability of syntactic constructions—into experimental tools.

Finally, while the method of cases 2.0 overcomes the limitations of the method of cases 1.0 and has many advantages, it is not the only empirical method available to the naturalistic conceptual analyst. Historical, anthropological, or sociological linguistics can provide important evidence relevant to describing concepts of philosophical interest. Historians of science have often relied on this type of evidence to study past scientific concepts. In fact, these methods and the method of cases 2.0 nicely complement each other. The former provide more ecologically valid evidence, the second more controlled evidence.

It may be tempted to object that an empirical, to say nothing of an experimental, approach to concepts is not always needed to fulfill philosophers' goals. To press the point, a critic could note that scientists are routinely engaged in prescriptive conceptual analysis, but don't feel the need to set up experiments to examine the concepts they plan to reform. Why should it be any different in philosophy? But, first, scientists' prescriptive conceptual analysis is very much in line with the characterization proposed in Section 7.3. In particular, recommendation always takes place against the background of the description of existing concepts. Literature reviews lay out the content of these concepts. Furthermore, scientists seem sensitive to the conservatism embodied in the similarity criterion, although it is naturally balanced by the utility of the reformed concepts. And the description of existing concepts is broadly empirical: Literature reviews examine the actual uses of concepts in scientific practice. Perhaps a critic would concede these points, but insist that, while empirical, the description of existing concepts in science is not experimental. The reason for this, however, is in part that being elitist and individualistic is not an issue there: Scientists are exclusively concerned with the concepts they and their colleagues possess. And, as noted in Section 7.3, a detailed description of concepts is often not needed for prescriptive purposes. Finally, experimental analyses may be useful in science too, for example when one suspects that the use of a concept in writing is different from its spontaneous use in thought (Stotz et al., 2004; Machery, 2016a).[27]

---

[27] For discussion of the experimental turn in the philosophy of science, see Machery (2016a).

7.7 A Case Study: The Lay Concept of Innateness

To illustrate naturalized conceptual analysis and the method of cases 2.0, I provide a fleshed-out example, focusing on the following question: How should we think about the development of organisms? In particular, is the concept of innateness useful to characterize the ontogeny of some traits? This question has been at the center of an intense and protracted controversy in ethology (e.g., Konrad Lorenz), comparative psychology (e.g., Daniel Lehrman), psychobiology (e.g., Gilbert Gottlieb), and the philosophy of biology (e.g., Paul Griffiths).[28] Addressing this question requires understanding how people think about innate traits, and having some relevant knowledge about development—exactly what naturalized conceptual analysis is for. Answering it would allow the theorist to decide whether a lay concept, INNATENESS, can be used in the scientific study of biological (including psychological) development or whether it should be eliminated. It would also contribute to squaring the manifest and the scientific images of the world by revealing whether, and in which respect, the two are at odds with respect to biological development.

Following Griffiths (2002), Griffiths et al. (2009) have proposed a particular analysis of the lay concept of innateness (see also Linquist et al., 2011). Innate traits are proposed to be the expression of what people view as the inner nature of organisms (e.g., dogs, cats, etc.). These traits have the three following features:

1. *Fixity*—they are hard to change; their development is insensitive to environmental inputs in development; it appears goal-directed, or resistant to perturbation.
2. *Typicality*—they are part of what it is to be an organism of that kind; every individual has them, or every individual that is not malformed, or every individual of a certain age, sex, or other natural subcategory.
3. *Teleology*—this is how the organism is meant to develop; to lack the innate trait is to be malformed; environments that disrupt the development of this trait are themselves abnormal.

We are not proposing to analyze INNATENESS by means of a set of necessary and sufficient conditions called "Typicality," "Fixity," and "Teleology." The three-feature analysis has a similar status to accounts of other concepts developed by psychologists and cognitive anthropologists. It treats the vernacular concept of innateness as a cognitive structure (a body of information) that has its origin in folk biology. If the three-feature analysis is correct, then the cognitive structure that underpins the use of the term "innate" is an implicit theory that views organisms as having inner natures that are expressed in traits that are likely to be typical, fixed, and teleological.

---

[28] This issue is different from, and indeed prior to, the debate between nativists and anti-nativists about the extent of the innate endowment of the mind.

In line with the call for greater sophistication in the models of concepts naturalistic conceptual analysts should put forward, we were explicit in proposing that Typicality, Fixity, and Teleology contribute *additively* to judgments about whether some trait is innate. That is, each feature contributes to the judgment that a trait is innate independently of whether that trait has the other two features. Suppose that we were wrong, and that people only take one feature—Fixity, for example—to be characteristic of traits that express inner natures; suppose also that people use the other two features as suggestive cues for whether the defining feature is present (perhaps because they believe that the corresponding properties tend to co-occur). This alternative to the three-feature theory predicts an interaction among the three features. Direct evidence that the trait is not fixed will reduce the influence of evidence that the trait is typical or teleological on the final judgment about its innateness.

Finally, we wanted to find out the weight of each of these three features—how much each feature influences the judgment that a trait is innate—although we did not have any a priori hypothesis about this.

To assess our hypotheses and to determine the weight of the three features, we appealed to empirical methods. In a series of experiments, lay people were presented with examples of birdsong. Each example had the same structure. The case began with a standard paragraph about research on birdsong, designed to convince participants that there is a wealth of well-established scientific knowledge about birdsong. The next paragraph began with one or two sentences naming a specific bird and providing some neutral information about it. This was designed to convince participants that this is a real animal. The remainder of this paragraph stated whether the song of the male of this species is fixed, typical, teleological, or their opposites, using one of each of these pairs of statements:

Fixed/plastic

0.   Studies on _____ show that the song an adult male produces depends on which songs they hear when they are young.
1.   Studies on _____ show that the song an adult male produces does not depend on which songs they hear when they are young.

Typical/not typical

0.   Studies also show that different males in this species sing different songs.
1.   Studies also show that all males of this species sing the same song.

Teleology/no teleology

0.   Close observations of these birds reveal that the males' song is not used to attract mates or to defend territories. Scientists therefore agree that this feature of the bird has no real function, like the appendix in humans.

1.   Close observations of these birds reveal that the males' song attracts mates and helps to defend their territory. Scientists therefore agree that this feature of the bird has a real function, like the heart in humans.

To illustrate, the case describing a species of bird in which birdsong is not typical, is fixed, and has a function read as follows:

Birdsong is one of the most intensively studied aspects of animal behavior. Since the 1950s scientists have used recordings and sound spectrograms to uncover the structure and function of birdsong. Neuroscientists have investigated in great detail the areas of the brain that allow birds to develop and produce their songs. Other scientists have done ecological fieldwork to study what role song plays in the lives of different birds.

The Alder Flycatcher (*Empidonax alnorum*) is a migratory neo-tropical bird which breeds in southern Canada and the northern USA. Studies on the Alder Flycatcher show that the song an adult male produces does not depend on which songs they hear when they are young. Studies also show that different males in this species sing different songs. Furthermore, close observations of these birds reveal that the males' song attracts mates and helps to defend their territory. Scientists therefore agree that the bird's song has a real function, like the heart in humans.

On a 7-point scale, 1 meaning strongly disagree and 7 meaning strongly agree, how would you respond to the following statement?

"The song of the male Alder Flycatcher is innate."

Statistical analysis of the data obtained in several studies confirmed that people are more likely to judge that a trait is innate when it is fixed, typical, and has a function, and that these three features contribute independently to people's judgment. Furthermore, we were able to determine that teleology only plays a small role in innateness judgment (Figure 7.1).[29]

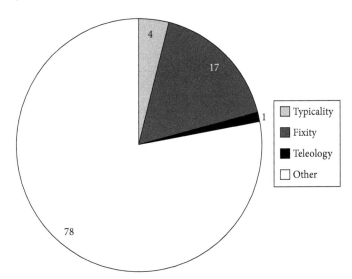

Figure 7.1 Proportion of the variance independently predicted by fixity, typicality, and teleology (based on Study 1 of Griffiths et al., 2009).

[29] A limitation of this study was that we did not attempt to determine whether these bliefs are retrieved by default.

In light of these results, we challenged the empirical validity of the concept of innateness. This concept leads people to infer that a trait is universal from the fact that it evolved; it leads them to conclude that a trait has a function from the fact that it is universal, and so on. That is, people are disposed to follow, e.g., the inferences:

Trait x is universal   Trait x is innate

Trait x is innate   Trait x is functional

This inference pattern as well as the other inference patterns between the universality of a trait, its plasticity, and its function are not empirically valid. Evolutionary biology tells us that a universal trait is not particularly likely to be functional, that traits that are not plastic may be functional, etc. The lay concept of innateness thus promotes unreliable inferences, and should be either modified or eliminated. A central aspect of our manifest image of development turns out to be incompatible with the scientific image.

7.8 Conclusion

We should refrain from embracing the last fad of conceptual-analysis bashing or the long-standing skepticism among naturalistic philosophers: Naturalized, conceptual analysis is immune to the issues that plague other forms of conceptual analysis, and it has important roles to play. Naturalistic philosophers should not shy away from it; after all, scientists routinely analyze concepts, and some important contributions to the history of science are conceptual analyses (e.g., Lehrman, 1953 on the concepts of instinct and innateness).

Naturalized conceptual analysis is not your grandfather's conceptual analysis. It focuses on concepts delineated psychologically instead of semantically, and it has no truck with gaining knowledge in a priori manner. It does not fall prey to the usual objections to a prioristic conceptual analysis. Most important perhaps, its goal is not to identify analytically true propositions; rather, its most fundamental goal is to identify the inferences our minds are prone to draw in order to assess them. Finally, the method of cases 1.0 is often a poor way to complete this task, and we philosophers must revamp it thoroughly. When it is used to analyze concepts, the method of cases 1.0 is elitist and individualistic; it is blind to variation; it is geared toward simplistic models of concepts; it is useless for measuring the weights of component concepts; and it may not even be very good at identifying the properties represented by concepts. If we care about analyzing concepts for some philosophical purpose, the experimental method—the method of cases 2.0—is our best tool.

Postscript

Debates about the limits of philosophical knowledge go way back, and philosophers fall roughly into two distinct traditions. Some, like Plato, Aristotle, Descartes, and Leibniz, are optimistic about the reach of philosophizing; others, like Hume, Dewey, and James, incline toward thinking that philosophical knowledge is limited and emphasize the critical role of philosophy: On their view, philosophy corrects erroneous, empty, or misleading ideas. Each tradition is of course quite diverse, but each is also unified by its optimism or pessimism about philosophical knowledge. *Philosophy Within Its Proper Bounds* clearly belongs to the second tradition: Resolving philosophical issues that require modally immodest philosophical knowledge, such as physicalism and the necessary conditions for knowledge and responsibility, is beyond our reach.

Philosophers need not power off their laptop. Modally immodest philosophical issues have modally modest counterparts, which are both intricate and exciting. Philosophers can also, in a naturalistic spirit, contribute to the growth of empirical knowledge. And, finally, conceptual analysis should take back the place it once had among philosophers. Understanding concepts, a thoroughly empirical matter, is valuable in itself—it gives us insight into how people deal, sometimes with great success, with issues of philosophical interest—and instrumentally: It opens the door for articulating the manifest and scientific images and for criticizing and reforming lay concepts.

For much of the history of philosophy, philosophers could not have imagined their philosophizing as separate from not only mathematics, but also the empirical sciences. Perhaps because they felt threatened by the apparently unstoppable growth of the sciences, philosophers started carving their own kingdom, far removed from scientists' interests and methods. Modally immodest philosophical issues may seem to play a central role in building a wall between philosophy and the sciences, but in fact they are not the safe haven they are cracked up to be. These issues are beyond our epistemic reach and we should set them aside in order to turn our attention toward issues we can fruitfully theorize about. The development of the empirical method of cases 2.0 to analyze concepts is part and parcel of this reorientation of philosophy. Hopefully, it will, at least partly, close the gap that emerged decades ago between science and philosophy.

Bibliography

Abarbanell, L., & Hauser, M. D. (2010). Mayan morality: An exploration of permissible harms. *Cognition*, 115, 207–24.

Adams, F., & Steadman, A. (2004). Intentional action in ordinary language: Core concept or pragmatic understanding? *Analysis*, 64, 173–81.

Adleberg, T., Thompson, M., & Nahmias, E. (2015). Do women and men have different philosophical intuitions? Further data. *Philosophical Psychology*, 28, 615–41.

Ahlenius, H., & Tännsjö, T. (2012). Chinese and Westerners respond differently to the trolley dilemmas. *Journal of Cognition and Culture*, 12, 195–201.

Alexander, J. (2012). *Experimental philosophy: An introduction*. Cambridge: Polity.

Alexander, J., & Weinberg, J. M. (2007). Analytic epistemology and experimental philosophy. *Philosophy Compass*, 2, 56–80.

Alexander, J., & Weinberg, J. M. (2014). The "unreliability" of epistemic intuitions. In E. O'Neill and E. Machery (Eds.), *Current controversies in experimental philosophy* (pp. 128–45). New York: Routledge.

Alicke, M. D. (1992). Culpable causation. *Journal of Personality and Social Psychology*, 63, 368–78.

Alicke, M. D. (2000). Culpable control and the psychology of blame. *Psychological Bulletin*, 126, 556–74.

Alston, W. P. (1993). Epistemic desiderata. *Philosophy and Phenomenological Research*, 53, 527–51.

Alston, W. P. (1995). How to think about reliability. *Philosophical Topics*, 23, 1–29.

Alston, W. P. (2005). *Beyond "justification": Dimensions of epistemic evaluation*. Ithaca, NY: Cornell University Press.

Andow, J. (2015). Expecting philosophers to be reliable. *Dialectica*, 69, 205–20.

Anscombe, G. E. M. (1958). Modern moral philosophy. *Philosophy*, 33, 1–19.

Antognazza, M. R. (2015). The benefit to philosophy of the study of its history. *British Journal for the History of Philosophy*, 23, 161–84.

Arkes, H. R. (2001). Overconfidence in judgmental forecasting. In J. S. Armstrong (Ed.), *Principles of forecasting: A handbook for researchers and practitioners* (pp. 495–516). Boston: Kluwer Academic.

Audi, R. (1997). *Moral knowledge and ethical character*. Oxford: Oxford University Press.

Austin, J. L. (1956). A plea for excuses. *Proceedings of the Aristotelian Society*, 57, 1–30.

Ayer, A. J. (1954). *Philosophical essays*. London: MacMillan.

Balaguer, M. (2009). The metaphysical irrelevance of the compatibilism debate (and, more generally, of conceptual analysis). *The Southern Journal of Philosophy*, 47, 1–24.

Banerjee, K., Huebner, B., & Hauser, M. (2010). Intuitive moral judgments are robust across variation in gender, education, politics and religion: A large-scale web-based study. *Journal of Cognition and Culture*, 10, 253–81.

Bargh, J. A. (1994). The four horsemen of automaticity: Intention, awareness, efficiency, and control as separate issues. In R. Wyer and T. Srull (Eds.), *Handbook of social cognition* (pp. 1–40). Hillsdale, NJ: Lawrence Erlbaum.

Barsalou, L. W. (1987). The instability of graded structure: Implications for the nature of concepts. In U. Neisser (Ed.), *Concepts and conceptual development: Ecological and intellectual factors in categorization* (pp. 101–40). Cambridge: Cambridge University Press.

Bartels, D. M. (2008). Principled moral sentiment and the flexibility of moral judgment and decision making. *Cognition*, 108, 381–417.

Bartels, D. M., & Pizarro, D. A. (2011). The mismeasure of morals: Antisocial personality traits predict utilitarian responses to moral dilemmas. *Cognition*, 121, 154–61.

Baz, A. (2012). Must philosophers rely on intuitions? *The Journal of Philosophy*, 109, 316–37.

Baz, A. (2015). On going nowhere with our words: New skepticism about the philosophical method of cases. *Philosophical Psychology*, 29, 64–83.

Bealer, G. (1992). The incoherence of empiricism. *Proceedings of the Aristotelian Society, Supplementary Volumes*, 66, 99–143.

Bealer, G. (1996). A priori knowledge and the scope of philosophy. *Philosophical Studies*, 81, 121–42.

Bealer, G. (1998). Intuition and the autonomy of philosophy. In M. R. DePaul and W. Ramsey (Eds.), *Rethinking intuition: The psychology of intuition and its role in philosophical inquiry* (pp. 201–40). Lanham, MD: Rowman & Littlefield Publishers.

Bechtel, W., & Mundale, J. (1999). Multiple realizability revisited: Linking cognitive and neural states. *Philosophy of Science*, 66, 175–207.

Beebe, J. R. (2004). The generality problem, statistical relevance and the tri-level hypothesis. *Noûs*, 38, 177–95.

Beebe, J. R., & Buckwalter, W. (2010). The epistemic side-effect effect. *Mind & Language*, 25, 474–98.

Beebe, J. R., & Jensen, M. (2012). Surprising connections between knowledge and action: The robustness of the epistemic side-effect effect. *Philosophical Psychology*, 25, 689–715.

Beebe, J. R., & Undercoffer, R. J. (2015). Moral valence and semantic intuitions. *Erkenntnis*, 80, 445–66.

Beebe, J. R., & Undercoffer, R. J. (2016). Individual and cross-cultural differences in semantic intuitions: New experimental findings. *Journal of Cognition and Culture*, 16, 322–57.

Belnap, N. D. (1962). Tonk, plonk and plink. *Analysis*, 22, 130–4.

Bengson, J. (2015). The intellectual given. *Mind*, 124, 707–60.

Bishop, M. A. (1992). The possibility of conceptual clarity in philosophy. *American Philosophical Quarterly*, 29, 267–77.

Bishop, M. A., & Trout, J. D. (2005). *Epistemology and the psychology of human judgment*. Oxford: Oxford University Press.

Björnsson, G., & Finlay, S. (2010). Metaethical contextualism defended. *Ethics*, 121, 7–36.

Block, N. (1978). Troubles with functionalism. In C. W. Savage (Ed.), *Minnesota studies in the philosophy of science*, vol. 9 (pp. 261–325). Minneapolis: University of Minnesota Press.

Block, N. (1995). On a confusion about a function of consciousness. *Behavioral and Brain Sciences*, 18, 227–47.

Block, N., & Stalnaker, R. (1999). Conceptual analysis, dualism, and the explanatory gap. *The Philosophical Review*, 108, 1–46.

Boghossian, P. A. (1996). Analyticity reconsidered. *Noûs*, 30, 360–91.

Boghossian, P. A. (2003). Epistemic analyticity: A defense. *Grazer Philosophische Studien*, 66, 15–35.

BonJour, L. (1980). Externalist theories of empirical knowledge. *Midwest Studies in Philosophy*, 5, 53–74.

BonJour, L. (1998). *In defense of pure reason: A rationalist account of a priori justification.* Cambridge: Cambridge University Press.

Boyd, R. N. (1988). How to be a moral realist. In P. K. Moser & J. D. Trout (Eds.), *Contemporary materialism: A reader* (pp. 307–70). London: Routledge.

Bradner, A., Weekes Schroer, J., & Chin-Parker, S. (ms). When the violinist is your half-sibling: Using experimental philosophy to assess the Stranger's objection to Thomson's classic thought experiment.

Brandom, R. (1994). *Making it explicit: Reasoning, representing, and discursive commitment.* Cambridge, MA: Harvard University Press.

Brandom, R. (2001). Reason, expression, and the philosophical enterprise. In C. P. Ragland and S. Heidt (Eds.), *What Is Philosophy?* (pp. 74–95). New Haven: Yale University Press.

Broad, C. D. (1940). Conscience and conscientious action. *Philosophy*, 15, 115–30.

Brown, H. I. (1985). Galileo on the telescope and the eye. *Journal of the History of Ideas*, 46, 487–501.

Buckwalter, W. (2010). Knowledge isn't closed on Saturday: A study in ordinary language. *Review of Philosophy and Psychology*, 1, 395–406.

Buckwalter, W. (2012). Non-traditional factors in judgments about knowledge. *Philosophy Compass*, 7, 278–89.

Buckwalter, W. (2014). Gettier made ESEE. *Philosophical Psychology*, 27, 368–83.

Buckwalter, W. (2016). Intuition fail: Philosophical activity and the limits of expertise. *Philosophy and Phenomenological Research*, 92, 378–410.

Buckwalter, W., Rose, D., & Turri, J. (2013). Belief through thick and thin. *Noûs*, doi: 10.1111/nous.12048.

Buckwalter, W., & Stich, S. (2015). Gender and philosophical intuition. In J. Knobe & S. Nichols (Eds.), *Experimental philosophy*, vol. 2 (pp. 307–46). Oxford: Oxford University Press.

Buhrmester, M., Kwang, T., & Gosling, S. D. (2011). Amazon's Mechanical Turk a new source of inexpensive, yet high-quality, data? *Perspectives on Psychological Science*, 6, 3–5.

Burge, T. (1979). Individualism and the mental. *Midwest Studies in Philosophy*, 4, 73–121.

Burgess, A., & Plunkett, D. (2013a). Conceptual ethics I. *Philosophy Compass*, 8, 1091–101.

Burgess, A., & Plunkett, D. (2013b). Conceptual ethics II. *Philosophy Compass*, 8, 1102–10.

Burnyeat, M. F. (1982). Idealism and Greek philosophy: What Descartes saw and Berkeley missed. *Royal Institute of Philosophy Lecture Series*, 13, 19–50.

Cappelen, H. (2012). *Philosophy without intuitions.* Oxford: Oxford University Press.

Carey, S. (2009). *The origin of concepts.* Oxford: Oxford University Press.

Carnap, R. (1950). *Logical foundations of probability.* Chicago: University of Chicago Press.

Carnap, R. (1963). P. F. Strawson on linguistic naturalism. In P. Schilpp (Ed.), *The philosophy of Rudolf Carnap* (pp. 933–40). Lasalle: Open Court.

Casasanto, D., & Lupyan, G. (2015). All concepts are ad hoc concepts. In E. Margolis & S. Laurence (Eds.), *Concepts: new directions* (pp. 543–66). Cambridge, MA: MIT Press.

Chalmers, D. (2014). Intuitions in philosophy: A minimal defense. *Philosophical Studies*, 171, 535–44.

Chalmers, D. J. (1996). *The conscious mind.* Oxford: Oxford University Press.

Chalmers, D. J. (2011). Verbal disputes. *Philosophical Review*, 120, 515–66.

Chalmers, D. J. (2012). *Constructing the world*. Oxford: Oxford University Press.

Chalmers, D. J. (2015). Why isn't there more progress in philosophy? *Philosophy*, 90, 3–31.

Chalmers, D. J., & Jackson, F. (2001). Conceptual analysis and reductive explanation. *The Philosophical Review*, 110, 315–60.

Choe, S. Y., & Min, K.-H. (2011). Who makes utilitarian judgments? The influences of emotions on utilitarian judgments. *Judgment and Decision Making*, 6, 580–92.

Christensen, D. (2007). Epistemology of disagreement: The good news. *Philosophical Review*, 116, 187–217.

Christensen, D. (2009). Disagreement as evidence: The epistemology of controversy. *Philosophy Compass*, 4, 756–67.

Chudnoff, E. (2013). *Intuition*. Oxford: Oxford University Press.

Cikara, M., Farnsworth, R. A., Harris, L. T., & Fiske, S. T. (2010). On the wrong side of the trolley track: Neural correlates of relative social valuation. *Social Cognitive and Affective Neuroscience*, 5, 404–13.

CNN (2003). Runaway freight train derails near Los Angeles. CNN.com/US. Available at http://edition.cnn.com/2003/US/West/06/20/train.derails/. Accessed July 5, 2016.

Cohen, J. (1992). A power primer. *Psychological Bulletin*, 112, 155–9.

Cokely, E. T., & Feltz, A. (2009). Individual differences, judgment biases, and theory-of-mind: Deconstructing the intentional action side effect asymmetry. *Journal of Research in Personality*, 43, 18–24.

Colaço, D., Buckwalter, W., Stich, S. P., & Machery, E. (2014). Epistemic intuitions in fake-barn thought experiments. *Episteme*, 11, 199–212.

Colaço, D., Kneer, M., Alexander, J., & Machery, E. (ms). On second thoughts.

Colaço, D., & Machery, E. (2017). The intuitive is a red herring. *Inquiry*, 60, 403–19.

Collins, J., Hall, N., & Paul, L. A. (2004). Counterfactuals and causation: History, problems, and prospects. In J. Collins, N. Hall, & L. A. Paul (Eds.), *Causation and counterfactuals* (pp. 1–57). Cambridge, MA: MIT Press.

Conee, E., & Feldman, R. (1998). The generality problem for reliabilism. *Philosophical Studies*, 89, 1–29.

Costa, A., Foucart, A., Hayakawa, S., Aparici, M., Apesteguia, J., Heafner, J., & Keysar, B. (2014). Your morals depend on language. *PLOS ONE*, 9, e94842.

Côté, S., Piff, P. K., & Willer, R. (2013). For whom do the ends justify the means? Social class and utilitarian moral judgment. *Journal of Personality and Social Psychology*, 104, 490–503.

Cova, F., & Pain, N. (2012). Can folk aesthetics ground aesthetic realism? *The Monist*, 95, 241–63.

Craig, E. (1990). *Knowledge and the state of nature: An essay in conceptual synthesis*. Oxford: Oxford University Press.

Crockett, M. J., Clark, L., Hauser, M. D., & Robbins, T. W. (2010). Serotonin selectively influences moral judgment and behavior through effects on harm aversion. *Proceedings of the National Academy of Sciences*, 107, 17433–8.

Cullen, S. (2010). Survey-driven romanticism. *Review of Philosophy and Psychology*, 1, 275–96.

Cummins, R. (1998). Reflection on reflective equilibrum. In M. R. DePaul & W. Ramsey (Eds.), *Rethinking intuition: The psychology of intuition and its role in philosophical inquiry* (pp. 113–28). Lanham, MD: Rowman & Littlefield Publishers.

Cushman, F., & Mele, A. (2008). Intentional action: Two-and-a-half folk concepts? In J. Knobe & S. Nichols (Eds.), *Experimental Philosophy* (pp. 171–88). Oxford: Oxford University Press.

Cushman, F., Young, L., & Hauser, M. (2006). The role of conscious reasoning and intuition in moral judgment testing three principles of harm. *Psychological Science*, 17, 1082–9.

Danks, D. (2014). *Unifying the mind: Cognitive representations as graphical models*. Cambridge, MA: MIT Press.

Danks, D., Rose, D., & Machery, E. (2014). Demoralizing causation. *Philosophical Studies*, 171, 251–77.

Davidson, D. (1987). Knowing one's own mind. *Proceedings and Addresses of the American Philosophical Association*, 60, 441–58.

De Brigard, F. (2010). If you like it, does it matter if it's real? *Philosophical Psychology*, 23, 43–57.

Demaree-Cotton, J. (2016). Do framing effects make moral intuitions unreliable? *Philosophical Psychology*, 29, 1–22.

Dennett, D. C. (1993). *Consciousness explained*. London: Penguin.

Dennett, D. C. (2005). *Sweet dreams: Philosophical obstacles to a science of consciousness*. Cambridge, MA: MIT Press.

Dennett, D. C. (2013). *Intuition pumps and other tools for thinking*. New York: W.W. Norton & Company.

Descartes (1999). *Discourse on method*, trans. D. A. Cress. Indianapolis: Hackett Publishing Company.

Deutsch, M. (2009). Experimental philosophy and the theory of reference. *Mind & Language*, 24, 445–66.

Deutsch, M. (2015). *The myth of the intuitive*. Cambridge, MA: MIT Press.

Devitt, M. (2011). Experimental semantics. *Philosophy and Phenomenological Research*, 82, 418–35.

Devitt, M. (2012). Whither experimental semantics? *Theoria*, 72, 5–36.

Devitt, M. (2014). We don't learn about the world by examining concepts: A response to Carrie Jenkins. In R. Neta (Ed.), *Current controversies in epistemology* (pp. 23–33). New York: Routledge.

Dewey, J. (1910). *The influence of Darwin in philosophy and other essays in contemporary thought*. New York: Henry Holt and Company.

Dietrich, F., & Spiekermann, K. (2013a). Independent opinions? On the causal foundations of belief formation and jury theorems. *Mind*, 122, 655–85.

Dietrich, F., & Spiekermann, K. (2013b). Epistemic democracy with defensible premises. *Economics and Philosophy*, 29, 87–120.

Dretske, F. I. (1970). Epistemic operators. *The Journal of Philosophy*, 67, 1007–23.

Dummett, M. (1973). *Frege: Philosophy of language*. London: Duckworth.

Dunaway, B., Edmonds, A. & Manley, D. (2013). The folk probably do think what you think they think. *Australasian Journal of Philosophy*, 91, 421–41.

Dupré, J. (1981). Natural kinds and biological taxa. *The Philosophical Review*, 90, 66–90.

Dutant, J. (2015). The legend of the justified true belief analysis. *Philosophical Perspectives*, 29, 95–145.

Einhorn, H. J., & Hogarth, R. M. (1978). Confidence in judgment: Persistence of the illusion of validity. *Psychological Review*, 85, 395–416.

Elga, A. (2007). Reflection and disagreement. *Noûs*, 41, 478–502.

Elster, J. (2011). How outlandish can imaginary cases be? *Journal of Applied Philosophy*, 28, 241–58.

Epstein, S., Pacini, R., Denes-Raj, V., & Heier, H. (1996). Individual differences in intuitive-experiential and analytical–rational thinking styles. *Journal of Personality and Social Psychology*, 71, 390.

Evans, G. (1973). The causal theory of names. *Proceedings of the Aristotelian Society, Supplementary Volumes*, 47, 187–225.

Faul, F., Erdfelder, E., Lang, A. G., & Buchner, A. (2007). G* Power 3: A flexible statistical power analysis program for the social, behavioral, and biomedical sciences. *Behavior Research Methods*, 39, 175–91.

Feldman, R. (1985). Reliability and justification. *The Monist*, 68, 159–74.

Feldman, R. (2006). Epistemological puzzles about disagreement. In S. Hetherington (Ed.), *Epistemology futures* (pp. 216–36). New York: Oxford University Press.

Feltz, A., & Cokely, E. (2011). Individual differences in theory-of-mind judgments: Order effects and side effects. *Philosophical Psychology*, 24, 343–55.

Feltz, A., & Cokely, E. T. (2009). Do judgments about freedom and responsibility depend on who you are? Personality differences in intuitions about compatibilism and incompatibilism. *Consciousness and Cognition*, 18, 342–50.

Feltz, A., & Cokely, E. T. (2012). The philosophical personality argument. *Philosophical Studies*, 161, 227–46.

Feltz, A., Harris, M., & Perez, A. (2012). Perspective in intentional action attribution. *Philosophical Psychology*, 25, 673–87.

Feltz, A., & Zarpentine, C. (2010). Do you know more when it matters less? *Philosophical Psychology*, 23, 683–706.

Fine, K. (1994). Essence and modality. *Philosophical Perspectives*, 8, 1–16.

Fischer, J. M. (2010). The Frankfurt cases: The moral of the stories. *Philosophical Review*, 119, 315–36.

Flikschuh, K. (2014). The idea of philosophical fieldwork: Global justice, moral ignorance, and intellectual attitudes. *The Journal of Political Philosophy*, 22, 1–26.

Fodor, J. A. (1964). On knowing what we would say. *The Philosophical Review*, 73, 198–212.

Fodor, J. A. (1987). *Psychosemantics: The problem of meaning in the philosophy of mind*. Cambridge, MA: MIT Press.

Fodor, J. A. (1994). *The elm and the expert*. Cambridge, MA: MIT Press.

Frankfurt, H. G. (1969). Alternate possibilities and moral responsibility. *The Journal of Philosophy*, 66, 829–39.

Frederick, S. (2005). Cognitive reflection and decision making. *Journal of Economic Perspectives*, 19, 25–42.

Friedman, M. (2001). *Dynamics of reason*. Stanford: CSLI Publications.

Friesdorf, R., Conway, P., & Gawronski, B. (2015). Gender differences in responses to moral dilemmas: A process dissociation analysis. *Personality and Social Psychology Bulletin*, 41, 696–713.

Fumagali, M., Vergari, M., Pasqualetti, P., Marceglia, S., Mameli, F., Ferruci, R, Mrakic-Sposta, S., Zago, S., Satori, G., Pravettoni, G., Barbieri, S., Cappa, S., & Priori, A. (2010). Brain switches utilitarian behavior: Does gender make the difference? *PLOS ONE*, 5, e8865.

Gao, Y., & Tang, S. (2013). Psychopathic personality and utilitarian moral judgment in college students. *Journal of Criminal Justice*, 41, 342–9.

Geipel, J., Hadjichristidis, C., & Surian, L. (2015). The foreign language effect on moral judgment: The role of emotions and norms. *PLOS ONE*, 10(7), e0131529.

Gendler, T. S. (2007). Philosophical thought experiments, intuitions, and cognitive equilibrium. *Midwest Studies in Philosophy*, 31, 68–89.

Gendler, T. S., & Hawthorne, J. (2005). The real guide to fake barns: A catalogue of gifts for your epistemic enemies. *Philosophical Studies*, 124, 331–52.

Gerken, M., & Beebe, J. R. (2016). Knowledge in and out of contrast. *Noûs*, 50, 133–64.

Gettier, E. L. (1963). Is justified true belief knowledge? *Analysis*, 23, 121–3.

Gilligan, C. (1982). *In a different voice*. Cambridge, MA: Harvard University Press.

Glasgow, J. (2009). *A theory of race*. New York: Routledge.

Gleichgerrcht, E., & Young, L. (2013). Low levels of empathic concern predict utilitarian moral judgment. *PLOS ONE*, 8, e60418.

Glenn, A. L., Koleva, S., Iyer, R., Graham, J., & Ditto, P. H. (2010). Moral identity in psychopathy. *Judgment and Decision Making*, 5, 497–505.

Glymour, C. (2015). Probability and the explanatory virtues. *The British Journal for the Philosophy of Science*, 66, 591–604.

Godfrey-Smith, P. (2009). *Darwinian populations and natural selection*. Oxford: Oxford University Press.

Gold, N., Colman, A. M., & Pulford, B. D. (2014a). Cultural differences in responses to real-life and hypothetical trolley problems. *Judgment and Decision Making*, 9, 65–76.

Gold, N., Pulford, B. D., & Colman, A. M. (2014b). The outlandish, the realistic, and the real: Contextual manipulation and agent role effects in trolley problems. *Frontiers in Psychology: Cognitive Science*, 5, 35.

Goldman, A. (2008). Reliabilist epistemology. In E. Z. Zalta (Ed.), *The Stanford Encyclopedia of Philosophy* (Winter 2015 Edition), <http://plato.stanford.edu/archives/win2015/entries/reliabilism/>.

Goldman, A. I. (1976). Discrimination and perceptual knowledge. *The Journal of Philosophy*, 73, 771–91.

Goldman, A. I. (1979). What is justified belief? In G. Pappas (Ed.), *Justification and knowledge* (pp. 1–23). Dordrecht: Reidel Publishing Company.

Goldman, A. I. (1988). Strong and weak justification. *Philosophical perspectives*, 2, 51–69.

Goldman, A. I. (2007). Philosophical intuitions: Their target, their source, and their epistemic status. *Grazer Philosophische Studien*, 74, 1–26.

Goldman, A. I. (2010). Philosophical naturalism and intuitional methodology. In *Proceedings and addresses of the American Philosophical Association* (pp. 115–50). American Philosophical Association.

Goldman, A. I., & Pust, J. (1998). Philosophical theory and intuitional evidence. In M. R. DePaul and W. Ramsey (Eds.), *Rethinking intuition: The psychology of intuition and its role in philosophical inquiry* (pp. 179–200). Lanham, MD: Rowman & Littlefield Publishers.

Gonnerman, C., Reuter, S., & Weinberg, J. M. (2011). *More oversensitive intuitions: Print fonts and could choose otherwise*. Paper presented at the One Hundred Eighth Annual Meeting of the American Philosophical Association, Central Division, Minneapolis, MN.

Gopnik, A., & Schwitzgebel, E. (1998). Whose concepts are they, anyway? The role of philosophical intuition in empirical psychology. In M. R. dePaul (Ed.), *Rethinking intuition* (pp. 75–91). Lanham, MD: Rowman & Littlefield.

Graham, G., & Horgan, T. (1994). Southern fundamentalism and the end of philosophy. *Philosophical Issues*, 5, 219–47.

Gramsci, A. (2000). *The Gramsci reader: Selected writings, 1916–1935*, edited by D. Forgacs. New York: New York University Press.

Greene, J. (2014). *Moral tribes: emotion, reason and the gap between us and them*. New York: Penguin Press.

Greene, J. D., Cushman, F. A., Stewart, L. E., Lowenberg, K., Nystrom, L. E., & Cohen, J. D. (2009). Pushing moral buttons: The interaction between personal force and intention in moral judgment. *Cognition*, 111, 364–71.

Grice, H. P. (1989). *Study in the way of words*. Cambridge, MA: Harvard University Press.

Grice, H. P., & Strawson, P. F. (1956). In defense of a dogma. *The Philosophical Review*, 65, 141–58.

Griffiths, P. E. (2002). What is innateness? *The Monist*, 85, 70–85.

Griffiths, P. E., Machery, E., & Linquist, S. (2009). The vernacular concept of innateness. *Mind & Language*, 24, 605–30.

Gyekye, K. (1997). *Tradition and modernity: Philosophical reflections on the African experience*. Oxford: Oxford University Press.

Hacker, P. M. S. (2009). A philosopher of philosophy. *The Philosophical Quarterly*, 59, 337–48.

Hacking, I. (2007). The contingencies of ambiguity. *Analysis*, 67, 269–77.

Hadjichristidis, C., Geipel, J., & Savadori, L. (2015). The effect of foreign language in judgments of risk and benefit: The role of affect. *Journal of Experimental Psychology: Applied*, 21, 117–29.

Haggqvist, S. (1996). *Thought experiments in philosophy*. Stockholm: Almqvist & Wiksell International.

Hales, S. D. (2006). *Relativism and the foundations of philosophy*. Cambridge, MA: MIT Press.

Hales, S. D. (2012). The faculty of intuition. *Analytic Philosophy*, 53, 180–207.

Hall, N. (2004). Two concepts of causation. In J. Collins, N. Hall, & L. A. Paul (Eds.), *Causation and counterfactuals* (pp. 225–76). Cambridge, MA: MIT Press.

Hansen, C. (1981). Linguistic skepticism in the Lao Tzu. *Philosophy East and West*, 31, 321–36.

Hardimon, M. O. (2003). The ordinary concept of race. *The Journal of Philosophy*, 100, 437–55.

Hare, R. M. (1981). *Moral thinking: Its levels, method, and point*. Oxford: Clarendon Press.

Harman, G. (1968). Knowledge, inference, and explanation. *American Philosophical Quarterly*, 5, 164–73.

Hart, H. L. (1961). *The concept of law*. Oxford: Clarendon Press.

Haslanger, S. (2000). Gender and race: (What) are they? (What) do we want them to be? *Noûs*, 34, 31–55.

Haslanger, S. (2006). Philosophical analysis and social kinds. *Proceedings of the Aristotelian Society, Supplementary Volumes*, 80, 89–118.

Haslanger, S. (2010). Language, politics and "the folk": Looking for "the meaning" of "race." *The Monist*, 93, 169–87.

Hauser, M., Cushman, F., Young, L., Kang-Xing Jin, R., & Mikhail, J. (2007). A dissociation between moral judgments and justifications. *Mind & Language*, 22, 1–21.

Hausman, D. M., & Woodward, J. (1999). Independence, invariance and the causal Markov condition. *The British Journal for the Philosophy of Science*, 50, 521–83.

Helzer, E. G., & Pizarro, D. A. (2011). Dirty liberals! Reminders of physical cleanliness influence moral and political attitudes. *Psychological Science*, 22, 517–22.

Hertwig, R., & Erev, I. (2009). The description–experience gap in risky choice. *Trends in Cognitive Sciences*, 13, 517–23.

Hintikka, J. (1999). The emperor's new intuitions. *The Journal of Philosophy*, 96, 127–47.

Hitchcock, C. (2007). Three concepts of causation. *Philosophy Compass*, 2, 508–16.

Hitchcock, C., & Knobe, J. (2009). Cause and norm. *Journal of Philosophy*, 11, 587–612.

Hogarth, R. M., & Einhorn, H. J. (1992). Order effects in belief updating: The belief-adjustment model. *Cognitive Psychology*, 24, 1–55.

Horgan, T., & Timmons, M. (1991). New wave moral realism meets moral twin earth. *Journal of Philosophical Research*, 16, 447–65.

Horne, Z., & Livengood, J. (2017). Ordering effects, updating effects, and the specter of global skepticism. *Synthese*, 194, 1189–1218.

Horne, Z., Powell, D., & Spino, J. (2013). Belief updating in moral dilemmas. *Review of Philosophy and Psychology*, 4, 705–14.

Horowitz, T. (1998). Philosophical intuitions and psychological theory. *Ethics*, 108, 367–85.

Horvath, J. (2010). How (not) to react to experimental philosophy. *Philosophical Psychology*, 23, 447–80.

Horvath, J. (2015). Thought experiments and experimental philosophy. In C. Daly (Ed.), *The Palgrave handbook of philosophical methods* (pp. 386–418). London: Palgrave Macmillan UK.

Horvath, J., & Wiegmann, A. (2016). Intuitive expertise and intuitions about knowledge. *Philosophical Studies*, 173, 2701–26.

Huemer, M. (2005). *Ethical intuitionism*. New York: Palgrave Macmillan.

Huemer, M. (2008). Revisionary intuitionism. *Social Philosophy and Policy*, 25, 368–92.

Hume, D. (1999). *An enquiry concerning human understanding*, edited by T. Beauchamp. Oxford: Oxford University Press.

Hyde, J. S. (2005). The gender similarities hypothesis. *American Psychologist*, 60, 581–92.

Ichikawa, J., Maitra, I., & Weatherson, B. (2012). In defense of a Kripkean dogma. *Philosophy and Phenomenological Research*, 85, 56–68.

Jackson, F. (1986). What Mary didn't know. *The Journal of Philosophy*, 83, 291–5.

Jackson, F. (1998). *From metaphysics to ethics: A defence of conceptual analysis*. Oxford: Oxford University Press.

Jackson, F. (2011). On gettier holdouts. *Mind & Language*, 26, 468–81.

James, W. (1904). The pragmatic method. *The Journal of Philosophy, Psychology and Scientific Methods*, 1, 673–87.

Jones, E. E., & Nisbett, R. E. (1972). The actor and the observer: Divergent perceptions of the causes of behavior. In E. E. Jones, D. Kanouse, H. H. Kelley, R. E. Nisbett, S. Valins, & B. Weiner (Eds.), *Attribution: Perceiving the causes of behavior*. Morristown, NJ: General Learning Press.

Justus, J. (2012). Carnap on concept determination: Methodology for philosophy of science. *European Journal for Philosophy of Science*, 2, 161–79.

Kahane, G., Everett, J. A., Earp, B. D., Farias, M., & Savulescu, J. (2015). "Utilitarian" judgments in sacrificial moral dilemmas do not reflect impartial concern for the greater good. *Cognition*, 134, 193–209.

Kahneman, D. (2011). *Thinking fast and slow*. New York: Farrar, Strauss and Giroux.

Kahneman, D., & Tversky, A. (1982). Variants of uncertainty. *Cognition*, 11, 143–57.

Kamm, F. M. (1993). *Morality, mortality*. Oxford: Oxford University Press.

Kamm, F. M. (2006). *Intricate ethics: Rights, responsibilities, and permissible harm*. Oxford: Oxford University Press.

Kauppinen, A. (2007). The rise and fall of experimental philosophy. *Philosophical explorations*, 10, 95–118.

Kelly, D., Machery, E., & Mallon, R. (2010). Race and racial cognition. In J. M. Doris and the Moral Psychology Research Group (Eds.), *The moral psychology handbook* (pp. 463–72). Oxford: Oxford University Press.

Kelly, K. T. (2007). A new solution to the puzzle of simplicity. *Philosophy of Science*, 74, 561–73.

Kelly, T. (2005). The epistemic significance of disagreement. *Oxford Studies in Epistemology*, 1, 167–96.

Kelly, T. (2010). Peer disagreement and higher order evidence. In A. I. Goldman & D. Whitcomb (Eds.), *Social epistemology: Essential readings* (pp. 183–217). Oxford: Oxford University Press.

Kim, M., & Yuan, Y. (2015). No cross-cultural differences in the Gettier car case intuition: A replication study of Weinberg et al. 2001. *Episteme*, 12, 355–61.

Knobe, J. (2003). Intentional action and side effects in ordinary language. *Analysis*, 63, 181–7.

Knobe, J. (2004). Intention, intentional action and moral considerations. *Analysis*, 64, 190–3.

Knobe, J. (2006). The concept of intentional action: A case study in the uses of folk psychology. *Philosophical Studies*, 130, 203–31.

Knobe, J., & Burra, A. (2006). Intention and intentional action: A cross-cultural study. *Journal of Culture and Cognition*, 1–2, 113–32.

Knobe, J., & Nichols, S. (2008). An experimental philosophy manifesto. In J. Knobe & S. Nichols (Eds.), *Experimental philosophy* (pp. 3–14). Oxford: Oxford University Press.

Koenigs, M., Kruepke, M., Zeier, J., & Newman, J. P. (2012). Utilitarian moral judgment in psychopathy. *Social Cognitive and Affective Neuroscience*, 7, 708–14.

Kornblith, H. (1998). The role of intuition in philosophical inquiry: an account with no unnatural ingredients. In M. DePaul & W. Ramsey (Eds.), *Rethinking intuition: The psychology of intuition and its role in philosophical inquiry* (pp. 129–41). Lanham, MD: Rowman & Littlefield.

Kornblith, H. (2007). Naturalism and intuitions. *Grazer Philosophische Studien*, 74, 27–49.

Kornblith, H. (2014). Is there room for armchair theorizing in epistemology? In M. C. Haug (Ed.), *The armchair or the laboratory?* (pp. 195–216). New York: Routledge.

Kripke, S. (1977). Speaker's reference and semantic reference. *Midwest Studies in Philosophy*, 2, 255–76.

Kripke, S. (1980). *Naming and necessity*. Cambridge, MA: Harvard University Press.

Kuhn, D. (1991). *The skills of argument*. Cambridge: Cambridge University Press.

Kupperman, J. (1999). *Learning from Asian philosophy*. Oxford: Oxford University Press.

Kupperman, J. J. (2010). Confucian civility. *Dao*, 9, 11–23.

Lam, B. (2010). Are Cantonese-speakers really descriptivists? Revisiting cross-cultural semantics. *Cognition*, 115, 320–9.

Lanteri, A., Chelini, C., & Rizzello, S. (2008). An experimental investigation of emotions and reasoning in the trolley problem. *Journal of Business Ethics*, 83, 789–804.

LaPorte, J. (2004). *Natural kinds and conceptual change*. Cambridge: Cambridge University Press.

Laurence, S., & Margolis, E. (2003). Concepts and conceptual analysis. *Philosophy and Phenomenological Research*, 67, 253–82.

Lavers, G. (2012). On the Quinean-analyticity of mathematical propositions. *Philosophical Studies*, 159, 299–319.

Lehrer, K. (1990). *Theory of knowledge*. Boulder, CO: Westview Press.

Lehrman, D. S. (1953). A critique of Konrad Lorenz's theory of instinctive behavior. *The Quarterly Review of Biology*, 28, 337–63.

Levin, J. (2005). The evidential status of philosophical intuition. *Philosophical Studies*, 121, 193–224.

Levy, N. (2014). Intuitions and experimental philosophy: Comfortable bedfellows. In M. C. Haug (Ed.), *The armchair or the laboratory?* (pp. 381–97). New York: Routledge.

Lewis, D. (1996). Elusive knowledge. *Australasian Journal of Philosophy*, 74, 549–67.

Lewis, D. K. (1983). Mad pain and Martian pain. In D. K. Lewis, *Philosophical papers*, vol. 1 (pp. 122–32). Oxford: Oxford University Press.

Lewis, D. K. (1986). Causation. In D. K. Lewis, *Philosophical papers*, vol. 2 (pp. 159–213). Oxford: Oxford University Press.

Liao, S. (2016). Are philosophers good intuition predictors? *Philosophical Psychology*, 28, 1004–14.

Liao, S. M., Wiegmann, A., Alexander, J., & Vong, G. (2012). Putting the trolley in order: Experimental philosophy and the loop case. *Philosophical Psychology*, 25, 661–71.

Linquist, S., Machery, E., Griffiths, P. E., & Stotz, K. (2011). Exploring the folk biological conception of human nature. *Philosophical Transactions of the Royal Society B*, 366, 444–53.

Livengood, J., & Machery, E. (2007). The folk probably don't think what you think they think: Experiments on causation by absence. *Midwest Studies in Philosophy*, 31, 107–27.

Livengood, J., Sytsma, J., Feltz, A., Scheines, R., & Machery, E. (2010). Philosophical temperament. *Philosophical Psychology*, 33, 313–30.

Löhr, G. (forthcoming). Abstract concepts, compositionality, and the contextualism-invariantism debate. *Philosophical Psychology*.

Lombrozo, T. (2009). The role of moral commitments in moral judgment. *Cognitive Science*, 33, 273–86.

Love, A. C. (2013). Experiments, intuitions and images of philosophy and science. *Analysis Reviews*, 73, 785–97.

Ludwig, K. (2007). The epistemology of thought experiments: First person versus third person approaches. *Midwest Studies in Philosophy*, 31, 128–59.

Ludwig, K. (2014). Methods in analytic epistemology. In M. C. Haug (Ed.), *The armchair or the laboratory?* (pp. 197–239). New York: Routledge.

Lycan, W. (2006). On the Gettier problem problem. In S. Hetherington (Ed.), *Epistemology futures* (pp. 146–68). Oxford: Clarendon Press.

Machery, E. (2005). Concepts are not a natural kind. *Philosophy of Science*, 72, 444–67.

Machery, E. (2006). Two dogmas of neo-empiricism. *Philosophy Compass*, 1, 398–412.

Machery, E. (2007). Concept empiricism: A methodological critique. *Cognition*, 104, 19–46.

Machery, E. (2009). *Doing without concepts*. New York: Oxford University Press.

Machery, E. (2010a). Precis of doing without concepts. *Behavioral and Brain Sciences*, 33, 195–206.

Machery, E. (2010b). The notion of concept in psychology and philosophy and the elimination of "concept." *Behavioral and Brain Sciences*, 33, 231–44.

Machery, E. (2010c). Replies to my critics. *Philosophical Studies*, 149, 429–36.

Machery, E. (2011a). Thought experiments and philosophical knowledge. *Metaphilosophy*, 42, 191–214.

Machery, E. (2011b). Variation in intuitions about reference and ontological disagreement. In S. D. Hales (Ed.), *A companion to relativism* (pp. 118–36). Malden, MA: Wiley-Blackwell.

Machery, E. (2011c). Concepts: A tutorial. In R. Belohlavek & G. J. Klir (Eds.), *Concepts and fuzzy logic* (pp. 13–44). Cambridge, MA: MIT Press.

Machery, E. (2012a). Expertise and intuitions about reference. *Theoria*, 72, 37–54.

Machery, E. (2012b). Why I stopped worrying about the definition of life … and why you should as well. *Synthese*, 185, 145–64.

Machery, E. (2014). What is the significance of the demographic variation in semantic intuitions? In E. Machery & E. O'Neill (Eds.), *Current controversies in experimental philosophy* (pp. 3–16). New York: Routledge.

Machery, E. (2015a). By default. In S. Laurence & E. Margolis (Eds.), *The conceptual mind: New directions in the study of concepts* (pp. 567–88). Cambridge, MA: MIT Press.

Machery, E. (2015b). The illusion of expertise. In E. Fischer & J. Collins (Eds.), *Experimental philosophy, rationalism, and naturalism: Rethinking philosophical method* (pp. 188–203). London: Routledge.

Machery, E. (2015c). A broad Rylean argument against reference. In J. Haukioja (Ed.), *Advances in experimental philosophy of language* (pp. 65–83). London: Bloomsbury Academic.

Machery, E. (2016a). Experimental philosophy of science. In J. Sytsma & W. Buckwalter (Eds.), *A companion to experimental philosophy* (pp. 475–90). New York: John Wiley & Sons.

Machery, E. (2016b). The amodal brain and the offloading hypothesis. *Psychonomic Bulletin & Review*, 23, 1090–5.

Machery, E., Deutsch, M., Sytsma, J., Mallon, R., Nichols, S., & Stich, S. P. (2010). Semantic intuitions: Reply to Lam. *Cognition*, 117, 361–6.

Machery, E., & Doris, J. (forthcoming). An open letter to our students: Doing interdisciplinary moral psychology. In B. G. Voyer & T. Tarantola (Eds.), *Moral psychology: A multidisciplinary guide*. Berlin: Springer.

Machery, E., & Faucher, L. (2005). Social construction and the concept of race. *Philosophy of Science*, 72, 1208–19.

Machery, E., & Faucher, L. (forthcoming). The folk concept of race. In T. Marques & Asa Wikforss (Eds.), *Shifting concepts: The philosophy and psychology of conceptual variability*. Oxford: Oxford University Press.

Machery, E., & Lederer, L. G. (2012). Simple heuristics for concept composition. In M. Werning, W. Hinzen, & E. Machery (Eds.), *The Oxford handbook of compositionality* (pp. 454–72). Oxford: Oxford University Press.

Machery, E., Mallon, R., Nichols, S., & Stich, S. P. (2004). Semantics, cross-cultural style. *Cognition*, 92, B1–B12.

Machery, E., Mallon, R., Nichols, S., & Stich, S. P. (2013). If intuitions vary, then what? *Philosophy and Phenomenological Research*, 86, 618–35.

Machery, E., Olivola, C., & De Blanc, M. (2009). Linguistic and metalinguistic intuitions in the philosophy of language. *Analysis*, 69, 689–94.

Machery, E., Olivola, C. Y., Cheon, H., Kurniawan, I. T., Mauro, C., Struchiner, N., Susianto, H. (ms). Is folk essentialism a fundamental feature of human cognition?

Machery, E., and Stich, S. P. (2012). The role of experiment in the philosophy of language. In G. Russell & D. G. Fara (Eds.), *The Routledge companion to the philosophy of language* (pp. 495–512). New York: Routledge.

Machery, E., Stich, S. P., Rose, D., Alai, M., Angelucci, A., Berniunas, R., Buchtel, E. E., Chatterjee, A., Cheon, H., Cho, I.-R., Cohnitz, D., Cova, F., Dranselka, V., Lagos, A. E., Ghadakpour,

L., Grinberg, M., Hashimoto, T., Horowitz, A., Hristova, E., Jraissati, Y., Kadreva, V., Karasawa, K., Kim, H., Kim, Y., Lee, M., Mauro, C., Mizumoto, M., Moruzzi, S., Olivola, C. Y., Ornelas J., Osimani, B., Romero, C., Rosas Lopez, A., Sangoi, M., Sereni, A., Songhorian, S., Sousa, P., Struchiner, N., Tripodi, V., Usui, N., Vazquez del Mercado, A., Volpe, G., Vosperichian, H. A., Zhang, X., and Zhu, J. (Forthcoming c). The Gettier intuition from South America to Asia *The Journal of Indian Council of Philosophical Research*.

Machery, E., Stich, S. P., Rose, D., Chatterjee, A., Karasawa, K., Struchiner, N., Sirker, S., Usui, N., and Hashimoto, T. (forthcoming a). Gettier across cultures. *Noûs*, doi: 10.1111/nous.12110.

Machery, E., Stich, S. P., Rose, D., Chatterjee, A., Karasawa, K., Struchiner, N., Sirker, S., Usui, N., and Hashimoto, T. (forthcoming b). Gettier was framed! In M. Mizumoto, S. P. Stich, & E. McCready (Eds.), *Epistemology for the rest of the world*. Oxford: Oxford University Press.

Machery, E., Sytsma, J., & Deutsch, M. (2015). Speaker's reference and cross-cultural semantics. In A. Bianchi (Ed.), *On reference* (pp. 62–76). Oxford: Oxford University Press.

Mackie, J. L. (1977). *Ethics: Inventing right and wrong*. Harmondsworth: Penguin Books.

Malle, B. F. (2006). The actor-observer asymmetry in attribution: A (surprising) meta-analysis. *Psychological Bulletin*, 132, 895–919.

Mallon, R., Machery, E., Nichols, S., & Stich, S. P. (2009). Against arguments from reference. *Philosophy and Phenomenological Research*, 79, 332–56.

Malmgren, A. S. (2011). Rationalism and the content of intuitive judgements. *Mind*, 120, 263–327.

Margalit, A. (1979). Open texture. In A. Margalit (Ed.), *Meaning and use* (pp. 141–52). Dordrecht: Springer.

Martí, G. (2009). Against semantic multi-culturalism. *Analysis*, 69, 42–8.

May, J., Sinnott-Armstrong, W., Hull, J. G., & Zimmerman, A. (2010). Practical interests, relevant alternatives, and knowledge attributions: An empirical study. *Review of Philosophy and Psychology*, 1, 265–73.

Metz, T. (2007). Toward an African moral theory. *The Journal of Political Philosophy*, 15, 321–41.

Michelin, C., Pellizzoni, S., Tallandini, M. A., & Siegal, M. (2010). Should more be saved? Diversity in utilitarian moral judgment. *Journal of Cognition and Culture*, 10, 153–69.

Mikhail, J. (2011). *Elements of moral cognition: Rawls' linguistic analogy and the cognitive science of moral and legal judgment*. New York: Cambridge University Press.

Miller, D. (2008). Political philosophy for earthlings. In D. Leopold & M. Stears (Eds.), *Political theory: Methods and approaches* (pp. 29–48). Oxford: Oxford University Press.

Millikan, R. G. (1984). *Language, thought, and other biological categories: New foundations for realism*. Cambridge, MA: MIT press.

Mizrahi, M. (2015). Three arguments against the expertise defense. *Metaphilosophy*, 46, 52–64.

Moore, A. B., Clark, B. A., & Kane, M. J. (2008). Who shalt not kill? Individual differences in working memory capacity, executive control, and moral judgment. *Psychological Science*, 19, 549–57.

Moore, A. B., Lee, N. Y. L., Clark, B. A. M., & Conway, A. R. A. (2011). In defense of the personal/impersonal distinction in moral psychology research: Cross-cultural validation of the dual process model of moral judgment. *Judgment and Decision Making*, 6, 186–95.

Murdoch, I. (1970). *The sovereignty of good*. London: Routledge and Kegan Paul.

Murphy, G. L. (2002). *The big book of concepts*. Cambridge, MA: MIT Press.

Murray, D., Sytsma, J., & Livengood, J. (2013). God knows (but does God believe?). *Philosophical Studies*, 166, 83–107.

Musen, J. D. (2010). *The moral psychology of obligations to help those in need*. Bachelor of Arts, Harvard.

Myers-Schulz, B., & Schwitzgebel, E. (2013). Knowing that P without believing that P. *Noûs*, 47, 371–84.

Nadelhoffer, T., & Feltz, A. (2008). The actor-observer bias and moral intuitions: Adding fuel to Sinnott-Armstrong's fire. *Neuroethics*, 1, 133–44.

Nadelhoffer, T., Kvaran, T., & Nahmias, E. (2009). Temperament and intuition: A commentary on Feltz and Cokely. *Consciousness and cognition*, 18, 351–5.

Nadelhoffer, T., & Nahmias, E. (2007). The past and future of experimental philosophy. *Philosophical Explorations*, 10, 123–49.

Nado, J. (2014a). Why intuition? *Philosophy and Phenomenological Research*, 89, 15–41.

Nado, J. (2014b). Philosophical expertise. *Philosophy Compass*, 9, 631–41.

Nado, J. (2015). Philosophical expertise and scientific expertise. *Philosophical Psychology*, 28, 1026–44.

Nagel, J. (2012). Intuitions and experiments: A defense of the case method in epistemology. *Philosophy and Phenomenological Research*, 85, 495–527.

Nagel, J. (2013). Defending the evidential value of epistemic intuitions: A reply to Stich. *Philosophy and Phenomenological Research*, 87, 179–99.

Nagel, J., San Juan, V., & Mar, R. A. (2013). Lay denial of knowledge for justified true beliefs. *Cognition*, 129, 652–61.

Nahmias, E., Morris, S. G., Nadelhoffer, T., & Turner, J. (2006). Is incompatibilism intuitive? *Philosophy and Phenomenological Research*, 73, 28–53.

Nichols, S. (2004). Folk concepts and intuitions: From philosophy to cognitive science. *Trends in Cognitive Sciences*, 8, 514–18.

Nichols, S., & Knobe, J. (2007). Moral responsibility and determinism: The cognitive science of folk intuitions. *Noûs*, 41, 663–85.

Nichols, S., & Stich, S. P. (2003). *Mindreading: An integrated account of pretence, self-awareness, and understanding other minds*. Oxford: Oxford University Press.

Nichols, S. & Ulatowski, J. (2007). Intuitions and individual differences: The Knobe effect revisited. *Mind & Language*, 22, 346–65.

Nisbett, R. E. (2003). *The geography of thought*. New York: The Free Press.

Norcross, A. (2008). Off her trolley? Frances Kamm and the metaphysics of morality. *Utilitas*, 20, 65–80.

Norton, J. (2008). Must evidence underdetermine theory? In M. Carrier, D. Howard, & J. Kourani (Eds.), *The challenge of the social and the pressure of practice: Science and values revisited* (pp. 17–44). Pittsburgh: University of Pittsburgh Press.

Norton, J. (ms). *The material theory of induction*. Available at http://www.pitt.edu/~jdnorton/homepage/cv.html#material_theory.

Nozick, R. (1974). *Anarchy, state and utopia*. New York: Basic Books.

Nussbaum, M. C. (1990). *Love's knowledge: Essays on philosophy and literature*. Oxford: Oxford University Press.

O'Neill, E., & Machery, E. (2014). Experimental philosophy: What is it good for? In E. Machery & E. O'Neill (Eds.), *Current controversies in experimental philosophy* (pp. vii–xxix). New York: Routledge.

O'Neill, P., & Petrinovich, L. (1998). A preliminary cross-cultural study of moral intuitions. *Evolution and Human Behavior*, 19, 349–67.

Olivola, C. Y., Machery, E., Cheon, H., Kurniawan, I. T., Mauro, C., Struchiner, N., & Susianto, H. (ms). Reality does not bite: Universal aversion to illusory experiences.

Palmira, M. (2015). How to condorcet a Goldman. *Episteme*, 12, 413–25.

Papineau, D. (2011). What is x-phi good for? *The Philosophers' Magazine*, 52, 83–8.

Papineau, D. (2014). The poverty of conceptual analysis. In M. C. Haug (Ed.), *Philosophical methodology: The armchair or the laboratory?* (pp. 166–94). New York: Routledge.

Parfit, D. (1984). *Reasons and persons*. Oxford: Oxford University Press.

Pasnau, R. (2013). Epistemology idealized. *Mind*, 122, 987–1021.

Pastötter, B., Gleixner, S., Neuhauser, T., & Bäuml, K.H. T. (2013). To push or not to push? Affective influences on moral judgment depend on decision frame. *Cognition*, 126, 373–7.

Paul, L. A. (2012). Metaphysics as modeling: The handmaiden's tale. *Philosophical Studies*, 160, 1–29.

Paxton, J. M., & Greene, J. D. (2010). Moral reasoning: Hints and allegations. *Topics in Cognitive Science*, 2, 511–27.

Paxton, J. M., Ungar, L., & Greene, J. D. (2012). Reflection and reasoning in moral judgment. *Cognitive Science*, 36, 163–77.

Peacocke, C. (1992). *A study of concepts*. Cambridge, MA: MIT Press.

Peirce, C. S. (2001). How to make our ideas clear. In M. P. Lynch (Ed.), *The nature of truth: Classic and contemporary perspectives* (pp. 193–209). Cambridge, MA: MIT Press.

Petrinovich, L., & O'Neill, P. (1996). Influence of wording and framing effects on moral intuitions. *Ethology and Sociobiology*, 17, 145–71.

Petrinovich, L., O'Neill, P., & Jorgensen, M. (1993). An empirical study of moral intuitions: Toward an evolutionary ethics. *Journal of Personality and Social Psychology*, 64, 467–78.

Pinillos, N. Á., Smith, N., Nair, G. S., Marchetto, P., & Mun, C. (2011). Philosophy's new challenge: Experiments and intentional action. *Mind & Language*, 26, 115–39.

Plato (2004). *Republic*, trans. C. D. Reeve. Indianapolis: Hackett Publishing Company.

Plunkett, D. (2015). Which concepts should we use? Metalinguistic negotiations and the methodology of philosophy. *Inquiry*, 58, 828–74.

Pogge, T. W. (1990). The effects of prevalent moral conceptions. *Social Research*, 57, 649–63.

Polger, T. W., & Shapiro, L. A. (2016). *The multiple realization book*. Oxford: Oxford University Press.

Pollock, J. L. (1984). Reliability and justified belief. *Canadian Journal of Philosophy*, 14, 103–14.

Popper, K. R. (1959). *The logic of scientific discovery*. London: Hutchinson.

Prinz, J. (2002). *Furnishing the mind*. Cambridge, MA: MIT Press.

Prior, A. N. (1960). The runabout inference-ticket. *Analysis*, 21, 38–9.

Pujara, M., Motzkin, J. C., Newman, J. P., Kiehl, K. A., & Koenigs, M. (2013). Neural correlates of reward and loss sensitivity in psychopathy. *Social Cognitive and Affective Neuroscience*, 6, 794–801.

Putnam, H. (1975a). The analytic and the synthetic. In. H. Putnam (Ed.), *Mind, language and reality*, vol. 2 (pp. 33–69). Cambridge: Cambridge University Press.

Putnam, H. (1975b). The meaning of "meaning." In. H. Putnam (Ed.), *Mind, language and reality*, vol. 2 (pp. 215–71). Cambridge: Cambridge University Press.

Quine, W. V. O. (1960). *Word and object*. Cambridge, MA: MIT Press.

Quinn, W. (1993). Actions, intentions, and consequences: The doctrine of doing and allowing. In W. Quinn, *Morality and Action*. Cambridge: Cambridge University Press.

Rachels, J. (1975). Active and passive euthanasia. *New England Journal of Medicine*, 292, 78–80.

Radford, C. (1966). Knowledge: By examples. *Analysis*, 27, 1–11.

Ramsey, W. (1992). Prototypes and conceptual analysis. *Topoi*, 11, 59–70.

Rawls, J. (1980). Kantian constructivism in moral theory. *The Journal of Philosophy*, 77, 515–72.

Reichenbach, H. (1938). *Experience and prediction: An analysis of the foundations and the structure of knowledge*. Chicago: University of Chicago Press.

Reuter, K. (2011). Distinguishing the appearance from the reality of pain. *Journal of Consciousness Studies*, 18, 9–10.

Rey, G. (2010). Concepts versus conceptions (again). *Behavioral and Brain Sciences*, 33, 221–2.

Rini, R. A. (2014). Analogies, moral intuitions, and the expertise defence. *Review of Philosophy and Psychology*, 5, 169–81.

Rini, R. A. (2015). How not to test for philosophical expertise. *Synthese*, 192, 431–52.

Robbins, E., Shepard, J., & Rochat, P. (2017). Variations in judgments of intentional action and moral evaluation across eight cultures. *Cognition, 164*, 22–30.

Rosen, G. (1990). Modal fictionalism. *Mind*, 99, 327–54.

Rosen, G. (2004). Skepticism about moral responsibility. *Philosophical Perspectives*, 18, 295–313.

Rosen, G. (2006). The limits of contingency. In F. MacBride (Ed.), *Identity and modality* (pp.13–39). Oxford: Oxford University Press.

Roskies, A. L., & Nichols, S. (2008). Bringing moral responsibility down to earth. *The Journal of Philosophy*, 105, 371–88.

Routley, R. (1973). Is there a need for a new environmental ethic? *Proceedings of the Fifteenth World Congress in Philosophy*.

Russell, B. (1948). *Human knowledge: Its scope and its limits*. London: Allen & Unwin.

Rust, J., & Schwitzgebel, E. (2013). Ethicists' and nonethicists' responsiveness to student e-mails: Relationships among expressed normative attitude, self-described behavior, and empirically observed behavior. *Metaphilosophy*, 44, 350–71.

Ryberg, J. (2013). Moral intuitions and the expertise defence. *Analysis*, 73, 3–9.

Ryle, G. (1953). Ordinary language. *The Philosophical Review*, 62, 167–86.

Sarkissian, H. (2014). Ritual and rightness in the Analects. *Dao companion to the Analects* (pp. 95–116). Dordrecht: Springer.

Sarkissian, H., Chatterjee, A., de Brigard, F., Knobe, J., Nichols, S., & Sirker, S. (2010). Is belief in free will a cultural universal? *Mind & Language*, 25, 346–58.

Sartwell, C. (1991). Knowledge is merely true belief. *American Philosophical Quarterly*, 28, 157–65.

Scholl, B. (ms). Two kinds of experimental philosophy (and their experimental dangers).

Schroeter, L. (2004). The limits of conceptual analysis. *Pacific Philosophical Quarterly*, 85, 425–53.

Schulz, E., Cokely, E. T., & Feltz, A. (2011). Persistent bias in expert judgments about free will and moral responsibility: A test of the expertise defense. *Consciousness and cognition*, 20, 1722–31.

Schupbach, J. N. (2011). Comparing probabilistic measures of explanatory power. *Philosophy of Science*, 78, 813–29.

Schupbach, J. N. (2017). Experimental explication. *Philosophy and Phenomenological Research*, 94, 672–710.

Schupbach, J. N., & Sprenger, J. (2011). The logic of explanatory power. *Philosophy of Science*, 78, 105–27.

Schwitzgebel, E. (2009). Do ethicists steal more books? *Philosophical Psychology*, 22, 711–25.

Schwitzgebel, E., & Cushman, F. (2012). Expertise in moral reasoning? Order effects on moral judgment in professional philosophers and non-philosophers. *Mind & Language*, 27, 135–53.

Schwitzgebel, E., & Cushman, F. (2015). Philosophers' biased judgments persist despite training, expertise and reflection. *Cognition*, 141, 127–37.

Schwitzgebel, E., & Rust, J. (2009). The moral behaviour of ethicists: Peer opinion. *Mind*, 118, 1043–105.

Schwitzgebel, E., & Rust, J. (2010). Do ethicists and political philosophers vote more often than other professors? *Review of Philosophy and Psychology*, 1, 189–99.

Schwitzgebel, E., & Rust, J. (2014). The moral behavior of ethics professors: Relationships among self-reported behavior, expressed normative attitude, and directly observed behavior. *Philosophical Psychology*, 27, 293–327.

Schwitzgebel, E., Rust, J., Huang, L. T. L., Moore, A. T., & Coates, J. (2012). Ethicists' courtesy at philosophy conferences. *Philosophical Psychology*, 25, 331–40.

Searle, J. R. (1980). Minds, brains, and programs. *Behavioral and Brain Sciences*, 3, 417–24.

Sellars, W. (1963). *Science, perception, and reality*. New York: Humanities Press.

Seyedsayamdost, H. (2015a). On normativity and epistemic intuitions: Failure of replication. *Episteme*, 12, 95–116.

Seyedsayamdost, H. (2015b). On gender and philosophical intuition: Failure of replication and other negative results. *Philosophical Psychology*, 28, 642–73.

Shapiro, L. A. (2004). *The mind incarnate*. Cambridge, MA: MIT Press.

Shech, E., & Hatleback, E. (ms). The material intricacies of Coulomb's 1785 electric torsion balance experiment.

Shepherd, J., & Justus, J. (2015). X-phi and Carnapian explication. *Erkenntnis*, 80, 381–402.

Shoemaker, S. (1963). *Self-knowledge and self-identity*. Ithaca, NY: Cornell University Press.

Shope, R. K. (1983). *The analysis of knowing: A decade of research*. Princeton, NJ: Princeton University Press.

Shtulman, A. (2015). How lay cognition constrains scientific cognition. *Philosophy Compass*, 10, 785–98.

Sider, T. (2011). *Writing the book of the world*. Oxford: Oxford University Press.

Sidgwick, H. (1876). Professor Calderwood on intuitionism in morals. *Mind*, 1, 563–6.

Sidgwick, H. (1883). *Method of ethics*. London: MacMillan.

Singer, P. (1972). Moral experts. *Analysis*, 32, 115–17.

Sinnott-Armstrong, W. (2008). Framing moral intuitions. In W. Sinnott-Armstrong (Ed.), *Moral psychology*, vol. 2: *The cognitive science of morality* (pp. 47–76). Cambridge, MA: MIT Press.

Sober, E. (2015). *Ockham's razors: A user's manual*. Cambridge: Cambridge University Press.

Solomon, R. C. (2001). "What is philosophy?" The status of non-western philosophy in the profession. *Philosophy East and West*, 51, 100–4.

Sorensen, R. A. (1992). *Thought experiments*. Oxford: Oxford University Press.

Sosa, E. (1998). Minimal Intuition. In M. DePaul & W. Ramsey (Eds.), *Rethinking intuition* (pp. 257–70). Lanham, MD: Rowman and Littlefield Press.

Sosa, E. (2007). Experimental philosophy and philosophical intuition. *Philosophical Studies*, 132, 99–107.

Sosa, E. (2009). A defense of the use of intuitions in philosophy. In M. Bishop & D. Murphy (Eds.), *Stich and his critics* (pp. 101–12). Oxford: Blackwell.

Sosa, E. (2010). The epistemology of disagreement. In A. Haddock & A. Millar (Eds.), *Social epistemology* (pp. 278–97). Oxford: Oxford University Press.

Spirtes, P., Glymour, C. N., & Scheines, R. (2000). *Causation, prediction, and search*. Cambridge, MA: MIT Press.

Sprouse, J., & Almeida, D. (2012). Assessing the reliability of textbook data in syntax: Adger's Core Syntax. *Journal of Linguistics*, 48, 609–52.

Sprouse, J., Schütze, C. T., & Almeida, D. (2013). A comparison of informal and formal acceptability judgments using a random sample from Linguistic Inquiry 2001–2010. *Lingua*, 134, 219–48.

Stanford, P. K. (2010). *Exceeding our grasp: Science, history, and the problem of unconceived alternatives*. New York: Oxford University Press.

Starmans, C., & Friedman, O. (2012). The folk conception of knowledge. *Cognition*, 124, 272–83.

Stevens, S. S., & Galanter, E. H. (1957). Ratio scales and category scales for a dozen perceptual continua. *Journal of Experimental Psychology*, 54, 377–411.

Stich, S. P. (1993). Moral philosophy and mental representation. In M. Hechter, L. Nadel, & R. Michod (Eds.), *The origin of values* (pp. 215–28). New York: Aldine De Gruter.

Stich, S. P. (2013). Do different groups have different epistemic intuitions? A reply to Jennifer Nagel. *Philosophy and Phenomenological Research*, 87, 151–78.

Stich, S. P., & Tobia, K. P. (2016). Experimental philosophy and the philosophical tradition. In J. Sytsma & W. Buckwalter (Eds.), *A Companion to experimental philosophy* (pp. 5–21). New York: John Wiley & Sons.

Stoltz, J. (2007). Gettier and factivity in Indo-Tibetan epistemology. *The Philosophical Quarterly*, 57, 394–415.

Stotz, K., Griffiths, P. E., & Knight, R. (2004). How biologists conceptualize genes: An empirical study. *Studies in History and Philosophy of Science Part C: Studies in History and Philosophy of Biological and Biomedical Sciences*, 35, 647–73.

Strawson, P. F. (1963). Carnap's views on constructed systems versus natural languages in analytic philosophy. In P. Schilpp (Ed.), *The philosophy of Rudolf Carnap* (pp. 503–18). Lasalle: Open Court.

Strohminger, N., Lewis, R. L., & Meyer, D. E. (2011). Divergent effects of different positive emotions on moral judgment. *Cognition*, 119(2), 295–300.

Swain, S., Alexander, J., & Weinberg, J. M. (2008). The instability of philosophical intuitions: Running hot and cold on Truetemp. *Philosophy and Phenomenological Research*, 76, 138–55.

Sytsma, J., & Livengood, J. (2015). *The theory and practice of experimental philosophy*. Peterborough: Broadview Press.

Sytsma, J., Livengood, J., Sato, R., & Oguchi, M. (2015). Reference in the Land of the Rising Sun: A cross-cultural study on the reference of proper names. *Review of Philosophy and Psychology*, 6, 213–30.

Sytsma, J., & Machery, E. (2010). Two conceptions of subjective experience. *Philosophical Studies*, 151, 299–327.

Talbot, B. (2013). Reforming intuition pumps: When are the old ways the best? *Philosophical Studies*, 165, 315–34.

Talbot, B. (2014). Why so negative? Evidence aggregation and armchair philosophy. *Synthese*, 191, 3865–96.

Tassy, S., Oullier, O., Mancini, J., & Wicker, B. (2013). Discrepancies between judgment and choice of action in moral dilemmas. *Frontiers in Psychology*, 4, No. 250. http://dx.doi.org/10.3389/fpsyg.2013.00250.

Tetlock, P. E. (2005). *Expert political judgment: How good is it? How can we know?* Princeton, NJ: Princeton University Press.

Thomson, J. J. (1971). A defense of abortion. *Philosophy & Public Affairs*, 1, 47–66.

Thomson, J. J. (1985). The trolley problem. *Yale Law Journal*, 94, 1395–415.

Tittle, P. (2005). *What if? Collected thought experiments in philosophy.* New York: Pearson.

Tobia, K., Buckwalter, W., & Stich, S. (2013). Moral intuitions: Are philosophers experts? *Philosophical Psychology*, 26, 629–38.

Tobia, K., Chapman, G., & Stich, S. (2013). Cleanliness is next to morality, even for philosophers. *Journal of Consciousness Studies*, 20, 195–204.

Turri, J. (2013). A conspicuous art: Putting Gettier to the test. *Philosophers' Imprint*, 13, 1–16.

Turri, J. (2015). Unreliable knowledge. *Philosophy and Phenomenological Research*, 90, 529–45.

Turri, J. (2016). Knowledge judgments in "Gettier" cases. In J. Sytsma & W. Buckwalter (Eds.), *A companion to experimental philosophy* (pp. 337–48). New York: John Wiley & Sons.

Turri, J., Buckwalter, W., & Blouw, P. (2015). Knowledge and luck. *Psychonomic Bulletin & Review*, 22, 378–90.

Turri, J., & Friedman, O. (2014). Winners and losers in the folk epistemology of lotteries. In J. Beebe (Ed.), *Advances in experimental epistemology* (pp. 45–69). London: Bloomsbury Publishing.

Tversky, A., & Kahneman, D. (1971). Belief in the law of small numbers. *Psychological Bulletin*, 76, 105–10.

Tversky, A., & Kahneman, D. (1974). Judgment under uncertainty: Heuristics and biases. *Science*, 185, 1124–31.

Tversky, A., & Kahneman, D. (1983). Extensional versus intuitive reasoning: The conjunction fallacy in probability judgment. *Psychological Review*, 90, 293–315.

Uhlmann, E. L., Pizarro, D. A., Tannenbaum, D., & Ditto, P. H. (2009). The motivated use of moral principles. *Judgment and Decision Making*, 4, 476–91.

Unger, P. K. (1996). *Living high and letting die: Our illusion of innocence.* New York: Oxford University Press.

Vacha-Haase, T., & Thompson, B. (2004). How to estimate and interpret various effect sizes. *Journal of Counseling Psychology*, 51, 473–81.

Vaidya, A. J. (2010). Philosophical methodology: The current debate. *Philosophical Psychology*, 23, 391–417.

Valdesolo, P., & DeSteno, D. (2006). Manipulations of emotional context shape moral judgment. *Psychological Science*, 17, 476–7.

Van Fraassen, B. C. (1980). *The scientific image.* Oxford: Oxford University Press.

Van Fraassen, B. C. (1999). The manifest image and the scientific image. In D. Aerts (Ed.), *Einstein meets Magritte: The White Book—an interdisciplinary reflection* (pp. 29–52). Dordrecht: Kluwer.

Van Helden, A. (1974). The telescope in the seventeenth century. *Isis*, 65, 38–58.

Van Helden, A. (1977). The invention of the telescope. *Transactions of the American Philosophical Society*, 67, 1–67.

Vargas, M. R. (2015). *Building better beings: A theory of moral responsibility.* Oxford: Oxford University Press.

Waismann, F. (1945). Symposium: verifiability. *Proceedings of the Aristotelian Society, Supplementary Volumes*, 19, 119–50.

Wasserman, R. (2015). Material constitution. In E. N. Zalta (Ed.), *The Stanford Encyclopedia of Philosophy* (Spring 2015 Edition), <http://plato.stanford.edu/archives/spr2015/entries/material-constitution/>.

Waterman, J., Gonnerman, C., Yan, K., & Alexander, J. (forthcoming). Infallibilism, certainty, skepticism: A cross-cultural study. In M. Mizumoto, S. P. Stich, & E. McCready, (Eds.), *Epistemology for the rest of the world*. Oxford: Oxford University Press.

Weatherson, B. (2003). What good are counterexamples? *Philosophical Studies*, 115, 1–31.

Weatherson, B. (2013). Margins and errors. *Inquiry*, 56, 63–76.

Weinberg, J. M. (2007). How to challenge intuitions empirically without risking skepticism. *Midwest Studies in Philosophy*, 31, 318–43.

Weinberg, J. M. (2014). Cappelen between rock and a hard place. *Philosophical Studies*, 171, 545–53.

Weinberg, J. M., & Alexander, J. (2014). The challenge of sticking with intuitions through thick and thin. In A. R. Booth & D. P. Rowbottom (Eds.), *Intuitions* (pp. 187–212). Oxford: Oxford University Press.

Weinberg, J. M., Alexander, J., Gonnerman, C., & Reuter, S. (2012). Restrictionism and reflection: Challenge deflected, or simply redirected? *The Monist*, 95(2), 200–22.

Weinberg, J. M., Gonnerman, C., Buckner, C., & Alexander, J. (2010). Are philosophers expert intuiters? *Philosophical Psychology*, 23, 331–55.

Weinberg, J. M., Nichols, S., & Stich, S. (2001). Normativity and epistemic intuitions. *Philosophical Topics*, 29, 429–60.

Weisberg, D. S., & Goodstein, J. (2009). What belongs in a fictional world? *Journal of Cognition and Culture*, 9, 69–78.

Weisberg, D. S. (2014). The development of imaginative cognition. *Royal Institute of Philosophy Supplement*, 75, 85-103.

Whewell, W. (1847). *The philosophy of the inductive sciences, founded upon their history*, 2nd ed. London.

Wiech, K., Kahane, G., Shackel, N., Farias, M., Savulescu, J., & Tracey, I. (2013). Cold or calculating? Reduced activity in the subgenual cingulate cortex reflects decreased emotional aversion to harming in counterintuitive utilitarian judgment. *Cognition*, 126, 364–72.

Wiegmann, A., Horvath, J., & Meyer, K. (ms). Intuitive expertise and irrelevant options.

Wiegmann, A., Lippold, M., & Grigull, R. (ms). On the robustness of intuitions in the two best-known trolley dilemmas.

Wiegmann, A., Okan, J., & Nagel, J. (2012). Order effects in moral judgment. *Philosophical Psychology*, 25, 813–36.

Wiegmann, A., & Waldmann, M. R. (2014). Transfer effects between moral dilemmas: A causal model theory. *Cognition*, 131, 28–43.

Wilkes, K. V. (1988). *Real people: Personal identity without thought experiments*. Oxford: Clarendon Press.

Williams, B. (1970). The self and the future. *The Philosophical Review*, 79, 161–80.

Williams, B. (1985). *Ethics and the limits of philosophy*. Cambridge, MA: Harvard University Press.

Williamson, T. (2004). Philosophical "intuitions" and scepticism about judgement. *Dialectica*, 58, 109–53.

Williamson, T. (2007). *The philosophy of philosophy*. Oxford: Blackwell.

Williamson, T. (2010). Philosophy vs. imitation psychology. *New York Times*, August 19, 2010, available at http://www.nytimes.com/roomfordebate/2010/08/19/x-phis-new-take-on-old-problems/philosophy-vs-imitation-psychology?

Williamson, T. (2011). Philosophical expertise and the burden of proof. *Metaphilosophy*, 42, 215–29.

Williamson, T. (2013). *Modal logic as metaphysics*. Oxford: Oxford University Press.

Williamson, T. (2016). Philosophical criticisms of experimental philosophy. In J. Sytsma & W. Buckwalter (Eds.), *A companion to experimental philosophy* (pp. 22–36). New York: John Wiley & Sons.

Wilson, M. (2006). *Wandering significance: An essay on conceptual behavior*. Oxford: Oxford University Press.

Winawer, J., Witthoft, N., Frank, M. C., Wu, L., Wade, A. R., & Boroditsky, L. (2007). Russian blues reveal effects of language on color discrimination. *Proceedings of the National Academy of Sciences*, 104, 7780–5.

Wiredu, K. (1996). *Cultural universals and particulars: An African perspective*. Bloomington: Indiana University Press.

Wittgenstein, L. (1953). *Philosophical investigations*. 2nd ed. trans. G. E. M. Anscombe. Oxford: Blackwell.

Wolters, G. (2013). European humanities in times of globalized parochialism. *Bollettino della Società Filosofica Italiana*, 208, 3–18.

Wood, A. (2008). Cross-cultural moral philosophy: Reflections on Thaddeus Metz: "Toward an African moral theory." *South African Journal of Philosophy*, 26, 336–46.

Woodward, J. (2014). Simplicity in the best systems account of laws of nature. *The British Journal for the Philosophy of Science*, 65, 91–123.

Woodward, J. (2017). Interventionism and the missing metaphysics: A dialogue. In M. Slater & Z. Yudell (Eds.), *Metaphysics and the philosophy of science: New essays* (pp. 193–228). Oxford: Oxford University Press.

Woolfolk, R. L. (2011). Empirical tests of philosophical intuitions. *Consciousness and Cognition*, 20, 415–16.

Woolfolk, R. L. (2013). Experimental philosophy: A methodological critique. *Metaphilosophy*, 44, 79–87.

Worsnip, A. (2014). Disagreement about disagreement? What disagreement about disagreement? *Philosophers' Imprint*, 14, 1–20.

Wright, J. (2013). Tracking instability in our philosophical judgments: Is it intuitive? *Philosophical Psychology*, 26, 485–501.

Wright, J. C. (2010). On intuitional stability: The clear, the strong, and the paradigmatic. *Cognition*, 115, 491–503.

Xiang, L. (2014). *Would the Buddha push the man off the footbridge? Systematic variations in the moral judgment and punishment tendencies of Han Chinese, Tibetans and Americans*. Bachelor of Arts, Harvard.

Young, O. A., Willer, R., & Keltner, D. (2013). "Thou shalt not kill": Religious fundamentalism, conservatism, and rule-based moral processing. *Psychology of Religion and Spirituality*, 5, 110–15.

Zagzebski, L. (1994). The inescapability of Gettier problems. *The Philosophical Quarterly*, 44, 65–73.

Zamzow, J., & Nichols, S. (2009). Variations in ethical intuitions. *Philosophical Issues*, 19, 368–88.

Index